THE TRIAL OF GUSTAV GRAEF

THE TRIAL OF GUSTAV GRAEF

ART, SEX, AND SCANDAL IN LATE NINETEENTH-CENTURY GERMANY

BARNET HARTSTON

NIU Press / DeKalb, IL

Northern Illinois University Press, DeKalb 60115

Printed in the United States of America
26 25 24 23 22 21 20 19 18 17 1 2 3 4 5
978-0-87580-767-6 (cloth)
978-1-60909-226-9 (e-book)
Book and cover design by Yuni Dorr

Library of Congress Cataloging-in-Publication Data
Names: Hartston, Barnet P. (Barnet Peretz), 1969– author.
Title: The trial of Gustav Graef : art, sex, and scandal in late nineteenth-century Germany / Barnet Hartston.
Description: DeKalb, IL : Northern Illinois University Press, 2017. | Includes bibliographical references and index.
Identifiers: LCCN 2017034856 (print) | LCCN 2017035546 (ebook) | ISBN 9781609092269 (ebook) | ISBN 9780875807676 (hardback)
Subjects: LCSH: Graef, Gustav, 1821–1895—Trials, litigation, etc. | Trials (Perjury)—Germany—Berlin—19th century. | Artists' models—Germany—Berlin—19th century. | Artists—Germany—Berlin—19th century. | Nudes in art—19th century. | BISAC: HISTORY / Europe / Germany. | ART / Art & Politics. | HISTORY / Modern / 19th Century.
Classification: LCC KK69.G73 (ebook) | LCC KK69.G73 H37 2017 (print) | DDC 345.43/0234—dc23
LC record available at https://lccn.loc.gov/2017034856

For Gloria Leifer-Hartston and Michelle Hartston

TABLE OF CONTENTS

List of Illustrations viii
List of Abbreviations ix
Acknowledgments xi

PROLOGUE 3

INTRODUCTION 9
A Society in Transformation 9
A Culture of Honor 12
Filth and Trash 17
A Note on Method 18

CHAPTER ONE | THE RISE AND FALL OF GUSTAV GRAEF 23
A Portrait of the Artist as a Young Man 23
From Obscurity to Respectability 26
In Pursuit of Beauty 33
A Change of Fortune 37

CHAPTER TWO | THE TRIAL AS PUBLIC SPECTACLE 41
Venue and Cast 43
Disorder in the Court 45
Love Poetry and *The Fairy Tale* 49
The Graef Trial and "New Journalism" 54
A Verdict, but Not an Ending 57

CHAPTER THREE | ARTISTS AND PHILISTINES 61
Naturalism and Idealism 62
The "Model Market" 66
Three Pamphlets 69
The Artists' Declaration 79
The Revolution and Its Victims 86

CHAPTER FOUR | WOMEN'S VOICES / WOMEN'S SILENCES 93
Prostitution and the "Fallen Woman" in Imperial Germany 95
Constructing a Fairy Tale Model 104
The Graef Trial and German Feminism 107
Assuming Femininity 114

CHAPTER FIVE | STORIES ABOUT OTHERS 117
A Dark and Uncivilized World 120
A Case of Madness or Dissimulation? 127
Defiance and Agency 130
A Powerful Example of the Jewish Question 133

CHAPTER SIX | A CRIMINAL JUSTICE SYSTEM IN CRISIS 144
New Codes, New Problems 145
In the Throes of Perjury Fever 148
Art and Obscenity 151
Closing the Courtroom 162
From Lex Graef to Lex Heinze 174

CHAPTER SEVEN | POWER CONFLICTS IN THE COURTROOM 186
The Almighty Prosecutor 190
The Absolute Discretion of Judges 195
A Lawyers' World 199
There Are Still Juries in Berlin! 204

EPILOGUE 214

CONCLUSION 225

NOTES 235
BIBLIOGRAPHY 271
INDEX 281

LIST OF ILLUSTRATIONS

FIGURE 1 Photograph of Gustav Graef (1885) 5
FIGURE 2 Photograph of Bertha Rother (1885) 6
FIGURE 3 Gustav Graef, *Auszug der ostpreußischen Landwehr ins Feld 1813 nach deren Einsegnung in der Kirche* [The East Prussian Militia takes to the field in 1813 after receiving a blessing in the Church at Königsberg], 1860–1861 27
FIGURE 4 Gustav Graef, *Vaterlandsliebe im Jahre 1813—Ferdinande von Schmettau opfert ihr Haar für das Vaterland* [Love of the Fatherland in 1813: Ferdinande von Schmettau sacrifices her hair on the altar of the Fatherland], 1863 28
FIGURE 5 Art Card of Gustav Graef's *Félicie* 31
FIGURE 6 Henri Gervex, *Rolla* (1878) 32
FIGURE 7 Gustav Graef, *Das Märchen* [The Fairy Tale] 35
FIGURE 8 Postcard of the Criminal Court Building in Berlin-Moabit (1905) 42
FIGURE 9 Newspaper advertisement for a posttrial brochure from E. Bartels Press 53
FIGURE 10 Sketch of Karl Frenzel 69
FIGURE 11 Newspaper advertisement for Max Heinemann's brochure *Der Prozeß Graef und die deutsche Kunst* [The Graef trial and German art] 71
FIGURE 12 Photograph of Paul Lindau 74
FIGURE 13 Photograph of Adolph Menzel with Anton von Werner 81
FIGURE 14 Letter from Bertha Rother to the Police-Presidium Berlin 92
FIGURE 15 A flyer from the Schulze publishing house reporting the trial verdict 154
FIGURE 16 Sketch of Bertha Rother in costume (1887) 220

LIST OF ABBREVIATIONS

AdF:	General German Women's Association (*Allgemeine deutsche Frauenverein*)
ALR:	Prussian General Code (*Allgemeinen Landrecht für die preußischen Staaten*)
BArch:	Bundesarchiv Berlin-Lichterfelde
DLA Marbach:	Deutsches Literaturarchiv Marbach
GStA PK:	Geheimes Staatsarchiv Preußischer Kulturbesitz
GVG:	German Court Organization Law (*Gerichtsverfassungsgesetz*)
LAB:	Landesarchiv Berlin
PrAdK:	Historisches Archiv: Archiv der Preußischen Akademie der Künste
SAPD:	Socialist Workers' Party of Germany (Sozialistische Arbeiterpartei Deutschlands)
StGB:	Criminal Code (*Strafgesetzbuch*)

ACKNOWLEDGMENTS

There is nothing better than a good story. I first stumbled upon the Graef trial while engaging in research for my dissertation in 1996. Although I was captivated by the richness and strangeness of the case, it did not fit into my existing research agenda, and I decided to shelve it—at least temporarily. Unfortunately, it took me more than a decade and a half to return to the case; the wait, however, was well worthwhile. I have enjoyed this project as much as any I have ever engaged in. I can only hope that a fraction of the joy I found in the research and writing of this book will be found in the reading of it as well.

My journey toward this book first began with a rambling and unfocused presentation at a 2012 DAAD Workshop on Weimar Legal Culture at Vanderbilt's Max Kade Center for German and European Studies, hosted by Henning Grunwald and Helmut Walser Smith. I am grateful to those who attended not only for their extraordinary patience, but also for their encouragement at such an early stage of my research. I should also mention the essential role of a 2010 DAAD Faculty Summer Seminar on "Violence and the Law in German Cultures of Modernity" at Cornell University, which was hosted by Isabel Hull. Those who attended this six-week seminar will clearly recognize the influence of our common readings and discussions on the law in German history in my approach to this research project. I am deeply indebted to them, and also to the DAAD for their generous support of such work. The substantial research required for this project would not have been possible without the Lloyd W. Chapin Faculty Research Fellowship, which provided generous support for my long research stays in Berlin. I therefore owe a special debt of gratitude to Eckerd College, Lloyd Chapin, and particularly to Helmar Nielsen, who is responsible for this wonderful endowment.

Sace Elder was generous with her time and refreshingly blunt with her feedback, and the detailed reviews of Ann Goldberg and Sarah Leonard (as well as their own wonderful record of scholarship) helped make this a better book. Many others, including Benjamin Hett, Richard Wetzell, Theresa Smith, Lee Irby, and David Pinto also provided both welcome advice and encouragement along the way. A number of archivists were instrumental in pointing me to sources that I otherwise may have missed—especially Julian Schulenburg of the Geheimes Staatsarchiv Preussischer Kulturbesitz, whose extensive research advice proved particularly fruitful. Thanks are also due to the staff at the Landesarchiv Berlin, the

Bundesarchiv Berlin-Lichterfelde, the Staatsbibliothek zu Berlin and the Deutsches Literaturarchiv in Marbach.

The staff at Northern Illinois University Press have been wonderful to work with, especially Amy Farranto and Nathan Holmes, whose patience and good advice made the process of getting this manuscript into print a very positive one. I would also like to express my gratitude to Elizabeth Dale, editor of the journal *Law and History Review*, for allowing me to use portions of my forthcoming article "Closing the Courtroom: Press Restrictions and Criminal Trials in Late Nineteenth-Century Germany" in this book.

Finally, I would also like to thank my daughters McKenzie, Tess, and Sofia Augusta, and my son Daniel Hartston, each of whom make every day both a joy and an adventure. Heidi, Paul, and Ruby Epstein; Amos, Thuy, Spencer, and Ryan Hartston; and Eve, David, Zoe, Elliot, and Ian Fleck have all contributed to my work—even if they never read a word. My heartfelt appreciation also goes to the two people without whom this book would never have happened: Gloria Leifer-Hartston, who has provided a lifetime of love, encouragement, and ample inspiration through her example as a scholar and teacher, and Michelle Hartston, whose rapt attention to the details of my daily journeys to nineteenth-century Berlin may occasionally have been feigned, but whose love and support were always genuine. This book is dedicated to them.

THE TRIAL OF GUSTAV GRAEF

PROLOGUE

An Arresting Story

There are no surviving descriptions of the scene, but one can easily imagine the chaos. First, the sudden, sharp knock at the front door as police officers demanded entry into the apartment. Then, a frenzied search of the residence as the elderly professor, his wife, and his two adult children looked on in disbelief. Perhaps an awkward fumbling for keys as the police ordered the professor to open the locked drawers in his office desk, and pleas from the family left unanswered as the men stuffed confiscated papers into their satchels. Finally, the biggest shock of all: the police officers announced that the sixty-three-year-old Gustav Graef was now under arrest and would be taken to police headquarters at the Molkenmarkt in Central Berlin. In just a few minutes, a man's hard-earned reputation was ruined and a family's long struggle for prosperity was imperiled. For the prisoner, Gustav Graef, was no ordinary man. He was a respected professor, a member of the Royal Academy of Arts, and one of the most famous painters in Berlin.

Despite his own protestations of innocence and appeals by his family, Gustav Graef was not allowed to post bail. This was in part due to the serious nature of the crimes with which he had been charged: perjury, subornation of perjury, and two counts of inappropriate relations with female models under the age of fourteen. Because of the ongoing investigation, a backlog of cases in the court system, the sickness of key witnesses, as well as the traditional summer recess for Berlin criminal courts, Gustav Graef would spend the next six months in pretrial custody.[1] Although the arrest itself in March 1885 generated only minimal press attention, the trial of Gustav Graef the following September would result in one of the most sensational *causes célèbres* of this era.

Ironically, for many observers the central figure of the Graef affair was not the painter himself, but his favorite young model, alleged victim, *and codefendant*, Bertha Rother. For complicated reasons that will be explained in chapter one, Bertha was also taken into custody by Berlin police along with her mother and younger sister. The three members of the Rother family would remain incarcerated for the next six months, and they would eventually sit beside Graef as defendants at trial. While the arrest of Gustav Graef threatened to destroy his public reputation, the arrest of Bertha Rother had exactly the opposite effect on her public status. From a poor and troubled childhood in Berlin's Moabit district, this twenty-one-year-old woman was suddenly and spectacularly elevated into an international celebrity, a symbol of feminine beauty, and an alternately worshipped or reviled object of sexual desire. Bertha was viewed by many as the young siren so incredibly beautiful that she had not only inspired an accomplished artist, but also allegedly tempted him to lose his moral compass and throw away both his career and his reputation.

By the midpoint of the trial, the public fascination with Bertha Rother had become a public obsession. Young men crowded around the courthouse in the hope of catching a glimpse of her, and a few allegedly offered enormous sums of money for coveted seats inside the courtroom. One enterprising admirer even succeeded in slipping past security to give her a bouquet of flowers while she walked in an internal hallway between the courtroom and her jail cell. Meanwhile, photographs and sketches of Bertha, along with "art cards" featuring Graef's nude paintings of her, appeared and disappeared from the front windows of local bookstores and art shops faster than they could be replaced. Berlin police even banned street corner sales of publications that bore Bertha's image in fear of the public unrest that might result. For a time, as one Canadian newspaper claimed, Bertha Rother was "the best-known woman in Germany outside of the royal family."[2]

Although a variety of images of Bertha Rother, both clothed and unclothed, flooded the shops and bookstores of Berlin (and soon spread to the rest of Germany and across Europe), one image in particular was most highly sought after. It was the painting that Gustav Graef had intended to be his masterpiece: *Das Märchen* (*The Fairy Tale*) (see figure 7). This painting depicts a story of obscure origins, and it is not entirely clear how much of it was inspired by traditional German fairy tales and how much was Graef's personal creation. According to his own description of the work, it portrays a young princess who had earlier been transformed into a fish by an evil witch, at the exact moment she emerges from the water, sloughs off her scales, and frees herself from the witch's curse. At the same time, a raven—perhaps representing a prince cursed by the same witch—swoops down to grasp the fish scales with his beak to help pull them away. The image was intended by Graef to capture the precise moment of the young princess's liberation, where the glorious beauty of her body is revealed in the glimmering

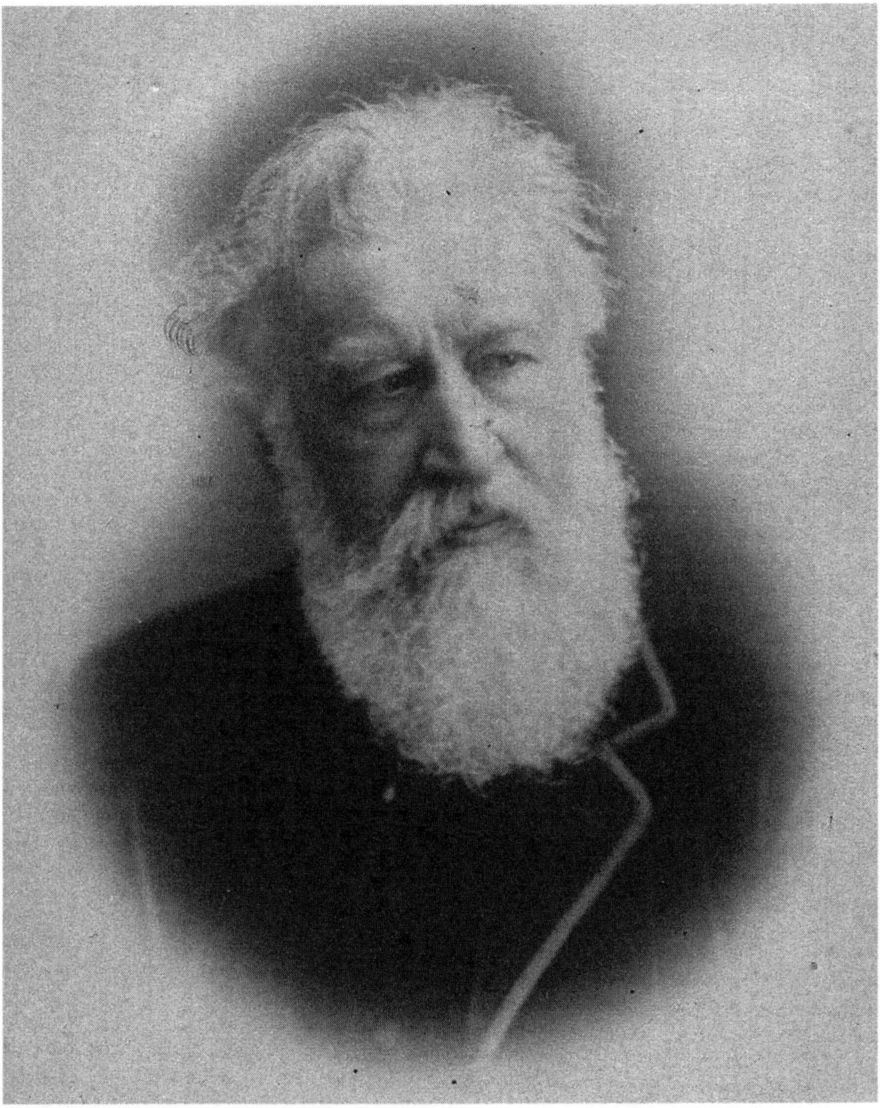

FIGURE 1. Photograph of Gustav Graef (1885). Courtesy of the SLUB Dresden / Digitale Sammlungen aus: Op.var.950-32, misc.8.

sunlight.[3] This painting was Gustav Graef's admitted obsession, and he labored on it for more than five years—even reworking it one last time during his long pretrial incarceration. One might even suggest that *The Fairy Tale* itself was put on trial alongside its creator. Not only was it formally submitted as evidence during

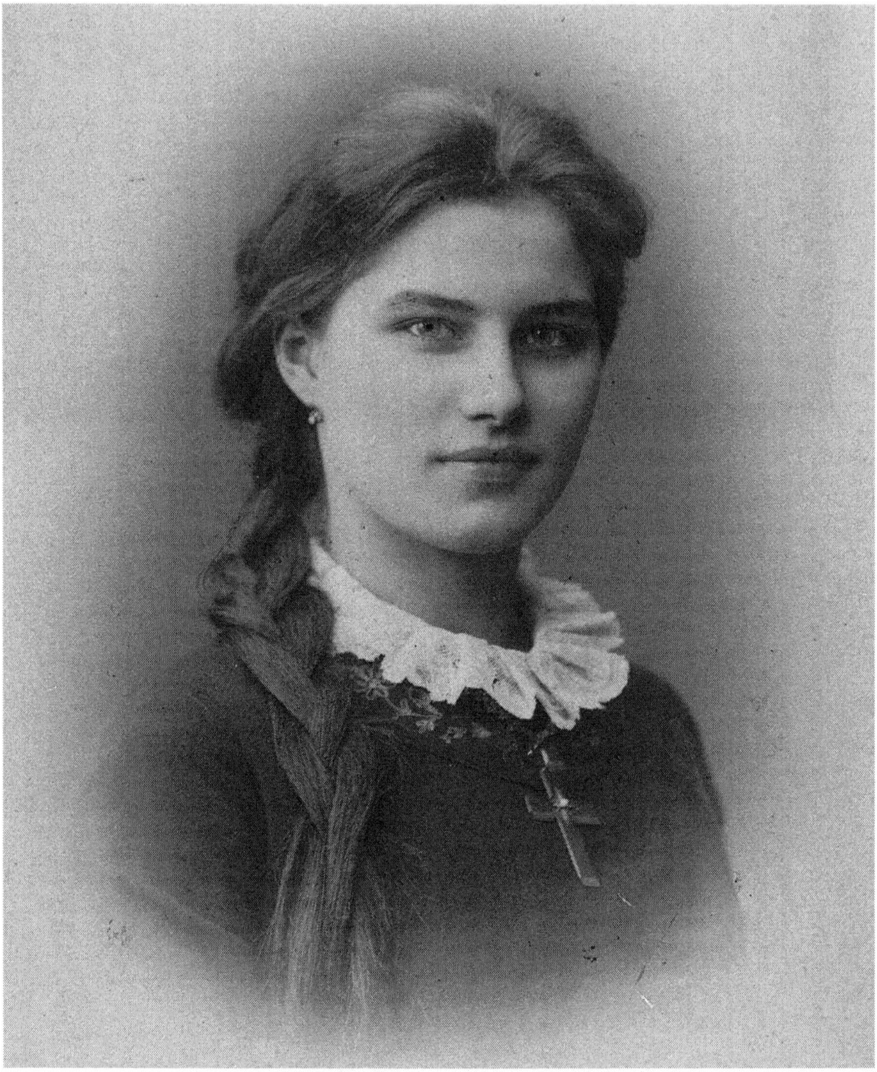

FIGURE 2. Photograph of Bertha Rother (1885). Courtesy of the SLUB Dresden / Digitale Sammlungen aus: Op.var.950-32, misc.8.

the proceedings, but it was also the subject of both internal police deliberations and heated public debates about whether it was a true work of art or an obscene and vulgar image. Such debates lasted long after a verdict in the Graef trial was delivered by the jury.

Although Graef's painting was intended to depict a moment of joy and triumph, a celebration of beauty, and the victory of good over evil, the historical episode surrounding it is much darker and more morally ambiguous—perhaps reminiscent of original tales from the Brothers Grimm rather than their sanitized modern versions. Because of her legendary beauty and her association with Gustav Graef's controversial painting, Bertha Rother was occasionally described by observers as the "Fairy Tale Model." For Rother, however, as well as for Gustav Graef and many other characters in this real-life drama, this tale would have no happy ending. Regardless of what one might conclude about the personal credibility or moral depravity of individual defendants and trial participants, it is clear that the trial left permanent scars on almost everyone it touched.

It is perhaps a bit surprising that the "Graef Affair" is so little remembered in Germany, especially considering the intense attention paid by the German and international press and Gustav Graef's substantial reputation at the time. In some respects, this scandal was part of a general pattern of sensational trials that occupied the public imagination in turn-of-the-century Germany; however, this case was also unique in many ways. It provoked fierce public debates about issues far beyond the guilt or innocence of a single man or the beauty of a particular woman, including arguments about art and obscenity, gender and class relations, the allegedly corruptive influence of Jews on German culture, and perceived flaws in German legal codes. The Graef trial, therefore, is much more than simply a fascinating story; it can also serve as a useful window into political, social, and cultural tensions within German society during this era.

INTRODUCTION

To help us understand the behavior of the participants in the Graef trial as well as the reactions of observers, it is essential to appreciate at least three basic facts about German society in the 1880s. First, Germany was in the midst of a difficult transformation that had begun to undermine traditional social relations and political institutions. Put simply, rapid industrialization and urbanization were altering everyday life in German cities. Second, in part as a response to the social upheaval caused by this transformation, German society developed a rather complex and pervasive honor culture that emphasized education, experience, courage, and other typically "masculine" characteristics. This honor culture served many purposes, the most important of which was to separate out those entitled to a measure of honor and respect (bourgeois gentlemen) from those with little or no inherent honor (women, children, and the working classes). Notably, this honor culture was closely tied to a "crisis of masculinity" that developed as German women began to campaign more vocally for greater rights in society. Finally, there was also a widespread perception at the time that standards of morality within German society had declined substantially, and that pornographic art and literature, as well as prostitution and deviant sexual behavior, now posed a grave threat to the basic fabric of society. Because the three themes of socioeconomic transformation, bourgeois masculine honor, and obsession with cultural and moral decline will run throughout this book, a slightly longer discussion of each one may be useful at this point.

A SOCIETY IN TRANSFORMATION

On January 18, 1871, in the Hall of Mirrors at the Versailles Palace, Otto von Bismarck joined with dozens of military officers and the princes of various

German states to proclaim the founding of a new German Empire. The diverse German lands, long divided into kingdoms, duchies, and principalities, were at long last unified into a single nation under the rule of Kaiser Wilhelm, the former king of Prussia.[1] The founding of the German Empire was reason enough for German nationalists to celebrate. However, this triumphal moment also came on the heels of a spectacular victory over the rival French army at Sedan, which included not only the crushing of French forces, but also the capture of Emperor Napoleon III. It was also followed, in part due to an influx of cash from French reparations, by an economic boom and a dramatic rise in the value of stocks. This was, or so it seemed, the beginning of a golden age for Germany.

The exuberance did not last long. In 1873, a financial panic spread across Europe and America as major stock markets crashed, taking with them the solvency of dozens of companies and the personal savings of both the affluent and those whose wealth was merely aspirational. This financial crisis would help trigger the Great Depression of the nineteenth century, which would last (with short periods of recovery) until 1896. For many German elites, anguish over the financial crisis of 1873 was accompanied by a growing anxiety over rapid industrialization and urbanization. Beginning in the 1880s, waves of rural migrants from central and eastern Europe flooded into major cities such as Berlin and into the boom towns of the Rhine and Ruhr valleys. The changing character of urban society led to mounting fears about squalor and declining health, increased crime, and the potentially dangerous (and revolutionary) character of the lower classes.[2]

The initial optimism of unification began to break down in other ways as well. Political rivalries, for example, became more intense during the 1870s as Bismarck labeled many of his opponents "enemies of the Reich" and launched campaigns to limit the influence of the Catholic Church. Even the adoption of new law codes, which were intended to balance Prussian traditions with those of the smaller German states, left neither side satisfied. In other words, the work of political and legal unification was begun in 1871, but it would continue to be an uncomfortable and divisive process for at least a generation.

The decade of the 1870s also included the formation of the Socialist Workers' Party of Germany (SAPD) under the leadership of Wilhelm Liebknecht and August Bebel. Because this party followed Marxist principles and advocated an eventual violent overthrow of both the monarchy and economic elites, it was treated as a dangerous pariah organization by Chancellor Otto von Bismarck and most other politicians across the spectrum. Bismarck would seek to win workers away from socialism in the 1880s, at first by tacitly supporting the alternative

Christian-Social Party, and later by passing landmark social legislation—including sickness insurance, accident insurance, and old age and disability insurance. In addition, Protestant leaders launched urban missions to aid the lower classes and bring them back within the Christian fold, and others would form "morality associations" both to campaign for stronger laws regarding immoral behavior and to assist prostitutes and other lower-class "fallen women."[3] In the meantime, Otto von Bismarck did his level best to destroy the infrastructure of the SAPD. He used a pair of assassination attempts on Kaiser Wilhelm in 1878 as a justification to officially ban the party, and he would use the power of the public prosecutor to harass, intimidate, and repeatedly jail those Socialists who dared to publish critiques of his policies. While German Socialists would later consider the decade of the 1880s to be a "heroic period" of resistance, for many Germans it was the time when a deep and abiding fear of working-class militancy became prevalent.

Finally, although Imperial Germany was far from what we might call a modern democracy, there is substantial evidence that a process of democratization was beginning to take place during this period of demographic transformation. As Margaret Anderson suggests in her exceptional book *Practicing Democracy*, the institution of voting by universal manhood suffrage for delegates in the Reichstag (lower house of parliament) helped to create a diverse and powerful grassroots political culture before the turn of the century; as she puts it, Germans were busy "rapidly transforming a segmentary, authoritarian, and communal culture that professed to abhor partisanship of any kind into a nationalized, participatory, public culture, one in which partisan loyalties organized expectations and structured much of public life."[4] Thus, despite the institutional advantages still enjoyed by government officials and conservative elites (including an unelected executive and a lack of ministerial responsibility), this electoral system provided real room for political dissent and reinforced new cultural norms—especially greater public awareness of legal rights and guarantees of fair election procedures.[5] If the institutions of German democracy were not yet fully developed, Anderson argues, then at least the rules of democratic procedure could still be used to challenge the will of the government and to delimit the government's possible responses to political opposition.

Not surprisingly, Imperial Germany has frequently been described by historians as a "hybrid state": a nation with both democratic institutions and authoritarian leaders, modern social programs and reactionary social traditions, a flourishing political press and a government determined to silence and punish its severest critics. To some degree all societies are hybrid, as they occupy tenuous and often contentious middle grounds between centralized power and devolution and between tradition and change. In Imperial Germany, however, such tensions were especially pronounced, and anxiety about the state of society, and about the development and direction of public opinion and popular culture, was intensified through the echo chamber of an active political press. This work will venture some limited comparisons between the Graef Affair and similar episodes in contemporary British society. Although such comparisons will undoubtedly highlight peculiarities of the German experience, they will also tend to suggest that German society in this period was on a twisted road toward modernity rather than in the midst of an inexorable decline toward fascism.

A CULTURE OF HONOR

At the start of chapter one, we will trace the unexpected rise of the artist Gustav Graef from a childhood of poverty in Eastern Prussia to a life of luxury and privilege as one of the most respected painters in Berlin. If this brief summary of his life story vaguely resembles one of those books by Horatio Alger that were popular in the United States in the mid-nineteenth century, in which a young man relies on honest hard work and a bit of good fortune to rise from "rags to riches," it is important to note that the world of class and status in Imperial Germany was far more complex and variegated than simply "rags" and "riches." Gustav Graef had not entered the world as a simple bootblack sleeping on the streets or wallowing in the workhouses; he may have been born poor, but his family, which included both professors and pastors, was not without status. As for Graef's meteoric rise, it was an ascent into the highest echelons of a particular part of the bourgeoisie, the *Bildungsbürgertum*, an educated and cultured bourgeois elite.[6] Membership in this social class was marked not by rank or title, but by a complex code of honor that could vary slightly depending on one's exact position and level of education. The core of this honor culture was an ethic of work, thrift, honesty, moderation, and sexual chastity. The careful and even obsessive maintenance of this sense of honor and reputation was essential to maintaining social standing—and to ensuring an appropriate amount of power, respect, and deference in social relations.[7] As the historian Ann Goldberg suggests, honor was a form of currency that could be turned into concrete services (including social status, jobs, credit, marriage, and power), but it could just as easily be squandered and lost.[8] Understanding this code of honor is essential to understanding the gravity of the charges against Gustav Graef: this case, it turns out, revolved much more around potential breaches of bourgeois standards of honor than the achievement of justice for young lower-class victims of sexual exploitation.

The intricate, contradictory, and occasionally absurd demands of this "bourgeois culture of honor" have been the focus of a wide range of scholarly studies. Beginning in the 1990s, for example, Ute Frevert, V. G. Kiernan, and Kevin McAleer examined a resurgence of dueling culture (with both swords and pistols) during the late nineteenth century.[9] Although the duel originated in aristocratic rituals of honor during the early-modern period, it now served both in university dueling clubs and in public life as an ultimate symbolic measure of bourgeois values of honor, courage, and masculine self-discipline. Dueling was technically considered a criminal act in Imperial Germany; however, it was usually punished with a slap on the wrist or a small jail sentence. A refusal to duel, on the other hand, could have much more serious consequences—including public humiliation and even dismissal from the military. Honor was thus, quite literally in some cases, a matter of life or death. The hypocritical attitude of German authorities toward the duel is especially evident in the practices of the German Military Honor Courts (*militärische Ehrengerichte*), which had originally been designed to forestall duels by providing judgments in matters of military honor. By the 1880s, these courts seemed to be having the opposite effect. Although officials of the Honor Courts discouraged dueling, they also now offered to attend the duels to make sure they were properly carried out.[10]

The revival of dueling in Imperial Germany was accompanied by a stunning growth in public denunciations and honor-related litigation. In her landmark 2010 book, *Honor, Politics, and the Law in Imperial Germany*, Ann Goldberg argues that Germany's honor culture was far more juridified than that in most other countries. On the one hand, libel laws provided a powerful method for the government to silence dissent and intimidate political enemies. When Otto von Bismarck labeled German Catholics, Socialists, and even some Junker nobles who were critical of his policies as "enemies of the Reich," he backed up this rhetoric with explicit orders that public prosecutors vigorously pursue slander and libel cases against these groups. The more significant development in German society, however, was not the use of slander and libel laws as tools of political oppression, but their use in regulating disputes involving personal honor. As Goldberg reports, there were 52,645 criminal indictments for libel in Germany in 1883; in 1910 there were 84,058 indictments. These figures dwarf the number of libel prosecutions in France, and they do not include the tens of thousands of libel suits in Germany that were settled out of court. They also do not include the large numbers of so-called *Privatklage* (private suits), where allegations of slander could be filed by private plaintiffs and litigated under criminal law before local magistrates.[11] The obsession with maintaining personal honor was so powerful, it created an overwhelming burden for German criminal and civil courts.

Special Honor Courts also played an increasingly important role in the regulation of German professions, beginning with law and medicine and gradually extending into a variety of fields. These Honor Courts policed professional standards and personal behavior, and they also served as a way to sharpen professional identity by emphasizing standards of honor, masculine self-discipline, and specialized knowledge in an attempt to distinguish experts from "laypeople."[12] Even in professions without a formal system of Honor Courts, breaches of honor could be informally policed by various clubs or professional associations. Inappropriate behavior could bring private reprimands or, in more extreme cases, even shunning or expulsion—a kind of excommunication from the professional community. As we will see, this was even true for Gustav Graef and his artistic peers in Berlin, whose community was informally unified and regulated by membership in the Association of Berlin Artists (*Verein Berliner Künstler*).[13]

It is difficult to overstate the pervasiveness of this culture of honor within the German elites. As Goldberg again explains: "No social interaction, no gesture or statement, however trivial, seemed immune from denunciation and litigation. The motives and interests behind these lawsuits were extremely varied: revenge, rage, jealousy, setting the record straight, restoring one's reputation, defeating an opponent, shaming an enemy."[14] At its core, this obsession with honor was not a sign of stability and self-confidence within the German bourgeoisie, but a product of the deep anxieties formed within a society in the midst of a dramatic transformation. In a sense, this obsession with honor can be seen as a reaction against modernity—an attempt to reinforce traditional values against the perceived social and moral degeneration of the modern world.

Those groups excluded from this world of bourgeois honor, including women, Jews, and members of the lower classes—as well as deviants, criminals, and lunatics—were frequently characterized as unsuited for participation in the public sphere since they were considered uncultured, irrational, and essentially "feminine" in nature.[15] In fact, political discourse in Imperial Germany was frequently shaped by debates about how to deal with these troublesome populations, including a large pamphlet literature dedicated to answering a "Jewish Question" (*Judenfrage*) alongside a "Women's Question" (*Frauenfrage*) and a "Social Question" (*soziale Frage*). The threats these groups posed seemed not just to endanger the power and status of bourgeois men, but the very stability of the nation as a whole.

It is important to note here that members of these "outsider" populations could occasionally make use of the courtroom to press their own claims for public honor and respect, although usually with only limited effectiveness. German women, especially after the turn of the century, would begin to step forward in public to defend their honor—even sometimes seeking to shame the men (or the government officials) they felt had caused their own disgrace.[16] Typical notions of female honor, however, were far different from those commonly attributed to men. Female honor was much more closely tied to sexual honor, and once sullied, this sexual honor could not be easily repaired. As Ute Frevert suggests: "A woman who had forfeited this integrity by giving her body to a man who had no 'right' to it (or by being forced to do so) also forfeited her honour. It was only logical that women whose physical honour had been forfeited in such a manner could not restore it by their own physical efforts. Honour which had been 'besmirched' by a man, could only be 'rehabilitated' by a man."[17] Women, in other words, were usually dependent on a male "guardian" (or on the justice system) to seek vengeance for their damaged honor and reputation. The notion of a woman fighting a duel would have seemed entirely ridiculous to most Germans; in fact, it was commonly accepted that a woman who had insulted a man was simply to be disregarded or the matter was to be taken up with her husband or family.[18]

It is not surprising, therefore, that after Gustav Graef began to achieve substantial success as a painter, his wife Franziska would retreat from her various occupations back into the home. Although she did host a popular weekly salon, her primary responsibilities as a bourgeois wife were now to manage the servants and dedicate herself to the successful upbringing of her children. It is also not surprising that Franziska's voice is almost entirely missing from the historical record of this affair; in respectable German society, it was not a wife's role to publicly comment or to defend her husband against scandalous accusations—even though her own standing and reputation in society was as much at stake as his.[19]

Interestingly, most public conflicts between German Jews and anti-Semites during this era did not lead to direct challenges, either in formal duels or in a court of law. On the one hand, a duel would have been a tacit acknowledgment of the slanderer's honor and his "ability to grant satisfaction." On the other hand, a private slander suit might also expose a Jewish defendant to court costs and to future targeting by other anti-Semitic agitators. Unfortunately, most requests by German Jews that state prosecutors target anti-Semites for egregious cases of slander and libel, or for publicly insulting an established religion, fell on deaf ears.[20] There were, however, a small but growing number of Jews who were willing and even eager to defend themselves in public. Perhaps the best example during the 1880s was the prominent journalist and Orthodox rabbi Hirsch Hildesheimer, who would willingly slander anti-Semites in the most outrageous manner possible in the hopes of forcing them to sue him. At trial, Hildesheimer and his lawyers would then attempt to systematically demonstrate the truth of their defamatory comments while publicly defending their own manhood and bravery in the press.[21] Although one could argue that legal actions filed by Hildesheimer and later Jewish "defense organizations" seriously impacted the fortunes of individual anti-Semitic agitators, it would be much more difficult to prove that they reduced the pervasiveness of anti-Jewish sentiments in any significant way.

There were also a growing number of cases during this era in which working-class men used slander laws as a tool in labor disputes, suing strikebreakers or even employers for comments that disparaged their honor. For Ann Goldberg, this suggests that alongside the hierarchical and class-based nature of honor culture in Imperial Germany, there was also a growing "democratization of honor."[22] In early modern Germany, such suits would have seemed incomprehensible; in Imperial Germany, they were a sign of a growing discourse of citizenship and legal equality. Goldberg does admit, however, that slander lawsuits filed by workers against employers usually went nowhere, primarily because §193 of the Penal Code proscribed suits against employers for criticizing their subordinates.[23] If members of the lower classes were more willing to make claims of honor based upon their citizenship and equality before the law, those claims were often ineffective in a society still so visibly divided by class and status.

The triumphant ascent of Gustav Graef and his family from poverty into a life of comfort, privilege, and honor, then, was also entry into a world where a single misstep could be personally devastating for a man of status. Certainly, accusations of sexual impropriety with a minor and perjury under oath were among the most serious charges a respected bourgeois gentleman could face. In a society so obsessed with public honor, the mere insinuation that one might have engaged in indecent or immoral behavior could be as personally and socially devastating as an actual conviction in court.

FILTH AND TRASH

A third important characteristic of Imperial German society was a growing obsession with the amount of *Schmutz- und Schundliteratur* (filth and trash literature) publicly available in German society. The ready accessibility of erotic books and pornographic photographs, often characterized as "filth," and the spread of inexpensive and low-quality pulp fiction, labeled as "trash," created a general sense in upper echelons of society that German culture and standards of morality were under serious threat.[24] The peak of this paranoia came in the 1890s, after an especially lurid murder trial for the killing of a Berlin night watchman, the so-called Heinze case, filled the headlines. Critics blamed the widespread availability of "filth and trash" not only for such gruesome cases as the Heinze murder, but also for much of what was wrong with German society, including the spread of sexual perversions and venereal diseases, and dramatic increases in prostitution and criminality in general.[25] The Heinze case thus sparked a "moral panic" in Germany, and it spurred a decade-long battle over the so-called Lex Heinze: a series of laws pushed by a coalition of "morality associations" designed to root out the moral corruption that was poisoning the social body—especially by restricting literature, theater performances, and artworks that violated a public "sense of shame."[26]

The "moral panic" in the decade after the 1891 Heinze case had its roots in much earlier developments. Beginning in midcentury, the development of wood cellulose paper, the high-speed rotary press, and new photographic techniques helped to expand the range of available and affordable printed material. This resulted in a dramatic increase in the number of newspapers, cheap novels, plays, and pamphlets—as well as pornographic texts and images.[27] Print culture had heretofore been the domain of social elites; now, however, inexpensive reading material of questionable quality was available to all. Instead of being exposed to classical art and literature which would enrich and ennoble them, the most vulnerable populations of the Reich, including women, children, and members of the working class, were being bombarded by filth and trash that, it was feared, would inevitably lead to moral corruption and the undermining of the social order.[28]

Gary Stark argues that comprehending the role of nationalism in the German *Kaiserreich* is also essential to understanding this obsession with rooting out "filth and trash." Rising popular nationalism, as well as the emergence of theories of racial competition produced by men like the Comte de Gobineau, led to concerns about the need to maintain high birthrates and also to efforts to restrict sexual activity to heterosexual marriage and reproduction for the good of the nation.[29]

Indeed, growing concerns about the effects of "filth and trash" on the public were not limited to Imperial Germany; as Gary Stark suggests, similar trends and a similar paranoia about indecent texts and images occurred in France, England, and the United States.[30] Although the Heinze case is remembered as the primary trigger for the moral panic of the 1890s, the trial of Gustav Graef, which occurred only six years earlier, undoubtedly also played an important role in stoking rising levels of public anxiety. Sensational journalistic accounts of the Graef case, as well as the widespread circulation of photos of Bertha Rother (both nude and clothed), generated substantial public outrage and even led to the passing of explicit laws that restricted press coverage of sensational trials.

One might anticipate in a fairly authoritarian state such as Imperial Germany that courtroom conflicts about obscene texts and images might be reduced to a simple struggle between conservative police, prosecutors, and government officials on the one hand, and radical intellectuals, artists, and smut-peddlers who wished to protect freedom of expression at all costs, on the other. This is simply not the case. Indeed, as we will see, the Graef case exposed serious disagreements and internal dissention between various police authorities, justice officials, and private jurists about when legal intervention could be justified and what methods of intervention would be most effective. Such dissention was equally apparent among German artists and writers.

A NOTE ON METHOD

This book, of course, is not the first work of history to focus on a single trial (or group of trials) as a tool to gain insight into a particular cultural milieu. By now, microhistory as a subdiscipline has developed a significant history of its own, from classic works by Carlo Ginsburg and Natalie Zemon Davis to more recent books by Edward Berenson and Helmut Walser Smith.[31] Although the authors of small-scale histories do not always share the same methodological framework, they do usually proceed from a common assumption: by starting with individual stories rather than broader trends, historians can often more easily recognize the nuances, contradictions, and complexities that are hidden within the broader picture. Only by tugging at the threads of individuals' life stories can one get a real sense of the complex cultural fabric within which their lives were intertwined. In the story of the Graef trial we will encounter a social and cultural world so very similar to, and yet so very different from our own.

The Graef case was not the first trial used by the German press to both attract readers and score political points, and it was certainly also not the last. A number of impressive studies have appeared in recent years that reveal a pattern of sensational trials during the Imperial era and examine their effects on German political culture.[32] There are a number of causes célèbres to choose from, including the Heinze murder trial of 1891 and a later series of sex scandals that implicated members of Kaiser Wilhelm's inner circle in orgies and homosexual trysts. As Martin Kohlrausch argues in his book *Der Monarch im Skandal* (The Monarch in Scandal), it was the withering press coverage of such sex scandals that helped to decisively undermine both Kaiser Wilhelm II's personal image and damage the sacred aura surrounding the German monarchy.[33] Kohlrausch, like many scholars who have researched public scandals in Imperial Germany, begins his analysis in the 1890s. This decade, he suggests, was the pivotal period in which a German "mass media" first came of age and became a powerful force in driving criticism of the political system. The idea that the 1890s were a transformative decade in German political and cultural history has been a common assertion, but it is also a bit of an exaggeration.[34] As we will see, press coverage of the 1885 Graef trial also drove political debates on a number of fronts, and it directly influenced the actions of both government officials and legislators. The Graef trial was no mere prelude to these later scandals, but part of a longer pattern of causes célèbres that dominated the entire history of the German Empire.

There is, of course, an inherent danger in attempting to use a public scandal as a tool to make generalizations about the German criminal justice system or about Imperial German society as a whole. These extraordinary scandals are by definition outside of the norm and therefore are not truly representative of everyday political and legal practices. In her recent book *Machtvolle Verhandlungen* (Powerful Proceedings), Alexandra Ortmann warns us that the "subtleties of contemporary practices can only be measured and judged in the everyday, not in the scandalous."[35] Ortmann is certainly right in advising caution, and her focus on criminal justice in the rural Allgäu (Swabia) provides insights that would be missed in any mere study of urban causes célèbres. However, it is important to remember that in Imperial Germany (and in many other nations at this time), extraordinary scandals had become a fairly typical phenomenon. The extraordinary, in other words, was becoming ever more ordinary in German life. It is also true that sensational trials can sometimes reveal tensions within a society in ways that local conflicts do not. As Frank Bösch argues, public scandals are not merely a reflection of social norms within a society, they can also be a powerful driver of political, legal, and cultural change.[36] Where once historians might have perceived these sorts of sensational stories as worthy only for trashy Pitaval, modern historians see in these scandals a remarkable opportunity for analysis.

This book will begin with a brief examination of the life of Gustav Graef, his development as an artist, and his rise into the upper echelons of bourgeois society. Graef's own personal history overlaps with the remarkable transformation of German art during the nineteenth century from romanticism to historical realism, and eventually to German naturalism and impressionism. Although Graef tended to follow these trends rather than set them, his work was well known, and he achieved national and even international recognition. Finally, the chapter will chronicle his fall from grace, with the dramatic story of his alleged crimes and eventual arrest.

The second chapter will examine the trial as the sort of public spectacle that would become increasingly common in Imperial Germany. Although salacious trials were not entirely new, a controversial new style of sensationalist journalism evident during this case would spark protracted debates about the potentially deleterious effects of sensationalized press coverage on the German public. More specifically, journalists who covered the Graef trial, and especially those who worked for liberal newspapers, were now assailed as dishonorable, ungentlemanly, and a danger to the social and moral health of the nation.

Chapter three will examine the complex repercussions of the Graef Affair in the world of German art. Although the trial took place more than a decade before the Berlin Secession and the revolutionary changes brought about by German impressionism and expressionism, it nonetheless both exposed and exacerbated rifts within the Berlin artistic community. Gustav Graef had never before been a figure of controversy; during and after the trial, however, he was attacked by some as a symbol of all that was wrong with modern art, and defended by others as a victim of reactionary moralists who were clinging to stale and outdated traditions. While the Berlin artistic community was far from unified during the trial, many prominent artistic voices would step forward to vigorously defend the honor of the guild—even at the expense of one of their former colleagues.

Chapter four will pay closer attention to the voices of women in this episode, and it will focus especially on the fascinating figure of Bertha Rother, the so-called "Fairy Tale Model." Unfortunately, the voices of women as both participants and observers of the Graef Affair are not easily accessible in the historical record. This is especially true for Bertha Rother, whose life story was filtered and distorted through the opinions and fantasies of male journalists, authors, and politicians.

Despite this, I will investigate the life of Bertha Rother more closely—if not to uncover her own perspective, then at least to imagine what her own experiences might have been like and to unpack the stereotypes that were often used to frame her as a character for public consumption.

Chapter five will focus on how public debates during and after the Graef trial tended to contribute to the "othering" of two additional social groups: the urban lower classes and German Jews. In the first part of the chapter, I will examine class divisions in German society, both real and imagined, and I will discuss how stereotypes about the poor were reflected in depictions of the trial. The steady stream of witnesses from the poorest areas of Berlin provided a spectacle that journalists, including the well-known novelist, playwright, and cultural critic Paul Lindau, were all too eager to describe in melodramatic and often scornful detail. For Lindau, the behavior of lower-class witnesses at trial (especially compared to the noble bearing of Gustav Graef) was proof of their utter lack of honor or dignity. Surprisingly, the Graef trial was also proclaimed by German anti-Semites as proof of the inherent criminality of Jews and the cultural degeneracy caused by Jewish influence. This case became a valuable propaganda weapon for German anti-Semites *despite the fact that Gustav Graef himself was not Jewish.*

Chapter six will focus on the trial's place in the legal culture of Imperial Germany. The Graef case occurred in the midst of a crisis of confidence in the German criminal justice system. Most legal experts and lay observers at the time agreed that the trial had been an absolute disaster and had reinforced the sense that both the Criminal Code and Code of Criminal Procedure were deeply flawed. In the aftermath of the trial, criticism from the political press was extraordinarily intense as journalists, politicians, and legal experts all weighed in with their own specific complaints and demands for reform. Press coverage of the Graef trial not only helped to drive legal debates over the next several years, but in at least one case these debates had a significant influence on the making of new law.

Finally, chapter seven will return to the courthouse itself, where we will examine the interactions between legal officials in the case—including judges, prosecutors, defense lawyers, and jurors—in order to expose the changing relationships between these parts of the Imperial criminal justice system. As it turns out, it was not only the criminal law codes that were under attack in the new Reich, but also the various roles of court officials themselves, who were desperate to defend their own power, status, and professional honor.

When I first began my research on this topic, there were few substantial works of scholarship focused specifically on the Graef trial. In July of 2014, however, after most of my manuscript had been completed, Dagmar Reese published an excellent monograph on the trial, entitled *Akt und Anstand: Die Skandal um den Gustav Graef Prozess* (Decency and the Nude: The Scandal Surrounding the Gustav Graef Trial), which she describes as a microhistory that helps readers get a more nuanced picture of life in the *Kaiserreich*.[37] Although our two monographs both center on the same 1885 trial, our end products are different in both scope and approach. Reese's book is primarily concerned with tensions within the German art world that were revealed by the Graef trial, including the growing commercialization of art, the increased use of nude female models, and the changing relationship between artists and the models they employed—topics that I touch on only in passing. On the other hand, although Reese devotes some attention to the impact of the trial on debates about class, gender, and honor culture, she does so in rather less depth and with less reference to accumulated scholarship than I have attempted to do here. Interestingly, Reese also tends to straightforwardly depict Gustav Graef as the innocent victim of an overzealous prosecutor and a campaign by moralists and critics of modernity in German art. I offer no conclusions here about Gustav Graef's "guilt"; however, I would suggest the evidence about his behavior is far more contradictory than Reese's depiction suggests. The same, by the way, might be said about the degree to which Graef was personally rehabilitated after the trial. Although I have here stressed some of the differences between our two books, I would also readily praise Dagmar Reese for her research and analysis, from which I have learned much.

Unfortunately, both Dagmar Reese and I have had to pursue our research without any original court records from the Graef trial itself, since they no longer exist in German archives. Thankfully, fairly detailed records of the trial proceedings are preserved through trial transcripts published in leading newspapers of the time as well as in booklets put up for public sale after the verdict. The complex and contentious aftermath of the Graef case is also evident in exchanges between political newspapers and in booklets, specialized legal journals, parliamentary debates, internal government documents, and exchanges of letters—including personal letters sent by Gustav Graef that are in the collection of his daughter, Sabine Lepsius, housed in the Deutsches Literaturarchiv Marbach. This wide range of sources has provided a wealth of interesting, sometimes perplexing, and occasionally surprising insights into this fascinating historical episode.

CHAPTER ONE

THE RISE AND FALL OF GUSTAV GRAEF

The story of Gustav Graef's life is almost as remarkable as the story of the trial that destroyed his career and reputation. From a childhood in relative poverty at the eastern edges of the Prussian kingdom, Graef gradually earned a national reputation and built a very comfortable life for his family. His own personal and artistic path, as well as his rise to wealth and respectability in Berlin society, made him seem a relatively unlikely candidate for such a scandal—thus making his sudden downfall all the more dramatic.

A PORTRAIT OF THE ARTIST AS A YOUNG MAN

Gustav Graef was born into a prominent family in the East Prussian city of Königsberg, now the Russian city of Kaliningrad, on December 14, 1821.[1] Much of his family's reputation came through the achievements of his paternal grandfather, Christoph Hartmann Graef, who had been a professor of theology at the Albertus University of Königsberg—often referred to as the "Albertina." Christoph Graef had served multiple terms as rector (chancellor) and as prorector (vice chancellor) of the university, and his career had overlapped with both the last years of the Albertina's most famous faculty member and former alumnus, Immanuel Kant, and the short but tumultuous presence of Johann Gottlieb Fichte in 1806–1807. Perhaps inevitably, Christoph Graef fell short of the reputation of those two illustrious colleagues; a report on the state of the Albertina commissioned by the Prussian Interior Ministry characterized him only as a "morally honorable man, who approaches his teaching position with honesty and the best of intentions."[2] Despite this rather backhanded compliment, there is ample evidence that Christoph Graef was both honored by his colleagues at the Albertina and celebrated by his students.

In addition to his work as a professor, Christoph Graef was notable for his zealous Prussian nationalism and devout Protestantism. He had been an early member of the Royal German Society of Königsberg (*Königliche Deutsche Gesellschaft*), an association that was formed in the 1740s to encourage the study of German literature and culture. This organization was sponsored by the king of Prussia, Friedrich Wilhelm III, and it remained fiercely loyal to this "father of the fatherland" even during the most perilous years of the Napoleonic Wars.[3] Notably, in the years after 1808, Christoph Graef took the position of prorector (vice chancellor) at the Albertina only because he, along with other members of the faculty senate, had symbolically offered the permanent rectorship to the thirteen-year-old Prussian crown prince (later King Friedrich Wilhelm IV) as a symbol of their reverence for the Prussian monarchy. In addition to his overt patriotism, this patriarch of the Graef family was also known as a religious leader, serving first as an army chaplain during the War of Bavarian Succession, and later as a pastor at the Königsberg cathedral.

Many of the children of Christoph Graef followed in the footsteps of their renowned father. Two sons, Johann Friedrich Graef and Johann Polycarpus Gottfried Graef, were pastors, and a son-in-law, Samuel Wald, was both a pastor and professor of Greek language at the Albertina. Another son, Johann August Ferdinand Graef—the father of Gustav—went in a different direction. J. A. F. Graef became neither a professor nor a pastor; perhaps in part because of relatively limited family funds, he did not pursue the same educational path as his older siblings and ended up in middle-level civil service positions, first as a city clerk (*Stadt-Sekretär*) and then later as a clerk at the High Regional Court (*Oberlandesgerichtssekretär*) in Königsberg.[4] Like Gustav Graef's grandfather, his father was also a member of the nationalistic Royal German Society, and in 1808 he penned and published his own poem to celebrate the birthday of Friedrich Wilhelm III.[5] Unfortunately, he also committed suicide at a young age, leaving his young widow with several children and stepchildren from an earlier marriage and with very little money or potential sources of income. Only through immense effort did Gustav Graef's mother and older siblings succeed in keeping the family together in these difficult circumstances.[6]

Gustav Graef remembered having been attracted to art from a very early point in his childhood. According to an account written much later by his daughter, Sabine Lepsius, Graef had fondly described his own memories of finger-painting great battle scenes on fogged-up windows at a time when his family couldn't afford paint or pencils. As a young student, he was even skilled enough to earn some extra money for the family by sketching portraits. Despite this growing artistic talent, Graef agreed to follow his mother's wishes and study medicine at the Albertina. During his time at the university, he produced one of his earliest known works, an 1843 lithograph of the student club *Corpslandsmannschaft Normania*. In this drawing, Graef depicted his student peers outdoors in their characteristic club uniforms, engaging in drinking, debating, and playing cards. Graef also included himself in the work, sitting on a tree stump while observing and sketching the group.[7] Soon after this sketch was completed, Graef, at the age of twenty-two, decided to abandon his study of medicine and take up the study of art. Somehow he had managed to convince his mother to let him attend the Royal Art Academy in Düsseldorf.

For the young Graef, the move to Düsseldorf must have been a dream come true. At the time, the Düsseldorf Academy was internationally famous as a center for the so-called "Düsseldorf School" of German romantic art. The director of the Academy, Wilhelm von Schadow, was the son of the illustrious sculptor Gottfried Schadow, who still led the Royal Academy of the Arts in Berlin and had designed the famous quadriga atop the Brandenburg Gate. According to the historian Peter Paret, the younger Schadow was a gifted administrator and teacher who fostered a strong sense of community among the artists in training. Under Schadow's tutelage, young artists could enroll in a long course of study, where they could learn everything from portraiture to historical, religious, and genre painting.[8]

Graef's earliest works from this time demonstrate the influence of Wilhelm von Schadow, especially in his choice of religious and mythical subjects. His 1846 oil painting *Chriemhilde Asks Hagen to Protect her Husband Siegfried*, for example, was based upon the Nibelung cycle, and his 1851 painting *Jeptha Meets his Daughter* took a story from the Book of Exodus as its inspiration. Like many other aspiring painters of the time, Graef's formal training at the Academy was followed by journeys to cultural centers such as Antwerp, Paris, and Munich as well as longer stays in Italy, England, and Scotland. Once Graef returned to Königsberg, however, he struggled to make a living. In 1852, Graef finally relocated to Berlin, where he would spend the rest of his life.

Before he left Königsberg for Berlin, Graef met and fell in love with a student in one of his painting classes named Franziska Liebreich. The pair was married in 1853 after a three-year courtship. Known for both her beauty and artistic talent, Franziska came from a prominent Jewish family in Königsberg. Her father was a successful dentist, and her four brothers were all engaged in medical or scientific pursuits.[9] Such mixed marriages were not entirely uncommon during this era, as up to 25–30 percent of young Jewish women in mid-nineteenth-century Prussia entered into marriages with non-Jews. What was particularly unconventional here is that Franziska may have actually *lost* relative social status through her marriage to a poor painter, as opposed to raising her social status by marrying outside her faith.[10]

Gustav and Franziska had three children together, and the younger two would go on to international prominence. Botho Graef eventually became a renowned archaeologist and art historian, while his younger sister Sabine would follow in her father's footsteps and become a famous painter in her own right—along with her equally successful husband, Reinhold Lepsius. As a young man who was starting a family, however, Gustav Graef continued to struggle to find work and build a reputation. To help bring in income, Franziska gave French lessons and painted her own pictures of composers such as Beethoven, Schubert, and Schumann. Meanwhile, her husband took on any job available—even reportedly painting railway signs.[11]

FROM OBSCURITY TO RESPECTABILITY

Gustav Graef's first major commission was to paint frescoes to adorn the southern domed hall of the New Museum in Berlin. These frescoes were not Graef's own composition; they were based on sketches by the director of the Munich Art Academy, Wilhelm von Kaulbach, and were part of a project that would employ teams of artists over a fifteen-year period. This was nonetheless an important early project for Graef, since Kaulbach was at the height of his popularity and had been commissioned directly by King Friedrich Wilhelm IV. Graef's primary contribution here was to complete the frescoes *The Reconciliation of Widukind with Charlemagne* and *A Half-figure of Caesar Augustus*. Based on his successful work with Kaulbach, Graef was asked in 1859 to paint four additional frescoes from the Hercules myth for the entry hall of the Old Museum in Berlin.[12]

Even as Graef labored on these early works following the lead of older mentors such as Schadow and Kaulbach, younger generations of German artists were already beginning to move away from depictions of biblical stories or mythical tales and to turn instead toward historical realism. The transition away from romantic idealism toward historical realism was not sudden; however, it was rather dramatic. As the historian Peter Paret explains: "The slow turning away . . . from the overtly symbolic, in which the idea is given absolute precedence over documented fact, toward attempts at a realistic interpretation of events that had

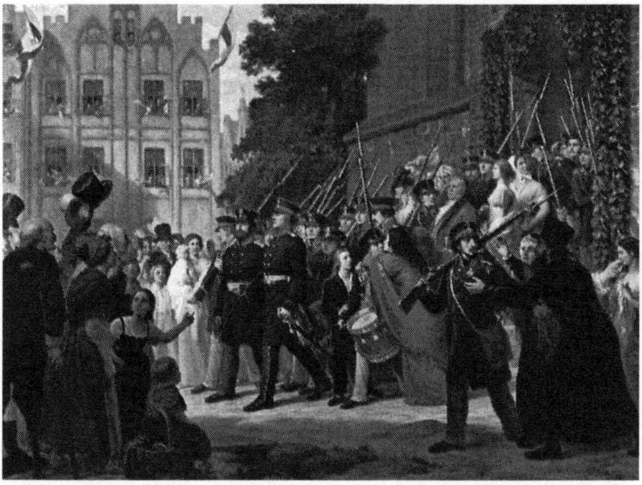

FIGURE 3. Gustav Graef, *Aufzug der ostpreussischen Landwehr ins Feld 1813 nach deren Einsegnung in der Kirche* [The East Prussian Militia Takes to the Field in 1813 after Receiving a Blessing in the Church at Königsberg], 1860–1861. *Preussen. Versuch einer Bilanz* (Reinbek bei Hamburg: Rowohlt, 1981).

actually occurred, represented a basic change in outlook.... Gradually, conventionally timeless robes and stylized 'medieval' smocks and armor gave way to greater detail and an increasing effort to differentiate periods and social groups."[13]

In his own development as a painter—especially after his relocation to Berlin—there is little doubt that the young Graef was also influenced by the work of the quintessential German realist painter, Adolph Menzel. Although only six years his senior, Menzel had already achieved a reputation in Berlin by the time Graef was beginning his studies in Düsseldorf. Born in Silesia and largely self-taught as an artist, Adolph Menzel got his first break in 1839, when he was commissioned to provide a series of almost four hundred woodcut illustrations for Franz Kugler's popular biography of Frederick the Great. To create his illustrations, Menzel buried himself in thousands of historical primary and secondary sources on the life of Frederick. Menzel even provided an appendix to the book called "Historical Documentation to Aid the Reader in Interpreting Some of the Illustrations." His insistence on such painstaking historical research was an attempt to achieve absolute authenticity in his depictions, including the accurate representations of popular dress and customs from a given era.[14] After the success of these illustrations, Menzel produced a series of oil paintings, many of which focused on critical episodes in the life of Frederick. While Menzel and other realists tended to focus on leading historical personalities, they were also

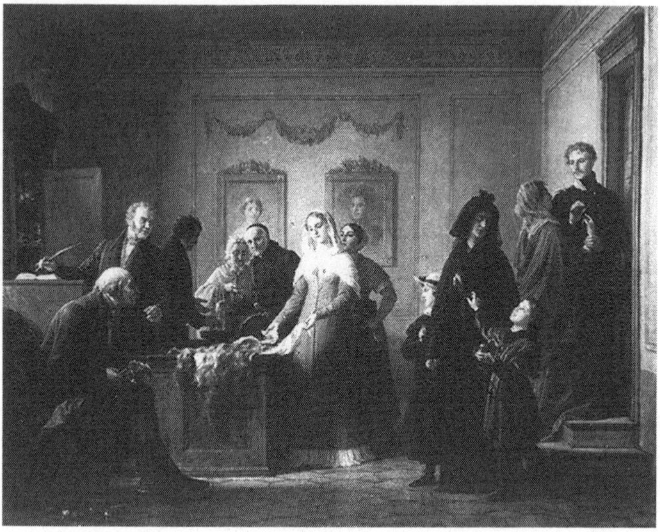

FIGURE 4. Gustav Graef, *Vaterlandsliebe im Jahre 1813—Ferdinande von Schmettau opfert ihr Haar für das Vaterland* [Love of the Fatherland in 1813: Ferdinande von Schmettau Sacrifices Her Hair on the Altar of the Fatherland], 1863.

interested in the accurate depiction of ordinary people. In fact, it was allegedly in response to demands from realist artists such as Menzel that the first German encyclopedia of costume was issued.[15]

Gustav Graef, meanwhile, was still struggling in relative anonymity. His initial attempts to engage in large historical paintings in the early 1860s, while not groundbreaking in method, would offer him a first chance at notoriety. In 1861, Graef began a series of large oil paintings depicting scenes from the Napoleonic Wars. Like many Prussians who grew up in the immediate aftermath of these wars, Graef had long been obsessed with heroic stories about the liberation of the Prussian people from the shame of French domination. In addition, the Prussian government at this time was already making extensive preparations for the upcoming fiftieth anniversary celebration of the crucial victory over Napoleon at the Battle of Leipzig. These preparations included the commissioning of artists to paint patriotic and historical works that would be publicly exhibited in Berlin and around Prussia.

Of all the paintings commissioned for these patriotic exhibits, those created by Gustav Graef were perhaps the most famous and best remembered. The first one, *The East Prussian Militia Takes to the Field in 1813 after Receiving a Blessing in the Church at Königsberg*, was finished in 1861 (see figure 3).[16] This painting is memorable because of its vivid representation of Prussian soldiers being embraced by family members and hailed by local citizens as they leave a church service and prepare to march off to war. However, the painting is also remarkable for another feature: in the right foreground, a Jewish soldier, separated from the mass of soldiers emerging from the church, breaks from an embrace with his traditionally garbed Orthodox father to join his countrymen in battle. The implication here is clear. Although the painting explicitly links the patriotic cause of Prussia with the blessings of a Christian God, the rather prominent inclusion of the Jewish soldier makes clear the importance of tolerance in the Prussian state. Despite the fact that he is clearly emerging from a separate tradition, the Jewish soldier's patriotic spirit is no less profound, and his sacrifice on the battlefield is no less sacred or honorable.[17]

The next year, Graef painted one of his most iconic works, *Love of the Fatherland: Ferdinande von Schmettau Sacrifices Her Hair on the Altar of the Fatherland* (see figure 4).[18] This painting celebrated a famous incident from the Napoleonic Wars. When ordinary Prussian citizens had been asked to contribute money and personal goods to support the military effort against the French, a fifteen-year-old girl, Ferdinande von Schmettau, insisted on cutting and donating her beautiful blonde hair since she had nothing else to give to her country. At the time, news of this incident spread quickly, and the story was used by the Prussian government to boost morale and encourage public sacrifice. Fifty years later, on the anniversary of the Prussian declaration of war against Napoleon, Gustav Graef's depiction of this story caused a public sensation. The novelist Theodor Fontane, for example, wrote a glowing review of the painting in the prominent newspaper the *Kreuzzeitung*, and he also took the time to write directly to Graef to offer his congratulations.[19] Many other rave reviews followed. The painting was taken (along with other patriotic works by artists such as Anselm Feuerbach) on a long tour around Prussia, with stops in Stettin, Danzig, and Königsberg. But that was not all. When the Prussian king Wilhelm I (later Kaiser Wilhelm I) found out that the real Ferdinande von Schmettau was still alive but mired in poverty, he ordered her to be publicly fêted as a heroine and granted a substantial pension. A grateful Ferdinande sent a letter to Gustav Graef expressing thanks for reminding people about her story, and she included a lock of her famous hair for him to keep.[20]

Graef, still in fairly tight financial circumstances, worried about finding a buyer for the painting. However, the painting not only sold—it was eventually acquired directly by Wilhelm I and bequeathed to the National Gallery in Berlin. This iconic image was celebrated long beyond the anniversary of Prussian liberation. In fact, over the next several decades it became an important symbolic representation of Prussian (and later German) nationalism—even finding its way into many schoolbooks as a concrete lesson on patriotism and self-sacrifice.[21] Shortly after finishing his painting of Ferdinande von Schmettau, Graef completed one final large historical genre painting: *The Farewell of a Lithuanian Militiaman to his Beloved in 1813*.[22] Although not as successful as the painting of Ferdinande von Schmettau, this bittersweet image of a young soldier and his sweetheart carving a symbol of their love into a tree before parting was also very well received.

Graef's growing reputation led to a new commission in 1868—this time to help decorate the inside of the new *Aula* (main hall) of the Albertina in Königsberg with frescoes. The project was spearheaded by the leader of the Königsberg Art Academy, Ludwig Rosenfelder, and featured several other local artists, including Johannes Heydeck, Maximilian Piotrowski, and Emil Neide (who later instructed Käthe Kollwitz during her time in Königsberg). These painters were asked to depict classical models for each of the areas of study at the university. Graef's submission included three separate frescoes: *Juris Prudentia*, a scene where the Greek ruler Solon allows the Athenian senate to take an oath before his laws; *Eloquencia*, a depiction of Demosthenes's speech about the crown; and *Artium Historia*, a representation of Phidias showing Pericles and Aspasia the shield of Athena Parthenos.[23] This project, which occupied Graef over the next three years, would have surely been a proud homecoming for someone whose ancestors had such a long tradition at the Albertina.

Although it was his frescoes and historical paintings that first brought Graef public attention, it was his special talent for portraiture that would finally bring him financial stability. Graef had always painted portraits, but beginning in the mid-1860s he began to dedicate himself to them more energetically. By the 1870s, Graef and his colleague Gustav Richter had become the two most prominent portrait painters in Berlin. Portraits were in great demand by successful members of the Berlin bourgeoisie, who were often eager to document their growing wealth and status in the first years of the new German Reich. Some of Graef's best-known subjects included the "railroad king" Bethel Henry Strousberg and his wife Mary Ann in 1870; the Prussian ambassador to Rome (and his old friend from Königsberg) Robert von Keudell and his wife in 1874; and the eminent jurist Bernhard Windscheid in 1883.[24] Many other portraits from this period are not included in posthumous lists of Graef's paintings, including a well-received portrait of the young Sybille von Arnim (a niece of Otto von Bismarck and the new wife to Bismarck's youngest son Wilhelm).[25] Graef also corresponded with Otto von

Bismarck's daughter, Marie, in the hopes of painting a portrait of the chancellor himself—although no record of such a painting exists.[26]

It was during these years that the career of Gustav Graef reached its peak. In 1874, he was honored by the Royal Academy of Arts with the Small Gold Medal, four years later he earned the honorary title of professor, and finally, in 1880, he was elected as a full member of the Royal Academy of Arts, Section for Visual Arts. These were all tremendous honors, and they secured his standing and public reputation as an artist. These honors also symbolized a dramatic change in social status for the Graef family. From their rather poor start in Königsberg, the Graefs now had a steady enough income to relocate into luxurious lodgings in one of the most prestigious neighborhoods in Berlin—on the first floor of Lützowplatz 10, just to the south of the Berlin Tiergarten. Graef was able to maintain a large studio next to his family's living quarters, while another floor of the building served as a workspace for the prominent Berlin architects Martin Gropius and Heino Schmieden.[27]

At the same time, Graef's wife Franziska had also become deeply engaged in the salon life of the city. Franziska held regular gatherings on Thursdays that welcomed very prominent guests, including Robert von Keudell, the ambassador to Rome; Julian Lessing, the director of the Museum of Applied Arts

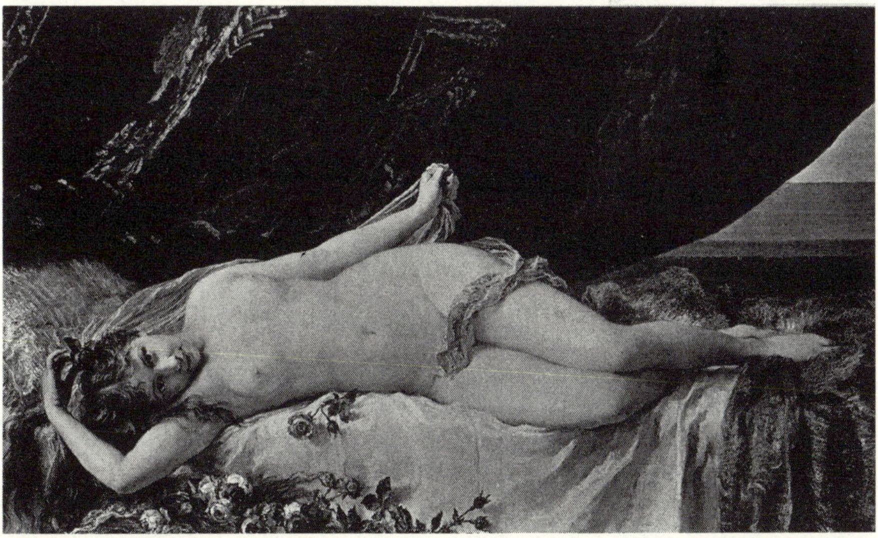

FIGURE 5. Art Card of *Félicie* by Gustav Graef. With permission from the Geheimes Staatsarchiv Preussischer Kulturbesitz (GStAPK I. HA rep. 77, tit. 657, nr. 3, bd. 1, p. 135).

(*Kunstgewerbemuseum*); Julian Schmidt, an accomplished literary historian; Arthur Hobrecht, the former mayor of Berlin (*Oberbürgermeister*) and future Prussian finance minister; and Babette Meyer, a well-known salonnière who was taking art lessons from Gustav Graef.[28] These were all people with considerable status and social connections, and Keudell and Meyer were close friends with Otto von Bismarck and other members of the chancellor's family. Meanwhile, Gustav and Franziska Graef also opened their home to host several gifted young friends of the Graef children, Sabine and Botho. These included the young philosopher and sociologist Georg Simmel, for whom the Graef household became almost a second home after the death of his father in 1874. It was through Sabine Graef that Simmel met his future wife, Gertrud Kinel, who had studied art with Sabine at the Académie Julian in Paris.[29]

As one might imagine, the Graef household was abuzz with creativity. Although Gustav Graef was clearly now the breadwinner in the family, both Franziska and Sabine Graef remained active. Franziska no longer produced art for public consumption, but she did not completely give up her artistic identity. She was listed as

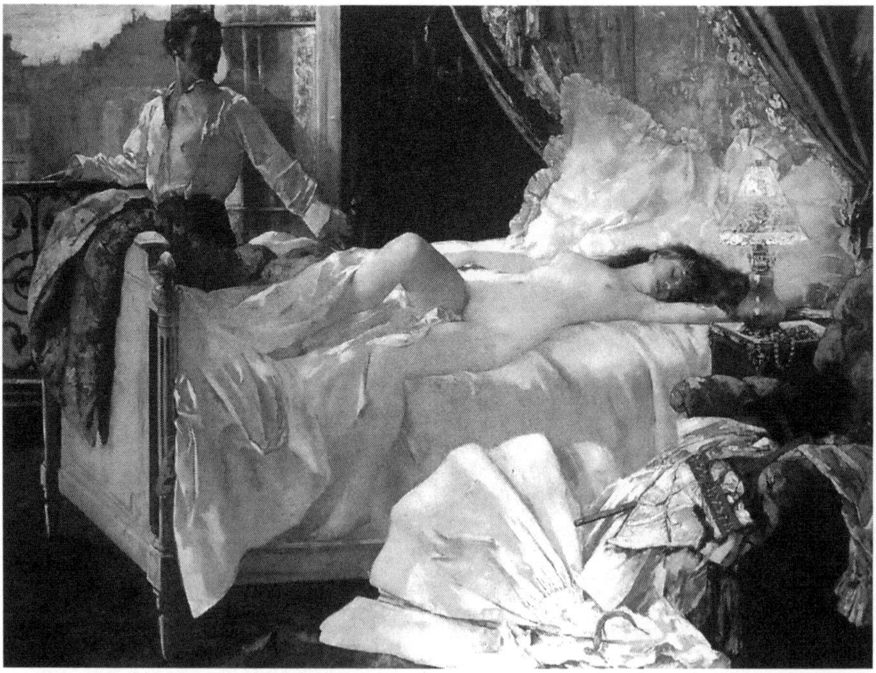

FIGURE 6. Henri Gervex, *Rolla* (1878).

a member of the Association of Female Artists in Berlin (*Verein Berliner Künstlerinnen*) from 1871 until 1884.[30]

IN PURSUIT OF BEAUTY

The late 1870s and early 1880s were thus a golden age for Gustav Graef and his family. Berlin was the center of German portraiture, and Gustav Graef was one of the two most popular portrait painters in the city. However, while portraiture ensured a substantial income for Graef, it did not necessarily fulfill his artistic ambitions. Like many artists during this period, Graef felt that portraiture was a kind of "poor man's bread" (*Sklavenbrot*) which forced him to comply with the tastes and whims of the person who commissioned the work.[31] Even during the height of his success as a portraitist, therefore, Graef was already experimenting with more fanciful and idealistic images, including nature studies and allegorical images involving nude female figures.

One of his first such efforts came in 1875, with a painting entitled *Pensierosa.* The painting enjoyed modest success, and it was greeted as groundbreaking when put on display at the 1876 Centennial Art Exhibition in Philadelphia.[32] Three years later came a further success when Graef was apparently commissioned by a wealthy young man in Paris to paint his lover in the nude. Graef worked on this painting in France, and he then finished it at a studio in Berlin with the help of a local young model named Bertha Rother. The work that resulted was entitled *Félicie,* and it caused quite a stir when it was first displayed publicly at the annual exhibit of the Berlin Royal Academy of Arts in 1879 (see figure 5).[33] *Félicie* depicts a beautiful young woman reclining rather seductively on a lounge, looking directly at the viewer while placing a rose in her hair. Her left hand is outstretched and grasps the edge of a sheet behind her as if she has just revealed herself to the viewer; a rumpled corner of the same sheet, which is suspiciously phallic in shape, extends across her left leg to cover her genitalia.

It is possible that Graef (or his mysterious benefactor) had been inspired to create *Félicie* in part by the work of the young French painter Henri Gervex, whose painting *Rolla* had caused a sensation in Paris in 1878 after it was rejected by the Paris Salon (see figure 6). Gervex had intended his artwork to depict the last lines of a poem by Alfred de Musset, which featured a desperate young man in poor financial straits who chose to spend his last night in the arms of a prostitute before leaping out a window to his death. Gervex depicted the gentleman (Rolla) standing at the window as he took one last look back at the nude woman still sleeping in his bed. Apparently, what the Paris Salon found improper about *Rolla* was not the nude figure itself, but the discarded petticoat and corset on the floor next to her—which made direct reference to the sexual act and also implied her status as a lower-class prostitute rather than a lover. It is not clear if Gervex had expected his painting to be rejected, but it is clear that this rejection brought the artist and his painting increased notoriety.[34]

Graef's *Félicie* had some superficial similarities to Gervex's *Rolla*, but it lacked the discarded clothing and avoided anything that might explicitly reference prostitution or class differences. Still, the painting provoked both enthusiastic and overtly hostile reactions among Berlin artists and art critics. The writer and art critic Paul Lindau later recalled being shocked at the notion that this rather traditional portraitist and painter of historical scenes—then approaching his sixtieth birthday—could be responsible for such a startlingly sensual painting. Lindau claimed that there were many "moral Pharisees" who were appalled by the rather risqué image, but he suggested that most artists at the exhibit recognized the beauty of the painting and the enormous skill it took to produce it.[35]

The most gushing praise for *Félicie* came from the pen of Adolf Rosenberg, a leading art historian and critic who regularly published art and theater reviews in a variety of newspapers. In his review of the 1879 Academy exhibit for *Die Grenzboten*, Rosenberg singled out *Félicie* for special praise, suggesting that it was a masterwork that was unlike anything else being currently exhibited. Rosenberg related to his readers the story of the painting's origin, and he suggested that this extraordinary commission—to preserve the beauty of a young lover from the vagaries of time—had produced extraordinary results.[36] For Rosenberg, Graef's painting was far from scandalous or provocative; in the childlike and innocent countenance of the young woman, he suggested, one finds no trace of sensuality—only an uninhibited figure lost in graceful reverie. Although he pointed to minor flaws in coloring that prevented the painting from reaching perfection, Rosenberg also compared the work to Titian's nudes and suggested that it was far superior to anything that French artists currently had to offer: "With its soft curves and rosy flesh, its inner warmth that seems almost to give the sense of actual blood coursing through her veins, how differently this figure strikes the viewer as compared to those elegant but boring abstractions which the French, who are normally so fascinated by the nude figure, are now mucking around with."[37] After

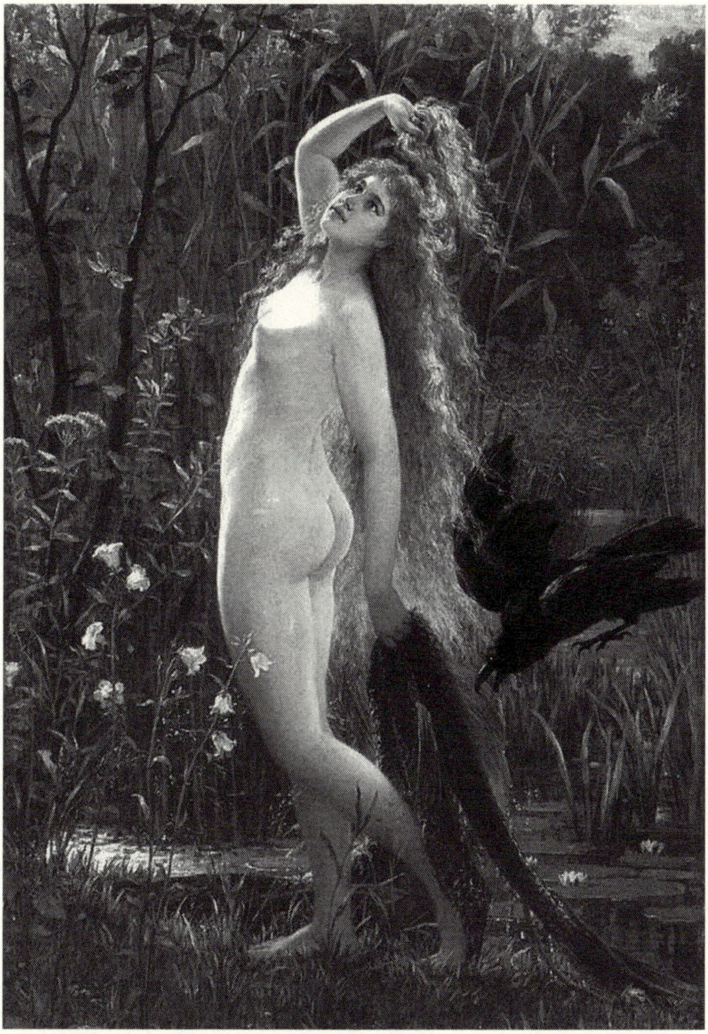

FIGURE 7. Gustav Graef, *Das Märchen* [The Fairy Tale].

the Berlin exhibition, Graef's *Félicie* reportedly caused a sensation—and some consternation—when it was shown in Düsseldorf and Wuppertal.[38]

By his own account, Gustav Graef's startling success with *Félicie* encouraged him to experiment further in this direction. He now began work on an uncommissioned painting that he hoped would be his masterpiece: *Das Märchen* (*The*

Fairy Tale). To paint this mythological picture, Gustav Graef again employed the same young model as he had used to help him complete *Félicie*: Bertha Rother. Much of the work on the painting took place in Berlin. However, while Graef was on a family vacation to the island of Rügen, he sent for Bertha to follow him. Graef found a secluded spot outside of the resort town of Binz where he could paint Bertha outside and take advantage of the natural light. This made him one of the first German painters of this era to experiment with the French fashion of painting *en plein air* rather than inside a studio.[39]

Graef submitted *The Fairy Tale* alongside several other paintings for the Fifty-Fifth Exhibit of the Royal Academy of Arts in 1881 (see figure 7). The new painting received a rave review from the left-liberal *Im neuen Reich*, which praised it as a masterwork as surprising as the exquisite *Félicie*, which Graef had offered two years earlier. Not only had Graef given the painting a truly poetic and fable-like atmosphere, the reviewer claimed, but "the incidental grace in the movement of this beautiful female body, her eyes filled with a look of happiness and limbs pulsating with beauty, seems far removed from any kind of sophisticated sensuality and lewdness—a quality that is happily also shared by his 'Félicie.'"[40]

Unfortunately for Graef, not all the reviews were positive. Adolf Rosenberg, who had been so full of praise for *Félicie*, described *The Fairy Tale* as well intentioned but deeply flawed in both color and proportion. He pointed specifically to the extraordinary slimness of the female figure which tapered into an impossibly thin pair of legs. Worse yet, Rosenberg tied the problems in *The Fairy Tale* to a general decline in the overall quality of Graef's work, which now rarely rose above mediocrity.[41] In a review of another Academy exhibit three years later, Rosenberg continued his criticism of Graef. He asked rhetorically if there was now any portraitist as good as the recently deceased Gustav Richter. His answer was no: "For a while it seemed as if Gustav Graef might be his equal in the narrow field of portraiture; but this hope was only an illusion. Graef's use of color (*Kolorit*) has grown more clumsy and uninspiring with each passing year, while the construction (*Auffassung*) of his images has lost all of its power and warmth. Now he paints ordinary run-of-the-mill portraits which are indistinguishable from any other."[42]

It appears that Graef took this criticism to heart. Rather than giving up on *The Fairy Tale*, a painting he originally envisioned as his masterpiece, he decided that he would revise and rework the composition while once again employing Bertha Rother as his model.[43] Since this painting was not commissioned by a paying customer, Graef was forced to take long pauses in order to return to working on traditional portraits. His progress on the painting thus continued sporadically over the next five years. One might speculate about why Gustav Graef developed such an obsession with this particular painting. Was it a desperate attempt to restore his faltering reputation and regain the praise of critics such as Rosenberg? Was it an obsession with achieving an ideal of beauty that rivaled the great masters? Was it a rather convenient excuse to spend more time (illicitly or innocently) with his beautiful young model? Or was there perhaps some less obvious or conscious motive? Did he somehow see himself as the raven in *The Fairy Tale*, peeling away the ugly scales of Bertha's poverty and poor upbringing to expose the startling beauty underneath? Or perhaps he, like the raven, fervently wished to be transformed back into a young man so he could sweep her away as a lover? Certainly, there are rich opportunities here for analysis and perhaps even psychoanalysis—opportunities that I will leave for readers to explore. For it was here, in his work on *The Fairy Tale* and in his relationship with Bertha Rother, that Gustav Graef got himself into trouble.

A CHANGE OF FORTUNE

It was common during this era for artists to employ young women as models for their artwork—a job that often included long hours spent posing in the nude. Such women were often as young as fourteen years old and occasionally even younger. Graef's contemporaries in Berlin frequently shared models with one another and talked openly of the young girls they used. Models typically came from very poor families; many were also the product of deeply dysfunctional homes and occasionally also engaged in prostitution to support themselves. If Graef and his fellow artists were consciously exploiting the vulnerable situation of these poor young women, they were also making themselves vulnerable as well. In a society where masculine honor was paramount, blackmail could be a very powerful weapon.

Graef's difficulties began in December of 1883, in an incident involving a thirteen-year-old model named Helene Hammermann, who had been recommended to Graef by another prominent artist, August von Heyden. According to Graef, he had invited Helene into his studio and asked her to disrobe; after finding her form acceptable, he asked his daughter Sabine to record her address and send her home. Helene Hammermann's version of the encounter was quite different. According to a summary of the incident written some years later, Helene claimed that Graef had held her down while fondling her breasts and inserting his fingers inside her. When she resisted and threatened to tell her parents, Graef allegedly said to her: "You wouldn't be so dumb as to say anything about this. You're no longer a child."[44]

According to Graef, his first notion that something was amiss came when Antonie Hammermann, the stepmother of Helene, confronted him at his home and accused him of having abused her daughter. Graef vigorously denied the accusation, but he later admitted having given her ten Marks in an attempt to get her to leave. A few days later, Antonie Hammermann sent a representative named Krischen, who pretended to be sympathetic to Graef but nonetheless demanded 1,000 Marks from him to convince the Hammermanns not to make their accusations public.[45] Graef refused outright, and immediately asked Krischen to leave. Graef quickly discovered, however, that he was not the only artist who had been accused of sexual abuse by Helene and Antonie Hammermann. Graef's colleague, the seventy-two-year-old Hermann Kretzschmer, reported that the Hammermanns had made similar accusations against him and had sent the same Krischen to demand 1,000 Marks.[46] Hearing this, Graef decided to report the matter to the police, who immediately launched an investigation.

In June of 1884, both Antonie Hammermann, the stepmother of Helene Hammermann, and her representative, Krischen, were put on trial for attempted blackmail. At trial, their defense attorneys attempted to impeach Gustav Graef's credibility by suggesting that he possessed an amorous nature and a long history of relationships with other underage models. They were particularly interested in questioning the young Bertha Rother, who was known to have modeled extensively for Graef over the past several years. Defense attorneys, however, mistakenly called Bertha's sister Anna, assuming that it was she who had been employed by Graef. Anna Rother denied any affair with Graef, and (after the mistaken identity was discovered) she also denied any knowledge of a relationship between Professor Graef and her sister Bertha. Gustav Graef was then asked under oath about a relationship with either Anna or Bertha Rother. At the time, he was advised by the judge that he had the right to refuse his testimony under §54 of the Code of Criminal Procedure (*Strafprozessordnung*), since any admission of an affair would incriminate him by putting him in danger of prosecution for adultery. Graef did not make use of his rights, and he firmly insisted that there was no relationship with either Anna or Bertha Rother. Faced with denials on all sides, the defense's attacks against Graef's character went nowhere. A jury convicted Antonie Hammermann of blackmail and sentenced her to two years in prison; her accomplice, Krischen, was sentenced to eighteen months.[47]

Over the following year, Antonie Hammermann's husband Wilhelm worked tirelessly to get his wife out of jail. He first sent several letters to Graef begging for clemency and even sent him a statement signed by his daughter in which she apologized and retracted her allegations. When this didn't work, he reversed course and threatened Graef with further "revelations." Eventually, when he heard rumors that Graef had indeed been engaged in a sexual relationship with Bertha Rother, Hammermann saw his chance for revenge. Through friendly contacts within the Rother household, Hammermann found out that Graef had not only regularly paid the Rother family huge sums of money, but he had also visited them regularly, traveled extensively with Bertha Rother by his side, and, of course, frequently painted her in the nude. Some witnesses from the neighborhood reported that they had overheard Bertha openly admitting an affair with the artist, while others provided damning eyewitness testimony about their trysts. In March of 1885, seven months after his wife's conviction, Wilhelm Hammermann gathered this mass of hearsay and circumstantial evidence and denounced Graef to the Berlin police.

After interviewing a number of Hammermann's witnesses, police decided to search Gustav Graef's house, where in a locked desk drawer they found fairly risqué poems that were obviously directed at Bertha Rother. Police also found receipts which showed that in addition to taking Bertha on trips to Rügen, Braunschweig, London, and Boulogne, Graef had also paid for Bertha's training as an actress and had given the Rother family upwards of 35,000 Marks over a period of several years—an enormous sum of money. This evidence was enough to cause prosecutors to order Gustav Graef's arrest on charges of perjury, subornation of perjury, and two counts of lewd behavior with minors under fourteen (namely Helene Hammermann and Bertha Rother). Prosecutors also suspected that Graef had initiated a sexual relationship with Bertha Rother's youngest sister Lieschen, who would have been approximately thirteen years old at the time of the investigation. Graef was not formally charged with this act, however, since Lieschen's exact age could not be positively ascertained until after the trial began.[48]

Prosecutors did not stop with their charges against Graef. In a clear sign of the seriousness with which authorities took the crime of perjury, they also filed charges against three members of the Rother family.[49] Bertha Rother, the model whom Graef was alleged to have molested when she was a minor, was charged with subornation of perjury for allegedly pressuring her sister, Anna, to lie under oath about the existence of the affair. Anna herself was charged with perjury for having denied knowledge of the relationship at trial; and finally, Auguste Rother, the mother of both Bertha and Anna, was charged with aggravated procuring (*schweren Kuppelei*) for allegedly providing her own young daughters for Graef to sexually exploit. Gustav Graef and the three members of the Rother family would spend the next six months in custody while they awaited trial.

CHAPTER TWO

THE TRIAL AS PUBLIC SPECTACLE

If one believes many of the newspaper articles and pamphlets printed at the time, the trial of Gustav Graef and the Rother family was an event of profound cultural and historical importance and even a "landmark case in the history of German jurisprudence."[1] Of course, we cannot take such descriptions completely at face value. To a certain degree, this kind of rhetoric reflects the hyperbole that is common in press coverage of sensational trials; after all, in the struggle to attract readers, intrepid journalists, editors, and authors sometimes treat every case as if it were a "trial of the century." The Graef trial was *not* a watershed moment for German jurisprudence; however, it did set important legal and cultural precedents. For example, as the historian Uwe Wilhelm claims, the Graef case was one of the first clear demonstrations of the power of the German press to drive public criticism of the legal system. During and after the trial, sustained critiques of the justice system were present on a daily basis in almost every major newspaper. Such critiques came not only from journalists and politicians, but also from prominent legal theorists and even trial participants who stepped forward to share their various diagnoses and proposed reforms.[2] One of the most important lessons of the Graef trial for many contemporaries, therefore, was its demonstration of the growing influence of the political press and its potential impact on public opinion.

The German press in the 1880s was in the midst of a transformation. The number of newspapers had increased dramatically in the wake of unification, as had the number of subscribers. Although even the most successful German newspapers, such as the *Berliner Tageblatt*, rarely had more than 30,000 total postal subscribers, such newspapers were also widely available at inns and restaurants and thus available to a much broader reading public than subscription numbers might suggest.[3] It is also important to note that the German press during this period was primarily a political press. Individual newspapers often represented

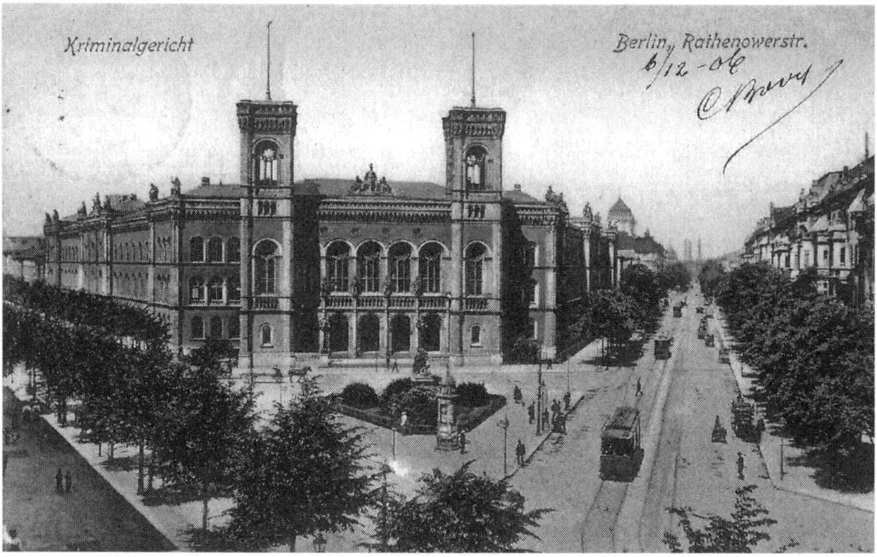

FIGURE 8. Postcard of the Criminal Court Building in Berlin-Moabit (1905).

the viewpoint of particular politicians or political factions, and such newspapers regularly engaged in running arguments with other newspapers that represented rival viewpoints. In fact, the German political press provided an essential platform for partisan debates and political opposition in early Imperial Germany—perhaps even more important than the German Reichstag itself. Not surprisingly, the growing power and influence of the press did not please everyone. The new cacophony of journalistic voices seemed to many observers to be uncouth, uncivilized, and even un-German.

Although journalists in this period could seize on almost any issue to launch political attacks against one another, against political opponents, or against the government, there is no doubt that sensational trials provided a common trigger. Legal cases served as opportunities both to criticize the justice system and to moralize about the state of German society, and they had the added benefit of containing the kind of melodrama that might attract and keep new readers. Explicitly political prosecutions such as the 1872 trial of Socialist leaders August Bebel and Wilhelm Liebknecht, as well as the 1874 treason trial of Otto von Bismarck's personal rival, Prince Harry von Arnim, were ready-made vehicles for political criticism within the press. Even in ordinary criminal trials, however, dramatic reportage could frequently be useful both for scoring political points and for selling newspapers.

VENUE AND CAST

The Graef trial began on September 29, 1885 in the Great Jury Hall of the Berlin Regional Court (*Berlin Landgericht I*) in the Moabit district of Berlin. As the historian Benjamin Hett suggests, the Great Jury Hall was "as much a theater as a judicial arena."[4] The courthouse had been completed only three years prior to the trial, and its twin towers, grand entrance, and classic *Rundbogenstil* arches made it stand out in the midst of the otherwise semideveloped slums of northern Berlin (see figure 8). The interior of the Great Jury Hall was perhaps even more impressive than the exterior of the building. Its dimensions were enormous by any standard: it was 20.4 meters long and 11.25 meters wide, and its ceilings were a stunning 12 meters high. Within this large space, there was seating for 250 spectators, and two additional loges were reserved for prominent official guests.[5] Neo-Gothic arches framed the ends of the hall, and five stained glass windows looked out onto Alt-Moabit, the main avenue outside. If this churchlike architecture failed to instill the required solemnity into the proceedings, pithy quotations painted on the walls were intended to remind both participants and observers of the sacredness of the occasion.[6] These surroundings undoubtedly lent an air of gravity to the proceedings, and they almost certainly added to the dramatic tension as well.

The Graef trial, like many other great legal dramas enacted in this building, attracted significant crowds. In the weeks before the case opened, the court had been besieged by requests for tickets to attend the proceedings—almost all of which had been rejected. In fact, because of the sensitive nature of the charges, the lead judge in the case, Boguslaw Müller, ordered the trial to be closed to the public. He did, however, allow those with a "special interest" in the case to attend. This exception was interpreted quite broadly, meaning that the courtroom was filled each day not only with family members of the defendants, but also with fellow artists, scholars, authors, lawyers, and even some high justice officials and military personnel.[7] Officials in the Prussian Justice Ministry were following the case closely, and newspapers commented on the presence of several leading government officials in the audience, including the notorious prosecutor and anti-Socialist crusader, Hermann Tessendorf.[8] Judge Müller also allowed a few members of the press to attend, with the admonition that they not publish "sensitive" parts of the proceedings. Despite the "closed" courtroom, then, many newspapers across Germany would print detailed daily reports on the trial proceedings, some of which would later be collected and printed as pamphlets for public sale.

Judge Müller, by the way, was an experienced fifty-eight-year-old judge who had transferred to his post in Berlin from Posen two years before. At the time of Müller's transfer, Justice Minister Heinrich Friedberg had praised his diligence, efficiency, and extensive knowledge of the law, recommending him as "one of the best Regional Court Directors we currently have."[9] In jury trials such as these, the lead judge was accompanied by two associate judges—here named Freytag and Friedenthal—and a panel of twelve jurors and two alternates. The elected foreman of the jury was a city councilman named Schäfer; however, because the official court records of the Graef trial no longer exist, we know nothing about the other jurors in the case.[10] The defendants were assisted by five different lawyers, the most prominent of whom was John Simson, the younger brother of the illustrious president of the German Supreme Court (*Reichsgericht*), Eduard von Simson. John Simson grew up in Königsberg and studied at the Albertina University, where he had befriended Gustav Graef almost fifty years earlier. Thereafter, he and his brother Eduard had founded one of the most successful civil law firms in Berlin, where they would eventually be joined by Eduard's son, August von Simson.

John Simson was assisted by Wilhelm Kleinholz, an able attorney who would later serve as cocounsel for the journalist Maximilian Harden in the infamous Moltke-Harden trial.[11] Three additional attorneys represented the Rother family: Holz, Voigt, and Cassel.[12] Leading the prosecution was Max Heinemann, a forty-four-year-old prosecutor who was still at a relatively early stage in a long and distinguished career. Before coming to Berlin in 1882, he had served as a junior prosecutor alongside Judge Müller in Posen.[13]

Although official trial records for the Graef case no longer exist, summaries of the proceedings are preserved in exactly the form that the overwhelming majority of observers would have encountered them: in transcripts recorded by reporters in the courtroom. Such transcripts usually came from a few original sources, including Oskar Thiele, whose trial summaries were printed in a range of newspapers across the political spectrum. Not much is known about Thiele, but he and his colleague Hugo Friedländer were responsible for reporting on some of the most infamous trials of Imperial Germany, many of which Friedländer later recounted in a series of books entitled *Interesting Criminal Trials*.[14] These transcripts were not always a complete verbatim record of the proceedings because testimony that the court reporter thought was uninteresting or irrelevant was often summarized or skipped entirely. Also, in a case dealing with sensitive matters such as sexual relations, court reporters would often self-censor their own transcripts during disturbing or graphic testimony. As we will see, critics of the press would occasionally attack both trial transcripts and journalistic commentaries on this case as unreliable and inaccurate depictions of the proceedings.[15]

DISORDER IN THE COURT

Unique features of the German legal system frequently helped to accentuate the dramatic nature of trial proceedings. For example, while the modern American common-law system includes the right of a defendant to confront his or her accusers in court, very little actual "confrontation" is allowed. In an Imperial German trial, however, a judge might call upon witnesses to rebut one another's testimony face to face in front of the jury—thus leading to some very tense and melodramatic courtroom standoffs. Perhaps the best example of this came early in the trial, when Helene Hammermann, the young model who first claimed sexual abuse by Graef, was summoned to testify. After she had described her alleged abuse in detail, the defendant, Gustav Graef, was asked by the judge to respond directly; he denied her accusations without hesitation. This, however, was not enough. The prosecutor, Max Heinemann, asked Graef to step forward into the witness area so that Helene Hammermann could repeat her allegations directly to his face. She did exactly that, and added angrily, "I know exactly what happened to me in your studio!"[16] Graef, however, stood his ground and was steadfast in his denials. Then, Hermann Kretzschmer, another artist Helene Hammermann had accused of abuse, was also asked to step into the witness area to confront his accuser directly.[17] As he proclaimed his innocence to the court, Helene screamed at him, "You liar! I'm telling the truth! I know best what happened in your studio!"[18] Immediately thereafter, Helene Hammermann's stepmother was brought into the witness area to confront Graef and Kretzschmer directly, and the inevitable personal attacks once again flew back and forth in front of the jurors.

As one might expect in such a case, the majority of testimony involved witnesses who provided circumstantial evidence of Graef's affair with Bertha or those who refuted such evidence. Much of this testimony would be excluded as hearsay in modern American courtrooms. Judges in Imperial Germany, however, had wide latitude about what questions they would allow and what evidence they would admit. Hearsay testimony was often permitted, and it was assumed that the credibility of such statements could best be weighed by challenging witnesses directly or by forcing conflicting witnesses to face each other in person. Therefore, when witnesses offered shocking revelations, their testimony would inevitably be followed by angry confrontations with the defendants or with additional witnesses who directly refuted their accounts. The courtroom drama thus leaped from climax to climax, as battling witnesses exposed neighborhood fault lines and personal vendettas for all to see.

Perhaps the most important witness against the defendants was Concordia Intrau, a temporary resident of the Rother household who had overheard an angry fight between Bertha and Anna Rother, during which they had allegedly admitted the existence of an affair. Intrau also presented a wide range of further damning evidence against the defendants. She reported, for example, having overheard Anna say that Graef had also made sexual advances to her after concluding that Bertha was now "too used up." Intrau further claimed to have heard Auguste Rother trying to force her youngest daughter Elizabeth (Lieschen) on Graef, only to be met with Graef's desperate objection that he could not accept "establishing any new relationships since the one with Bertha had almost ruined him."[19] Finally, Intrau claimed that despite Graef's initial rejection of Lieschen, she later overheard compromising talk and obscene sounds coming from Lieschen's room that left no doubt of a sexual liaison. Intrau's descriptions of the sounds coming from Lieschen's bedroom were apparently graphic enough for the judge to exclude all other female witnesses and audience members from the courtroom. Although Intrau admitted that she had not seen Graef during this alleged encounter, she suggested that she knew when Graef was present because of his particular style of ringing the doorbell. Graef did not face any charges with regard to Lieschen, but this evidence was seen by many observers as potentially disastrous for his credibility.

Intrau's testimony was corroborated by another resident of the Rother household, a wainwright named Kühnle, who claimed to have once listened at the bedroom door of Lieschen Rother and heard the same kinds of graphic sounds that Intrau had described. Kühnle also suggested that he and others in the house were repeatedly sent away on errands during Graef's visits to see Lieschen. In addition, Kühnle reported that Bertha had once complained to him about being prostituted out by her own mother, and he testified that Bertha had openly bragged to him about having a relationship with Gustav Graef.

Graef, of course, rejected the testimony of Intrau and Kühnle, and he denied any affair with Lieschen. He insisted that the Rother doorbell was a simple pull lever and could not possibly be made to exhibit any "special" ringing, as Intrau had claimed. Bertha Rother also intervened to add that Intrau was not credible since she had a long history of quarreling with the Rother family, including a violent brawl with Lieschen during which the young girl had brandished a knife. She reported that Intrau had also feuded with Auguste Rother about accusations that she had abused her own young illegitimate son.[20] Intrau was forced to admit this long and bitter history with the Rother family, but she assured the court that her own testimony was not motivated by any ill will. Intrau also specifically rejected the charge made by defense lawyers that she, Kühnle, and the Hammermann family had been dining together at a local tavern during the trial; she claimed that it was coincidence that they all simply happened to like to eat at the same establishment near the courtroom.[21]

Two additional witnesses, the sisters Minna and Clara Adler, supported Intrau's account of conversations in the Rother household. However, Clara Adler also added another damning detail: that Bertha had complained bitterly about having had to give up her body regularly to Graef since she was thirteen years old for a "lousy thirty Marks." Bertha Rother responded by acknowledging the remark, but she insisted that "giving up her body" was a reference to the rather arduous task of standing daily as model and not to any sexual acts.[22]

As the trial continued, even the most unlikely of witnesses stepped forward to provide sensational evidence. A hotel manager named Potenberg from Binz, a small town on the resort island of Rügen, was summoned to testify about Gustav Graef's stay there with Bertha Rother. He related that two of his employees had eavesdropped at the front door to Graef's room and had heard Bertha call out: "Oh professor! That tickles!" Graef immediately interrupted to suggest that a perfectly innocent incident was being blown out of proportion. He insisted that he and Bertha had been forced to work indoors due both to Bertha's illness and to several days of inclement weather. Bertha's seemingly damning exclamation was simply a response to his clumsy attempts to treat her sore throat using a special throat brush.[23] Graef asked the judge to refer to his own diary, which had been confiscated by police. The judge ordered that an excerpt of the diary be read in court, and the relevant passage seemed to confirm both the weather and Bertha's illness. Potenberg, the hotel manager, remembered Bertha becoming ill during their stay, and he also recalled retrieving special medicine from a pharmacy for a sore throat. He testified that during their visit, the rest of the Graef family had traveled briefly from their own hotel across the island at Sassnitz to visit Graef—although he did not know if they all dined together with Bertha.[24]

The dramatic nature of these revelations and refutations could sometimes be exacerbated by the conduct of the presiding judge. Unlike in American courts, where judges are often cast in the role of referees between adversarial prosecutors and defense attorneys, in the Imperial German system, judges often played a much more active role in questioning and directing witnesses. One example comes from the testimony of Amanda Reuter, a young woman who had lived in the Rother household for several years and who had earlier been arrested alongside Bertha Rother for prostitution.[25] Initially, Reuter was an extremely uncooperative witness. During the pretrial investigation, she had admitted to having accidentally barged in on an intimate scene between Bertha and the professor. Now, however, Reuter cried on the stand and claimed to remember nothing about the events in question or even her own earlier testimony. An angry Judge Müller lectured Reuter on the dangers of perjury, but this only elicited more anguished cries. After a while, Reuter did start to give more details, although her story was altered. She now claimed that the incident in question had happened on a night when Bertha was scheduled to attend a ball at the Kroll Opera House. When Reuter tried to enter Bertha's dressing room, she had found it locked. In contradiction to her earlier testimony, however, she now claimed never to have seen Gustav Graef directly in Bertha's room. After a brief court recess, a clearly frustrated Judge Müller decided to put off further examination of Amanda Reuter after finding out that she had apparently downed three cognacs and a half-liter of beer in her short time outside the court.[26]

A very different example is offered by the exculpatory testimony of Marie Reim, a close friend to Bertha who also lived with the Rother family for two years, and who apparently accompanied Bertha and Professor Graef on several international voyages. In contrast to the relatively damning testimony of witnesses such as Intrau, Kühnle, and Adler, Reim insisted that Graef's behavior had always been honorable. Reim admitted that she was at first quite suspicious of the relationship between the two, and she even dared to ask Graef directly if the two were having an affair. Graef assured her that he only wanted to help Bertha, and would do his best to support her family as long as she maintained her reputation. Reim claimed that the three always had separate rooms on their travels, and she testified that she never observed any inappropriate behavior. There was occasional kissing or caressing, but only the kind one might expect from father and daughter, and almost always in the presence of Bertha's family members. Reim claimed to be very close to Bertha Rother, and she told the court that Bertha was very open with her about all of her secrets—even her dalliances with other men during the time she was posing for Graef. While Bertha had openly admitted all of these affairs,

Reim claimed, she had always denied that her relationship with Graef had been anything other than platonic.

Under pointed questioning from Judge Müller, Reim went on to describe Bertha's lifestyle as sinful and profligate. Reim suggested that a young suitor, a law clerk from Magdeburg named Lange, rented an apartment for her so she could be independent from her family. When Lange was out of town, however, Bertha would often have actors and military officers call on her for nights filled with alcohol, dancing, and the card game Skat.[27] Judge Müller, glad to finally be eliciting what he thought was reliable testimony in this description of Bertha's decadent lifestyle, praised Reim's "better upbringing" compared to those of other witnesses in the case. When the judge asked her if Bertha's behavior offended other members of the Rother family, however, Reim became embarrassed and refused to answer.[28]

Until this point in the trial, for complicated reasons that we will discuss later, the prosecution had struggled to formally prove the charge of perjury; in other words, despite days of scandalous revelations that impugned the character of the defendants, the prosecutor had not yet definitively proven that Gustav Graef had lied at the Hammermann trial about having an illicit relationship with Bertha Rother. This may explain the decision by the prosecutor, Max Heinemann, to introduce the most controversial and sensational evidence in the case: a collection of papers that had been confiscated from a desk in Gustav Graef's study.

LOVE POETRY AND *THE FAIRY TALE*

Perhaps because of his struggles with poverty as a young man, Gustav Graef was apparently quite meticulous about money. The first envelope of private documents opened at trial contained a mountain of receipts, promissory notes, and IOUs that Graef had diligently used to document the huge sums of money he was spending on (or loaning to) Bertha and other members of the Rother family. Although the average amount on these documents was usually a few hundred Marks or less, together the entire stack of receipts added up to nearly 35,000 Marks (an amount that was nearly nine times the yearly salary of the prosecutor, Max Heinemann). Graef insisted that the larger amounts had been intended as loans to be paid back at 4 percent interest and that as time went on he gave money to the Rothers more and more reluctantly. Indeed, several letters were read out loud in which Graef bitterly complained about Auguste Rother's constant demands for more money.[29]

Other packages of documents were even more damaging. One contained a collection of poems written by Graef to (or about) Bertha Rother. This particular package came with a note attached to it asking his sons to leave the package unopened and burn it after his death. Graef tried to suggest that it had been his intent to allow his sons either to read or burn this package according to their own desires, but the judge suggested that the clear language of the note contradicted his assertion. In what must have been a humiliating experience for Graef, the judge asked for each one of these poems to be read out loud in court. This would turn out to be a fairly controversial decision, since many critics would later argue that the fairly small probative value of the poetry could not excuse the invasion of Graef's privacy and the public humiliation that would inevitably accompany it. In the view of these critics, no amount of poetry—regardless of how explicit—could ever be used as proof that sexual relations had occurred.

Still, the poetry was read out in court, and it was dutifully transcribed for the rapt audience outside the courtroom as well. Perhaps the most embarrassing poem for Graef was an acrostic, a poem in which the first letter of each line spells out a word. The poem reads roughly as follows:

Blossoming blonde child come here!
Eyes of blue so full of charm.
Rosy cheeks that tempt and cheer,
To gaze too deeply might cause harm.
Hot desire for lips so sweet
Ah! If only for a kiss!

Rose so slender and petite,
Open, petals! Give me bliss!
The dew gleaming on your breast,
Has renewed my youthful powers.
Enlivened by both love and lust,
Rose, within me your bloom flowers![30]

A much longer poem was named after the painting that became his obsession, *The Fairy Tale*:

You have granted to me, oh Art
Lovely images of life to see,
To lift me o'er life's common part,
Jacob's ladder you have built for me.

Found amidst tall weeds, this wild vine
Budding shoots so deeply concealed
Now I tend to her with thoughts so kind
Until her ripeness is revealed.

Swinging me up towards illusion
Fantasy's power now drives me hence,
Frees me from dust and confusion
And provides my art its countenance.

If both for good and for evil
The seeds are planted within each breast
From evil I would redeem her
Through all the skills that within me rest.

It may raise itself up as high
As my imagination sustains,
The picture will indeed comprise
Only that which my mind contains.

I ask that magic rule the day
To make this beauty so long endure,
Until my image can convey
the young girl I see so true and pure.

Two paths are there for you to take:
If only I might help choose your course
Follow one, the other escape
To flee the long torment of remorse

If perchance the fates do decree
That my very heart you know no more
My restless striving would not cease
But glancing heavenward I'd go forth.[31]

For each of the poems read out in court, Gustav Graef offered similarly innocent explanations and interpretations. First, he asserted, all poetry was based on fantasy and imagination, and these fantasies inspired poetry in the same way they inspired great works of art. To write or paint about such feelings, however, was not the same as seeking to act on them. Graef urged the court to call the novelist and cultural critic Paul Lindau as an expert witness to testify about the important differences between poetic fantasies and reality: a request that the court ultimately refused. Secondly, Graef claimed that many of his individual poems were inspired by completely innocent interactions. One poem, for example, closed with the lines "The sweet secret I hold here / of which I only am aware."[32] Graef described this poem as an expression of the feelings he had when accompanying Bertha Rother to the theater, a place where most people would not have known she was employed by him as a model. Again, this "secret" did not refer to any physical relationship, but to his musings about accompanying a beautiful and mysterious young woman. Graef admitted that his relationship with Bertha was complicated, but he insisted that all of these illusions and delusions were helpful to him as an artist. As he testified:

> I had a tenderness for Bertha, just as if she were my own child; since she was not in fact my child, there were certainly some sensual feelings mixed in. I did not give in to these feelings, however, but used them to inspire the aesthetic qualities of my work. If I had actually sought a physical satisfaction for these sensual feelings, then I would have been satisfied, and I would not have needed to express them in poetry. But if my relationship with Bertha had been sexual, it would not have been possible to preserve the illusions I created around her—and that was what was most important to me.[33]

In addition to the collection of poems, Judge Müller also read aloud a part of Gustav Graef's will, addressed to his sons, which included the following passage:

> My fantasies led me to idolize the girl who inspired me to create *The Fairy Tale*, and the close relationship that I engaged in with her gave me ever more inspiration to paint. This relationship has caused me great worry and also great sacrifices of money—all things that I endured because otherwise she would have moved on to another artist and thus would be lost to my work. I was never untrue to your mother, and I have always held her in high honor. My relatively young and excitable heart, however, requires stimulation now and then in order to strive and create, in part due to the oppressiveness I sometimes felt because of your mother's sickliness and occasional melancholy nature. I had to keep myself fresh. Ideals are not always reachable in life, but life teaches us that those with a striving nature that cannot be held back will necessarily seek substitutes to compensate for relationships that are unfulfilling. This is what I have done. I did not enter into this relationship flippantly, but to pursue higher goals; therefore I hope that you will regard me with the same honor as you always have before.[34]

These letters by themselves, of course, did not prove that a sexual relationship occurred. As circumstantial evidence, however, they did suggest to some observers that Graef's behavior may have been less than honorable.

Perhaps to counter the effects of these letters and poems, Graef and his lawyers put forward an unusual demand: they asked the judge to be able to display Graef's painting *The Fairy Tale* to the jurors. Graef suggested to Judge Müller that if he could show the jury a photo of the painting as it had been before his arrest, and then show how it had been improved during his stay in prison, the quality of the work would demonstrate to them that his "relationship" with Bertha was one directed toward artistic and not base sexual goals. Prosecutor Heinemann strenuously objected to this motion. Evidence had already been offered about Graef's obsession with the painting, he argued, and the quality of the work had absolutely nothing to do with whether or not there had been sexual contact or perjured statements. Bertha Rother's attorney also objected to a display of the nude painting, which he suggested would create a rather embarrassing situation for his client.

After a short consultation with his associate judges, Judge Müller reluctantly agreed to bring the painting into court. Müller claimed that displaying this painting in court was not just unpleasant, but also a grave violation of everyone's sense of decency (*Sittlichkeitsgefühl*): "This is not simply because the painting depicts a nude figure, a thing that is common enough in museums and is often worthy of admiration. What is distasteful here is that the display of this nude painting will inevitably lead to comparisons with 'the original'—the young woman who now sits at the defense table."[35] Judge Müller insisted that the dignity of the court (and not just the dignity of Bertha Rother) should be preserved as much as possible. Thus, he ordered the painting be brought into the courtroom under cover so that no one outside the court could view it, and he insisted on holding the viewing in the judges' chambers with only the defendants, lawyers, jurors, and a few expert witnesses present. Bertha Rother, not surprisingly, was excused from this part of the trial hearing. The viewing itself required only five minutes; there is no record of what was discussed or argued during this portion of the trial.[36]

These events were certainly salacious enough to provide titillation to the newspaper-reading public, even when reproduced in the otherwise dry form of trial transcripts. In the hands of talented journalists and authors, however, this kind of courtroom drama could be carefully edited and presented with élan and literary flair. In an article for the *Nationalzeitung*, for example, the author and literary critic Paul Lindau helped his audience read between the lines. He portrayed an animated and anguished Graef desperately pleading his innocence to the jury during confrontations with witnesses and then becoming so agitated at the reading of his private poems that at one point he turned ashen white and slammed copies of the documents down on the defense table.[37] Other accounts depicted a humble Graef stepping forward, despite his obvious embarrassment, to earnestly assist the court in deciphering his own handwriting—sometimes even completing poetic verses directly from memory.

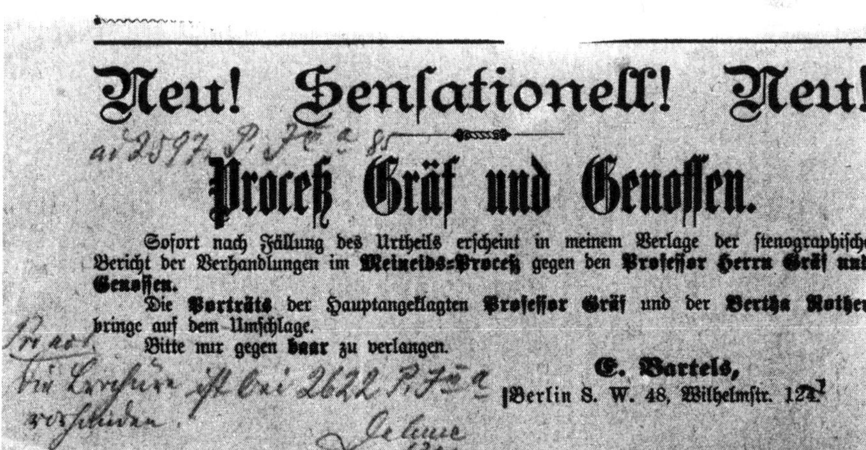

FIGURE 9. Newspaper advertisement for a posttrial brochure from E. Bartels Press. With permission from the Landesarchiv Berlin (LAB A pr. br. rep. 30 Berlin C, nr. 14751, p. 7).

In the hands of journalists, then, the Graef trial was put in narrative and descriptive form; it was turned from complex procedural drama into high tragedy. It is not surprising, therefore, that the provocative tenor of press coverage quickly became as common a topic in the German press as the actual trial itself. For many observers, the behavior of segments of the press during this trial were even more alarming than the allegations against the defendants.

THE GRAEF TRIAL AND "NEW JOURNALISM"

To many conservative journalists and politicians, the journalistic fascination with sensational trials seemed especially vulgar and improper. The most successful newspapers in Germany during the 1870s and 1880s tended to be liberal in orientation, and they were saddled by their conservative rivals with pejorative labels such as the "gutter press" (*Revolverpresse*) or more pointedly, the "Jew Press" (*Judenpresse*)—epithets that were intended to emphasize their corruptive effect on German morals and social institutions. While the editors of more conservative newspapers tended to portray themselves as responsible men who reported objectively in the interests of society, they portrayed liberal journalists as rogues who sought to create and exploit scandals simply to benefit their own political and pecuniary goals. It was also implied by these critics that in appealing to the emotions of their readers, liberal muckrakers were violating traditional notions of manliness that emphasized honor, self-control, and the absence of emotional expression. During the Graef trial, for example, the editors of the Catholic *Germania* suggested that their own newspaper had refrained from commenting on the proceedings while they were underway and that they were even reluctant to report on such a scandalous case after it was over. This restraint was clearly contrasted to the behavior of the liberal press and authors such as Paul Lindau, whom the *Germania* accused of seeking to use melodramatic reporting on the case to sway political opinion and even to influence the jury itself.[38]

Attacks on "ungentlemanly" journalists were quite common during this era, and such critiques had even been occasionally levelled by liberal journalists against their political rivals as well; during the 1870s and early 1880s, for example, when Catholic, Socialist, and even a few ultraconservative journalists were prosecuted for libelous attacks on Otto von Bismarck and National Liberal politicians, they were described by liberal journalists as having failed to engage in reasonable debates between "dueling" opinions, and instead resorting to *Attentate*—literally "assassinations" against the character of their opponents. The clear implication here was that those journalists who improperly attacked the honor of government officials were not gentlemen, and instead were just as disreputable and dangerous as those who might plot to murder leading political figures. At a time when actual assassination attempts on political leaders were not entirely infrequent, this was a powerful accusation.[39]

Public concern about sensational journalism was not limited to Germany during this era. In fact, there are important similarities between the Graef case and a case that was taking place simultaneously in London: the infamous "Maiden Tribute Affair." In her 1992 book *City of Dreadful Delight*, Judith Walkowitz examined the Maiden Tribute Affair (along with other sensational cases such as the Whitechapel murders of Jack the Ripper) in order to gain insight into gender relations in the complex social, cultural, and political world of late Victorian London. Direct comparisons between the Graef case and the Maiden Tribute Affair were fairly common in Germany and around Europe at the time, although they rarely progressed beyond a superficial level.[40] Some brief comparisons of these two affairs, therefore, may be useful here.

In July of 1885, the English journalist W. T. Stead began an investigative report for his newspaper, the *Pall Mall Gazette*, on the world of prostitution and child trafficking in London's poorer districts. Entitled "The Maiden Tribute of Modern Babylon," this series of articles electrified the public and set off debates about government regulation of prostitution and a perceived moral degeneration within English society. The particular intensity of the public reaction to the "Maiden Tribute" articles was partially due to the methods that W. T. Stead employed: rather than simply providing a series of moral lectures on the evils of prostitution, Stead posed as a potential client and infiltrated the London underworld—even going as far as to purchase a thirteen-year-old girl for sexual purposes. Stead published the lurid details of his adventures in a barely anonymous form, and he proclaimed it to be evidence of the decadence of English society and the special depravity of the upper classes. According to Judith Walkowitz, "The Maiden Tribute" series was one of the most successful pieces of scandal journalism in the nineteenth century.[41]

Critics of Stead and his reports railed against his "New Journalism," an approach that Judith Walkowitz describes as featuring a more personal and colloquial style, intimate detail, and a capacity to shock, amuse, and entertain. As Walkowitz suggests, Stead captured the attention of readers (and perhaps political sympathizers) by introducing "human interest stories that exposed the secrets of the rich and incited sympathy for the domestic plight of the poor."[42] For his journalistic rivals, some of whom were no doubt motivated by professional jealousy, this approach was both immoral and inappropriate for a journalistic professional. Accusations of unethical conduct against Stead eventually led to actual criminal charges. When it became clear that Stead had indeed engaged in the purchase of a thirteen-year-old girl, Eliza Armstrong, for his story, and when Eliza's parents claimed that she had been drugged and taken by an intermediary without their explicit approval, Stead was arrested and charged with kidnapping. Other prominent reformers, such as Bramwell Booth, the "General" of the Salvation Army, were also arrested for their roles in the scheme, while the feminist Josephine Butler escaped prosecution since she claimed that although she had introduced several participants in the plot she had not been aware of their plans. The trial of W. T. Stead and his fellow defendants occurred just two weeks after the end of the Graef trial, and it was almost as sensational a story as the original newspaper articles in the *Pall Mall Gazette* had been a few months before. Stead's conviction and his sentencing to three months in prison gratified his critics, who viewed him as a sensationalist huckster and a villain as depraved as the exploitative sexual "minotaurs" he had written about.[43] Stead himself, however, viewed this conviction as a badge of honor—even proudly donning his old prison uniform every year on the anniversary of his conviction until his death aboard the RMS *Titanic* twenty-seven years later.[44]

While liberal journalists in Germany did not instigate the Graef trial in the same way that Stead had initiated the "Maiden Tribute Affair," their trial coverage was condemned in much the same way as Stead's *Pall Mall Gazette*. The *Berliner Börsen-Courier* and the *Nationalzeitung* were especially singled out for their "feuilletonistic" coverage of the Graef trial—with "feuilleton" referring to the section of newspapers generally reserved for entertaining feature stories or serialized fiction. This kind of trial coverage, it was argued, encouraged the worst instincts of the public—something the arch-conservative *Kreuzzeitung* compared to spreading poison into the German soul. The *Kreuzzeitung* accused the *Börsen-Courier* of filling reports on the trial with sentimental coquetry about alley prostitutes and fallen women, and then attempting to "cover up the moral abyss uncovered by the trial with flowery rhetoric."[45] According to the ultraconservative *Reichsbote*, the *Nationalzeitung* was even worse:

> It is already a sign of confused moral principles for a newspaper to describe an ugly and scandalous trial held behind closed doors as a "gripping drama." The smarmy praise heaped on the leading figures of the trial is also absolutely disgusting. The "patient and humane" lead judge, the "warm-blooded" prosecutor, and the

> "pre-eminent jurist and eloquent advocate" Simson—how embarrassing this flattery must seem to an earnest and conscientious judge. One has to ask: what is this newspaper's goal? . . . Such behavior on the part of the press must be protested in the interests of public law and morality.[46]

During and after the trial, leading Catholic and conservative newspapers continuously lambasted these "ungentlemanly" liberal newspapers as muckraking scandal sheets that were engaged in a headlong rush for readers and profits. "Instead of working to lead and nurture the general public, as one might expect," the *Kreuzzeitung* complained, "they have instead become an obedient servant to their basest instincts."[47] As we will see in the following chapters, this growing outrage against the excesses of the liberal press would have important consequences, and it would give rise to explicit attempts to restrict the German press and enact legal penalties for inappropriate and "immoral" reporting.

A VERDICT, BUT NOT AN ENDING

Although daily accounts of criminal trials such as the Graef case provided public entertainment, the trials themselves were frequently long and exhausting experiences for everyone involved; the Graef trial, for example, featured approximately ninety witnesses spread over eight grueling days of testimony. Even the *Plädoyers*, or closing statements, given on the ninth day of the trial were not for the faint of heart; Max Heinemann's closing for the prosecution lasted for nearly five hours, with only a very short break in the middle. His speech was as much an attack on the German press and a defense of his own conduct as it was a review of the evidence against Graef and the Rother family. Heinemann condemned parts of the press for their sensationalism, their open support of Graef, and their alleged attempts to unduly influence the course of justice. He suggested that there was a clear difference between real "popular opinion" and a mere "opinion of the moment" (*Tagesmeinung*)—a debased thing that was formed in corridors and taverns and then spread by a tendentious press. Heinemann asked the jurors not to be swayed by this outside influence and to make sure that a guilty man did not go free.[48]

Heinemann also vigorously denied allegations from some liberal newspapers that he was using this trial to launch some kind of moral campaign against modern art. Sexual relations between an unmarried artist and his models, he said, would probably not have led to a prosecution; indeed, even sexual relations with underage models may not have caused him to file charges—*if not for the fact that perjury was also committed.*[49] This was no moral inquisition, therefore, and certainly not the kind of attack on artistic freedom that certain segments of the press had described.

Heinemann focused the jurors' attention on the receipts, letters, love poetry, and other documents that he argued had clearly revealed a deeper relationship than an artist would normally have with a model. It was ridiculous to argue, as the defense did, that Graef's poetry was sensual without being inspired by real carnal knowledge. Heinemann suggested a parallel example in the work of Johann Wolfgang von Goethe. He argued that Goethe's poems written about his unrequited love for Lilli Schönemann had been written almost entirely in idealistic terms, while those poems that characterized his relationship with his mistress and later wife, Christine Vulpius, were much more openly sensual.[50] This latter kind of open sensuality was clearly evident in Graef's poetry, and according to Heinemann this clearly indicated a relationship that was far from platonic.

Finally, Heinemann also argued that there were plenty of other indications of a sexual relationship, including both witness testimony and clear references to Graef's own unsatisfactory marital relationship in his will. Why, for example, would Gustav Graef have had to excuse his conduct to his sons in the will? Why make excuses if one has a clear conscience?[51] It is impossible to believe, Heinemann suggested, that an artist would pursue an artistic ideal into the home of such a disreputable family, and it was equally unlikely that Graef had a simple "fatherly" relationship with Bertha, a young woman who already had a substantial police record for prostitution.[52] Heinemann ended by suggesting to the jurors that it had made him sick to bring charges against such a highly respected man as Gustav Graef, but he hoped the jurors would not acquit Graef because of any wariness about convicting a man of high status of such terrible crimes.[53]

After a short pause, the lead defense attorney for Gustav Graef, John Simson, was given the opportunity to begin his own closing statement. Like Heinemann, Simson began by addressing the role and influence of the German press; however, his description was quite different from the prosecutor's. Simson admitted that large sections of the press had openly expressed sympathy for Gustav Graef; this was not an attempt to sway public opinion, he argued, but instead an actual reflection of public opinion. As Simson put it:

> Public opinion, Mr. Prosecutor, stands against you in this case. The public believes that in order to charge such a man as Gustav Graef with such grave crimes, you

> should have had more substantial and credible evidence than you have presented here. The public believes that it is not right to swear in convicted criminals, including one who has already partially served a sentence for her crimes, to testify about their own innocence. The public believes that such things can only bring about a regrettable state of legal confusion.[54]

The heart of Simson's argument lay in making a clear contrast between the character and reputation of Gustav Graef and the character of those who testified against him. Simson told the jury that he had personally known Graef since he was seventeen, and they had both attended the Albertina in Königsberg together. Even after the two went their separate ways, they had still remained personally close. Simson, therefore, claimed to be able to say authoritatively not only as a defense attorney, but also as a character witness, that Graef was extraordinarily generous, thoroughly honorable, and a true patriot. Simson did admit that Graef was perhaps less clever when it came to matters of practical life, even though he was a very intelligent, creative, and successful man.

In stark contrast to his description of the sterling character of Graef, Simson painted a far different picture of the Hammermann family. This entire tragedy, Simson argued, had begun with a piece of knavery devised by the Hammermanns, who hoped to use their daughter to squeeze money out of two honorable men. When this failed, and when his wife ended up in prison instead, Wilhelm Hammermann decided that he would get his revenge by hook or by crook. Simson ridiculed the idea that the young model Helene Hammermann had any credibility at all. He described her accusations against the painter Hermann Kretzschmer as absurd, not only because of his excellent personal reputation, but also because he was a man of age seventy-five, who had recently recovered from a stroke and who probably did not have much longer to live. Simson pointedly referred to Helene Hammermann as a "Canaille" (piece of scum), who grew up in a house with hucksters and criminals, and who was clearly capable of all kinds of misdeeds herself. Simson even suggested that an abhorrent voice, like the one she possessed, was often a reliable sign of a crude character. The jurors had a clear choice in figuring out what happened in the original Hammermann case, Simson concluded; they could believe in the testimony of honorable citizens such as Graef and Kretzschmer, or they could believe the testimony of people such as the Hammermann family and their loyal "agent" Krischen.

After Simson finished, there were still additional closing arguments by a second counselor for Graef as well as separate attorneys for the other defendants:

Bertha, Anna, and Auguste Rother. Unfortunately, even after listening to a full day and evening of closing arguments, the jurors' responsibilities were not yet complete. There were still rebuttals and counter-rebuttals by all of the attorneys, as well as lengthy instructions by the judge. The jurors were finally released for deliberations at 10:15 in the evening—after thirteen total hours of closing arguments. Their deliberations, thankfully, took only ninety minutes, and their verdict was read some time after midnight. In the end, all four of the defendants were acquitted of all charges.

After the verdict was announced in court, Gustav Graef tearfully embraced both his lawyers and members of his own family. Meanwhile, outside the court, an enormous crowd of as many as 3,000 people had gathered to hear the outcome. According to several newspaper descriptions, this crowd cheered wildly as word of the decision came out.[55] The crush of spectators was so great as the defendants were released—even at nearly 2:00 a.m.—that they had to be quietly shepherded out through a side door in the jury room. Although the long and grueling trial was finally over, this was far from the end of the drama. In fact, the public repercussions of the Graef case were only just beginning to be felt.

CHAPTER THREE

ARTISTS AND PHILISTINES

The name Gustav Graef appears only rarely in modern texts about the history of German art, perhaps in the form of a passing reference to his famous 1863 painting of the Prussian heroine Ferdinande von Schmettau or a quick nod to his general skill as a portraitist. This is not entirely surprising, especially since Graef—as successful as he was at the time of his trial—never achieved the international reputation of other nineteenth-century German painters such as Caspar David Friedrich, Wilhelm von Schadow, or Adolph Menzel. Of course, it is also quite common for reputations to ebb and flow after the death of a particular artist. Even a painter such as Wilhelm von Kaulbach, a man who had been lionized as a master by his peers at midcentury, was virtually forgotten just a few decades after his death.[1] Still, there is something peculiar about this particular case of historical amnesia. Gustav Graef's name was not simply forgotten over time, it was erased from the history of German art. His name, for example, is conspicuously absent from the historical membership roster of the Association of Berlin Artists, and very little evidence of his career or his correspondences is preserved in the archives of the Royal Academy of Arts. In addition, the published histories of these art institutions contain no explicit mention of Graef's work or the impact of his trial on the German art world. It is almost as if Gustav Graef never existed and his infamous trial never took place.

The purging of Gustav Graef from the history of German art was undoubtedly a product of the lasting damage to his reputation caused by the charges filed against him. However, there is more to the story. The trial itself triggered fierce debates in the German press about the character and future of German art, and it gave both artists and others a chance to weigh in on these discussions. For a time, Gustav Graef became an unwitting symbol of all that was wrong with modern art in Germany—or for some of his defenders, he became a martyr to a moral "philistinism" that threatened to keep modern art rooted in sterile old traditions. The 1880s are sometimes described as a period of relative quiet in the German art world—a calm before the first waves of impressionism and then expressionism breached the fiercely defended fortress of German artistic traditions. The debates surrounding the Graef case, however, demonstrate that long before these revolutions began in earnest, the German art world was already in turmoil.

NATURALISM AND IDEALISM

Even before a verdict in the Graef trial had been reached, newspapers such as the conservative *Kreuzzeitung* and the Catholic *Germania* were using the case to suggest that there was something deeply wrong both with German high culture and with German society as a whole. This, of course, was not a new revelation for critics of modern German culture; it reflected a deep pessimism that was common during this time. As Fritz Stern described in his classic work, the *Politics of Cultural Despair*, the cultural pessimism of this era can be traced in part back to the philosophical works of Arthur Schopenhauer early in the century and through later works by Friedrich Nietzsche, Paul de Lagarde, and Julius Langbehn.[2] While these four authors differed in their approaches, their focus, and their prescriptions for the future, they often selected similar targets to blame for this decline: liberalism, capitalism, and the development of an increasingly crass popular culture. Cultural pessimism in Imperial Germany was not confined to only a small cadre of elite intellectuals; it also extended across political and social divisions from conservative and Catholic elites well into the middle classes. Paired with the fear of revolutionary Marxism, this pessimism gave many the sense that Germany, and perhaps Europe as a whole, was heading towards some sort of cataclysm. To be fair, conservative and Catholic newspapers such as the *Kreuzzeitung* and *Germania* did not cite Nietzsche, Lagarde, or other cultural pessimists directly in their editorials about the Graef trial; however, one can clearly read in these newspapers the sense that modern German culture had become shallow, debased, and immoral.[3]

In addition to making general complaints about the decline of German traditions, many conservative newspapers were also beginning to take specific aim at the rise of "naturalism" in German art and literature—a movement inspired by the influence of the French novelist, Émile Zola. Beginning in the early 1870s, Zola had dedicated himself to a long sequence of novels called the Rougon-Marcquart series, which explored the lives of main characters descended from a common ancestor. Instead of presenting a hero coming to terms with his world, Zola depicted the complex personal development and social relations of his characters, often members of the lower classes, warts and all.[4] Zola described his own novels as almost scientific or experimental in nature: he would create characters and then follow them as the effects of heredity, as well as social and environmental influences, carried them forward within their milieu. Zola's work, therefore, tended to emphasize the social ills of the urban landscape and the personal damage caused by modernization and industrialization.

Zola's influence was first felt in Germany after the seventh novel in his Rougon-Marcquart series, *L'Assommoir*, which tackled the life experience of the working classes of Paris, including a blunt examination of the effects of alcohol and poverty. Zola's characters employed the "language of the street," and he himself described the novel as "a work of truth, the first novel about the people which doesn't lie to us and which presents to us the odor of the people."[5] Although *L'Assommoir* was not translated into German until 1879, almost two years after it appeared in France, it still provoked immediate negative reviews from German literary critics for its elaborate descriptions of the lowest levels of the social ladder and what one critic called the "ugliest and most disgusting of things."[6]

Even those German critics who recognized Zola's talent were not altogether uncritical of his work. One example was the well-known literary historian Julian Schmidt, a close colleague of the famous novelist Gustav Freytag and later a prominent member of Gustav Graef's social circle. Schmidt, along with Freytag, had been a key figure in the founding of German literary realism in the wake of the Revolution of 1848. He had famously admonished German writers that "the novel should look for the German people where they are at their best, namely at their work."[7] This motto served as the inspiration for Freytag's famous novel *Soll und Haben*, which had provoked controversy upon its release in 1855 for its rather realistic view of ordinary people. By the time Zola's work began to reach Germany two decades later, however, Schmidt made it clear that this was not the kind of realism he had had in mind. Schmidt was sympathetic to the efforts of Zola, whom he described as a "great talent" and as someone who possessed a gift for describing both people and nature.[8] However, in an 1878 essay, he complained that in emphasizing the ugliness and crudeness of the working class and the constant battle between social classes, Zola had presented a biased story that pushed the reading public toward socialism.[9] For Schmidt, true literature should not seek simply to reflect the world in its chaotic messiness; instead, an author should observe reality, and then use the ideals of truth, beauty, and the good to produce a sense of what ought to be (*ein Seinsollendes*) as a poetically transfigured image (*poetisch-verklärendes Bild*). The novels of Zola, in other words, contained *too much reality*. In the aftermath of the stock market crash of 1873 and the economic and social upheaval that followed, works that focused unsparingly on the plight of the working classes were frequently viewed with suspicion. What Schmidt desired, therefore, was something quite different from Zola's naturalism: an idealism, rooted in the real world, that suggested workers could improve their lives through individual effort and spirit rather than through social revolution.[10]

In an 1885 essay in the *Preußische Jahrbücher*, Schmidt celebrated the seventieth birthday of the German realist painter Adolph Menzel by once again distinguishing the "idealist realism" that Menzel was known for from crude naturalism. "Considered more deeply," Schmidt wrote, "one might even call [his] realistic exactness a kind of idealism, since the true nature of something is its reality. The true realist painter does not create a photograph that reproduces nature exactly; instead the image that he perceives with his own senses, he must first spiritually reproduce (*geistig reproducieren*)."[11] Menzel's selection of subjects was also not random, according to Schmidt, and it was certainly no accident that he frequently chose to portray the grand figures of Prussian history, including Frederick the Great. In other words, although a clear break from romantic idealism, the realism of Menzel was quite distinct from the naturalism of Zola.

Despite the rather harsh critical reception given by Schmidt and others, Zola and his naturalist approach slowly began to gain more admirers in Germany. Heinrich and Julius Hart, who founded the journal *Kritische Waffengänge* (Critical Encounters) in 1882, used it both to popularize Zola's work and to vigorously defend it against criticism.[12] The publication of Zola's epic novel *Germinal* in early 1885—which appeared almost immediately in German after it had been serialized in French newspapers—improved his reputation further and helped German naturalism to coalesce as a movement. Later in this year, the same year as the Graef Affair, the Munich literary critic Michael Georg Conrad founded the journal *Die Gesellschaft* to support the work of German naturalists, and Wilhelm Arent published the first anthology of the work of Berlin naturalists, entitled *Moderne Dichtercharaktere*.[13]

For German critics of naturalism, this new approach was positioned in stark opposition to an idealism that had supposedly nourished German art and literature over the previous centuries. German idealists, in general, emphasized traditional notions of beauty and viewed the primary purpose of art as the education and inspiration of ordinary people through the exaltation of proper civic virtues.[14] Defenders of idealism tended to be suspicious of innovation in artistic techniques or aesthetic principles, and they were generally dismissive of artistic subjects that did not either extol German nationalism or portray both the good and great within humanity.[15]

Perhaps most importantly, idealists linked naturalism with French influence and therefore portrayed it as a fundamental threat to German culture. Cultural Francophobia had been fostered by German nationalists since the start of the nineteenth century, in part out of a desire to forge a common German identity that was distinct from French and Napoleonic influence. Even after the question of military superiority between Germany and France was (temporarily) settled in 1871, the question of cultural superiority was still a very sensitive matter in the newly united German Empire. As the director of the Munich Academy, Ferdinand von Miller, put it in a request for funding support: "This hereditary foe persists in making war on us by another, perhaps more damaging means. French taste, formed by art, and the French sense of beauty, have subjugated the whole world, including us Germans."[16] The fear of succumbing to French influence led many leaders in the German art world to rigidly distance themselves from French trends and innovations, especially the rise of impressionism and *plein air* painting. These French novelties were described as having a "frivolity, shallowness, and superficial virtuosity" that contrasted with German "depth, spirituality, and thoroughness."[17] Eventually, for many of these German cultural nationalists, "naturalism" ceased to refer to a particular artistic method or approach and instead became a general pejorative term for any form of art that broke with tradition or that seemed "modern," shallow, inferior, or French.[18]

There were other powerful reasons for German nationalists to cling to idealism and resist the incursion of "French" naturalism. As the art historian Robin Lenman argues, many idealists believed that the purpose of art was to distract public attention from the imperfections of the world and help them to contemplate the perfect, the ideal, and the eternal. Naturalist art, which often required viewers to confront poverty and social strife, was seen as a force that would only serve to increase public angst about contemporary social and economic tensions. As Lenman concludes about the German focus on monumental art in this period: "[A large] segment of German art production might be crudely interpreted as a symbolic denial of the new industrial and urban reality, and in psycho-cultural terms, along with much of contemporary literature, as a kind of steadying sea-anchor for society on its plunge toward modernity."[19] For idealists, then, naturalism was a morally dangerous trend that bordered on political subversion. Although the battle between idealists and naturalists did not begin with the Graef trial, the controversies surrounding this particular case brought the conflict very powerfully into the public sphere.

THE "MODEL MARKET"

Gustav Graef was an easy target for those looking for evidence of cultural corruption. The Catholic *Germania*, for example, expressed alarm that an elderly painter might have had sexual relations with underage models; however, the editors were even more distressed by the fact that Graef, or any prominent artist, would ever stoop to using former prostitutes for artistic inspiration in the first place. This was viewed as a violation of both social and artistic norms that must necessarily shock the conscience. As the *Germania* commented the day after the verdict:

> Something else was on trial alongside Professor Graef: the direction of modern art [*die moderne Kunstrichtung*]. Despite the acquittal of the individual defendants, modern art itself was subjected to a far more scathing verdict. What kind of art is it that seeks inspiration among the castoffs of society? What flights of fancy can come from an artist who spends his time wallowing in the sewers? . . . Art requires ideal compositions . . . and the deeper the artist can penetrate into the mysteries of the soul and the character of humans, the more profound his art. It is absolutely psychologically impossible, however, for an artist who views only the common, and who thinks that the castoffs of society are good enough for his inspiration, to produce art of superior quality.[20]

The *Germania* lamented the disappearance of great historical painters and portraitists, and their replacement by a "cult of the naked" which produced images that elicited shame rather than inspiration. "Art has become degenerate," the editors complained, "and philistinism [*Banausenthum*] now holds the brushes and palettes."[21] The *Germania* ended this article by calling on the German government to follow Aristotle's old recommendation to ban all forms of art that had a corrosive moral influence in society.

One of the first responses to the *Germania* came from the art critic Adolf Rosenberg—the same critic who had suggested in the early 1880s that Graef's work had been slipping in quality. Rosenberg penned a long commentary for the

Free Conservative paper *Die Post*, which had generally been pro-Graef during the trial. This essay mocked *Germania*'s call for a return to "morally pure" artists by recounting the rather colorful life story of Fra Filippo Lippi, the sixteenth-century artist who was still a favorite within the Catholic Church despite his own rather scandalous background. Lippi had selected the beautiful Lucretia Buti to serve as the model for his painting of the Madonna. Then, in violation of his sacred vows, the middle-aged artist had abducted her from the convent and lived with her in sin (thus producing his equally famous son, Fillipino Lippi). Apparently, Rosenberg opined, the Catholic Church had chosen not to discipline Lippi at the time and instead continued to sponsor his work—thus suggesting that the Catholic Church in the "good old days" had a much more flexible moral code than the one the *Germania* was assuming now.[22]

The liberal *Berliner Börsen-Courier* reached even further back in art history to provide its own counterexamples to the chaste idealism praised by the *Germania*. The newspaper featured a page-long article recounting the life of Phryne, the famous Greek hetaera and model. Phryne was reputed to have possessed such beauty that she was almost irresistible to men—only the philosopher Xenocrates had apparently succeeded in withstanding her charms. Among Phryne's many lovers was the orator Hypereides, who successfully defended her against the charge of impiety before the Athenian high court (*Areopagus*). Unable to sway the court through his rhetoric, Hypereides allegedly ripped off her cloak to reveal her naked bosom to the judges, who were so awed by what they saw that they summarily voted to acquit.[23] As suggested by the *Börsen-Courier*, it was Phryne's beauty that eventually allowed her to gain great wealth and to flaunt the moral codes of Athens, including her occasional swims in the nude during the sacred festival of Poseidon. Rather than condemning her behavior, however, the *Börsen-Courier* instead recounted the long list of famous artworks that were associated with her name, including the Aphrodite of Knidos and several other sculptures by her lover Praxiteles. Even contemporary artists, novelists, and poets, such as Otto Franz Gensichen and Ernst von Wildenbruch, the newspaper argued, were still enthralled and inspired centuries later by the beauty of this legendary young woman. Although the *Börsen-Courier* did not make an explicit link between Phryne and Bertha Rother, the implication was clear: an extraordinarily beautiful woman may lead some men to scandalous behavior, but she may also help an accomplished artist to create timeless masterpieces.[24]

Interestingly enough, while some articles in the *Börsen-Courier* seemed to celebrate the sordid history of artists and their models, other articles took a very different tack. To counter conservative portrayals of an immoral trade in models (*Modellwirtschaft*) and a "model-nuisance" (*Modellunwesen*) in modern Berlin, the *Börsen-Courier* suggested that the artist's studio was far from a den of immorality. It was instead a special space where ordinary standards of modesty and decency were suspended for higher aims and purposes. Just days after the end of the trial, the paper published an exposé of what it called the "Berlin Model Market" in the main foyer of the Royal Academy of Arts. This exposé, however, was not meant to reveal the scandalous behavior and secret moral decadence of such a location. Instead, the paper portrayed the world of artists and models as a rather curious but harmless place, where not just societal castoffs but a broad range of people could find employment. The sense of wonderment with which this strange world is described was evident even in the article's opening sentence: "What a strange and colorful collection of bohemians (*Bohème*) is this group of people called models."[25] Although the *Börsen-Courier* admitted that many young women were driven to modeling out of desperation, and although it also admitted that some women—even middle-class women—had been seduced (literally and figuratively) by an artist's invitations to model, the newspaper still depicted the model market itself as a rather sterile place, without any hint of sexual exploitation. Male and female models were separated on different sides of the hall, and women were never allowed in the general halls used for male nude modeling; they were instead escorted to private modeling rooms to help maintain their dignity. The newspaper singled out several individual models by name—focusing primarily on adult men and some elderly men and women—who were prized by artists for particular characteristics. Several of these models were also explicitly linked to the famous paintings that they had helped inspire. This place, in other words, served as a direct refutation of the *Germania*'s claim that great art could not be inspired by "ordinary" models.

This is not to say that the *Börsen-Courier* tried to disguise the fundamentally economic relationship between artists and models in this "model market." As described by the *Börsen-Courier*, models always tended to straighten up their postures or assume common modeling poses when artists passed through the hall in the vain hope of being selected and thus earning the one Mark fee common for adult models. The models described by the newspaper, however, were far from passive victims of an exploitative system. An older male model named Adami, for example, was depicted as always standing up to leave immediately after the contracted time was up, even if the artist begged him to stay for a few minutes longer. The article described Adami as strutting out of the hall as proud as a peacock

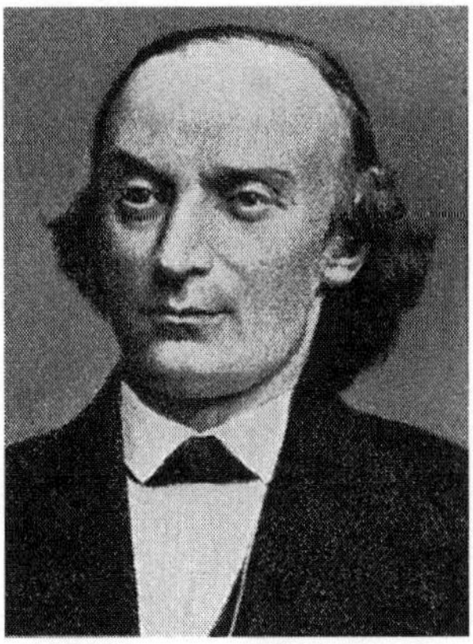

FIGURE 10. Sketch of Karl Frenzel. Wilhelm Speeman, *Spemanns goldenes Buch des Theaters* (1902).

while telling a desperate sculptor: "I'm not willing to give away even an extra minute to the Academy."[26] In this "market," therefore, it was clear that those with especially attractive or interesting features could often have substantial leverage and leeway with their prospective employers. This was, in other words, a classically liberal market where free actors entered into mutually beneficial contracts. There was little to criticize here in terms of a violation of social or artistic norms. Although this world would undoubtedly seem rather strange to many readers of the *Börsen-Courier*, it was not depicted as particularly decadent, nor was it worthy of condemnation. For the authors of the article, then, this "*Modellwirtschaft*" (trade in models) was hardly a "*Modellunwesen*" (model-nuisance).[27]

THREE PAMPHLETS

In the midst of these newspaper exchanges about the character of modern art (and about the models used by artists) came three influential pamphlets in quick succession, each of which used the Graef trial as a platform to either attack or defend trends in contemporary German art. The first pamphlet was written by Karl Frenzel, a well-known novelist and cultural critic for the *Nationalzeitung*. Frenzel's pamphlet originally appeared as a long posttrial commentary in the feuilleton of the *Nationalzeitung* before it was published separately under the title *Art and Criminal Law*. At its core, this essay was a vigorous defense of Gustav Graef; however, it was also a clear attempt by Frenzel to defend art and artists from those he considered the real "Philistines" in German society.

Like the journalists of the *Berliner Börsen-Courier*, Frenzel suggested that the world of artists was simply different from the world of ordinary people—as he suggested it should be. He asked his readers to think about what would have happened if writers such as George Sand and Lord Byron, and early humanists such as Petrarch, had been forced into the narrow confines of an ordinary life.[28] Not all artists and writers were necessarily led astray by their passions; in fact, while one painter might be enthralled by his model, a second might marry her, and a third might be entirely indifferent to her. What is absolutely certain, he argued, was that a degree of sensuality was often required for the great artists and writers to produce their greatest work.[29]

What differentiated Frenzel's pamphlet from the articles in the *Berliner Börsen-Courier* was both the extreme nature of his rhetoric and the specificity of his target. Frenzel took direct aim at the prosecutor in the Graef case, Max Heinemann, who he suggested was one of the great enemies of modern German art. By pressing charges against Gustav Graef, Heinemann had not simply intended to bring a single alleged perjurer to justice but also to attack the very practice of using nude models for artistic purposes. Frenzel compared Heinemann's alleged moral campaign to Girolamo Savonarola's public burning of works by Petrarch and Boccaccio in Renaissance Florence and also to the later prosecution of the Renaissance painter Paolo Veronese by the Inquisition. "As enduring as the name of the accused will be in the history of art," he wrote, "so will the infamy of the man who prosecuted him."[30]

For Frenzel, the actions of a prosecutor like Heinemann were not simply a nuisance, but a direct threat to artistic freedom. As he put it:

> Without models there would simply be no painting or sculpture; without original archetypes in society or events in the real world, there would be no poetry. If every paragraph of the penal code is now to be ruthlessly enforced, then no theater troupes can exist. The arts are sustained not only by reference to the real world in general, but unfortunately also by the dirt and filth of the world as well; they require sensuality and passion: they unleash the same human drives that the penal code seeks to limit, tame, and subdue.[31]

Frenzel openly wondered how far such moralists might go in their quest to stamp out all traces of sensuality in art and literature. He asked his readers to imagine the ridiculousness of an actor playing a half-crazed Othello in the act of approaching the bedchamber of Desdemona or an impassioned Mortimer declaring his love

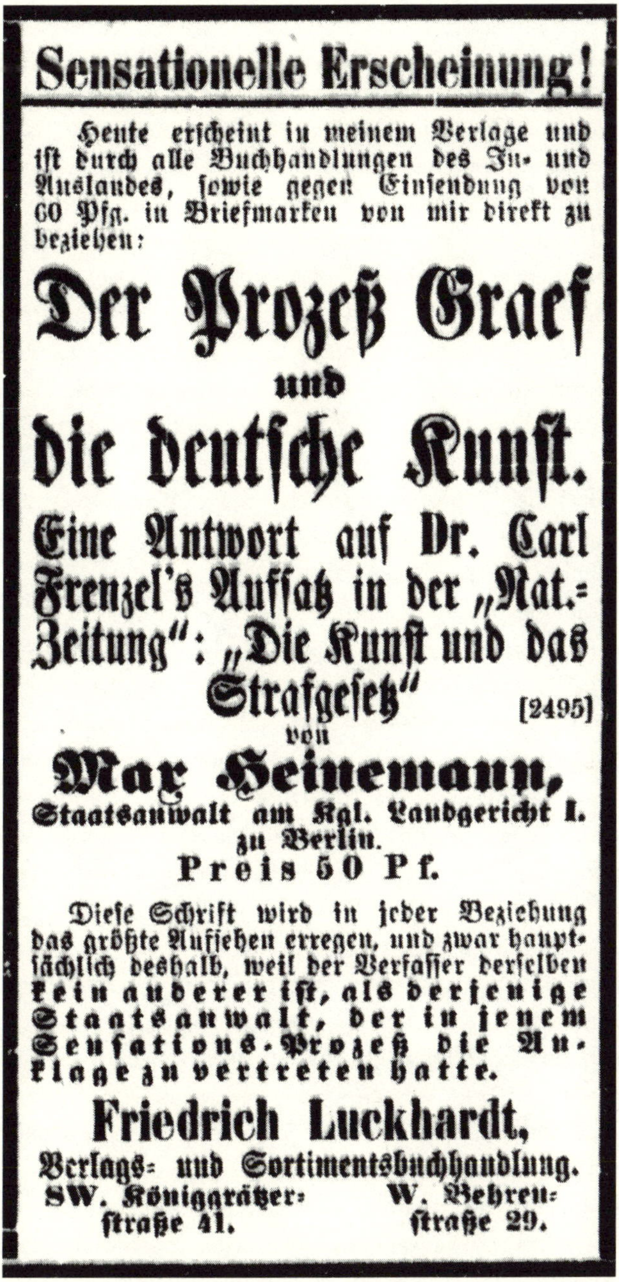

FIGURE 11. Newspaper advertisement for Max Heinemann's brochure *Der Prozeß Graef und die deutsche Kunst* [The Graef Trial and German Art]. *Reichsbote*, no. 240 (October 14, 1885), Beiblatt. Courtesy of the Staatsbibiothek zu Berlin—Preußischer Kulturbesitz.

for Mary Stuart, only to have to stop after each step and ask politely: "Am I coming a bit too close to you, miss? Is my touch too bold?"[32] In this kind of sterile world, every time an artist touched a model or an actor touched an actress it might make them subject to state prosecution. Frenzel's mocking tone aside, his argument here was actually a stark and radical one. As he concluded near the end of his essay: "Art and jurisprudence are absolute, incompatible, and irreconcilable opposites."[33]

Frenzel did also add very pointedly that he was not suggesting that artists should be completely exempt from the law. As he put it: "No one is demanding a special set of laws for artists in all things mine and yours, or for treason or manslaughter, and forgery or fraud will never be mitigated or excused by someone's artistic reputation; but in matters related to sensuality, the artist will require a different approach from the nonartist."[34] Although the Graef trial had resulted in an acquittal, Frenzel still fretted that such a case would provide a platform for narrow-minded conservatives to pressure justice officials into curtailing the free expression enjoyed by German artists. The Graef case, therefore, should serve as a warning to all those who cared about artistic freedom.

Frenzel's brochure brought an immediate response from a rather surprising source: Max Heinemann, the lead prosecutor in the Graef case. Heinemann quickly published his own pamphlet called *The Graef Trial and German Art*. Such a public statement from a state prosecutor was extraordinary, but perhaps also not surprising for a man who had been so incredibly sensitive to outside criticism during the Graef trial itself. In reality, Heinemann was far from a cultural dilettante, and he was deeply insulted by Frenzel's insinuation that he was a fanatical moral campaigner and sworn enemy of modern art. As his supporters in the press noted, Heinemann was a longtime patron of the arts, brother to a gifted novelist, and a talented musician in his own right. What those newspapers did not reveal was that Heinemann appears also to have been a part of a lively social and intellectual circle in Berlin that centered on the philosopher Paul Reé and the author Lou von Salomé. In fact, Heinemann had returned from a Swiss vacation with Reé and Salomé only a few months before the Graef trial began. He was apparently serving as a replacement for Friedrich Nietzsche, who had recently abandoned his unconventional triangle relationship with Reé and von Salomé over feelings of jealousy.[35] Given this background, it is not surprising that Heinemann would be outraged at being lectured by someone like Frenzel about art and morality.

Heinemann's response to Frenzel was at times playfully sarcastic and at other times deadly serious. He began his essay by defending his behavior as a prosecutor. He had never meant to put Graef's art or even his poetry on trial; the only reason these were entered as evidence was that they helped to corroborate the witness statements and provided additional evidence that an intimate relationship between painter and model had existed.[36] Heinemann also repeated his assertion that "leaving aside the age of the models, it was not an amorous relationship between artist and model that was on trial, but the falsely sworn **oath** that no intimate relationship existed."[37] It was here that Heinemann turned especially defiant. It may be true, he wrote, that according to Ovid, Jupiter on high laughs at the lies of lovers, "but thank goodness our notion of German justice does not yet laugh about the taking of an oath, neither one taken by lovers nor by any other person. The German people will hardly approve of your conflation of a sensual relationship between an artist and model and a false oath taken about such a relationship."[38]

Heinemann went on to mock Frenzel for suggesting that artists should not be held to the same ethical standards as ordinary people, and also for his assertion that artists' ability to adhere to moral codes was primarily a matter of individual temperament. These arguments were not only unreasonable, he claimed, but downright dangerous to the social order:

> Go ahead and try to convince the common people that artists have different rights than they do, and see if they believe you. Every person that you encounter will give you a different answer. On one side you'll hear "An artist is a man just like me!" and on the other side: "I think I have a talent for art too!" Or perhaps one will tell you: "I'm not an artist, but I want to learn!" or even "You're just a joker and you don't really mean what you're saying!" Take your precious theory to the stores where young men packed themselves in to buy pictures of Bertha Rother, or to the places where they showered huge bouquets of flowers on her, and tell them that "morals are a matter of temperament—but only for artists!" Surely they will greet your caveat with laughter.[39]

It was not he who posed a danger for the future of German art, Heinemann insisted, but Frenzel himself. Frenzel's artistic principles were a clear sign of cultural decay and a distortion of "true" German culture:

> You have attempted to perform a service for the world of art, but I believe that the *true* art world will not be grateful for such a service. . . . [for] there is another kind of art and artist, a kind whose praise you would seek in vain. Your most dangerous opponents would not be the sanctimonious pseudo-artists or narrow-minded

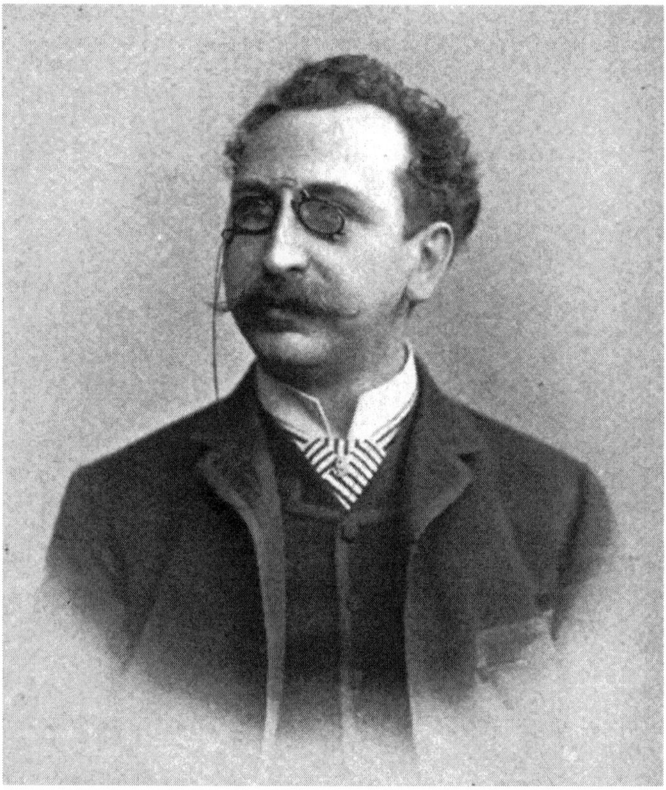

FIGURE 12. Photograph of Paul Lindau.

> dilettantes that you might expect; oh no, there are still real, great, true artists, who grant sensuality its place in life as well as in art, but who turn away in disgust at a lifestyle or an artistic philosophy that shuns morality and makes sensuality and fantasy its only guide.[40]

Heinemann took great pains to acknowledge that sensuality was indeed an important part of life, not just for artists, but also doctors, lawyers, or any other men who may struggle to find a balance between "sensual lust and a soul at peace."[41] Such internal struggles, he claimed, are a fact of life. Great artists, however, are not dominated by sensuality and lust, Heinemann wrote, but are inspired by things such as spirit, fantasy, as well as a reverence for the eternal. Although Heinemann admitted that his own views probably ran counter to the force of public opinion, he expressed his gratitude that there were still examples of such "pure art and pure artists" in Germany.[42]

Finally, Heinemann lamented his own ordeal during and after the Graef trial. He portrayed himself as a kind of martyr who had been targeted with threats and insults only for trying to stand up for what was right. Heinemann added that he had no doubt that Frenzel would have the last word on the matter, since a good portion of the German press stood at his disposal. If, however, Frenzel was right that the name of Heinemann would go down in art history for his prosecution of Gustav Graef, then he would certainly take pride in such an association.[43]

Although Heinemann's main target was Karl Frenzel, his essay also leveled an attack on another prominent Berlin cultural critic, Paul Lindau. The forty-six-year-old Lindau had already built a substantial reputation as a successful playwright and theater critic in Düsseldorf and Leipzig before relocating to Berlin in 1871, and he also edited several influential literary journals, including the monthly *Nord und Süd*. As the son of a Prussian justice commissar, Lindau developed a life-long interest in the justice system and the criminal underworld. Several of his own plays dealt with criminal trials, and just a few years after the Graef trial he published a very popular collection of sensational real-life trial stories.

Lindau had been a fairly visible figure during the Graef trial, and immediately after the verdict he published a long commentary in the *Nationalzeitung*, entitled "A Layperson's Perspective on the Graef Trial." In this article, he was quite critical of the prosecution and compared the reading of Graef's personal papers in court to the torture inflicted on suspects in the Middle Ages.[44] Heinemann was angered by the slights within Lindau's article, and he responded by attacking Lindau directly for his conduct during the trial. According to Heinemann, Lindau had frequently been seen drinking alongside the Rother family and other witnesses after the court proceedings had ended for the day. Heinemann also cited witnesses who claimed that one afternoon Lindau had called out to the large crowd assembled in front of the courthouse, saying: "We'll get rid of the prosecutor. First let's get an acquittal; then we'll get him out!"[45] Heinemann used these stories to ridicule the supposed objectivity of Lindau's journalistic "research" on the case, and he suggested that such behavior was especially revolting since Lindau had originally been proposed by the defense as an expert witness on artistic techniques.

Lindau responded to Heinemann's attack on him with an open letter published in the *Berliner Börsen-Courier*. He admitted to having associated with many witnesses in the case and even to spending time in the neighborhoods where the Rother and Hammermann families lived. If only Berlin prosecutors attempted the same degree of due diligence as he had in amassing evidence, Lindau pointedly remarked, they might have been able to spare themselves some embarrassment in court. Lindau, by the way, absolutely denied having made any of the public statements Heinemann attributed to him, and he mockingly expressed amazement that a state prosecutor would be so gullible as to accept hearsay without real corroboration. Despite this provocation, Lindau insisted that he would maintain his objective approach. His own pamphlet on the trial, which was planned for the November 1885 issue of his *Nord und Süd*, would reveal his real opinion of Heinemann: "that he pursued this thankless and difficult task without achieving success, but nonetheless with great vigor and talent."[46]

Lindau's essay on the Graef case in *Nord und Süd* would turn out to be a sixty-five-page-long article that covered all aspects of the case. He began this essay with a short statement about the problem of objectivity for any journalist or critic. It was not possible, he suggested, that any observer of such a contentious case could promise to be completely free of bias: "At some points, the author of these lines cannot honestly say 'I have described this exactly how it happened.' He can only ask one thing of himself: that out of all the contradictions, he has assiduously described what appeared to him to be most likely and what seemed subjectively true from his own point of view."[47] Despite this rather humble promise to serve as an honest observer, Lindau's trial summary reads as a full-throated defense of Gustav Graef, whom he describes as a foolish but well-meaning artist, and whom he labels the "hero of this tragedy."[48]

Lindau was certainly not as strident in tone as Karl Frenzel, but he did return to many of the same themes, including the difference between artists and ordinary mortals. Lindau rejected any suggestion that there should be a special set of moral laws for artists; however, he insisted that it was important to realize that artists and nonartists often had very different points of view:

> There is no denying that certain ideas seem natural and self-evident to an artist that would seem strange for a nonartist—including the relationship between artist and model. The unbridled joy of an artist at having found a perfect model . . . [or] the naiveté that might cause an artist to overlook the moral qualities of a girl because it is her physical qualities that inspire him . . . [are] things that seem more or less puzzling to laypeople and which can only be appreciated from the point of view of an artist.[49]

This distinction between the perspectives of artists and nonartists was the key problem in the Graef trial, according to Lindau, where artists and jurists seemed fundamentally unable to effectively communicate with one another:

> It was amazing to watch as Graef, who did not understand the jurist, would try to make the same point again and again, and then the jurist, who did not understand

> Graef the artist, would repeatedly demand another more plausible explanation to help make sense of what was otherwise incomprehensible to him. These repeated clashes are only understandable if you consider the vast difference in perspectives between the two sides.[50]

Only by understanding this difference, Lindau wrote, could one understand why Graef had willingly spent huge sums of money on Bertha Rother, or why he could overlook Bertha's sinful lifestyle or the greedy and shiftless nature of her mother. Even the "love" poems Graef wrote about Bertha Rother were an expression of what Lindau called "artistic-sensual delight" (*künstlerisch-sinnliches Wohlgefallen*), a feeling that had nothing to do with common lechery or lust—and was often their polar opposite.[51]

Perhaps the most remarkable thing about Lindau's essay is that at one point he gave way entirely to the voice of Gustav Graef himself. Lindau first cited several love poems that Graef had dedicated to his own wife that were not included in the trial transcripts; he then included extended passages from Graef's own "diaries," written after his arrest and during his long pretrial imprisonment, in which the defendant carefully explained his own past behavior. These diary excerpts do not read as a true diary, and appear instead to be Graef's personal closing argument in his own defense. Graef, for example, wrote that he had been inspired by classical images of the female body since a very young age, and as a child he had often been mocked by his schoolmates for the idealistic way that he described nude figures. According to these diaries, therefore, Graef's obsessions with nude figures had never been about sexual gratification but about an ideal of feminine beauty. Indeed, Graef insisted that he had always been in control of his sexual desires and could never imagine himself either seducing an innocent girl or paying for another's affections.[52] He added that the long hours, days, and even months spent around the same nude models did not tend to increase desire, but instead served to make such exposure seem ordinary. Lindau wholeheartedly accepted all of Graef's explanations in these "diary" entries. Although he repeatedly admitted that Graef had behaved in a naïve, gullible, and foolish manner, Lindau attributed this to an obsession with a higher artistic calling and not to any debased sexual motives.[53]

If Gustav Graef was glad to have the public backing of such a well-known figure as Paul Lindau, this support did not come without a price. Soon after the publication of Lindau's article in *Nord und Süd*, Graef personally thanked him and offered to send him a signed photographic reproduction of *The Fairy Tale*. Lindau, however, made it clear that this gift would not be sufficient repayment. He mentioned that his own wife had previously published a well-regarded series of fairy tales, and he told Graef that he would like to be able to give her an original painting by him on a fairy tale theme as a Christmas gift. Although phrased politely, Lindau's request made it clear he would not take no for an answer: "If I'm not in a position to pay you for your work, I believe I have every right to expect this favor from you, especially since it will cost you relatively little time and effort. I think it's important to say that."[54] This was a rather extraordinary demand, especially considering that the letter was written only four days before Christmas. A second letter sent the following day suggests that Graef agreed to provide the painting to Lindau, but with an added plea that it could perhaps serve as a New Year's gift rather than a Christmas gift.[55] While this exchange does not necessarily prove a *quid pro quo* for Lindau's supportive articles and essays, it would not have been an isolated case. Several years later the banker Gerson von Bleichröder would bankroll Lindau's long voyage to Mexico in exchange for flattering articles about the country—at a time when Bleichröder was heavily invested in Mexican securities.[56]

As one might expect, these three pamphlets brought renewed debates within the press, both within Berlin and across Germany. Frenzel's controversial pamphlet was savaged in the ultraconservative and Catholic press, which denounced what was interpreted as a call for a special privilege for artists to commit immoral acts without punishment (*Freibrief der Unsittlichkeit*).[57] The ultraconservative *Reichsbote* suggested that this kind of artistic philosophy was "the direct opposite of morality," and its editors linked the effects of naturalism in modern art to troubling new trends in modern philosophy, literature, and the natural sciences, as well as the development of Marxist socialism and anarchism—all movements that aimed at the destruction of the influence of Christianity on the German people, and therefore all responsible for a catastrophic decline in German culture.[58]

Press reactions to this debate, however, did not necessarily follow a simple right versus left political divide. The moderate rightist "Free-Conservative" *Post*, for instance, insisted that rigid enforcement of a bourgeois moral code (and its conflation with the penal code) could have a deleterious impact on German art and artists. As the *Post* editors wrote: "Art cannot be subordinated to this code unless one wants to destroy it; one should remember the words on the frieze above the entrance to the New Museum in Berlin: *Artem non odit, nisi ignarus* [Only the ignorant scorn art]."[59] The liberal *Frankfurter Zeitung*, on the other hand, dismissed this idea and insisted that there could not be a moral double-standard within the German justice system: the law must be applied equally regardless of the identity or temperament of the defendant. The editors of the *Frankfurter Zeitung* added that although there was no room for prudery, "we cannot imagine a true art that is not thoroughly grounded in morality and directed towards the ideal. Artists should dwell at the highest levels of humanity, and may, when necessary, contemplate the common as well, but they must not descend and intermix with the base and then insist on carte blanche for their actions. An artist, by the grace of God, will always remain just a human . . . but the higher and purer his aspirations, the higher his art will soar."[60] The *Frankfurter Zeitung* concluded that "an art which does not recognize this, and which seeks to emancipate itself from common standards of morality, is already degenerate, and this degeneracy will become a danger for the morality of the people as a whole."[61]

THE ARTISTS' DECLARATION

In the midst of this lively public debate, one additional voice made itself heard: the Association of Berlin Artists. The Association had held a meeting on October 20, 1885, where an open declaration was circulated for members to sign. The statement was later circulated by mail to other members of the Association to give them the opportunity to add their signatures as well. Shortly thereafter, this "Artists' Declaration," addressed directly to Max Heinemann, the prosecutor in the Graef case, was published in several leading newspapers. It read as follows:

> Esteemed Sir!
> In your publication from the twelfth of this month, you address the statements by Dr. Frenzel published in the *Nationalzeitung*, which claimed that in certain circumstances there should be an exception made for artists from the demands of our common moral code. The undersigned artists believe it important, both due to the public nature of this exchange and to their own position and status in society, to state that on this point we are in complete agreement with you. [We] would gladly forgo this rather dishonorable distinction, and would instead wish to be viewed no differently than any other upstanding man, whether he be rich or poor, or whether he occupies a high office or not. The undersigned are convinced that it would harm neither artists nor art itself to satisfy the dictates of law and morality.[62]

This statement was accompanied by the signatures of 172 members of the Association, including many of the most prominent artists in Berlin.[63] Signers also included several artists who had testified favorably for Gustav Graef during his trial, including Paul Thumann and Konrad Dielitz. The original authorship of the document is unclear; it may have been written by the chair of the Association, Carl Becker; however, according to the *Kreuzzeitung*, the main instigator of the letter was Adolph Menzel, and his signature was the first one on the document.[64]

There was at least some resistance to the letter from within the group. One artist who had refused to sign, Paul Meyerheim, even sent an angry letter to the leadership of the Association that criticized the public statement as an unnecessary and unproductive step. It was fine, Meyerheim suggested, to protest Frenzel's argument that artists should be held to different moral standards; this was, however, something that could have been done with an open letter directed at Frenzel himself. To send such a letter to Heinemann was not only to take his side in an esoteric debate about art and morality but also to publicly lend support to a man who had ruthlessly prosecuted one of their own. Meyerheim's angry letter caused a stir in the Association of Berlin Artists, and the leadership group called for a discussion of the matter at their next meeting, scheduled for November 3, 1885. This undoubtedly put Meyerheim in a rather difficult position. First of all, he had long been on very friendly terms with leaders of the Association, including both Adolph Menzel and Anton von Werner. Secondly, the other major agenda item for the meeting was a vote to make Menzel a special "honored member" (*Ehrenmitglied*) of the Association in celebration of his upcoming seventieth birthday. There are no surviving minutes of the November meeting, but several newspapers reported that when the agenda turned to the matter (immediately after Menzel was honored), Meyerheim simply gave a brief statement asking his colleagues to forgive his hastiness and his harsh language, and expressing the hope that they wouldn't hold his knee-jerk reaction against him. With that apology, the matter was apparently closed. A response from Max Heinemann thanking the artists for their supportive declaration was read out in full, and it was gratefully added into the record.[65] Faced with what he perceived as a public rejection by his colleagues, Gustav Graef soon sent word of his resignation from the Association.[66]

The Artists' Declaration provoked outrage among many liberal newspapers in Berlin. The *Berliner Zeitung*, for example, blasted it in a long front-page article. It was ridiculous, the editors claimed, for the Association to have taken sides in this rather regrettable debate, especially when Karl Frenzel had never actually suggested that there should be *special laws* for artists; he had only argued that the topic of sensuality needed to be thought about differently for artists than for nonartists—something the editors of the *Berliner Zeitung* believed was self-evident. The newspaper also mocked the seeming hypocrisy of the Artists' Association:

> If what the artists say in their declaration is true, namely that they do not claim any special exemptions from the moral laws of society, then they are actually passing judgment against their own behavior. For isn't the entire practice of using models, at least when seen from the viewpoint of strict bourgeois morality, a clear case of immoral behavior? And don't artists therefore commonly ask for an exception from our traditional moral and legal codes, if only to allow them to pursue their noble artistic quest?[67]

Like Paul Meyerheim, the editors of the *Berliner Zeitung* expressed dismay that the declaration itself was addressed to the prosecutor, Max Heinemann. This gesture gave the appearance that the artists approved not only of Max Heinemann's view of artists, but also that they approved of his prosecution of Graef. The only motivation that could explain the issuance of such a declaration, the newspaper

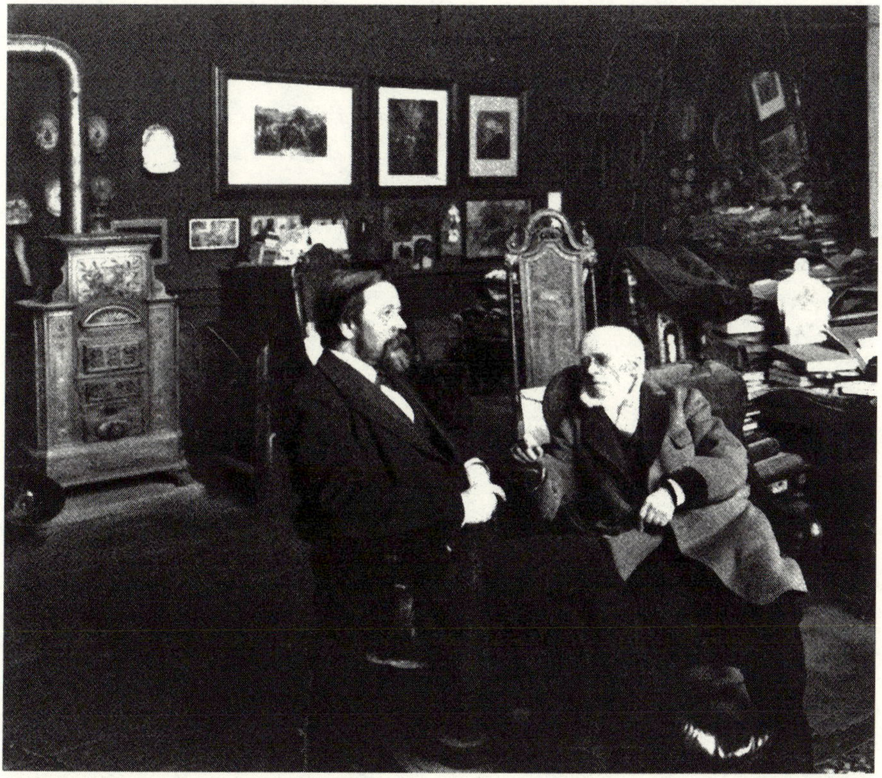

FIGURE 13. Photograph of Adolph Menzel with Anton von Werner. *Adolph von Menzel 1815–1905. Das Labyrinth der Wirklichkeit* (Berlin: 1997), 44.

claimed, was professional jealousy. Graef had been repeatedly described by Frenzel and others as an exceptional artist; since many members of the Association had previously had much less favorable reviews from Frenzel, this was perhaps a perfect opportunity to take their revenge against both men.

The claim by the *Berliner Zeitung* that the Artists' Declaration was motivated by professional jealousy seems specious at best. But the question remains: Why would the members of the Association have taken such a public step? In a 2004 article in the *Fontane Blätter*, Theresia Bach suggested that the willingness of so many artists to sign this declaration can be understood as a response to pressure "from above" for artists within the Association to renounce Frenzel and his support for sensuality in art. This outside pressure might help explain why a few artists, including Paul Meyerheim, first signed the declaration and then later asked for their names to be stricken from the document.[68] Bach also describes the declaration as a form of preemptive action by Berlin artists taken to avoid the potential for tougher legal restrictions on artistic freedom by the government. In other words, the Artists' Declaration was a kind of agreement about self-censorship—a promise to obey the rules, and a rebuke to those like Frenzel who sought to deviate from traditional cultural norms and traditions.[69] This explanation is a persuasive one, even if a lack of minutes or correspondences from the records of the Association of Berlin Artists makes it difficult to substantiate.[70]

We should also bear in mind that the Artists' Association was a historically conservative institution with strong ties to the monarchy. It was dominated by rather traditional realist painters such as Adolph Menzel, Carl Becker, and the younger but equally successful Anton von Werner. Like Menzel, Werner first became known for his monumental works on historical themes, and his most famous painting, *The Proclamation of the German Empire*, is an image still used by many German history textbooks today to depict the 1871 coronation of Kaiser Wilhelm I. Werner had been installed as the Director of the Royal Academy's art schools in 1875, and his personal contacts with both Otto von Bismarck and leading members of the Hohenzollern Dynasty won him both substantial commissions and also considerable influence within the Berlin artistic community. Not surprisingly, Werner became especially well known for his public support for idealism and his disdain for naturalism and all forms of French influence in German art.[71]

The leading figures of the Association of Berlin Artists not only held substantial influence over members of the organization, but they controlled purse strings as well. Anton von Werner, for example, was a prominent member of Prussia's

National Art Commission (*Landeskunstkommission*) from 1875 to 1877 and again from 1882 to 1911. It was this Commission that voted on which painters to support and which paintings should be purchased by the National Gallery using public funds. Under Werner's guidance, this committee became known not only for supporting traditional idealism and historical realism, but also for favoring those artists who had close ties to committee members themselves.[72] One might easily imagine, therefore, that an invitation by Anton von Werner to sign such a public declaration would have been a fairly difficult offer to refuse.

The full story, however, is even more complicated than this. Just two years before the Graef trial, Karl Frenzel had been involved in a very nasty public spat with Anton von Werner. The argument began after Frenzel published an angry response to a controversial satirical pamphlet by Julius Stinde (under the pseudonym Quidam) called *Berlin Art Criticism with Marginal Notes*.[73] In this work, Stinde had mocked the leading art critics of Berlin by printing side by side their very contradictory reviews of individual paintings from an 1883 Berlin art exhibition. The clear implication was that art critics knew nothing about art, and they were no more qualified to judge paintings and sculptures than ordinary observers. Although he had not been targeted personally in Stinde's book, Frenzel clearly felt offended. Taking his revenge in the pages of the *Nationalzeitung*, he defended the necessarily subjective nature of any art, theater, or literary critique, and he portrayed art critics as an absolutely vital link between German culture and the public. Frenzel's defense of critics, however, ended with some strong language directed at artists themselves. Although many artists liked to mock critics as ignorant interlopers, he claimed, they were also desperate for their attention and praise—without which their work would remain in obscurity. As he concluded, "Critics shrug their shoulders at such idle talk: they know that other geniuses and talents . . . will appear daily, hat in hand, standing at their front door."[74]

This last comment was taken by many Berlin artists as a deep insult, and it provoked intense anger and open mocking at the subsequent meetings of the Association of Berlin Artists. In an open letter to the *Nationalzeitung*, Anton von Werner responded by brusquely dismissing most art critics as dilettantes and suggesting that German art was not one whit better because of their commentary. In his opinion, both artists and the general public would actually be better off if such critics ceased to publish altogether. From this point onward, public exchanges between the two men degenerated into personal attacks, especially when Frenzel implied that Werner had sent free exhibition tickets to various art critics in the hope of influencing their reviews of his own work.[75] For Werner this was not just a simple personality conflict, it was clearly also a turf battle. As mentioned earlier, during this period it was artists and sculptors who dominated Prussia's National Art Commission, the committee that controlled museum purchases for the National Gallery. It was, therefore, artists such as Werner who believed themselves to be the experts on art and the "official" arbiters of artistic quality—not alleged pretenders such as Karl Frenzel.[76]

Although Frenzel would later attempt to walk back some of his most insulting comments, these wounds were almost certainly still raw even two years later. It seems clear, then, that the Artists' Declaration was neither a simple statement of moral principle nor the result of a long personal quarrel. This conflict was also a way for Anton von Werner and the leading artists of Berlin to lay a claim to a level of professional expertise and experience that no mere lay critic could compete with. The declaration may have been addressed to Heinemann, but the fusillade was aimed squarely at Frenzel and his fellow art critics. It would be artists themselves, not critics, who would set standards for the proper behavior of artists and determine the future direction of German art.

There are other reasons to believe that the signing of this public declaration was not simply a matter of simple obedience or self-preservation for members of the Artists' Association. The number of declaration signers, for example, represented approximately half of the total members of the Artists' Association, and there is no evidence that the careers of any nonsigners suffered as a result. Second, there is ample evidence that many members of the Berlin cultural elite, including Theodor Fontane, thought that Frenzel was simply off his rocker for suggesting that artists should be viewed differently from other people. Although Fontane knew Frenzel personally, and admired much of his work, his conclusion about Frenzel's commentary on the Graef trial was fairly blunt: "How could such a clever fellow write something so idiotic?"[77] Frenzel's argument apparently did not comport with Fontane's notion of artistic ideals or personal honor. Strains of cultural conservatism undoubtedly ran deep within the membership of the Association of Berlin Artists, and not just among its leaders. There are grounds, therefore, to assume that a significant portion of Berlin artists signed the Artists' Declaration voluntarily and not under duress.

Finally, even if there was significant unease among those signing the declaration, something that is difficult to measure, it is fairly clear that the Graef case was an awkward issue on which to make a public stand. Frenzel's essay was not only controversial, it was also a vigorous defense of Gustav Graef—someone whom many artists believed (despite his acquittal) had likely violated the most basic standards of honor and decency by engaging in love affairs with underage girls and lying about them under oath. In signing the declaration, then, the artists of Berlin were defending their own public honor and distancing themselves from a colleague who was widely seen to have transgressed social norms.

Regardless of the motivation of the members of the Association of Berlin Artists, or to what degree their apparent unanimity was real or forced, the Artists' Declaration was greeted enthusiastically among those journalists who had been critical of naturalism in German art. The conservative *Reichsbote*, for example, declared that the Graef trial "had pronounced a death sentence for naturalism in art," and the newspaper suggested that the exchange of pamphlets and the Artists' Declaration had only reinforced this conclusion.[78] In another long article entitled "Art and Morality," the *Reichsbote* expressed its gratitude that Berlin artists would join together to protest "against the naturalists who hoped to emancipate them from morality."[79] After sharply critiquing Frenzel for his ode to sensuality, the newspaper once again turned its attention directly to Gustav Graef and his infamous painting, *The Fairy Tale*:

> How can such a painter, for whom the world of spirit no longer exists, represent a fairy tale in a naked female figure? Should we really be surprised that such a man produces nothing more on his canvas than a sensual, lascivious woman—an image that mocks the purity and immediacy of our popular legends? The Brothers Grimm would have turned away in disgust if they had seen Graef's painting and heard someone say that the fairy tale should be represented by the figure of Phryne! ... In fact, this painting is a profanation of the fairy tales that cut every human soul to the quick, and of all the ideal figures that remain a part of our very soul after we first encounter them in childhood. If this painting were really a fairy tale, then what kind of mother could tell such a fairy tale to her children or give it to them to read?[80]

In the opinion of the *Reichsbote*, the influence of Zola and his German naturalist followers, a group in which they clearly lumped Karl Frenzel, Paul Lindau, and Gustav Graef, was a danger for the future of German art and for the morality of the German people. As they concluded: "Art has no greater enemy in our time than the naturalistic worldview, and we can only hope that the Graef trial, which has demonstrated just how deep of a moral abyss art has fallen into, can now help it to turn itself around."[81]

As we know in hindsight, the *Reichsbote*'s claim that the Graef trial had pronounced a death sentence for naturalism in Germany was both wishful thinking and disastrously poor prognostication. Although at the time one could never have guessed it from the publicly expressed sentiments within the Artists' Declaration, the German art world in the mid-1880s was on the verge of a revolution.

THE REVOLUTION AND ITS VICTIMS

The lines of battle seem fairly clear in this story. On the one side were the (typically younger) enthusiasts for naturalism and later impressionism, who were keenly attuned to French influence. On the other side were the conservatives, such as Anton von Werner and Adolph Menzel, men who opposed the influence of French "degeneracy" and who committed themselves to a desperate rearguard action to defend traditional German idealism. A closer inspection, however, suggests that we often tend to overestimate the distinctions and divisions between the two groups and to paint artists such as Menzel and Werner as rather one-dimensional reactionary figures. Menzel, for example, who was publicly renowned as the champion of German realism, had visited France repeatedly during the 1850s and 1860s (along with the young Paul Meyerheim) and had later engaged in experiments with light that mimicked the work of French greats such as Édouard Manet and Gustave Courbet.[82] According to Robin Lenman, Menzel was an enigmatic figure who was difficult to characterize: "Menzel never accepted the role of court painter or dynastic propagandist, stayed aloof from the academic establishment, and on political issues—such as official discouragement of Prussian artists' participation in the 1889 Paris Exhibition—he took a robustly independent line."[83] Even Anton von Werner, Lenman suggests, who openly acknowledged his reputation as the *bête noire* of the younger generation of German painters, was also a more nuanced figure than he is often portrayed. Not only did Werner vigorously defend artists' rights and single-handedly broaden the curriculum of the school at the Academy of Arts, Lenman argues, he was also a very public opponent of anti-Semitism.[84] The art historian Irmgard Wirth has also described several of Werner's paintings, including his 1882 *Im Garten* (In the Garden), as an "example of light experimentation (*Hellmalerei*) that was well down the path toward so-called Berlin Impressionism." As Wirth concludes about Werner, "it seems as if in secret he tried and succeeded in doing what he publicly condemned."[85]

There is no doubt, however, that during the 1880s and 1890s artists like Menzel and Werner would continue publicly to encourage art and artists that represented traditional notions of German idealism, while actively discouraging works that reflected naturalism, impressionism, or French influence. After 1888, their efforts would be emboldened by the crowning of a new emperor, Wilhelm II, who once referred to Paris as the "greatest whorehouse in the world" and who in an infamous 1901 speech denounced modern art for seeking to drag ordinary Germans down into the gutter rather than helping them to reach new cultural heights.[86] The opinions of the new kaiser, along with the influence of Werner, meant that French impressionism would make its way to Berlin cultural circles only very slowly, through private collections rather than exhibitions in state museums.

The first impressionist works prominently displayed in Berlin were brought in 1882 by the collectors Felicie and Carl Bernstein, who had purchased the paintings from their cousin Charles Ephrussi. In addition to being the director of the art journal *Gazette de Beaux-Arts*, Ephrussi had been a supporter of impressionism and a personal friend to Manet, Monet, and Degas. The exhibition of these paintings at the Bernstein house was not a private affair; Felicie Bernstein's role as a popular salonnière meant that prominent artists and intellectuals streamed into her home to examine and discuss the new artworks. Among the visitors was Adolph von Menzel, who was less than impressed. After examining a series of impressionist paintings, Menzel reportedly asked Carl Bernstein, "Did you really pay money for this garbage?" After realizing he may have insulted his host, Menzel backed down only slightly: "I'm very sorry to have said something so impolite about your collection. But that's my true opinion. These paintings are horrible."[87] Of course, not all visitors to the Bernstein home had the same reaction. Among those who were inspired by the collection were a young Max Liebermann and Hugo von Tschudi—two men who would be instrumental in the art revolution soon to come. As Gustav Graef's daughter, Sabine Lepsius, later wrote, the artworks displayed in the Bernstein home were "passionately admired or ridiculed, but always discussed, [and] they were the origin of plans which later coalesced in the founding of the [Berlin] Secession."[88]

Max Liebermann did not single-handedly create a revolution in the German art world, but as perhaps the most famous German impressionist painter, his influence was substantial. As early as 1883, the thirty-five-year-old Liebermann had already created controversy with his experiments in *plein air* painting. In reviewing the 1883 Munich International Exhibition, for example, the art critic Adolf Rosenberg had dismissively lumped Liebermann (along with Fritz von Uhde) in with the French participants, whose "figures look as though their heads, hands, and clothes were sprinkled with flour."[89] Despite this dismissive critical reception, other *plein-airistes* and naturalist painters such as Lesser Ury and Franz Skarbina continued to find an audience (and also willing buyers) for their experimental work during the 1880s. By the end of the decade, the tensions between these artists and the art establishment—often personified in the new chair of the Association of Berlin Artists, Anton von Werner—increased dramatically. Lieberman and a few other artists defied a semiofficial ban on participation in the 1889 Paris World Exhibition, and many of them sought alternate places to exhibit their art in Germany as well—outside the official exhibits commissioned by the Royal Academy of Arts or the Association of Berlin Artists.

The tension eventually came to a head in 1892, when Anton von Werner and other conservatives decided to close down an exhibit of the Norwegian artist Edvard Munch that the Association of Berlin Artists had previously agreed to sponsor. Angered by the decision, several artists, including Liebermann, joined together to form an independent group, called "The Eleven," that would sponsor its own exhibits of progressive paintings that were not favored by the more traditional art institutions of Berlin. The group was not unified by a single common artistic approach but by a common resistance to the conservatism of Werner, the Royal Academy of Arts, the Berlin Artists' Association, and their control over exhibition space, honors, and state funding.[90] The new group did not yet constitute a formal schism in the Berlin art world, but it was an important first blow.

The second blow came with the appointment of Hugo von Tschudi as the new director of the Berlin National Gallery in 1896. Since its founding, this museum had been dominated primarily by the kind of traditional historical and monumental paintings that were favored in mid-nineteenth-century Prussian art. Although Tschudi had not been a controversial figure before his appointment, he became a lightning rod for criticism after he solicited donations from some of Berlin's wealthiest art collectors and mounted an exhibit that included Courbet, Manet, Monet, and Degas.[91] From this point onward, Tschudi would serve as a fierce defender (and popularizer) of modern art, both in its French and German incarnations. He would regularly do battle with Werner, and he would do his best to help cultivate progressive trends within the Berlin art world.

By this time, a formal break within the Berlin art world was perhaps inevitable. Similar tensions in Munich had already led to the founding of the Munich Secession in 1893, and the Vienna Secession followed in 1897. The final break in Berlin apparently occurred in 1898, when Max Liebermann's friend and colleague Walter Leistikow had his painting *Grunewaldsee* rejected by the jury for the annual Academy of Arts exhibit. The Berlin Secession was officially founded on May 2, 1899, and Max Liebermann would serve as the organization's first president. The years ahead would not be easy. Liebermann and the Secession would have a difficult time battling against the disdain of the kaiser and the power of the traditional art establishment on one hand, and also the impending rise of even more radical movements that would view the work of Liebermann and other Secessionists as passé.[92] There would be further setbacks, such as when, in 1908, Hugo von Tschudi was temporarily forced out of the directorship of the National Gallery and replaced by Anton von Werner himself. By this time, however, there was no going back. The artistic revolution begun by Liebermann and Tschudi was profound and irreversible.[93]

Perhaps fittingly, one of Hugo von Tschudi's first exhibits after he took over as director of the National Gallery in 1896 was a posthumous tribute to a rather controversial artist: Gustav Graef. This exhibit of Graef's works at the National Gallery featured nearly one hundred oil paintings, studies, and sketches from different periods in the artist's life. The accompanying program for the exhibit presented a very brief biography of Graef that mentioned he had experimented with the painting of female nudes *en plein air*, but excluded any mention of his trial or the scandal surrounding his work. Both *Félicie* and *The Fairy Tale* were mentioned in the program, but neither painting was included in the exhibit itself.[94] As one might expect, not everyone was thrilled with the exhibit. Adolf Rosenberg, the critic who had first suggested in the early 1880s that Graef's artistic skills were declining, penned a very brief review of the exhibit in his *Journal for the Visual Arts*. In the article, he berated Tschudi for repeatedly displacing the permanent exhibit of Peter von Cornelius every four or five months to display the "odds and ends left behind by deceased lesser artists."[95] Rosenberg admitted that Graef's early nationalistic work ensured that his name would be remembered by future generations; however, Rosenberg also described his turn towards ideal figures and fantasy scenes later in his life as "a disastrous aberration." Rosenberg's review concluded with a very backhanded compliment: "As for his work as a painter of portraits and fashionable ladies, perhaps in a distant future, people searching for historical documents will discover and learn to treasure his art."[96]

Although conservative critics (rightly) worried at the time that Hugo von Tschudi might try to make radical changes at the National Gallery, there were also many other critics who feared that the new gallery director might not be forward-looking enough. One person who voiced this concern was the philosopher and sociologist Georg Simmel, who in 1896 published an anonymous essay entitled "Art Letter from Berlin" (*Berliner Kunstbrief*) in the prominent Viennese weekly *Die Zeit*.[97] Simmel criticized the National Gallery as having been one of the most poorly run museums in Germany, and he hoped that as its new director, Tschudi would breathe new life into an institution that had barely recognized anything but the most traditional forms of art. As an example of the narrow-mindedness of the previous director, Max Jordan, Simmel reported that the museum had passed over a beautiful portrait of the recently deceased Egyptologist Karl Richard Lepsius painted by his talented son Reinhold Lepsius, and instead purchased a clearly inferior portrait by another artist. The National Gallery did this, Simmel claimed, simply because Reinhold Lepsius had learned to paint in more progressive schools in Munich and Paris. One should remember that Simmel had a personal interest at stake here. After the death of his own father, Simmel had grown up in the Graef household, and he was still a close friend of Graef's daughter Sabine Lepsius and her husband Reinhold.[98]

If we can perhaps understand Simmel's attacks on the National Gallery and his anonymous support for the work of his friend, Reinhold Lepsius, the direction of the second half of Simmel's article is perhaps a bit surprising. As a further example of the reactionary nature of the National Gallery, Simmel pointed to the recent exhibition of an artist whom he characterized as both unmodern and decidedly mediocre: Gustav Graef. Simmel's critique of Graef's work was not entirely unkind, as he suggested that Graef's skill in representation would make him interesting for future generations. However, what made Graef's work so antiquated, Simmel argued, was his obsession with the portrayal of ideal beauty. As Simmel wrote:

> [For Graef] beauty is thus something different than for us moderns; he does not extract it from the genuine significance of phenomena, it does not reveal itself to him as the depths of life that lives each essence for itself, without comparison to all others, it does not accompany for him, as it does for us, as a *character indelibilis* of the autonomous movement of things.[99]

For Simmel, as well as for other artists who were determined to break away from the suffocating traditions of the past, the work of Gustav Graef represented a kind of superficial kitsch, the exact opposite of their own artistic ideals. Simmel suggested that Graef's posthumous exhibition featured the kind of "soft, flattering, and comforting" imagery that modern artists hoped to leave behind.[100]

In conclusion, it was not simply the scandal of his arrest and trial that led to the disappearance of Gustav Graef from the history of German art. Dismissed by conservative critics as an example of the corrosive influence of naturalism, French *plein-airisme*, and moral depravity, Graef's art was also rejected by modernists as hopelessly antiquated and superficial. Caught between naturalism and idealism, and between modernity and tradition, the work of Gustav Graef quickly fell into obscurity. By the time Germans marched off to war in 1914, both his work and his legacy as an artist had already drifted toward obscurity.

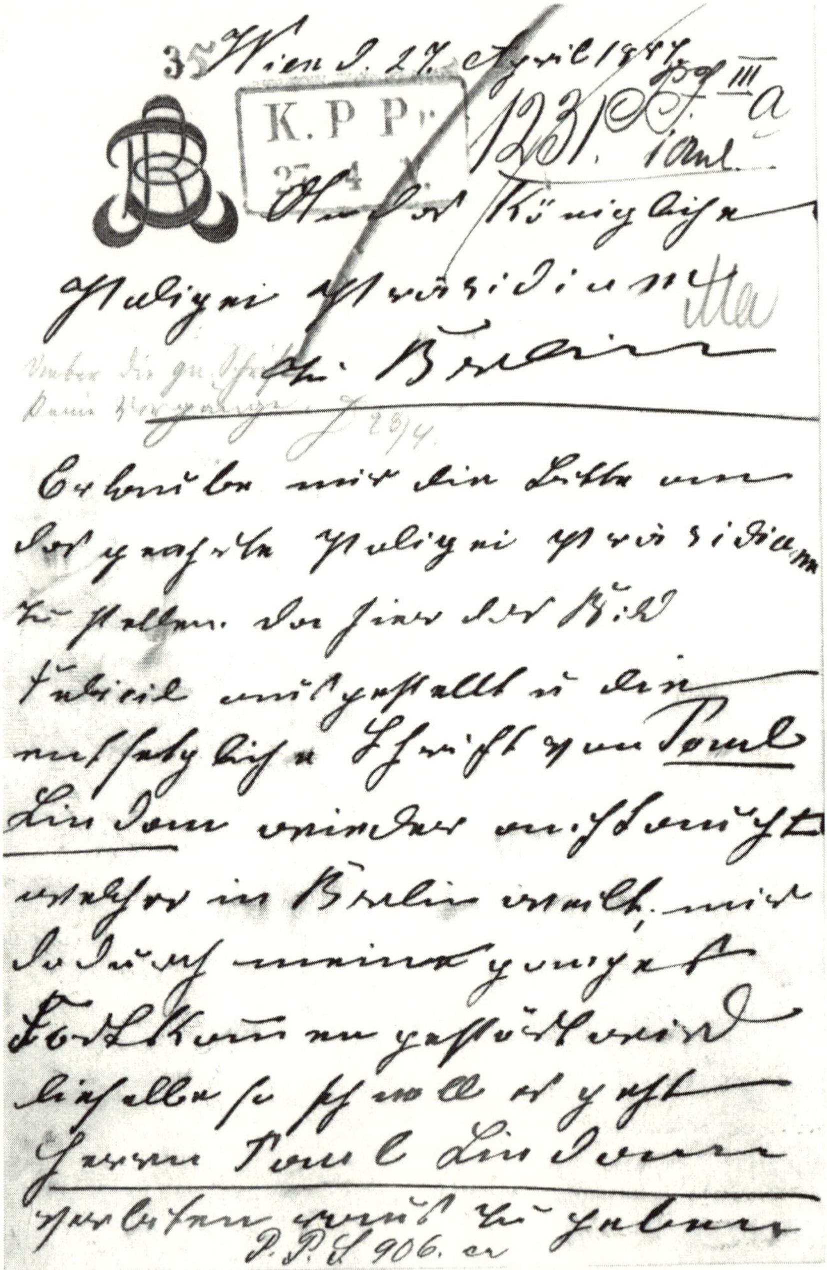

FIGURE 14. Letter from Bertha Rother to the Polizei Präsidium Berlin on her own personalized stationery, dated 27 April 1887. With permission from the Landesarchiv Berlin (LAB A pr. br. rep. 30 Berlin C, nr. 14751, p. 35).

CHAPTER FOUR

WOMEN'S VOICES / WOMEN'S SILENCES

The most dramatic moments of the Graef trial almost always involved the testimony of women. The accusations of Helene Hammermann and her stepmother, the denunciations of neighbors such as Concordia Intrau, and the pleas of innocence from Anna and Bertha Rother reverberated not only within the Moabit courtroom, but throughout the German press and into the wider public sphere. Here, then, in this sensational trial, women's voices from across the social spectrum could make themselves clearly heard. Or perhaps not—at least not in an unadulterated form. It is important to remember that almost everything we know about the women who testified at trial, as well as about the content and tenor of their testimony, was framed by the questioning of male judges and attorneys and mediated through the work of male court reporters, journalists, or authors—many of whom were clearly untrustworthy observers. Where, then, as historians, can we gain direct access to the voices and perspectives of the women involved in the Graef trial—either as defendants, witnesses, or observers? Unfortunately, the answer is far from encouraging. In the rich array of archival records, newspaper accounts, and pamphlets that are available on the Graef case, there are very few examples of the direct and unmediated voices of women.

Perhaps the most conspicuous example is the case of Bertha Rother, the young model who was both a codefendant and an alleged victim of Gustav Graef. During and after the trial, images of Bertha, both clothed and unclothed, sold well in Berlin and many other German and European cities. Indeed, paintings, photographs, and sketches of Bertha Rother, some of which she posed for in her brief career as a performer in Vienna after the trial, are still in existence today and are accessible on the Internet. Outside of her recorded testimony at trial, however, her own voice is almost entirely absent from the historical record—with one exception: a brief letter, hidden in police files within the *Landesarchiv Berlin*, which is perhaps the only surviving document written in Bertha Rother's own hand (see figure 14). In April of 1887, eighteen months after the trial, Bertha wrote to the Police Presidium of Berlin from her new apartment in Vienna. Her handwriting is not easy to read, and her grammar is far from perfect; her intent, however, is crystal clear. In this letter, written on stationery embossed with her own initials, Bertha pleaded with Berlin authorities to ban a new edition of Paul Lindau's pamphlet on the Graef trial, which had arrived in her newly adopted home city at the same time as a travelling exhibit of Graef's painting *Félicie*. She complained that Lindau's "revolting" work "will curse her entire fortunes" and suggested that he had already made more than enough money from the scandal. "I believe that's enough on the trial," she wrote, "and no more such writings need to be put into circulation there."[1] While Bertha Rother's success as a performer in Vienna was undoubtedly aided in part by her own infamy, this letter seems to reflect a clear desire to leave that past behind—or at least a revulsion at having to watch as Lindau, who was frequently less than complimentary to her family, used her infamy for his own private gain. There is no record of an official police response to Bertha's plea, but a brief note scribbled by authorities in the margins of her letter states simply: "No action will be taken against this book."[2] As we will see, in the published accounts of the trial, Bertha usually exists as a rather one-dimensional stereotype or caricature—as an object that could be the target of lust or revulsion, but rarely compassion or understanding. Despite the intense public obsession with Bertha, and especially with her body, there does not seem to have been much interest in protecting her as a person or in hearing the story from her point of view.[3]

Unfortunately, given these limitations, it is difficult to recover the perspective of Bertha Rother in any real sense. Thankfully, historians do have some special tricks up their sleeves for cases like this. One can, for example, try to approach her story indirectly by investigating what life may have been like for a young woman in her location and social position. One can also learn quite a bit about German society from the stories that were told *about* Bertha Rother and the various ways in which she was portrayed. Even if such stories are not directly enlightening about Bertha's thoughts and feelings, they help to delineate the expectations and stereotypes that she was forced to navigate. Finally, one can also learn from the voices of other women, including some of the most prominent German feminists of this era, who made an amelioration of the plight of poor women and the abolition of prostitution their most important goals.

PROSTITUTION AND THE "FALLEN WOMAN" IN IMPERIAL GERMANY

Although information about Bertha Rother's police record was left out of the press, we do have access to some of the details through journal articles written after the trial.[4] Bertha had first been picked up on suspicion of prostitution in July 1878 in the company of another woman who was living with the Rother family. Under interrogation at that time, Bertha claimed to have lost her virginity at least two years before (at age twelve) and to have been raped by an unknown assailant a year thereafter. Bertha was rearrested in June 1880 in the company of Amanda Reuter—another young woman who lived in the Rother household. In a compulsory medical exam, Bertha was found to have syphilis, and she was placed under supervision by the Berlin vice squad. A police report filed shortly afterward stated that Bertha worked for Graef as a model during the day while continuing to prostitute herself at night. There were various other reports of misbehavior in her record, including several reports of Bertha being warned by police for loitering in the evening along Unter den Linden, one of the main boulevards of the capital. Bertha's police files were then silent until 1884, by which time she had moved away from her mother's home and into a spacious apartment, allegedly paid for by a young law clerk she had met in Magdeburg. During this time, Bertha received police attention due to complaints that she was carousing and gambling with military officers and students in her new apartment. These reports, recorded in the year before her arrest, noted that Bertha now lived in luxury, attended the opera regularly, and only traveled in first-class carriages.[5]

These records thus suggest that Bertha Rother began working as a prostitute at the age of thirteen. As tragic and disturbing as this may seem from our own perspective, it was not entirely unusual for the time, as many of the prostitutes under police supervision by the Berlin vice squad were girls of thirteen or fourteen years of age.[6] It is also likely that Bertha grew up in an immediate milieu where prostitution was not only acceptable but common. Evidence offered at trial showed that Bertha's mother, Auguste Rother, rented rooms to numerous people, including several women who were also under supervision by the Berlin vice squad. It is certainly possible that Auguste knew how these tenants earned their rent but did not allow the entertainment of clients in her own home; it is more likely, however, that she served as the matron of a kind of private mini-bordello, where she encouraged individual tenants (and perhaps also her own daughters) to prostitute themselves in order to bring in extra income. Such small-scale secret bordellos were not entirely uncommon, especially on the fringes of society in households without a stable income. Prostitution here was an economic strategy and not simply the product of moral debasement or sexual deviance. Of course, such secret bordellos might occasionally lead to complaints and even denunciations by other renters who were not engaged in prostitution or who were raising children nearby—a fact that may explain the behavior of hostile witnesses such as Kühnle and Intrau in the Graef case.[7] Intrau, it should be noted, was married to a minor government official; thus, despite their common residence and background, she may have considered herself higher in social status than the Rother family.[8]

Prostitution in Imperial Germany existed in a complex legal and moral gray area. On the one hand, it had long been condemned by both Catholic and Protestant leaders as an immoral activity that violated the basic standards of Christian decency. On the other hand, many government officials and medical experts during the nineteenth century came to believe that prostitution served a lamentable but necessary social function, especially in large urban centers, university towns, military posts, and port cities where large numbers of unattached young men were present. Young single men in these areas were in a kind of social limbo; they were prevented from getting married and establishing a family either by their military commitments or by the expectation that they should set up a stable career first. At the peak of their sexual potency, it was therefore argued, they had no legitimate outlet for their natural desires.[9] While prostitution may have been morally repugnant, the alternative seemed even more worrisome for many public officials—that young men would instead seek their satisfaction among respectable lower- or middle-class women. Of course, this point of view reflected a common double standard of the time: while it was normal for young men to seek outlets for their natural drives, young women—at least those who were socially respectable—were expected to remain pure and free from sexual taint before they married.

For those who believed prostitution served a necessary societal function, the important question was how best to regulate and control it while keeping it hidden from public view. Prostitutes themselves were commonly viewed as sources of both medical and moral contagion; that is, they were seen as a threat to public health through the potential spread of venereal diseases and also a threat to morality through the potential weakening of ethical standards—especially when they came into contact with impressionable women and children. One possible solution was a kind of quarantine, the bordello, which could serve as a controlled atmosphere where prostitution could be carefully limited and concealed. Between

1794 and 1845, this was the preferred solution in many German states, including Prussia. Prostitution during this time was generally restricted to state-controlled brothels, which were often placed outside of city limits.[10] Government involvement in controlling bordellos was controversial throughout the nineteenth century, and many religious leaders viewed these policies as at best an official approval of prostitution and at worst as a government-supervised pandering business. In 1845, King Friedrich Wilhelm IV of Prussia reversed course and issued a royal decree banning bordellos in his kingdom. This action elicited enthusiastic support in some circles and consternation in others. Debates about prostitution, as well as pressure to change government policy, would wax and wane regularly through the formation of the North German Confederation in 1867 and German unification in 1871.[11]

Conflicting attitudes toward prostitution eventually led to legal contradictions within the new Imperial German Penal Code and also to fairly blatant disjunctures between the letter of the law and police or prosecutorial practice. On the one hand, §180 of the Penal Code outlawed pandering and (at least in theory) extended the ban on bordellos that had first been enacted in Prussia by royal decree in 1845. On the other hand, §361, part 6 of the Penal Code explicitly opened the door for prostitution to be tolerated under carefully limited circumstances. Under this law, women who were suspected of "professional acts of lewdness" (*gewerbsmäßiger Unzucht*) could be placed into a program of police supervision. Those who complied with police restrictions—which, the law stated, were in force to protect public health, order, and decency—were free to work. Meanwhile, those women who violated police restrictions on their activities, or who sought to ply their trade outside of police supervision, were threatened with severe punishment. In other words, while §180 threatened to prosecute those who arranged or supported prostitution, §361, part 6 not only allowed prostitution but placed it under a system of police oversight.

These laws became a bone of contention even before they came into effect for the entire German Reich. In 1871, for example, a married couple in Hamburg filed a complaint demanding that local authorities close a brothel in their neighborhood since it violated §180 of federal law (which at the time applied to Hamburg as part of the North German Confederation). The local prosecutor refused to press charges, however, since Hamburg police had sanctioned the opening of this brothel under §361, part 6 of the Penal Code. The couple and their lawyer decided to fight this ruling. Their attorney sent a questionnaire to sixteen leading law faculties asking them to offer opinions about whether police who sanctioned and supervised the operation of brothels were guilty of pandering, and whether the new federal laws should supersede state laws and traditions on such matters. Not all of the legal opinions were united, but the majority suggested that the local tolerance of bordellos was now in direct violation of federal law and must be halted. Armed with these legal opinions, the couple and their lawyer petitioned directly to Otto von Bismarck, who promised to intercede with Hamburg authorities. After the Hamburg Senate waffled on the matter, a complaint was sent to the *Bundesrat*, which in 1876 finally ordered Hamburg to close down all sanctioned brothels. The Hamburg authorities complied with this request, but only by officially disassociating themselves from the brothels—the prostitutes were allowed to remain and to pursue their livelihood at the same locations.[12] This kind of resistance to the new federal regulations was common: brothels remained open in Cologne until 1880, in Leipzig until 1889, and in other cities even longer.[13] Even in Berlin itself, bordellos were still tolerated by police long after the official Prussian ban, and a few brothels on the alley An der Königsmauer (near Alexanderplatz), which had served as a traditional red-light district for the city, remained open even into the early 1880s.[14]

Federal laws did not spell out any particular guidelines for police regulation of prostitution outside of bordellos, which meant that control was generally left up to local authorities. The result was a patchwork system in which officials could often follow their own inclinations and local traditions or adapt their policies to changing circumstances. While authorities in some German cities were overwhelmed by the number of prostitutes and took more draconian measures (such as restricting prostitutes to particular neighborhoods or launching periodic roundups), others found these kinds of actions unnecessary and suggested that their own traditional regulations had satisfactorily controlled and limited the problem.[15]

The most vocal opposition to this tacit government acceptance of prostitution came primarily from religious organizations, especially those tied to the Evangelical Church. In the early 1880s, this activism was organized on a local level and included speeches, sermons, and isolated actions of protest rather than a coordinated national campaign. Still, this opposition could cause problems for local authorities and even expose philosophical differences between police forces, local prosecutors, and higher justice officials. A short time after the Graef trial, for example, two prominent men in the city of Greifswald in Pomerania (a town approximately one hundred miles north of Berlin), namely Hermann Cremer, professor of theology at the University of Greifswald, and Wilhelm Philipps, a curate at the St. Marien Church, lodged a denunciation with local police in which they demanded the arrest of all known prostitutes in the town and also those landlords who knowingly rented apartments to them.[16] Philipps and Cremer had legal backing for their complaint, since just a few years earlier the Supreme Court in Leipzig had found that landlords who knowingly rented rooms to prostitutes for their "business" use could be charged with pandering.[17] Local prosecutors, however, refused to act. Philipps then pressed his complaint to the senior prosecutor (*Oberstaatsanwalt*) in Stettin, who finally agreed to press charges against a dozen landlords for renting apartments to known prostitutes under §180 of the Criminal Code. In the opinion of most Greifswald city officials and the local prosecutor, this wave of prosecutions was a terrible mistake. In a May 1886 report to the Prussian minister of the interior, Robert von Puttkamer, a local magistrate in Greifswald complained that many prostitutes had been forced out on the street since the prosecutions began, and that men looking for sex were already patronizing servant girls or even harassing the daughters of respected families.[18] Both the undersecretary of the interior, Ernst Herrfurth, and the senior prosecutor in Stettin who had originally agreed to the prosecutions, now recommended that no further charges should be sought and that additional actions against landlords should only be taken in special circumstances.[19]

In these ongoing internal discussions about how to deal with public complaints about prostitution, the police, prosecutors, and government officials occasionally did include concerns that poor young women might be made homeless or that landlords might be deprived of their livelihoods if every possible case under §180 were pursued; any reluctance to prosecute, however, was not based primarily on humanitarian grounds, but on the firm belief that a regulated system of prostitution was in the best interest of society and certainly safer than forcing the sex trade completely underground. In fact, many top Prussian officials expressed a distinct preference for a return to a system of bordellos, within which prostitution could be more carefully controlled and concealed.[20]

In this kind of patchwork system of regulation, the lives of young women who engaged in prostitution could be impacted by contact with police in very different ways. Local regulations for registered prostitutes in the town of Greifswald, for example, included not only required weekly gynecological exams and an obligation for official permission to travel or change addresses, but also a ban on the following: walking in groups or in the company of men in public places, walking on the street after 10:00 p.m., entering parks after sunset, entering train stations if not traveling, and living near a church, school, bar, or tavern. Berlin had similar restrictions, and although registered prostitutes could live almost anywhere in the city (as long as not near schools, churches, government buildings, or military barracks), they were banned from strolling conspicuously on major avenues such as Unter den Linden, and from loitering in public parks such as the Tiergarten.[21] Known prostitutes were also subject to weekly medical exams, and their apartments could be searched regularly by police. Although such supervision usually ended when the woman in question married or demonstrated stable income from a job, Berlin police were notoriously reluctant to strike women off of their supervision lists—at least not without embarrassing follow-up visits. Because prostitutes were ostensibly outlaws who were allowed to work only under the limited regulation and permission of police, they were also defenseless against the caprice of individual police officers. Women such as Bertha Rother, in other words, lived in a perpetual state of legal uncertainty.[22]

Perhaps not surprisingly, in a large city such as Berlin, actual enforcement of police regulations on prostitution was notoriously lax, and many of the restrictions mentioned above were commonly ignored.[23] To some degree this laxness came out of necessity. The Berlin vice squad was severely understaffed and directly supervised only a fraction of the registered prostitutes in the city. The decision about whom to place under supervision was made by the police themselves, and women with a long record of prostitution were more commonly selected than women who had other occupations but temporarily turned to prostitution for extra money. By one estimate, only 3,000 of the 15,000 to 30,000 registered prostitutes in Berlin were formally under supervision during the 1880s.[24] As Abraham Flexner wrote in his survey of prostitution in Europe just before World War One, the Berlin vice squad often tolerated streetwalkers on the major avenues and gathering points in the city as long as they were relatively inconspicuous and did not cause a scene.[25] Periodic police crackdowns and roundups were still common, however, especially following public complaints; Bertha Rother's warning for loitering on the famous promenade Unter den Linden was undoubtedly one such example. The vice squad also tended to turn a blind eye to the landlords who rented rooms to prostitutes unless there were clear denunciations from the public—which often came from angry neighbors, competitors, or women who had been gouged for high rents. To have systematically prosecuted landlords—as the Supreme Court decision suggested they should—would have paralyzed an already overburdened court system. Thus, although Berlin in the 1880s was still far from its future state at the turn of the century, when the number of prostitutes in the city would reach an estimated 100,000 to 200,000, the problem already seemed to many observers as if it were spiraling out of control.[26]

Although the direct supervision of prostitutes in Berlin seems to have generally been more lax than in other places in Germany, we should hold no illusions that the treatment of these young women was any more humane. Like other women who were placed under police observation, Bertha Rother was surely subjected to mandatory regular medical exams either in a hospital or at her home. As the historian Tanja Hommen reports, such examinations could often be brutal, painful, and humiliating. Many "respectable" victims of sexual assault during this era complained about their treatment during medical exams—which the Supreme Court ruled in 1886 could be carried out against their will to ascertain evidence of assault—and we can only assume that women suspected of prostitution were treated with even less compassion and consideration.[27] Vice squad officers in Berlin had the broad power to detain any women who were walking alone, or whose dress or behavior made them particularly suspect. These women would be released from custody when evidence surfaced of their productive employment or respectable family relations; however, the scar and shame of such an arrest would often remain. Although there seems to have been relatively little public concern about the treatment of prostitutes in these roundups, the power of police to arrest and interrogate any women in public places whom they deemed "suspicious" would eventually lead to a considerable backlash—especially among German feminists. It was thus not the mistreatment of prostitutes, but the fear that "honorable" women might also be caught up in police dragnets, that gradually fueled public calls to limit the powers of the Berlin vice squad.[28]

For those prostitutes, including Bertha Rother, who had been diagnosed with venereal diseases, the required medical treatment was even more rigorous and far more degrading. After her positive exam result, Bertha would likely have been detained and sent to the Charité hospital, where she would have probably been covered with an ointment containing mercury or forced to breathe in mercury vapors. Such treatments were not voluntary and often included repeated applications over a period of several weeks. As one might imagine, the side effects of exposure to mercury (vomiting, diarrhea, hair and tooth loss, difficulty breathing, and liver or kidney failure) could often be worse than the symptoms of the disease itself. Although doctors at the time reported success in their efforts to treat syphilis with heavy metals, they were also acutely aware of their patients' suffering and conscious that the side effects of such treatment could occasionally be fatal. To add insult to injury, those women who were forced to undergo such treatment were often required to pay for it themselves.[29]

For Bertha Rother, therefore, the prospect of escaping the streets to become a *femme entretenue*, or "kept woman," would not simply have meant additional income, but also an opportunity to free herself from some of the harsh conditions and restrictions placed upon her. Despite the long hours spent posing for paintings, a life as Gustav Graef's model (and/or concubine) also offered the opportunity to travel extensively, to dress in expensive clothes, and to attend concerts and balls from which she might ordinarily have been excluded. Her attendance at an elegant ball held at the Kroll Opera House, mentioned prominently during the Graef trial, was an example of just how far her social status had risen since her childhood. Although as a kept woman she was not an "authentic" member of the bourgeoisie, she was certainly far removed from the life of an ordinary street prostitute. Supported first by Gustav Graef and later by a young law clerk from Magdeburg, Bertha could now ride in first-class carriages along the streets she had once walked in search of clients. Of course, the life of any *femme entretenue* was entirely dependent on that woman's ability to find and then keep a male sponsor. Once a relationship was dissolved, someone like Bertha would need to quickly find a replacement or risk returning to the poverty she had so recently escaped.[30]

Bertha's training as a performer, an endeavor sponsored by Graef, contained perhaps the best prospect for her to escape the world of prostitution entirely. While actresses and singers were not always held in high regard in Imperial German society, such a career held out at least the possibility that she would no longer need to sell her own body—at least in a direct sexual sense. Contrary to the stereotypes of laziness and fecklessness that were often floated in regard to Bertha, there is little doubt that her everyday existence as a young woman had often been quite difficult. Whether it was meant to refer to her sexual exploitation or the rigors of modeling, there is still reason to take seriously her own bitter complaint reported at trial that she was tired of regularly giving up her body since she was thirteen years old for a "lousy thirty Marks."[31] As a successful performer, she might be able to free herself of all that. While the contemporary press complained that Bertha was attempting to profit from her notoriety, her eventual move to Vienna after the trial and her complaints about the reissuing of Paul Lindau's book seem to suggest someone determined to escape her own scandalous past rather than to revel in it.

This, of course, is not the portrayal of Bertha Rother that appeared in most newspapers and pamphlets of the time. Although a few journalists and legal commentators portrayed her as a victim of the legal process, or at least as the victim of a poor moral upbringing and corrupted urban environment, there seems to have been little or no public discussion of Bertha as a victim of sexual abuse. Even if one does not believe the allegations of an explicitly sexual relationship with Graef, who was more than forty years her senior, Bertha's police record included evidence that she had been sexually assaulted at a very young age and infected with syphilis either at this time or shortly thereafter. Ironically, in the Criminal Code of Imperial Germany, this kind of past history made it more difficult for charges of sexual abuse to be substantiated in the Graef case. The relevant law on sexual abuse of children was §176, part 3 of the Criminal Code, which banned all sexual contact with children under age fourteen. Violation of this law was punishable by up to ten years of hard labor (*Zuchthaus*), or in cases of mitigating circumstances no less than six months in prison. It was thus essential in the Graef trial that the prosecutor, Max Heinemann, be able to establish that sexual contact began before Bertha Rother's fourteenth birthday—something he was never effectively able to do. There was a further law on the books (§182 StGB) that applied to the seduction (*Verführung*) of girls under age sixteen. This law, however, applied only to a woman of unblemished character (*unbescholten*) and carried a maximum sentence of only one year in jail. This second law would not have been applicable to the Graef case since there was no reason to assume a "seduction" or any grounds for thinking that Bertha Rother was "unblemished" or still had any sexual honor that could have been violated. In other words, even if a sexual liaison had occurred with Bertha at the age of fourteen, it would not have been punishable because of her own sexual history.[32]

It is also true that during the 1880s there was relatively little importance attached to the possible emotional consequences of physical or sexual abuse. Scientists such as Richard von Krafft-Ebing were just beginning to investigate the psychological consequences of such abuse, and their conclusions usually focused on short-term behavioral impacts such as sleeplessness, nervousness, and nightmares. Once these symptoms had subsided after a few days or weeks, it was assumed there would be no additional psychological damage or need for treatment.[33]

From our own perspective, it might seem especially odd for Bertha to have been arrested and prosecuted side-by-side with her alleged molester; certainly, in the contemporary American legal system men are often prosecuted for sexual abuse even when the alleged victim denies under oath that any abuse took place—but rarely in our system are those alleged victims also prosecuted for their denials. The difference in priorities here is clear. In Imperial Germany, the alleged perjury was the more grievous crime, not the alleged molestation of an underage lower-class girl. This was especially true in the case of Bertha Rother, whose "sexual honor" was not an issue. The prosecutor, Max Heinemann, admitted this freely during the trial, when he suggested that charges may not have been filed against Gustav Graef for sexually exploiting an underage girl if he had not also perjured himself in a court hearing.[34] As a prostitute, therefore, Bertha warranted careful supervision and forced physical examinations. As an alleged transgressor against the sacred oath, she would feel the full force of the justice system mobilized against her. As a mere lower-class victim of sexual exploitation, however, she would not have drawn the attention of the German justice system at all.

CONSTRUCTING A FAIRY TALE MODEL

Most observers of the Graef case were not just unsympathetic toward Bertha Rother but openly disparaging of her character. Her critics frequently depicted her as a false, unscrupulous, and unrepentant young woman, who was willing to exploit her beauty, her newfound infamy, and the weaknesses of men for her own profit. The *Berliner Gerichtszeitung*, for example, described Bertha as a witness who "spoke in the extremely dramatic, elaborate, and affected manner of a person trained in theatrical performance."[35] The liberal *Vossische Zeitung* noted all the rumors circulating about Bertha's future employment and suggested she would do anything to use her notoriety to her own advantage; thankfully, the paper claimed, most Berliners were "not Yankee enough" to buy into any crass public stunts.[36]

There were occasional expressions of pity for Bertha in the press. The moderately conservative *Post*, for example, described an episode just before her arrest in which Bertha had single-handedly struggled to save her family from her deadbeat stepfather's attempts to sell off the family assets for his own benefit. The paper lamented that all her heroic efforts went for naught once she was arrested, since neighbors and creditors plundered what was left of the family belongings.[37] Other liberal newspapers suggested that Bertha's scandalous past was not solely of her own making but could be blamed instead on her parents and perhaps on society as a whole. Still others expressed sympathy for the rather public humiliation that Bertha faced in court and hoped that it would not lead her to return to a life of moral turpitude.[38] As conservative newspapers noted, however, defenses of Bertha Rother were rarely as passionate as those for Gustav Graef. The ultraconservative *Reichsbote*, for example, pointed out the hypocrisy of the liberal press, which still labeled Bertha Rother as "fallen" and "depraved" while giving the men who aided her fall—including, in the newspaper's opinion, Gustav Graef—a free pass. As the

Reichsbote wrote: "This truly immoral point of view, which is based on a heathen (*heidnischen*) view of women and which reduces women to being mere playthings for the lusts of men, must be openly protested in the interests of public morality."[39] This moral outrage against alleged liberal misogyny, however, did not translate into any real compassion for Bertha as an individual or any mitigation of her "fallen" and "depraved" status.

Perhaps the most interesting description of Bertha Rother came from the liberal *Nationalzeitung*, which had sparked controversy by publishing detailed and dramatized portrayals of the main players in the case:

> There are two different natures embodied in her. When she sits still with her head bowed and slowly raises up her eyes—at that moment one can see the image that must have given the artist his motivation. She appears truly as if she were out of a dream or fairy tale, a creature completely unconnected to the cares of this world. However, when she suddenly raises her head and looks around her with a cynical smile—at that moment she is once again the whore as alleged by the grave charges against her.[40]

While most newspapers covering the case described Bertha Rother as either a brazen whore or a corrupted innocent, the *Nationalzeitung* chose to unite both stereotypes—as if to suggest that these opposing character traits might be at war within all women. Readers of this newspaper may have consciously or unconsciously linked this description to Émile Zola's infamous portrayal of Nana Coupeau in his controversial 1880 novel *Nana*. In this book, Zola depicted a poor young woman whose astounding beauty helped her to rise from street prostitute to wealthy courtesan and actress. In Nana's first stage performance, given while scantily clad in front of a crowd of lustful men, Zola portrayed her as a woman with the same kind of bifurcated character: "All of a sudden, in the good-natured child the woman stood revealed, a disturbing woman with all the impulsive madness of her sex, opening the gates of the unknown world of desire. Nana was still smiling, but with the deadly smile of a man-eater."[41] The suggestion here is that women such as Nana and Bertha were initially innocent but that they also possessed an irrational and licentious nature buried deep within. Although their inherently lustful nature had first been unleashed by the desires of men, it would ultimately make these "man-eating" women a serious danger both to men and to society as a whole.[42]

If Bertha was an object of pity, revulsion, lust, and even fear, she was also a target for humor as well. Just after the end of the trial, a quickly authored one-act play appeared, penned by Martin Böhm, a prolific author of short parodies and bawdy theater pieces, and published under the pseudonym of Gustav Braun. The script of the play, entitled *In the Studio, or the Painter and His Model*, was reviewed and justifiably panned by most leading newspapers, and it is unclear if it was ever performed in public. It is interesting to note, however, that in this (barely) humorous version of reality, the hero is the old painter, who, although the butt of many jokes, successfully resists his wife's jealousy toward his patronage of underage models. At the end of the play he sees through his wife's schemes to catch him *in flagrante* with his young model Bertha Rosenduft (rose-scented) and gives her a lecture on art and morality: "An artist is someone oriented toward an ideal, a spirit that must constantly search for an inspiration for his work—but people do him wrong by suggesting that this kind of disposition is somehow depraved!"[43] The clear losers in this drama are Bertha and her family. The fictional Bertha shows her lack of morals by immediately offering to take off her clothes the moment she steps on stage; otherwise she is largely silent. Bertha's father, rather than her mother, rushes in at the end of the play to try to extort money for the artist's "mishandling" of his daughter. In the climactic scene, the artist and his servant throw Bertha and her father into the street and then sing a song to celebrate their triumph.

This was not the only satirical work of dubious quality penned after the trial. A short book called *The Fairy-Tale Model: A Model Fairy Tale for Children of Today* also appeared shortly after the verdict, which reduced Bertha Rother to an even less significant role in the affair.[44] This work, which was *not* designed for children, restaged the Graef affair in a mere sixty-four pages of poetry as a battle between the Greek gods Pluto and Apollo. In this retelling, Hermes is sent down to earth to help settle a bet between Apollo and Pluto about whether there is at least one artist in the world still imbued with pure idealism and not captivated by money. Hermes finds only old Professor Idealinski, a stand-in for Graef, who repeatedly swears to be an idealist and only to be interested in nude women for purely aesthetic reasons. In the end, Idealinski is forced to stand trial on Olympus for having attempted to pass off a painting of a hetaera (Greek concubine) as an example of ideal beauty. Fortunately for Idealinski, Zeus struggles to judge him without precise legal paragraphs to depend on. Many of the actual trial participants are directly or indirectly mocked here, including Graef as Idealinski and a brief appearance by Paul Lindau as Homer. Ironically, although the front cover of the pamphlet prominently features a sketch of Bertha Rother as the Fairy Tale Model (posing nude with a sack of gold above her head), she appears only briefly in the poem, has no lines of dialogue, and is simply referred to as a hetaera and a "flirtatious wench" (*kokette Frauenzimmer*). In fiction, as in the newspaper reportage of the time, Bertha Rother was given a face and body, but not a voice. She was treated as an object and a symbol, but never as a three-dimensional human being.

A brief comparison of this kind of rhetoric with the publicity surrounding a contemporary scandal in London, the so-called "Maiden Tribute Affair" unleashed by W. T. Stead, is worthwhile at this point. Not surprisingly, the depictions of Bertha Rother differed substantially from depictions by the London press of Eliza Armstrong, the young girl "purchased" by W. T. Stead in the "Maiden Tribute Affair." This difference was in part due to the very different circumstances of the "defilement" of each woman. On the one hand, Eliza was still only thirteen years old at the time of the trial and was portrayed exclusively as an innocent victim. According to Judith Walkowitz, Eliza Armstrong was a "muted" figure during the Stead trial, and "the most unsensational and uncontroversial witness." She showed remarkable calm during her testimony, and both prosecution and defense attorneys treated her as truthful, trustworthy, and sympathetic.[45] Eliza had been at great risk of losing her innocence and becoming a "fallen woman" due to the schemes of others; depictions of her cooperative behavior at trial, however, reinforced the idea that such a defilement had not taken place. Eliza Armstrong, in other words, was a relatively minor character in the Maiden Tribute Affair, who represented a passive object that had been put at risk by the lusts of men. While Eliza Armstrong had been an almost universal object of sympathy and pity, Bertha Rother was more commonly depicted as someone beyond either salvation or compassion. At the time of her trial, Bertha was twenty-one years old and had already accumulated a long record of prostitution. Her defilement had therefore happened long ago, and there was now little hope for redemption or room for pity. Bertha, in other words, had over time become a whore by choice and perhaps now remained one by nature as well. Even years after her acquittal, journalists both in Germany and elsewhere would continue to sarcastically chronicle Bertha Rother's adventures and misadventures, ridicule her attempts to build a new life, and take substantial pleasure in her long, slow, and painful fall out of the limelight.[46]

THE GRAEF TRIAL AND GERMAN FEMINISM

Aside from the very different portrayal of the victim at the center of the case, the Maiden Tribute Affair is starkly different from the Graef case in another way: the voice and influence of the British feminist Josephine Butler. W. T. Stead's sensational exposé on child prostitution was inspired in part by Butler, who had long sought his support for her campaigns against the controversial Contagious Disease Acts. These laws, the first of which were passed in 1864, had allowed for limited and regulated prostitution, but they also empowered police to subject suspected prostitutes to forced gynecological exams to contain the potential spread of venereal diseases. At the time, these laws were defended by the British government as public health measures. Critics such as Butler, however, pointed out the clear double standard that the Contagious Disease Acts reinforced: while large numbers of prostitutes were targeted by police, clients of these prostitutes were never subjected to exams and only rarely prosecuted.

Butler had originally started her public work as an advocate for the care, education, and religious salvation of "fallen women" through local charitable associations. The passage of the Contagious Disease Acts in the 1860s, however, helped push her beyond local welfare work into a national campaign against regulated prostitution. In 1869, Butler, along with Elisabeth Wolstenholme, founded the Ladies National Association for the Repeal of the Contagious Diseases Acts, and she began traveling the country to deliver public speeches denouncing what she viewed as official government support for the sexual exploitation of poor women. In 1874, Butler began a tour of Italy, France, and Germany to build broader European support for the outlawing of prostitution. Upon her return to England, she formed the British, Continental, and General Federation for the Abolition of State Regulation of Prostitution, which would hold annual meetings in different European cities.[47] As Judith Walkowitz suggests, the Maiden Tribute Affair played a key role in this campaign because British feminists such as Butler could use the episode as an opening to discuss sensitive sexual matters in public, to "voice their own fears about sexual danger and to attack institutions of male power that encouraged violence against women."[48] It was in part the tireless activism of Josephine Butler—along with the outrage generated by the Maiden Tribute Affair—that eventually helped lead to the Criminal Law Amendment Act of 1885, which raised the age of sexual consent from thirteen to sixteen. The controversy over these articles also helped to galvanize a disparate coalition of feminists, religious leaders, temperance advocates, Socialists, and trade unionists for a repeal of the Contagious Disease Acts, which occurred in the following year.[49] In sum, the "Maiden Tribute Affair" encouraged women to speak out publicly for social reform, and it also emboldened middle-class women to express solidarity with women from the lower classes.[50]

The same could hardly be said of the aftermath of the Graef trial in Germany; there, the absence of any significant female voices commenting publicly on the

Graef case seems quite extraordinary. Why was there no Josephine Butler in Germany at this time? Or better put, why were there no female voices willing to use the Graef case to demand measures that would protect poor women from sexual exploitation? To some extent, this difference was a result of the much stricter exclusion of German women from public politics. In the wake of the failed Revolution of 1848, several German states, including Prussia and Bavaria, had passed laws banning women from participating in clubs dedicated to political issues or from attending public meetings that discussed political topics.[51] Although women could still found and join organizations dedicated to social welfare or educational policy, these organizations and their leaders were often subject to police surveillance, and their meetings were immediately terminated if they ventured beyond acceptable discourse. In Prussia, this ban on women's participation in political meetings would continue in force until 1908. The practical effect of such laws was to dampen most public calls for female suffrage and to instead divert the efforts of most middle-class feminists toward improving women's social conditions, their access to education, and their ability to seek employment opportunities outside the home.[52]

Despite these restrictions on their participation in the German public sphere, women were far from silent on social issues during this period. The most prominent example was Louise Otto-Peters, who is often credited with being the founder of organized feminism in Germany. Otto-Peters first gained notoriety as a poet and novelist from the city of Meißen in Saxony, but her early work was far from apolitical and occasionally provoked the ire of government censors. During the Revolution of 1848, for example, Otto-Peters stirred controversy with her *Adresse eines Mädchens* (Address from a Girl), in which she insisted that the representatives in the new government of Saxony remember the interests of women when they considered how to improve the lives of the working class. Soon after, Otto-Peters founded the newspaper *Frauen-Zeitung* (or Women's Newspaper), which she published under the motto "I seek female citizens for the realm of freedom."[53] Her newspaper generally supported the liberal values of the revolution, but also sought openly to discuss women's issues from the perspective of women themselves and to fight for new economic, social, and educational rights. Once the Revolution faltered, however, Saxon authorities closed her newspaper after passing what was referred to as a *Lex Otto*, a law that explicitly banned women from the profession of newspaper editor. Otto-Peters was forced temporarily to move her operation to neighboring Thuringia, where she continued to publish, although in an admittedly more moderate voice.[54]

Scholars are often divided about how to interpret the career of Louise Otto-Peters after 1850. On the one hand, she continued to vigorously advocate for better economic and educational opportunities for women. For example, Otto-Peters helped to found the General German Women's Association or AdF (*Allgemeine deutsche Frauenverein*) in Leipzig in 1865. This organization sought to build an alliance of like-minded associations across all German-speaking lands with the goal of "raising the educational level of the female sex and the removal of all obstacles standing in the way of women's work."[55] Although the AdF never truly became a national organization, through its meetings and through the publication of its bimonthly journal *Neue Bahnen* (New Paths) it nonetheless became one of the most important voices for feminist activism in Germany.[56] On the other hand, in her own writings and her work with the AdF, Otto-Peters did not directly challenge most contemporary moral or political norms. She dressed conservatively and fostered a relatively modest and reserved public image; she did not publicly demand suffrage for women, and her writings advocated improvements for women that still emphasized their traditional place in the home raising children and serving their husbands. Certainly Otto-Peters was far removed from the more radical feminism of Louise Ashton, a German author and poet who demanded equality with men and, like the French novelist George Sand, occasionally dressed in men's clothing. Still, the moderate nature of Louise Otto-Peters's activism does not overshadow its ultimate significance. As Ruth-Ellen Joeres suggests: "In what was no doubt a strategic move, she thereby presented an impression of modesty, silence, passivity, and deference, while nevertheless managing almost single-handedly to set in motion a women's rights movement that would change the face of German society."[57]

Louise Otto-Peters was still very active at the time of the Graef trial, including serving as coeditor of the AdF journal, *Neue Bahnen*, along with her colleague Auguste Schmidt. However, the pages of this journal exhibit absolutely no trace of the Graef affair—even though the plight of poor women was a relatively common theme. This silence is perhaps not as surprising as it might seem. Discussing the Graef case openly in a publication written by women for women may have brought attention from police censors—especially because of the salacious nature of the case and the fact that it had become a politically charged topic. It is also reasonable to assume, however, that Otto-Peters may not have viewed Bertha Rother as an appropriate model to evoke sympathy for poor women who were unfairly exploited in German society. As we have seen, Bertha was often portrayed in a very different way from the young innocent Eliza Armstrong in the Maiden Tribute Affair; instead of an innocent, she was often described as a corrupted harlot who was complicit in her own fate. Without direct evidence, it is impossible to assume what Louise Otto-Peters might have thought or said about Bertha Rother; her public silence may have been as much a conscious choice as a legal necessity.

There were, of course, a number of other feminists active in Germany during the 1880s, including some who were much more willing to challenge the government directly on issues such as prostitution and the sexual exploitation of women. One prominent example was Gertrud Guillaume-Schack, the daughter of a liberally minded Silesian count, who was inspired by both Louise Otto-Peters and Josephine Butler to become an activist for the plight of poor women. Guillaume-Schack first joined Otto-Peters's AdF, and then in 1880 she joined with fellow AdF member Lina Morgenstern to found the Cultural Alliance for the Abolition of Officially Regulated Prostitution (*Kulturbund zur Abschaffung der behördlich konzessionierten Prostitution*)—otherwise known as the "*Kulturbund*." This organization, in practice, was a branch organization of Josephine Butler's British, Continental, and General Federation. The primary efforts of the *Kulturbund* were focused on the moral and sexual education of poor young women, and especially education about the dangers of sexually transmitted diseases. However, the core of their public rhetoric was aimed at challenging a moral system that demonized and dehumanized young prostitutes while leaving their clients untouched. Guillaume-Schack was relentless in her campaign against these kinds of misogynistic double standards, and her frequent motto was echoed in the first clause of the official program of the *Kulturbund*: "There is only one moral law (*Sittengesetz*), and it is the same for both sexes."[58]

As the feminist Helene Lange later recalled in her memoirs, Guillaume-Schack had been one of the first German women to speak so bluntly and openly in challenging government regulation of prostitution, and in doing so she frequently received police attention.[59] Public meetings of the *Kulturbund* were regularly attended by police observers, and they were often cut short or even forbidden. An 1882 speech in Darmstadt, for example, was interrupted by police who filed charges against Guillaume-Schack that resulted in a sensational criminal trial and eventual acquittal.

Although police authorities were concerned that Guillaume-Schack and other members of the *Kulturbund* were discussing titillating issues such as prostitution in "mixed" audiences, they were even more worried that these meetings were secretly aimed at recruiting support for German Socialism. Guillaume-Schack had a long history of advocating social reforms, and she focused much of her efforts on the plight of working women; however, despite government suspicions, there seems to have been little contact between Guillaume-Schack and German

Socialist leaders before the mid-1880s. Radicalized by her own conflicts with German authorities, however, and frustrated with the meekness of the middle-class feminist movement, she would eventually begin to reach out to Socialist leaders. By 1885, Guillaume-Schack had begun a correspondence with Friedrich Engels, and in the same year she founded the Club for the Interests of Working Women (*Verein zur Vertretung der Interessen der Arbeiterinnen*), also known simply as the "*Arbeiterinnenverein*."[60] In the following year, Guillaume-Schack founded a weekly newspaper called *Die Staatsbürgerin* (The Female Citizen), which was the first newspaper specifically targeting working-class women in Germany.

This was, however, a dangerous time to be fostering links to the leaders of European socialism. Only a few years earlier, in 1878, after two assassination attempts on Kaiser Wilhelm I, Otto von Bismarck had pressured the Reichstag to pass the so-called Anti-Socialist Laws. While these laws did not automatically result in the arrest or exile of all who claimed to be Socialists, they did make all clubs, rallies, and publications that supported socialist ideals illegal. Thus, even as the Graef trial began, Berlin newspapers were reporting on police intervention in meetings of the *Kulturbund* and *Arbeiterinnenverein*. Just six months after its first issue was printed, *Die Staatsbürgerin* was closed by Berlin police. By late 1886, Guillaume-Schack herself had been exiled from Germany and had taken up residence in England.[61]

The perceived radicalism of women such as Gertrud Guillaume-Schack made cooperation with more conservative religious-minded opponents of prostitution difficult. In the early 1880s, there had been substantial overlap between the efforts of protestant clergy and the *Kulturbund*, including by Pastor Ludwig Weber from Mönchen-Gladbach, who sat on the organization's executive committee. By 1887, however, a clear split had developed.[62] An anonymous pamphlet issued that year spelled out these differences from the point of view of religious conservatives. Entitled *The Fallen Girls and the Vice Squad*, the pamphlet began by listing the stated goals of *Kulturbund* and suggesting that many of those goals would be shared by most Christian readers as well. However, over the next several pages, the pamphlet sharply criticized the *Kulturbund* for its insistence on including women in public debates about sensitive matters, its attacks on the Prussian government and the Berlin vice squad, and its alleged desire to use the issue of prostitution to spread radical political ideas. In addition to voicing critiques that were disloyal and occasionally even libelous, the anonymous author claimed, members of the *Kulturbund* had also impugned the honor of the military by suggesting that soldiers were often the best customers of prostitutes and one of the main avenues for spreading syphilis.[63] Instead of winning support among the German people (or government officials), it was argued, such an approach served only to alienate potential supporters of the campaign against prostitution. Thus, although the author of this anonymous pamphlet acknowledged some common ground with women such as Guillaume-Schack, this recognition came with a heavy dose of skepticism and disapproval of their overall tactics and goals.

Neither the pages of Guillaume-Schack's *Die Staatsbürgerin* nor the anonymous *Fallen Girls and the Vice Squad* contained any mention of the Graef trial. Although it is true that Guillaume-Schack's newspaper did not publish its first issue until January of 1886 and the anonymous pamphlet first appeared in 1887, this silence is still worth noting. The *Fallen Girls and the Vice Squad*, for example, did repeatedly point to a scandalous episode which had recently exposed the evils of prostitution for all to see: the Maiden Tribute Affair in London.[64] Certainly, we might expect that the anonymous author of this pamphlet, so keen to protect the honor of the German authorities, would rather emphasize the depravity of British society as a warning to readers rather than use the Graef trial to directly criticize his own society. In the case of Guillaume-Schack, however, it is harder to attribute this silence to either fear or deference to authorities, especially since her past harassment by police did not prevent her from holding further meetings or printing additional newspaper issues. We must assume, therefore, that Bertha Rother—at least the Bertha Rother described in press reports—provided a poor example for abolitionists of any political stripe to use as propaganda in their political and moral campaigns against sexual exploitation.

More systematic and organized opposition to government regulation of prostitution would eventually arise in Germany during the 1890s as the number of prostitutes in major cities increased exponentially. Calls for reform would grow especially loud after the sensational Heinze murder trial in 1891, when Kaiser Wilhelm II stepped forward to demand new laws against pandering and street prostitution as well as a police offensive against the sale or display of obscene texts and images. This reinvigorated abolitionist campaign would involve a variety of religious, social, and political groups—including Socialist activists who would speak out more openly after the lapse of the Anti-Socialist Laws in 1890. The Heinze trial and its aftermath will be discussed in more detail in the following chapter; the eventual result, however, would be at best a partial success for reformers. Unlike England after the Maiden Tribute Affair, reformers in Germany after the Graef trial (and the Heinze Affair) would fail to build a critical mass of public opinion against regulated prostitution and thus also fail to push the government toward a formal banning of the sex trade.

ASSUMING FEMININITY

In the midst of this conspicuous silence, there are two very interesting examples of women who did publicly comment on the Graef trial; although their comments were relatively brief, they can still tell us important things about the role and perception of women in German society during this era. Shortly after the verdict in the Graef case, a brief article appeared in the journal *Die Nation* entitled "The Basis for Judgment." According to the historian Uwe Wilhelm, this essay, submitted under the pseudonym of "Portia," was one of the first examples of women offering published commentary on legal issues in Germany. The choice of Portia as a pseudonym here is not accidental. In the climactic Act Four of William Shakespeare's *Merchant of Venice*, the character of Portia appears disguised as a male lawyer named Balthazar and succeeds not only in shielding her identity from everyone (including her lover Bassanio), but also in saving the merchant Antonio through her own clever logic. Although Shakespeare was sure to restore gender balance in the last act of his play, the example he provided of a woman's wisdom and superior legal reasoning was no doubt a powerful one. There are, however, many curious things about this particular article in *Die Nation*. After criticizing the fact that women in the courtroom gallery had been excluded from sensitive parts of the Graef trial, Portia proclaims that Gustav Graef had to be acquitted "according to the laws of Venice" since witnesses could not possibly recall precise testimony from a hearing two years earlier. She then added the following rather startling passage, which included an imaginary interaction with Gustav Graef:

> If only I had been a juror! I would have introduced myself to him after his acquittal, just as a hundred years earlier the daughter of an alderman in London introduced herself to a defendant in a political trial as he cheerfully left the courtroom: "The daughter of a juryman who just now acquitted you wishes to make your acquaintance." "It is with heartfelt joy that I meet a sister of mine." "How am I a sister?" "Indeed! Since your father gave new life to you twenty years ago just as he did for me a few minutes earlier."[65]

It is not entirely clear which English trial Portia had in mind, although it could easily have been the 1794 treason trial of Thomas Hardy or the 1780 trial of Lord George Gordon, both of whom were acquitted to popular acclaim. Regardless, the comparison is still clear: Gustav Graef is represented here as an innocent and justly acquitted political martyr. Of course, one might suggest that the quality of mercy shown to Graef in the passage seems to strain the author's allusion to *The*

Merchant of Venice. Is the elderly Gustav Graef her Bassanio, a lover whom she imagined freeing through her own wisdom and guile? Who, then, is Shylock? The Jewish prosecutor Max Heinemann?[66] Without pursuing this imagined drama any further, the author instead returns to her main point, which is to criticize German stenography as entirely inadequate compared to its counterpart in Britain. There is no mention of Bertha Rother in her article, and no sympathy for the other defendants. Apparently, both Portias, the anonymous author and Shakespeare's fictional character, jumped at the chance to demonstrate their own wisdom in a patriarchal world; however, both did so not primarily for their own benefit but for the purpose of freeing an unjustly accused man.

A second example is equally instructive. Less than a week after the trial, a long poem appeared in the *Breslauer Zeitung*, addressed to Gustav Graef and signed by "Frau K." The work was quickly attributed to Friederike Kempner, perhaps the most famous German female poet of this era. Originally appearing in the back pages of the newspaper between advertisements, the piece was picked up and reprinted in several additional newspapers in Berlin and across the country. In this poem, Kempner lamented the fate of poor Gustav Graef, the talented and innocent artist who had been assailed merely for following his artistic muse a bit too passionately. Although the fame and following of Friederike Kempner were certainly real, it is fairly likely that this particular poem was not authentic. Kempner was not only the most famous female poet in Germany at this time, she was also the most widely mocked and mimicked poet in the country. Kempner first became popular through an 1880 review of her work by Paul Lindau, who described the quality of her poetry in highly ironic and sarcastic terms, and praised her work especially for its unintentional humor.[67] By the time of the Graef trial in 1885, a popular canon of Kempner's work existed alongside a substantial catalog of anonymous poems that were penned to mock her style and artistic sense. Not surprisingly, the newspapers that printed her alleged poem on the Graef trial also took pleasure in adding their own sarcastic commentary. The *Berliner Volksblatt*, for example, singled out the last stanza:

> Though the people's court reigned,
> And freed you at last,
> On history a stain!
> It's good that's now past.[68]

According to the *Volksblatt*, the last line of this poem rang doubly true as it applied both to the Graef case and to the Kempner poem itself.

The curious texts attributed to "Portia" and Friederike Kempner raise interesting questions. If we were to assume the authenticity of their authorship, we can still readily perceive the mocking reaction of a largely male reading public. However, the more compelling and perhaps more likely account is that these short texts are examples of men appropriating a female identity in order to intentionally demean the intellectual abilities and rational powers of women.[69] In these texts, the female legal commentator and poet both rush in headlong to defend Gustav Graef as an innocent martyr—one of them even fantasizing a personal encounter with an imaginary version of Graef recast as a brave and witty young man. The poem itself reads as shallow farce, and the legal commentary is far from what we might expect to see in a specialized journal. Here, apparently, instead of simply ignoring the voices of women, male authors have apparently assumed female identities in order to mock the superficiality and irrationality of any women who might presume to be capable of poetry or sophisticated legal discourse.

One final important note about women's voices and the Graef case: just because prominent feminists of the time did not publish or speak publicly about the Graef affair does not mean it was a topic that German women tended to avoid. Certainly, it is impossible to believe that women were generally uninterested in the scandal, especially since conservative newspapers such as the *Kreuzzeitung* fretted over the fact that the crowds gathering outside shop windows to luridly gaze at nude images of Bertha Rother contained large numbers of women.[70] What did German women think about the Graef case? The absence of substantive evidence makes even general conclusions difficult. It is important, however, to avoid the inherent fallacy (and misogyny) of assuming that all women's voices should have somehow spoken in unison about the trial. Just as women's organizations were heterogeneous in Imperial Germany, it is safe to assume that women's voices were undoubtedly as conflicting and divergent as those of German men.

CHAPTER FIVE

STORIES ABOUT OTHERS

Class and Race in Imperial Berlin

"A description of the Rother family," Paul Lindau wrote in his summary of the Graef case, "would be an undertaking worthy of Zola."[1] This reference to the French novelist Émile Zola would have automatically struck a chord with Lindau's readers, especially since Zola's popular and controversial novel *Germinal* had been serialized in German newspapers just a few months before the Graef trial began.[2] Invoking the name of Zola was not simply a way for Lindau to refer to the dramatic nature of the Graef Affair, it was also a signifier for a particular view of social relations in the modern world. Naturalists such as Zola commonly focused on class divisions, and in books such as *Germinal* an ensemble of working-class protagonists suffered primarily as a result of economic exploitation and the deleterious environmental effects of modern industrial society.[3] Paul Lindau was himself a novelist, playwright, cultural critic, and journalist, and he often blurred the lines of these literary genres. Although he may not have set out to explicitly mimic the style of Zola, he did frame his observations of the Graef case—and especially his observations of lower-class participants in the trial—almost as if he were an anthropologist recounting an expedition into the dark urban jungles of Northern Berlin.[4] While the figures that Lindau described could occasionally provoke pity as the victims of urban poverty, they were more often portrayed as morally, physically, and spiritually corrupted beings who were all but beyond redemption.

The concern of German elites with the condition of the urban poor was certainly not a new phenomenon. However, this concern was heightened toward the end of the nineteenth century as urbanization and industrialization fundamentally changed the nature of cities. The thoroughness of this transformation cannot be adequately gauged by mere population statistics, although even the numbers themselves are remarkable. In 1849, Berlin had a population of just over 400,000. At the foundation of the German Empire in 1871, its new capital had surpassed

825,000 inhabitants. By 1895, the population of the city had more than doubled again to over 1.7 million people.[5] This astonishing growth produced as much fear as it did pride among German elites. Within this modern city, it seemed, respect for authority, religious belief, and family bonds were all weakened, and this lack of social control had inevitably led to the rise of prostitution, criminality, and drunkenness among the lower classes.[6] Rampant immorality within the lower classes was seen as a fundamental danger to the stability of German society. Even more of a danger, however, was the rising support for socialism among the lower classes—an ideology that supposedly undermined the sanctity of family, community, and nation and was thus every bit as diabolical as criminality and sexual vice. Public debates about the "Social Question" were a common fixture of political culture, and answers to this question could range from suggestions for ameliorative reform to demands for repressive action.[7]

It was fear as much as compassion that motivated the great social reform legislation of the 1880s, measures seen as necessary not just to improve the condition of the poor and arrest their moral decline, but also to achieve the practical goal of winning the working classes away from revolutionary socialism. This was the age of Bismarck's "Revolution from Above," in which he attempted to undermine the appeal of socialism through reforms such as sickness insurance (1883), accident insurance (1884), and old age and disability insurance (1889). A mix of fear and compassion was also evident in the work of the Inner Mission, first founded by Johann Hinrich Wichern in the 1840s, which had served as an internal evangelical mission for "at risk" populations around Germany. In addition to offering the gospel as a cure to the moral degeneration within the city, leaders of the Inner Mission also sought to pressure the government to restrict all kinds of sinful behavior, including prostitution, obscene literature and images, and even dance halls, which were seen as a locus for all kinds of depravity.[8] Adolf Stöcker's Berlin City Mission, which was founded in 1874 but traced its roots back to Wichern, was one of many organizations that made concerted efforts to bring salvation, morality, and political education to the unwashed masses in the capital. In addition to his work as a pastor in the Imperial court and his role as director of the Berlin City Mission, Stöcker founded the Christian-Social Worker's Party in 1878 as an explicit attempt to draw workers away from Socialist agitation into a more palatable conservative social reform movement. Stöcker had dedicated his life to fighting the twin evils of moral depravity and revolutionary socialism. Faced with his fringe party's failure to attract significant working-class support, he would soon add a third target for attack: Jewish-liberal "Manchesterite" capitalism. For Stöcker and many other Germans, the "Social Question" came to be explicitly linked to a "Jewish Question"—a debate about the need to reduce or eliminate Jewish influence in Germany.

Although anti-Semitism had periodically found fertile ground in German lands during the nineteenth century, the founding of the German Empire in 1871 seemed to signal an important advance for German Jews. The Prussian Law of Emancipation, which had been passed in 1869, now became valid for the entire German Reich—thus abolishing any remaining restrictions on Jewish civil rights and assuring equality before the law.[9] The relaxation of these constraints allowed Jews to move into occupations that had previously been excluded to them, and prominent Jews quickly assumed important positions in the political life of the new state, including Eduard Lasker and Ludwig Bamberger as leading figures in the National Liberal Party and Gerson von Bleichröder as a powerful banker and associate of Otto von Bismarck.[10] The founding of the new Reich thus seemed to promise that German Jews would be full and equal partners in its glory and prosperity.

Then, just a few years later, the stock market collapse of 1873 challenged this progress. Lost jobs, lost fortunes in the stock market, and lost optimism about the future of Germany led to recriminations against the government, against liberalism, and most pointedly against the influence of German Jews. A wide range of politicians and political journalists, including conservatives, Catholics, and Socialists blamed the "Manchesterite" ideal of cutthroat capitalism for the crisis and pointed their fingers directly at the group that had most energetically advocated this ideal—the National Liberal Party.[11] Because this party had prominent Jewish leaders, because several Jewish businessmen were implicated in financial scandals, and especially because of traditional stereotypes about Jews and money, public anger at the economic collapse was often expressed in anti-Jewish rhetoric. One problem facing Germany, it was argued, could not be solved without addressing the other. As Otto Glagau, one of the leading critics of German liberalism, put it simply, "the Social Question is the Jewish Question."[12]

As we will see in this chapter, many observers of the Graef trial argued that the case confirmed the "otherness" of both members of the lower classes and German Jews. In the imagination of many Germans, the slums of Berlin contained savages as uncivilized as any colonial population. Meanwhile, lurking elsewhere in the city were Jewish elites who pretended to be civilized but were equally uncultured and unprincipled. Both of these groups seemed to pose a clear and present danger to the stability and prosperity of German civilization.

A DARK AND UNCIVILIZED WORLD

Paul Lindau began his long essay on the Graef trial with a short aside about the difficult problem of impartiality for any observer of public behavior. He claimed that while his intent was to provide an objective portrayal of events surrounding the trial, he could only promise to be as judicious and careful as possible in putting forward what seemed from his perspective to be the most plausible explanations. Lindau's "research methodology" for his trial account included not only direct observations of the court proceedings, but also after-hours conversations with many of the witnesses in local taverns. He, like the English journalist W. T. Stead, portrayed himself as an intrepid investigator who immersed himself in the culture of social outsiders in an attempt to discover their true nature. The implication was that only through direct observation of the culture of the Berlin underclass could Lindau portray this strange and disturbing world accurately—warts and all.[13]

What is missing in Lindau's long essay is any call for systematic remediation of the social conditions of the Berlin poor. Although Lindau recognized the social and environmental contribution to criminality, he seems to have accepted the urban milieu that produced it as a given, and he made no specific calls for change.[14] In his initial posttrial commentary in the *Nationalzeitung*, for example, Lindau began with a long description of the lowest levels of society, the "homeless vagabonds who wallow in the filth and misery of the local tavern, who drink and eat things barely fit for human consumption, and who walk around in tattered clothes and sleep in the streets."[15] For these unfortunates, the modern prison, with its cleanliness and orderliness, with its modern health care and nutritious food, allegedly constituted a marked improvement. Lindau then added a note of resignation: "because of the imperfection of human institutions, this situation may never change."[16]

In fact, Lindau's narrative often served to reinforce traditional class stereotypes rather than challenging or undermining them. For example, Lindau depicted wealthy men such as Gustav Graef as firmly ensconced in a culture of honor, with all that culture's attendant benefits and risks. Poorer neighborhoods, on the other hand, were viewed as cesspools of immorality and barbarity whose denizens were occasionally noble, but more often unwilling or unable to live according to the moral codes of civilized society. This depiction was generally consistent with most contemporary assumptions about the social order in Germany—even among those social critics who sympathized with the plight of the less fortunate. There was an enormous gap between the worlds of rich and poor—the former civilized but occasionally corrupted, and the latter thoroughly corrupted and only rarely capable of real improvement.

Indeed, for many defenders of Gustav Graef in the German press, the most alarming part of this entire episode was that such a respected and honored gentleman could ever be suspected of a crime as grave as perjury. Meyer Heckscher, for example, who wrote a pamphlet criticizing the failure of the justice system in the Graef case, suggested that most observers naturally sympathized with the defendant since "their respect for the sacredness of the oath made it impossible for the majority of people to associate this crime with the ideal personality of the accused artist. One didn't really imagine that the man could be guilty, one felt only sadness that such a thing could happen."[17] Paul Lindau expressed very similar sentiments in his own essay and also voiced his dismay that a prosecutor should take the word of obviously disreputable characters over the word of a gentleman:

> [In such a situation,] I would have thought more carefully about whether I should really cast doubt on the sworn testimony of a respected sixty-year-old man, who has led a life free of any taint, based solely on these kinds of witness statements. Or whether I should have pursued the matter so relentlessly, in a manner that made it seem as if his guilt and future punishment were only a formality, by ordering his house to be searched, his most personal papers to be confiscated and opened, his freedom stolen from him for seven months while all attempts to offer bail were rejected—all because of the denunciation of a man like Hammermann, the stolen letters of a man like Kühnle, or the alleged conversations overheard by a woman like Intrau.[18]

Lindau's clear implication was *not* that all men (or women) should equally be given the benefit of the doubt, but that respected men of substance should be given that benefit over and above those with less cultivation or means. He drew a clear distinction between the upstanding and honest (if also obsessive and gullible) Professor Graef and the dregs of society he was drawn into contact with in the quest to retain his ideal model.

Not all of the city's poor were *necessarily* monstrous in Lindau's view; however, in the lowest levels of society there were a disproportionately high number of what might be called "criminal personalities," who in many cases were identifiable through physical abnormalities, deformities, or ugliness. For example, Lindau mockingly speculated that Krischen, the "agent" that Antonie Hammermann had hired to assist in her blackmail attempts, might actually be as honest as he claimed. However, after describing Krischen's gruesome physical features in detail, Lindau added that "if a character actor wanted to assume the visage of a cutthroat criminal, he could do no better than this remarkably strange apparition."[19] In his description of this kind of "criminal physiognomy," Lindau had clearly been influenced by the controversial theories of the Italian criminologist Cesare Lombroso, which were just beginning to gain popularity at the time in Germany. Lombroso asserted that criminal behavior was frequently the product, not of environment, but of inherited characteristics. In Lombroso's view, these atavistic traits were not just present in behavior, but were identifiable in physical appearance as well.[20] Although Lombroso's major works were not translated into German until after 1887, his ideas were already well known in Germany at the time of the Graef trial.

Lindau did not attribute the criminality rampant amongst the poorer classes solely to inherited characteristics. His descriptions seem more consistent with a Lamarckian (or Spencerian) approach to genetics. In other words, he argued that the corruptive urban environment had a significant impact in cultivating a debased moral and spiritual character among its poorest inhabitants; these acquired characteristics, however, could then be passed down hereditarily through the generations. For example, Lindau pointed to young models such as Helene Hammermann and the Rother daughters, whose brashness of character (*Dreistigkeit*) he believed was a product of their terrible upbringing. In the case of Helene Hammermann, Lindau argued that "[she] is the true product of ugly big-city precociousness." The term translated here as "big-city precociousness" is *großstädtischer Frühreife*, which literally means "early maturity caused by the big city" and is a clear reference to the debilitating environmental effects of an urban setting—especially on sexuality.[21] The Rother apartment was described as filthy and literally teeming with people: a place where any "normal" bourgeois sense of privacy, modesty, or domesticity was completely lacking. Ironically, one of the most powerful pieces of evidence of this kind of moral and sexual depravity came from a brief conversation between Judge Müller and the witness Wilhelm Hammermann during the trial. To the judge's horror, Hammermann proudly admitted that he kept a large nude sculpture of himself in his living room for all—including his own children—to see.[22] This work had been a gift from an artist for whom he had stood as a model. Although the sculpture would undoubtedly have been appropriate for exhibit in an art gallery or the house of a wealthy gentleman unrelated to the model, Lindau implied that its display in the family home of the model himself was a clear sign of immodesty and inappropriate sexual openness—and a moral corruption that would inevitably be passed on to his children.

The neighborhoods of the urban poor, as described by Paul Lindau, were also dangerous in that they were sites of inverted gender relations. Bourgeois women were almost entirely absent from Lindau's trial account; Gustav Graef's wife Franziska was never mentioned, and his daughter Sabine—who testified briefly at trial—received only a passing reference.[23] The women in and around the Rother and Hammermann households, on the other hand, were portrayed as aggressive and outspoken, while their husbands or lovers were usually ignorant, shiftless, or inebriated. Their world, to quote the historian Ellen Ross writing about contemporary depictions of London slums, was a place "where women were neither ladylike nor deferential, where men struggled to hold onto their authority over them, where 'sexual antagonism' was openly acknowledged."[24] This inversion of authority was especially apparent in the Rother household, which Lindau first described in the following manner:

> The head of the Rother family, a journeyman potter with wild and poorly kempt black hair and beard, a pinched nose, a jaundiced complexion, and the sort of listless, but generally friendly attitude that one often finds in heavy drinkers, did not fulfill his role with any sort of dignity. He worked little, if at all, and spent most of his time drunk, hanging around neighborhood taverns and distilleries. He let his wife worry about money and household matters, and his children were allowed to grow up without supervision.[25]

Women may have exercised more power in lower-class families, but in Lindau's depiction this power almost always contributed to disorder and moral decay rather than preventing it. Auguste Rother, for example, pushed her children into modeling and perhaps prostitution after wasting all the money given to her by Gustav Graef in poorly run business ventures. If Wilhelm Hammermann had been the one who feverishly gathered evidence against Graef and turned it over to prosecutors, it was his wife who had been the main figure behind the attempted blackmail of both Graef and Kretzschmer. Even peripheral female characters in the trial story were depicted by Lindau as rather aggressive purveyors of gossip, who were prone to start fights and hold grudges. In Lindau's eyes, these violations of common gender roles made poorer neighborhoods into a distorted mirror of civilized society—a pitiful but also barbarous manifestation of the evils of the modern city.

The imagined class differences delineated by Lindau were also described by other observers. Many commentators on the trial suggested that the mixing of the classes in the wrong circumstances could be very dangerous—as if the moral depravity so common among the poor could be transferred through excessive or inappropriate contact. Judge Müller, for example, was stunned by the mere suggestion that Gustav Graef would willingly associate with a family such as the Rothers. As he put it in his questioning of Graef:

> You are alleged to have engaged in a relationship with the Rother family that no man of your status in society should engage in. . . . Didn't you ever say to yourself that societal rules and other imperatives exist that draw boundaries one ought not transgress? Wouldn't you think that in a situation where something dishonorable was demanded of you, your duty would be to reject that demand even at the risk of losing a model?[26]

The Catholic newspaper *Germania* was revolted not just by the alleged charges of perjury and sexual misconduct but also by the very notion that "this silver-haired old man would visit his model in her apartment, and make polite conversation at the table next to her drunken father and the equally besotted coachman who was her mother's illicit lover."[27] Even the liberal *Frankfurter Zeitung* was disgusted by the "made-up and unmade-up women of vice that surrounded this artist, drawn from the lowest social levels of a metropolis" and expressed shock at "how close the heights of the art world have come to the abyss of the criminal underworld."[28] In fact, Paul Lindau himself was repeatedly attacked by critics for associating too closely with the dregs of Berlin society in the "research" for his article on the trial. The prosecutor in the Graef case, Max Heinemann, mocked Lindau for engaging in "objective research" on the case by regularly carousing in local Moabit wine bars with friends of the Rother and Hammermann families.[29] Lindau's pointed defense against these allegations, that Heinemann should know that it was essential—both for a journalist and a prosecutor—to actually get to know the people involved in the trial, undoubtedly fell on deaf ears.

In reality, of course, the worlds of the wealthy and poor in Berlin were not nearly as separate and distinct as they were made to seem. Interactions between members of different social classes were a daily occurrence in nineteenth-century Berlin in ways both trivial and profound. The poor of Berlin cobbled together an existence based largely on servicing the needs of the wealthy and middle class, and although it was rarely admitted, the upper classes of the city were largely dependent on those services—for things as diverse as transportation, cheap day labor, and sexual gratification. The social relations of the poor in Berlin were thus hidden in plain sight; interactions with the lower classes were simply rendered invisible or insignificant for most wealthy residents of the city unless they openly challenged or violated social norms. While most wealthy Berliners would never have deigned to visit the hovel of a poor family in the way that Graef visited the Rothers, the expressions of shock at the behavior and living conditions of the urban poor were probably much more a product of collective denial rather than real ignorance. The journalist Maximilian Harden later made exactly this case in his sarcastic summary of the infamous Heinze murder trial in 1891, which he suggested had really uncovered absolutely nothing new about urban life in Berlin. As in other previous criminal cases, Harden argued, sensation-seeking journalists used expressions of shock and dismay at the moral depravity endemic among the poor to attract readership, and the public—bored with the politics of the day—enthusiastically devoured such sensationalized stories. Most elites, Harden sarcastically suggested, feigned ignorance and surprise at how the lower classes lived, but perhaps only in the special case of Kaiser Wilhelm II might they truly have been so ignorant.[30]

Harden's sarcasm aside, these frequent "revelations" about the conditions of the lower classes were undoubtedly a symptom of growing fears about the detrimental effects of urbanization and industrialization and the concurrent rise of revolutionary socialism. Cities and towns in Germany had always had problems with crime, but criminals in the overcrowded urban centers of the German Empire seemed now to have become especially ruthless and depraved, and far better organized as well. Just a few months after the end of the Graef trial, an anonymous serialized essay appeared in a law journal that promised an insider perspective "into the unfathomable depths of wickedness in this strange and unknown realm of the criminal underworld [*ungekannte Reich der Verbrecherwelt*]."[31] The essay, entitled "The Criminal World of Berlin," which was quickly published as a stand-alone book for public consumption, had been penned anonymously by Max Heinemann's prosecutorial colleague at the Berlin Regional Court, Gustav Otto, and it took one of the cases he had recently prosecuted—the Dickhoff trial—as its point of departure. Otto framed his essay as an attempt to correct popular attitudes toward criminals in Berlin, which he felt exhibited far too much sympathy for offenders. According to Otto, the defendant in the Dickhoff case, Ernst Wilhelm Dickhoff, known as "Dicke" (or "Fatty") by his fellow criminals, was not at all worthy of popular sympathy. He was a new kind of criminal mastermind—a commissioned salesman who led a double life as the ruthless leader of a band of lower-class thieves and murderers; he was, as Otto suggested, the king of a secret ring of professional criminals (*gewerbsmässige Verbrechertum*) embedded deep within German society and was one of the most dangerous criminals who ever lived.[32]

According to Otto's account, Berlin detectives had suspected for years that Dickhoff had planned robberies that targeted older widows. Dickhoff allegedly identified his marks while working door-to-door as a salesman, and he then trained a small army of criminal specialists, lookouts, and thugs to carry out the dirty work. When necessary, this dirty work could be bloody as well. Despite suspicions and circumstantial evidence tying Dickhoff to dozens of robberies and a series of murders of wealthy widows, police found it impossible to substantiate charges—especially because he was rarely present while his underlings were carrying out crimes and could thus provide solid alibis.[33] After years of evading justice, Dickhoff was eventually convicted in November 1883 of being an accessory to aggravated robbery and murder; however, far from claiming this as a great victory for the forces of order, Gustav Otto used the case to suggest that Dickhoff was just the tip of the iceberg. He engaged in a long and detailed description of lower-class neighborhoods in Berlin and "the small, unhealthy, and overcrowded apartments, with their physical and spiritual filthiness, that serve as the true breeding ground of criminality."[34]

The criminal underworld described by Otto was not entirely chaotic and lawless; it had instead developed into a complex and distorted mirror of German society, with its own castes, traditions, secret systems of communication, and even a twisted code of honor. Although the members of this underworld were often savage and ruthless, they were far from ignorant. In fact, Otto described these characters as possessing a high degree of intelligence, cleverness, resourcefulness, and even a degree of humor as they planned and executed their crimes. Their activities were not exclusively geared toward profit but toward an opposition to the moral and legal codes of "legitimate society"—sometimes almost as a kind of sport. In this kind of corrupted urban atmosphere, populated by a self-regulated web of heavy boys and con men, blackmailers and shysters, counterfeiters and common thieves, prostitutes, pimps, and pederasts, even the best police force was easily overmatched.[35] Gustav Otto perhaps painted a more extreme view of criminal life among the poorer classes in Berlin than had been common before, but his views reflected a growing panic and paranoia about the "uncivilized" nature of life in Berlin slums.

It is striking how often descriptions of the urban poor, whether in the "anthropological expeditions" of Paul Lindau, the shocking revelations of Gustav Otto, or the missionary efforts of Adolf Stöcker, often adopted an almost colonialist tone—as if the poor neighborhoods of northern Berlin were a "dark continent" filled with uncivilized and potentially dangerous natives. Those who commented on the Graef case were almost universally appalled by the depravity they observed among the lower-class participants in the trial, which included drunkenness, mendacity, laziness, promiscuity, and mental weakness. These "savage" characteristics marked the urban poor not only as outsiders in German society who could be "civilized" only with some difficulty, but also in their unreformed state as an inherently corrupting influence on the moral fabric of the nation.

A CASE OF MADNESS OR DISSIMULATION?

If self-proclaimed experts such as Paul Lindau and Gustav Otto were willing to offer their "scientific" observations of the depravity of the urban poor, there were also actual scientific experts called to testify on this topic within the Graef trial itself. These experts were called primarily to interpret the strange behavior of one particular witness: Bertha Rother's younger sister Anna. In addition to being a defendant herself, Anna Rother was also a key witness for the prosecution. At an official interrogation in June 1885, two months after her arrest on suspicion of perjury, Anna had admitted to investigators that an affair between Bertha and Professor Graef had indeed taken place, and she told investigators that both Graef and her sister had bribed and intimidated her to lie under oath at the Hammermann trial. This testimony had been a core piece of evidence supporting charges of subornation of perjury against both Bertha Rother and Gustav Graef. In response to direct questioning from Judge Müller, however, Anna claimed in court to have no memory of her previous statements to investigators or her allegedly perjured testimony at the Hammermann trial. She denied having been pressured to lie by Professor Graef and her sister and claimed not to know why she might have given different answers under interrogation. Despite being confronted with her own clearly contradictory statements, Anna insisted to the judge that she *always* told the truth.

Anna and Bertha Rother also continuously frustrated Judge Müller with their courtroom behavior during the trial, earning several rebukes for smiling and laughing at inappropriate times. Judge Müller even temporarily dismissed Bertha from the courtroom at one point for shaking her head, nodding, and whispering during the judge's questioning of her sister.[36] At times Anna seemed completely coherent, but when pressed by the judge to respond to questions she would often break into loud sobs and give confused answers. One particularly frustrating incident took place when Concordia Intrau, a resident of the Rother household and key witness for the prosecution, testified about a fight between the two sisters after the Hammermann trial in which Anna Rother had called her sister a "professor-whore" and Bertha had responded by accusing her sister of having committed perjury at the Hammermann trial. In the midst of Intrau's testimony, Anna Rother leapt forward to interject that this fight had been misinterpreted by the witness. She had indeed called her sister a "professor-whore" in a fit of anger, but then Bertha had responded to her insult by saying, "If I *were* a professor-whore, then you *would be* a perjurer." A flustered Judge Müller halted the proceedings and asked Anna why she had seemed almost incoherent in earlier testimony, but now seemed alert and confident—and able to distinguish between declarative and conditional statements. Anna quickly retreated into vague answers, and when the judge pressed her further, she broke down in tears. After this incident, the prosecutor immediately called for a forensic medical expert, Dr. Carl Liman, to be summoned to the courtroom to observe Anna and assess her mental competence. The use of expert witnesses was not an entirely new practice in German courtrooms, but it was becoming more common and often more controversial.[37] In this case, of course, the issue of Anna's competence was important not only for establishing her own guilt on charges of perjury but also for weighing the value of her "confession"—an essential pillar of evidence against all four defendants.

To say that Carl Liman wrote the book on the mental competence of witnesses would not have been an exaggeration: his book *Questionable Mental States in Court* (*Zweifelhafte Geisteszustände vor Gericht*) first appeared in 1869.[38] At Liman's request, the judge ordered Anna to read out loud the transcript of her own confession given during interrogation several months earlier; Anna refused, and she instead broke down in a fit of crying.[39] Anna's mother insisted that it was widely known that she was feeble-minded (*geistesschwach*) and that she could not count, did not know her own address or the date, and suffered from severe cramps that frequently prevented her from attending school.[40] These cramps were apparently severe enough that with Graef's sponsorship she had been briefly sent to the *Johannesstift* in Moabit, a religious foundation that aided poor and sick children.

Judge Müller next summoned a judge named Johl, who had led the early investigation of the Graef case and had first interrogated Anna in jail. Based on his own long experience as an investigative judge, Johl insisted that he could tell that Anna Rother was *not* crazy. At their first meeting, Anna had spoken clearly and freely about her anger at both Bertha and Professor Graef for having intimidated her and forced her to lie on the stand. Judge Johl insisted that her confession had come without any prodding, and that it was far too clear and detailed to have been invented on the spot. Subsequent interrogations of Anna gave the same impression until, suddenly, she decided to change her story. According to Johl, Anna was simply a first-rate dissembler (*Simulantin*) and certainly not mentally incompetent. Judge Müller asked the expert witness Dr. Carl Liman if he had any comment about Johl's testimony or about Anna's reactions to it. To Müller's surprise, Liman announced that it would be his task to prove that Johl's characterization of Anna as a dissembler was false. Müller admonished Liman that his only job was to give an expert opinion and not to make any premature conclusions. According to at least one trial summary, Judge Müller also instructed Dr. Liman to stop speaking privately to the defense team following complaints by the prosecutor.[41]

To help investigate Anna's mental state further, the judge summoned the prison doctor, Leopold Lewin.[42] Lewin testified that when Anna was first incarcerated, many of the prison attendants were suspicious of her behavior. She had periodic episodes during which she would cry out in pain because of cramps and then go into convulsions once someone entered the cell. When one attendant splashed water in her face during one of these episodes, her angry reaction convinced many observers that she was faking her symptoms. Continued observation, however, convinced Dr. Lewin that this was *not* the case. Most laymen, Lewin argued, cannot tell the difference between someone who is sane and someone who merely appears to be sane. In the case of Anna Rother, her labile emotions, insomnia, frequent nightmares, poor memory and reasoning skills, apathy, and constant headaches pointed to only one conclusion: a mental illness tied to epilepsy that might properly be called *dementia epileptica*.[43] This sickness, according to Lewin, was clearly hereditary in nature: "The father is a heavy drinker, and the daughter is therefore hereditarily damaged [*erblich belastet*]."[44] Lewin added that even if Anna could appear lucid at times—including during a police interrogation—he would still have to classify her as mentally incompetent. He also reminded the court rather pointedly that scientific evidence demonstrated that epileptics often tend toward both lying and criminality.

A colleague of Carl Liman, Dr. Wolff, gave similar testimony as an expert witness. He concluded that over 60 percent of epilepsy cases were accompanied by intellectual deficits and occasionally also by the tendency for pathological lying. In addition, Anna's imbecility was apparent through her deformed facial features, in the sense that one half of her face was better developed than the other. Wolff did agree that it was entirely possible that her testimony under police interrogation had been honest; given her overall mental condition, however, her testimony could not be assumed to be reliable. Under questioning from

Judge Müller, Dr. Wolff suggested that Anna was not really capable of forming her own free will, nor was she entirely able to assist in her own defense.[45]

Finally, Carl Liman, the doctor first called in to observe Anna Rother's behavior in court, went even further in his conclusions. Liman claimed that 80 percent of all epileptics showed signs of reduced mental capability. Despite the fact that a few historical cases of epileptics, such as Caesar, Muhammad, and Napoleon, demonstrated that enormous willpower could overcome the symptoms of such an illness, this was certainly not the case for someone like Anna Rother. Anna was no idiot, he argued, but she was feeble-minded and unable to tell right from wrong or the truth from a lie. Judge Müller questioned all three expert witnesses about how someone as allegedly "feeble-minded" as Anna could have the mental capacity to create such a complex web of realistic-sounding lies. Dr. Wolff thought that Anna might have been capable, while the others suggested that a third party must have influenced her statements to investigators.[46]

The prosecutor, Max Heinemann, angrily rejected the testimony of all of these medical experts. Although he admitted that Anna had a relatively weak constitution and could have been pressured by Gustav Graef to commit perjury, in his opinion Anna Rother was a master manipulator and schemer rather than a poor victim of mental illness. According to his own experience in cases like this, such dissemblers were as likely to fool "experts" as they were to fool ordinary people. Common sense suggested that Anna had been in full control of her faculties when she lied in the Hammermann case, and then again when she admitted lying to investigators. It was only for her own benefit that she had put on a carefully crafted performance in court during the trial.[47] Heinemann was thus asking jurors to favor his own expertise and experience as a prosecutor against the expertise and experience of the three medical professionals. It is not entirely clear which portrayal of Anna Rother the jurors found most credible: the mentally feeble epileptic or the master dissimulator. When they acquitted Gustav Graef of perjury, an acquittal of Anna naturally followed. In either depiction, however, Anna Rother could serve as a powerful symbol of the depraved condition of the lower classes and of a modern society gone terribly wrong.

DEFIANCE AND AGENCY

Anna Rother was portrayed in summaries of the Graef trial as either a victim of her upbringing (and heredity) or as a fiendish manipulator of the system. What she was not—at least according to descriptions of the trial—was a rational actor following her own self-interest. Like other lower-class participants in the trial, Anna was rarely described as exerting purely rational agency; her behavior and choices were characterized by foolishness, labile emotions, and outright deceptiveness. If, however, we read between the lines, and if we reimagine the Graef trial through the point of view of Anna and her fellow witnesses, what often appears to be shiftlessness, fecklessness, or madness in trial summaries might sometimes be reinterpreted as a strategy of passive resistance and even open rebellion. In Simone de Beauvoir's *The Second Sex*, the philosopher argued that many stereotyped forms of female behavior in her own era—including lateness and inattention—should be interpreted as a conscious or unconscious form of protest against the masculine world that women were forced to navigate.[48] This could just as well be the case for witnesses in the Graef trial—especially for the young women who were accused by lawyers or judges of not taking the proceedings seriously. From this perspective, of course, the mysterious psychological symptoms of Anna Rother might also be interpreted much differently. We should remember that despite the common rhetoric about equality before the law, most citizens from the lower classes who entered a courtroom knew that the deck was stacked against them. Prosecutors and judges certainly did not represent a part of *their* social world and could often be hostile or dismissive toward them. They did not face a true jury of their peers but rather a carefully selected jury of their social betters. In these circumstances, one can certainly understand the defiance and open disdain that witnesses and defendants sometimes demonstrated in court.

Of course, the story of the Graef trial also suggests that members of the lower classes could exert real power within the legal system. It was Wilhelm Hammermann, after all, who succeeded both in convincing the prosecutor first to free his own wife from prison and then to file charges against the wealthy man who helped put her there. In that sense, the trial was Hammermann's attempt to exact revenge (or justice) from Graef for having broken up his family. Furthermore, once called upon by the court, witnesses such as Concordia Intrau were free to carry out their own pursuit of private justice by venting about personal grievances and reenacting past neighborhood battles. While journalists and newspaper readers alike may have shaken their heads at the petty disputes and brawls depicted in the Rother household, for those involved these conflicts were deadly serious. If the Graef trial was officially about pursuing justice for violations of codified law, for members of the lower classes it was also an opportunity to pursue their own form of "community justice" by settling private scores and exacting vengeance against personal rivals.[49] It should be added that winning the praise of judicial authorities did not always benefit members of the lower classes outside of court. Marie Reim, one of the few residents of the Rother household to receive praise from Judge Müller for her honest and straightforward testimony, responded on the witness stand to this praise with silence and obvious embarrassment. According to the *Nationalzeitung*, Reim was fired from her position as a bookkeeper for a local clothing store soon after the trial ended, allegedly because of complaints about her close association with the Rother family.[50]

Were there no public voices raised to counter the negative depictions of lower-class participants in the Graef trial? What about Socialist journalists and politicians in Germany? The Socialist press had largely been shuttered or exiled since the passing of the 1878 Anti-Socialist Laws, and those Socialist politicians and journalists still in the country may have chosen to avoid public critiques that could have led to prosecution. From its exile in Zurich, the German Socialist newspaper *Sozialdemokrat* poked fun at the false bourgeois morality of Paul Lindau, whom the newspaper referred to as "Bismarck's poodle," and editors also mocked the "garbage" that apparently passed for high art in German society. From their perspective, trials of wealthy gentlemen such as Graef exposed the German Criminal Code as not worth the paper it was printed on. In order to get a free pass from both the bourgeois legal and moral codes, it was suggested, one apparently only had to have a bit of artistic ability—or better yet (quoting Iago's advice in Shakespeare's *Othello*), one needed only to "put money in your purse!"[51] This newspaper, however, was a fairly solitary voice. Again, it is certainly possible that the fear of government prosecution limited the willingness of Socialist politicians within Germany to write or speak about such a contentious case; it is more likely, however, that Socialists may have found the Graef case—and any perceived support for disreputable characters such as the Rothers or Hammermanns—to be fairly problematic for exploitation as political propaganda.[52]

Interestingly, in her analysis of press coverage of the Maiden Tribute Affair in 1885 London, Judith Walkowitz describes similar allusions to inverted gender norms and colonialist discourse in descriptions of the London poor.[53] Walkowitz, however, also depicts a determined cadre of social and political activists who used the Maiden Tribute Affair not only to push specific social reforms, but also to help counter depictions of the working class as shiftless and barbaric by invoking new tropes about their exploitation by a morally degenerate bourgeoisie. In Germany—at least in the immediate aftermath of this particular trial—those kinds of narratives were much less common.

A POWERFUL EXAMPLE OF THE JEWISH QUESTION

At first glance, the Graef case might not seem a particularly fruitful source of anti-Semitic propaganda or a useful platform for its dissemination; after all, not only was Gustav Graef *not* Jewish, he came from a long line of Protestant ministers and his grandfather had been a respected pastor at the Königsberg Cathedral. There were several factors, however, that helped put the Graef case squarely in the middle of contemporary debates about the so-called "Jewish Question." Long-standing concerns about cultural degeneracy in Germany and fears about recent political, economic, and legal changes had already been tied both to the general rise of liberalism and also to the allegedly corrupting influence of German Jews. Since the Graef trial provoked complaints about cultural degeneracy, flawed liberal legal reforms, and the excesses of the liberal press, it should not be surprising that it also provided a public platform for calls to limit Jewish influence.

The Graef case occurred only a dozen years after the financial panic of 1873, and the intervening decade had been filled with increasing vitriol linking the economic collapse with Otto von Bismarck, German liberals, and European Jews. In December of 1874, an author named Otto Glagau published a series of articles that complained about Jewish influence on the German government and more specifically targeted Otto von Bismarck's personal banker, Gerson von Bleichröder, as a major culprit in the speculation that had led to the stock market crash. These articles were published in a rather surprising place: the *Gartenlaube*, a very popular middle-class family magazine that was generally considered to be apolitical. In these articles, Glagau viciously attacked Bismarck's economic policies, criticized the corruption inherent in German banks and stock exchanges, and also pinned the blame for the financial collapse of 1873 directly on the deceit of Jewish bankers.[54] In addition to his assertion that "the Social Question is the Jewish Question," his most infamous claim was that 90 percent of all promoters (*Gründer*) and stock exchange speculators were Jews.[55] These articles served as the inspiration for further attacks against Bismarck, including anonymous articles by Christoph Cremer in the Catholic *Germania*, by Franz Perrot in the ultraconservative *Kreuzzeitung*, and in several sensational books published by Otto von Diest-Daber—all of which angrily blamed Bismarck for allowing Jewish greed to undermine the German financial system.

The rhetoric of these articles was still echoing through the press several years later when Wilhelm Marr published his infamous *The Victory of Jewry over Germandom* in 1879. Marr's book is an unrelentingly pessimistic account of how the

Jewish race had finally emerged victorious during the 1870s in its eighteen-hundred-year-long battle against the German race. Marr suggested that Jewish dominance was a forgone conclusion not only in Germany, but in the rest of Europe as well.[56] This paranoid racial argument seemed to strike a chord in a German society still reeling from the economic crisis, where both liberalism and tolerance suddenly seemed to be on the wane. However, the overall importance of Marr's treatise was accentuated by two other factors. First, despite the overall pessimism of his book, Marr concluded with a call to action: he founded the first explicitly anti-Jewish political organization in Germany, which would eventually become known as the Anti-Semitic League (*Antisemitenliga*).[57] Marr's book may have also been the first to coin the term "anti-Semitism" (*Antisemitismus*)—a word that would quickly take on an obvious symbolic importance both to Jews and to those across the globe who sought to attack them.[58]

Marr's Anti-Semitic League did not last, but it inspired the formation of numerous splinter parties and local "reform clubs" that hosted anti-Semitic speakers, published petitions, and even founded their own small newspapers. In addition, the court chaplain (*Hofprediger*) Adolf Stöcker began in 1879 to use anti-Semitic speeches to attract support for his fledgling Christian-Social Party. Because of his position as one of the leading Protestant pastors in Germany, Stöcker's speeches gave anti-Semitic rhetoric more public respectability. Although all of these anti-Semitic organizations, including Stöcker's Christian-Social Party, had a relatively difficult time cooperating with one another or attracting a mass audience, they were still far more influential than their membership numbers might indicate. A petition to convince the German government to reduce Jewish influence, for example, was circulated by the anti-Semitic activist Bernhard Förster and gained 250,000 signatures by 1882; although this petition was ignored by Chancellor Otto von Bismarck, it nonetheless demonstrated the potential attractiveness of anti-Semitic propaganda in Imperial German society.

At the same time, rhetorical attacks by these fringe groups against Jewish interests were being reported (and sometimes echoed) by segments of the more mainstream political press. Leading ultraconservative newspapers such as the *Kreuzzeitung* and the *Reichsbote*, as well as the right-wing Catholic daily *Germania*, often adopted anti-Semitic rhetoric to attack Chancellor Bismarck's association with liberal parties or to needle rival liberal politicians. Thus, although specifically anti-Semitic political parties remained small fringe elements in the early German Empire, they were not without influence. In their small (but often provocative) newspapers, in public speeches, and in election campaigns, these agitators often succeeded in helping keep the "Jewish Question" in the public eye.[59]

Anti-Semitic rhetoric was a common element not only in political and journalistic debates of this era but also in literature that focused on the perceived degeneracy of modern German culture. Just as Jewish influence had allegedly corrupted German political and social institutions, so it had allegedly led to a precipitous decline of German cultural and intellectual traditions. The authoritative text here was Richard Wagner's 1850 essay "Jewry in Music" (*Das Judentum in der Musik*), which was originally published anonymously but then rereleased under his own name twenty years later. By the time Wagner died in 1883, two years before the Graef trial, his attacks on the alien nature of Jews and their pernicious influence on German culture had been adopted and expanded by a wide variety of admirers. One prominent example was an 1881 lecture given by Bernhard Förster, a prominent Wagnerite, cofounder of the infamous Anti-Semitic Petition of the early 1880s, and also the future despised brother-in-law of Friedrich Nietzsche. Although Förster's speech was given in front of the Berlin branch of the Wagnerite Bayreuth Patronage Society, it was meant for general public consumption and was quickly published as a pamphlet called *The Relationship of Modern Jewry to German Art*.

Förster began his speech by contrasting the documents, stories, and myths that supposedly formed the core of German and Jewish cultures. While Germans were raised on the work of Dürer, Goethe, Beethoven, and Wagner, he suggested, Jews were exposed instead to the characters of the Hebrew Bible. This difference led to fundamentally dissimilar moral models. As Förster put it:

> We can find the ideals of Judaism that first developed in their ancient ancestors within the Old Testament. These are figures who have a certain greatness, but if we strip away our perceptions of them learned as youth, and what art and poetry have made of them, they seem quite foreign to us, and except for a few people alongside Abraham, they would never have been able to acknowledge or accept our ideals. This demonstrates a lineage far removed from our own German essence.[60]

Förster's argument was not merely an attempt to distinguish between Aryan and "Semitic" cultures, but also to draw distinctions even between Jews and other Semitic peoples. While ancient Phoenicians and later Arabs had managed to develop advanced technology, create sophisticated architecture, pursue unique artistic styles, and even cultivate a certain chivalrousness (*Ritterlichkeit*), the Jews were allegedly utterly incapable of such achievements. According to Förster, since German cultural products were an outgrowth not only of German history but of the German soul, Jews were absolutely unable to create the same quality of art, literature, or music. Förster did admit that in recent decades Jews had become adept at mimicking German styles, but he claimed that in doing so they often had a destructive impact, causing "our ideals to wither and [making] them seem foreign to us."[61]

Förster, like Wagner, singled out particular Jewish artists and musicians for criticism—especially Jacob (Jacques) Offenbach—and he expressed outrage that such Jewish composers could be so popular in the land of Bach and Beethoven: "How would Dürer's knight [a reference to Albrecht Dürer's 1513 engraving 'Knight, Death, and the Devil'] have reacted, had he seen that nine-tenths of the modern 'educated class' listens with enthusiasm to their Music-Jews and Literature-Jews, whose prostituted business comes mostly from printed wisecracks and smut?"[62] Although Förster did not link any individual Jewish artists or composers with particular acts of immorality, the implication is clear: proud and sacred traditions of German culture were being debased by the "smutty" and "prostituted" influence of Jewish artists, writers, and composers.

Even more damaging to German culture, according to Förster, was the pernicious influence of Jewish professors, cultural critics, and especially the "Jew Press," all of which conspired to divert ordinary Germans away from true art and deprive great German artists of any public resonance for their work. By bombarding people with the trivial and inconsequential and by distracting them with the abstract, Jewish influence had allegedly already caused irreparable harm to German society. Given this kind of analysis, it is not surprising that many critics of Gustav Graef would find it so easy to believe that the painter's debased personal morals were a natural companion to his "prostituted" art and a clear sign of Jewish influence.

If the propaganda of Glagau and Marr, as well as the ideas of Wagner and Förster, provide a general background for the linking of the Graef trial to the "Jewish Question," a more proximate event was just as important. Just a few months before the Graef trial, the court chaplain Adolf Stöcker, one of the leading anti-Semitic politicians in Germany and founder of the Berlin City Mission and Christian-Social Party, had been publicly humiliated in a trial that had some superficial parallels to the Graef case. In October of 1884, Heinrich Bäcker, editor of a small liberal Berlin newspaper called the *Freie Zeitung*, published a pair of deliberately provocative articles that explicitly accused Stöcker of crimes ranging from slander to embezzlement and perjury. There was little subtlety in these slanderous articles; one of them ended with the statement in bold print: **"If Mr. Stöcker would like to sue us** . . . for the content of this article, **we will produce proof of its accuracy**."[63] Although in the past Stöcker had resisted the temptation to sue his critics because of his position as court chaplain, this time he apparently could not resist such an overt and explicit challenge to his honor.

The result was disastrous for Stöcker. On the witness stand, he was ambushed by the experienced defense attorney August Munckel and bombarded with such a variety of allegations and innuendoes that he could never hope to successfully defend himself against them all. Eventually, in June of 1885, a panel of three judges convicted Bäcker of slandering Stöcker, but they sentenced him to only three weeks in jail—far less than the five months demanded by prosecutors. In justifying this lenient sentence, the lead judge, Hermann Lüty, asserted that due to Stöcker's checkered past, the court was not "in any position to blame Bäcker . . . for reaching the conclusion that the witness [Stöcker] stood in conflict with the truth."[64] The verdict in the Stöcker-Bäcker case was a political bombshell. The liberal press jumped at the chance to ridicule Stöcker as the "truth-loving Court Chaplain" and the "perjured pastor." So great was the public humiliation that many of Stöcker's traditional allies now hesitated to come to his defense. Although Stöcker succeeded in holding on to his position as court chaplain for several more years (mostly due to the efforts of Crown Prince William—later Kaiser Wilhelm II), his credibility and political influence never fully recovered.[65]

Ironically, one of the most prominent anti-Semitic commentators to link the Graef trial to the Stöcker-Bäcker case was none other than Otto Glagau, the author of the original 1874 anti-Semitic articles in the *Gartenlaube*. At the time of the Graef trial, Glagau was the editor of the journal *Der Kulturkämpfer*, which served as his own mouthpiece to comment on various political, social, and cultural matters. Although the actual circulation of this journal may have been limited, Glagau was already well known in Germany because of his previous work. In fact, despite the fact that Glagau specifically refused to join or endorse any specific anti-Semitic party or faction, he had still been chosen to serve as president of a Second International Anti-Jewish Congress, which took place at Chemnitz in 1883. Glagau was never a close supporter of Stöcker, but he was outraged that such a public figure had been railroaded by a political press and a justice system that served Jewish interests. This anger was still palpable in his commentary on the Graef trial four months later.

In an essay of more than twenty pages published in *Der Kulturkämpfer*, Glagau reviewed the details of the Graef case and considered its legacy. For Glagau, the trial served as a "powerful example of the Jewish Question" and a clear demonstration of the corrupted state of modern German society.[66] He found it outrageous to read liberal complaints that Graef's allegedly perjured statements had only come in response to inappropriate and largely irrelevant questioning by defense attorneys. This seemed a perfect parallel to the Stöcker case, where an innocent "victim" of slanders was crucified on the witness stand by clever Jewish lawyers:

> We certainly cannot deny the alarming problems that our criminal law currently suffers from—for example, the failure to formally record statements given during interrogations before the court. But why are people just now discovering these issues during the Graef trial, and why are they only now reacting with such fervor?! Wasn't this even more evident in the case of Court Chaplain Stöcker against the Jewish *Freie Zeitung*? Weren't the evidentiary motions by Sachs and Munckel, the defense lawyers of the Jew Bäcker, just as interminable and outrageous? Wasn't circumstantial evidence raised about the silliest and most trivial of matters, about things that later were acknowledged to have had absolutely nothing to do with the case at hand? These almost unprecedented submissions of evidence occurred at the expense of poor Stöcker, who was thereby transformed from a mere witness into a defendant.[67]

Glagau also suggested that the Graef trial revealed that Jews played a primary role in Berlin prostitution, and he suggested that attempts by the "Jew Press" to assert a special legal amnesty for painters and models (*Atelier- und Modell-Freiheit*) were nothing less than a façade to protect their illicit business interests.

Of course, in referring to the "Jew Press," Glagau meant not only those newspapers that were specifically owned by Jews or were targeted to Jewish readers, but also mainstream liberal newspapers that he believed served "Jewish interests" by undermining German values and institutions. As Glagau put it:

> The greatest danger to threaten the German people, however, is from the Jew Press, which is always impertinent, is becoming ever more powerful, and regularly works to undermine the sacred tenets of our society: morality and faith, family and state. As the Graef trial clearly shows, the Jew Press also threatens both the legal process and the integrity of judges and jurors. Newspaper reports on such cases, and open public access to trial proceedings themselves, are capable of doing much damage, including poisoning the youth and corrupting the entire population.[68]

Thus, even two decades before the infamous *Protocols of the Elders of Zion* appeared in Russia as alleged proof of a Jewish world conspiracy, Glagau's rhetoric demonstrated that paranoid fears about the power and influence of a secret Jewish cabal were not uncommon in Germany.

Glagau's interpretation of the Graef case was not totally unique, and in the heat of press debates about the trial it is sometimes hard to distinguish Glagau's attacks from those of ultraconservative or right-wing Catholic newspapers. The conservative *Kreuzzeitung*, for example, suggested that if it were true that those who defended Graef in the press "descended from that alien tribe (*fremdartige Sippe*), which believes it is entitled to treat its own feelings and interests as if they were the feelings and interests of the German people, then this would explain why so much since the twenty-eighth of September [the start of the Graef trial] has seemed incomprehensible to our own 'Aryan' point of view."[69] The *Kreuzzeitung* also contrasted the behavior of journalists in the "Jew Press" during the Graef trial to their previous behavior during the Stöcker-Bäcker case a few months earlier. While their conduct during the earlier case had been motivated by tribal hatred (*Stammeshaß*) against Stöcker, the *Kreuzzeitung* claimed, their avid support of Graef was motivated by an equal degree of tribal affinity (*Stammesliebe*).

It is also worth noting that at the same time these comments on the Graef trial were appearing in mid-October 1885, the editor of the *Kreuzzeitung*, Wilhelm von Hammerstein, was in court facing charges of slandering the lead judge from the Stöcker-Bäcker case. After the end of that earlier trial, a few liberal newspapers had lauded Judge Lüty's willingness to criticize Stöcker with the famous phrase that celebrated judicial independence in Prussia: "There are still judges in Berlin!" (*il y a des juges à Berlin!*). Hammerstein, then, had responded angrily in his own paper with the phrase "There are still Jews in Berlin!" (*il y a des juifs à Berlin!*). This statement alone was apparently not grave enough to trigger a prosecution under §166 of the Penal Code, which outlawed the slander of religious groups. However, an allegation within the same article that Judge Lüty was inherently biased because he was the baptized son of Jewish parents resulted in a conviction for libel and a relatively modest fine of 150 Marks.[70]

Since the Graef trial occurred only a month before the November 1885 elections for the Prussian House of Representatives, it also provided a useful topic for anti-Semitic demagogues to attract attention in public speeches. Less than a week after the verdict, Dr. Ammann, a member of the fringe German Anti-Semites' League and former follower of Eugen Dühring, delivered a political speech in front of an estimated 1,000 people in Berlin. This speech was mostly a rehashing of the critiques of the trial made by Otto Glagau and by newspapers such as the *Kreuzzeitung*, *Reichsbote*, and *Germania*. He advised his listeners to boycott any bookstores that displayed images of Bertha Rother, and he stressed the difference between true Germans and those defenders of Graef.[71] According to the liberal

Nationalzeitung, which was far from friendly to Ammann and his political group, Ammann's speech was greeted by enthusiastic applause and even occasional cries of "Jews out!" (*Juden raus!*).[72]

Ammann's meeting was soon followed by a public meeting of the Christian-Social Party, at which the party's leader, Adolf Stöcker, took his turn at addressing the Graef controversy. Stöcker did not contrast the Graef case with his own experiences in court; instead, he directed public attention to the revolting behavior of the "Jew Press" and the dangers posed by Jewish influence on German culture. As he told his audience,

> I have heard directly from artists themselves that our art is suffering due to foreign, anti-Christian influences, and that an unpleasant Jewish influence is becoming more prominent in painting and music as well as in poetry and the writing of novels. . . . We will do battle against this immoral art, just as we will continue to praise true art and hope that it returns to dominance. It is perhaps a good thing that this trial was publicized: it was the beginning of self-awareness, which can be the start of improvement.[73]

The influence of Jews and Freemasons had already started to poison the life of the people, Stöcker argued, and it was his duty to bring them back to Christianity.[74]

Of course, as I mentioned earlier, Glagau, Ammann, Stöcker, as well as newspapers such as the *Reichsbote, Germania*, and *Kreuzzeitung* all treated this case as part of the "Jewish Question" despite the fact that Graef himself was not Jewish and despite the fact that Max Heinemann, the man who had so doggedly prosecuted him, had originally been born into a Jewish family—a detail that liberal newspapers such as the *Berlin Börsen-Zeitung* pointed out with some glee.[75] For critics of Graef, however, his *actual* ancestry was seemingly of no concern considering the debased nature of his morals and artwork. As Otto Glagau wrote:

> In reality, the Graef trial is once again a powerful example of the Jewish Question. The wife of Professor Graef is said to be of Jewish ancestry, and his daughter engaged to a Jewish boy. Almost everyone who marched into the courtroom and testified in his favor belonged to this foreign race. Just have a look at the names! Indeed, this is even true about the prosecutor Heinemann, which should not prevent any German natives from giving him the credit he is due. Only his five-hour long closing argument was long and boring. His dissection and explication of Graef's poetry was called "hair-raising" even by the defense. He did, however, make a fairly poor impression on the jurors, and that perhaps helped lead to Graef's acquittal.[76]

It may seem strange from our own perspective to see an anti-Semitic author perform the rather acrobatic feat of backhandedly praising a converted Jewish prosecutor for pursuing charges against a non-Jewish defendant for allegedly helping to "Jewify" German culture; religious or racial prejudices, however, are frequently logically inconsistent—even when laid out in excruciating detail by men like Glagau. This inconsistency is not necessarily a sign of opportunism in the choice of target, but rather a willingness to accept multiple forms of evidence that might help substantiate a conspiracy or prove the existential nature of the threat.

Even years after the trial ended, anti-Semitic agitators continued to cite the Graef case in their propaganda. Carl Paasch, one of the more infamous and unstable anti-Semitic agitators of the early 1890s, pointed to the Graef trial as the most disgusting example from a long list of acquittals of obvious Jewish criminals. Such miscarriages of justice, according to Paasch, served only to provoke outrage among the German populace:

> In this trial, where a great effort was expended to obtain the acquittal of a senile sinner, all of Berlin Jewry celebrated him as a hero and martyr. Simson, Lindau, Lessing, Wolff, Lewin, Siegmund, Frenzel, Davidsohn, Holdheim und Philipps, Dernburg, Rosenstock, Salomonsohn, Isaac, Bernstein *et tutti quanti* jumped in openly to support him, while the respectable public, on the other hand, turned away from him in disgust.[77]

As usual for someone as paranoid as Paasch, the conspiracies to protect Graef were not limited to the Jewish community but included officials in the highest ranks of the government. Paasch accused the Prussian justice minister, Hermann von Schelling, of being too close to the Hildesheimer family, who were influential leaders of Orthodox Jewry in Germany and whose newspaper, the *Jüdische Presse*, was a notorious critic of anti-Semitic activists. Paasch even suggested that Justice Minister Schelling may have had Jewish blood himself, and he proclaimed that Schelling's own secret sexual escapades dwarfed those of Graef. Paasch ended his essay by asserting that Germany was even more threatened by Jewish influence than France, where the Panama Scandal had already led to accusations that Jews were conspiring to destroy the country.[78] Obviously, for a worldview in which criminal acquittals were often considered greater proof of a Jewish conspiracy than convictions, and where allegations of sexual misconduct fit in nicely with preexisting racial stereotypes and well-rehearsed narratives about cultural decline, the Graef trial was a mother lode of propaganda.

Carl Paasch was a marginal figure in German society, and his wild accusations not only made him politically untouchable but also raised doubts about his mental competence. For many Germans, however, the acknowledged outrageousness of Paasch's allegations did not suggest that all anti-Jewish stereotypes were groundless or that the influence of Jews in German society was benign. As we have seen, newspapers on the political right commonly used anti-Semitic rhetoric to attack political liberalism and to complain about allegedly harmful Jewish influence on Germany's cultural, economic, and legal development. Most Germans at the time would have rejected being labeled as anti-Semitic—at least in terms of being associated with explicitly anti-Semitic fringe political parties; however, many would probably also have seen a kernel of truth in criticism of Jewish influence even if they did not buy into the elaborate conspiracies mapped out by Paasch and Glagau. Thus, although the extreme nature of the rhetoric of a Glagau or Paasch is important to note, it is not the virulence, but rather the breadth of voices resorting to anti-Semitic rhetoric (even during the trial of a non-Jewish artist) that is perhaps most significant here.

It is certainly tempting to see the paranoid conspiracies of Paasch and the readiness of significant segments of the German press to resort to anti-Jewish stereotypes as a sign of things to come in Germany—as the beginning of a long descent that would lead to the rise of National Socialism and the eventual perpetration of the Holocaust. Another comparison with the work of Judith Walkowitz, however, might lead us to exercise a bit more caution in making such a direct link. In the second half of her book, *The City of Dreadful Delight*, which focuses on sexual crimes in 1880s London, Walkowitz describes in detail the way that the Whitechapel murders of 1888, popularly known as the crimes of "Jack the Ripper," incited a substantial anti-Jewish backlash. She suggests that this burst of anti-Semitism was in part endemic to the East End and also was a response to an unstable economy, a severe housing crisis in the Whitechapel neighborhood, and an influx of eastern European Jews into the area.[79] Anti-Jewish sentiment in London had also been whipped up by sensationalist journalists, who not only suggested that it was impossible for any true Englishman to have committed such grisly crimes, but also claimed that the killings showed some similarity to Jewish ritual-murders that had been reported in central and eastern Europe over the previous decade. The series of murders were attributed by some radical dailies, including W. T. Stead's *Pall Mall Gazette*, to "Leather Apron"—a mysterious man with a butcher's knife, an apron, and marked "Hebrew features." Fear and anger in the neighborhood became so great that anti-Jewish riots resulted, and police were sent into the streets to prevent the situation from turning into a pogrom. One young Jewish man even turned himself in to police to avoid the fury of the crowd, which had become convinced he was a likely suspect.[80]

A comparative study of the breadth and depth of anti-Semitism in late nineteenth-century Germany and England is far beyond what can be attempted here. It is clear from even a very superficial comparison of these cases, however, that anti-Semitism, often exacerbated by social tensions, economic instability, and a sensationalist press, was a substantial force in both turn-of-the-century London and Berlin. During the 1880s, anti-Semitism in Germany could also occasionally turn violent, as the 1881 pogroms in West Prussia and Pomerania clearly demonstrated.[81] That violence, however, like the violence in the East End of London, was quickly controlled and suppressed by police and government authorities. The enduring legacy of these episodes, therefore, was not necessarily in setting a precedent for later violent actions against Jews but in contributing to the vast storehouse of anti-Jewish stereotypes and to the general sense that there was in fact a real "Jewish Question" which required substantial action.

CHAPTER SIX

A CRIMINAL JUSTICE SYSTEM IN CRISIS

Despite the daily drama presented in newspaper transcripts of the Graef trial, many observers—especially those with any legal training—knew that the prosecution was in deep trouble from the very first day of the proceedings. Before the most memorable moments of the trial had occurred, the case began with a review of original testimony from the Hammermann blackmail trial, at which both Gustav Graef and Anna Rother had allegedly committed perjury. The testimony of judges and lawyers from the original Hammermann case was especially vital since no actual transcript of the Hammermann proceedings had been recorded. In a fairly disastrous turn for the prosecution, witnesses could not agree on the precise phrasing of the key questions to which Graef had allegedly given perjured answers more than sixteen months earlier. All agreed that Graef had denied engaging in "a relationship" with Bertha; however, there were some serious doubts about exactly what this denial encompassed.

The lead judge in the Hammermann case, *Landgerichtsdirektor* Bachmann, recounted that he had realized almost immediately that the defense attorney in that case had mistakenly called Anna Rother as a witness (rather than Bertha). After Anna denied having an intimate relationship with Graef that included expensive gifts and travel, Bachmann stepped in directly to ask Graef if he had carried on "that kind of a relationship" with her sister Bertha—an accusation that Graef denied under oath. For Judge Bachmann, it seemed clear that Graef was not simply denying a sexual relationship with Bertha but also denying that he had provided substantial gifts to her.[1] Bachmann's memory of these proceedings was challenged by Graef, who claimed that the question about a "relationship" had referred explicitly to a sexual affair that would necessarily have constituted adultery and not to Bachmann's broader notion of "relationship." In fact, Graef claimed that Judge Bachmann had specifically asked him if he had *seduced* Bertha—a version of events that Bachmann rejected out of hand. Meanwhile, an associate judge from the Hammermann trial testified that Graef had openly discussed his gifts to Bertha during his testimony, thus lending some support to Graef's version of events.[2] This dispute, of course, was far from trivial. The case against Graef now hinged on the precise definition of the word *relationship* (*Verhältnis*) as it had been used in the Hammermann trial. Graef still maintained that there had never been any sexual contact with Bertha. However, if jurors believed that he could have reasonably interpreted "relationship" to refer only to specifically adulterous behavior, namely intercourse, then they would still have to acquit him of perjury even if they believed that inappropriate but "nonadulterous" sexual contact had indeed taken place.[3]

Even more critically, when grilled by Graef's primary defense attorney, John Simson, the judges or lawyers from the Hammermann case could not state with unanimity whether this key question had been phrased in the present or past tense. This was also an essential point. If the question had been phrased in the present tense and there was no *ongoing* relationship with Bertha, then Graef would technically not have committed perjury. To make things even more confusing, Antonie Hammermann's former defense attorney insisted that it was he, not the trial judge, who had asked Graef the critical questions about a relationship with Bertha. He also claimed to have used the word *seduced* in his question to Graef—exactly as Graef had remembered. In exasperation over all of these conflicting statements, Judge Müller summoned additional witnesses who had been present at the Hammermann trial—only to reveal even more contradictory accounts. Without a transcript of the proceedings to verify any single version, the court was left with a rather muddled story.[4]

After the final verdict had been reached, criticism in the German press on this issue was withering, and many newspapers scathingly described the spectacle of conflicting testimony by judges and lawyers as a farce and a public embarrassment. For many critics, however, this was not just a minor legal issue that could be remedied by more careful recordkeeping; it was tied to systematic and fundamental flaws in the German criminal justice system. There was considerable disagreement about the causes of this dysfunction; almost everyone, however, seemed to agree on one thing: the existing law codes were utterly inadequate to deal with the problems facing German society.

NEW CODES, NEW PROBLEMS

The law codes functioning at the time of the Graef trial were of recent origin. The Criminal Code (*Strafgesetzbuch*), enacted soon after German unification, was derived directly from the former Criminal Code of the North German Confederation, which in turn had been based largely on the earlier Prussian Criminal Code of 1851. The Code of Criminal Procedure (*Strafprozessordnung*), which contained the practical guidelines for prosecutions along with the rights of defendants, was created in a longer process after unification and was finally enacted with a new Code of Civil Procedure (*Zivilprozessordnung*) as part of the German Justice Laws of October 1879. All of these law codes were deeply influenced by liberal views about crime and punishment that had been dominant in Germany since the middle of the nineteenth century, and they were designed to move the country solidly on the path toward becoming a *Rechtsstaat*: a nation whose administration was based on values of uniformity, regularity, and certainty in decision-making.[5] In this new *Rechtsstaat*, the administration of justice would be governed by the "rule of law," which would ensure that all citizens would not only be equal before the law but also would have guarantees against governmental caprice.[6]

On the surface, then, these new law codes appeared to signal a triumph of liberal bourgeois principles that aimed at a broader inclusion of the general public in the justice system as a bulwark against state power and the influence of aristocratic elites. Two key principles of this reformed criminal justice system were *Öffentlichkeit* or "openness," a requirement for most court proceedings to be open to public viewing and participation, and *Mündlichkeit* or "orality," a reliance on oral rather than written testimony in the courtroom. From the beginning of the century onward, liberal legal reformers had pursued both greater public participation in the justice system—including the adoption of a system of jury courts—and greater openness for criminal trials themselves. These twin meanings of legal *Öffentlichkeit*, public participation and an open courtroom, were viewed as essential reforms in that they could prevent abuses of power by a judiciary composed mostly of landed elites. A public trial proceeding could potentially serve an educative function as well: many liberal legal theorists argued that opening criminal trials to public observation (and reporting by daily newspapers) could serve to morally educate ordinary citizens by demonstrating both the inner workings of a courtroom and the potential consequences of violating the law.[7]

These new law codes, however, were not enacted without serious resistance, and they enjoyed very little of what we might call a "honeymoon" period. In fact, the new law codes were fiercely attacked by a wide variety of critics almost from the moment they were first passed. Socialists, for example, considered the legal reforms of the 1870s as half measures at best, which promised equality before the law but in reality merely provided a thin facade for a system of "class justice." This kind of argument would be implied by the Socialist leader Wilhelm Liebknecht as he stood trial for treason in 1872, and then made even more forcefully and systematically by his son Karl Liebknecht in a famous speech thirty-five years later.[8] Many liberal observers were also frustrated with reforms they felt were incomplete, and which left in place a system that still favored state interests more than the rights of ordinary citizens. In 1882, for example, the Berlin lawyer Gustav Kauffmann founded the Association for Legal Protection and Justice Reform (*Verein für Rechtsschutz und Justizreform*), an organization intended to draw both experts and laymen into the campaign for further legal changes, including reductions in court costs, limitations on prosecutorial powers, a broadening of the appeals process, and an expansion of the kinds of cases that would be brought before jury courts.[9]

Even high government officials frequently complained that reckless reforms and wrongheaded compromises within the new Penal Code and Code of Criminal Procedure had now led to confusion, inconsistency, inefficiency, and widespread frustration within the criminal justice system. For example, while many legal officials outside of Prussia were unhappy with having to adjust to norms adopted from Prussian statutes, many Prussian jurists believed there had been entirely too much compromise with the legal traditions of other states. In summing up his own dissatisfaction, the Prussian justice minister, Heinrich von Friedberg, wrote to Chancellor Otto von Bismarck lamenting that "the Imperial Justice Laws of 1879 took much away from us Prussians that had served us well before, and in some areas the achievement of legal unity was acquired at the expense of introducing legal norms into our land that both laymen and jurists view as regrettable, and as a serious deterioration of our previous circumstances."[10]

There were also more complicated reasons for wariness about liberal reforms—even among liberal jurists themselves. Alexandra Ortmann's recent book, *Machtvolle Verhandlungen* (Powerful Proceedings), makes a convincing case that enthusiasm about principles such as an open courtroom, open admission to the bar, and trial by jury had begun to wane as early as midcentury among many liberal legal professionals, and such enthusiasm had all but disappeared by the end of the century.[11] Ortmann suggests that most liberal reformers at the beginning of the century associated "the public" with a predominantly bourgeois public sphere. By the time of German unification, however, this public was now more frequently identified as an uncultured, ignorant, and potentially dangerous working class. Whereas liberal reformers early in the century were committed to democratizing the legal institutions of Germany, Ortmann suggests that by the time of unification there were growing calls among both liberal and conservative jurists to prevent such institutions from being compromised or corrupted by the uneducated masses.

Thus, alongside Socialists and left-liberals who claimed previous legal reforms had been only superficial and incomplete, there were also a significant number of conservative critics, high justice officials, and bourgeois jurists who worried that recent reforms had seriously weakened the criminal justice system and opened it up to new dangers.[12] The Graef trial in 1885 would provide the perfect vehicle for critics of all stripes to voice their fears and grievances. The most prominent debates focused particularly on three issues: an increase in perjury cases and the ineffectiveness of legal oaths, disagreements on how the government should deal with obscene images and texts, and the potential risks and benefits of maintaining an open courtroom. These debates were not limited to legal specialists; they also took place in the political press and in full view of a public that was keenly attuned to problems within the criminal justice system.

IN THE THROES OF PERJURY FEVER

As we know, the prosecutor in the Graef trial, Max Heinemann, suggested in his closing argument that he may never have filed charges against Gustav Graef for the sexual molestation of underage models if not for the fact that perjury had also been committed.[13] While this statement offers some insight into the relative unimportance of sexual violations against poor young women in German society, it also provides evidence of the deadly seriousness with which prosecutors viewed the sanctity of the oath itself. In a society where masculine honor was so valued, it is not surprising that a case of alleged perjury committed by a well-known and respected gentleman would create outrage. However, Heinemann's comment to the jury was undoubtedly also motivated by a growing panic about the number of perjury cases flooding German courtrooms. Just a few years earlier, German officials and politicians began voicing concern about excessive numbers of perjury cases across the country. An 1883 article from the liberal *Vossische Zeitung*, for example, referred to a "perjury fever" (*Meineidsfieber*) that had been plaguing the court system of Frankfurt. The newspaper argued that since the only crimes that were more serious than perjury were perhaps murder and arson, substantial reforms would have to come soon.[14] Anxiety also reached the German Reichstag and the Prussian House of Deputies, which debated the possible causes of this epidemic almost as intensely as the potential solutions. In any legal system, oaths to tell the truth are intended to be sacred; in an overtly religious and honor-obsessed society such as Imperial Germany, this was especially so. A charge of perjury, therefore, was exceptionally grave because it suggested a lack of honor and, at least implicitly, a transgression against the God to whom the oath was sworn. It was generally agreed by all stakeholders that something needed to be done.

It is not surprising, therefore, that the Graef case would help to reignite both internal government discussions and public debates about this apparent epidemic of perjury cases. For those who believed that Gustav Graef had indeed committed perjury, such as the prosecutor Max Heinemann, a prosecution was absolutely necessary to defend the standards of honor that were fundamental both to the justice system and to the maintenance of the social order. To fail to prosecute Graef for perjury would not only allow a violation of the law to go unpunished, it might also help reinforce the notion that such sacred oaths could be violated without consequence.

But if perjury was a real concern, why had no record been made of Graef's original sworn testimony in the Hammermann case? Some observers blamed the increased emphasis on the legal principle of orality (*Mündlichkeit*). In Prussia earlier in the century, it had been common for witnesses to have their testimony recorded in writing, after which they would have a chance to review these written statements for accuracy before swearing that their testimony had been truthful. Oral arguments by attorneys and oral statements by witnesses could still play an important role in those cases, but they were primarily used to clear up vagueness or inconsistencies within the written record. In both the new Code of Civil Procedure and the Code of Criminal Procedure, however, it was now oral testimony that took center stage while written evidence was relegated to a subordinate role. The greater emphasis on oral proceedings seemed to make a detailed trial transcript less practical and less necessary, and judges frequently interpreted §273 of the Code of Criminal Procedure as requiring the verbatim recording of witness statements only in special circumstances. This, of course, proved to be catastrophic for the prosecution in the Graef case. Without any written record of exactly who had asked Gustav Graef the key questions in the Hammermann trial or what specific wording or tense they used in asking him, there was relatively little hope for a perjury conviction.

Ironically, the Prussian Justice Ministry had been worried about the accurate recording of witness statements even before the Graef trial. In December of 1882, the Prussian justice minister, Heinrich von Friedberg, had issued a general order (*allgemeine Verfügung*) pointing out the difficulties that often arose when key sworn testimony was not recorded. In fact, formal legislation to remedy this problem had been included in a series of legal reforms proposed by Otto von Bismarck just a few months before the Graef trial. In particular, these reforms would have required that jury courts carefully record the most important points in witness testimony and also would have given all trial participants the right to clarify the trial record and to demand that a more detailed protocol be recorded.[15] When the proposed 1885 legal reforms stalled in the Reichstag, however, this particular legislation stalled as well. In the wake of the Graef trial and the wave of public criticism that came after, the best that von Friedberg could do was to issue another decree in November 1885 that once again strongly reminded judges to diligently enter the essential content of all sworn testimony into the trial record.[16]

Meanwhile, several newspapers put forward additional ideas for restoring the sanctity of the oath, which was seen as having been damaged by the flood of perjury cases. These suggestions did not include the idea that prosecutors should ignore minor cases of potential perjury; they instead focused on eliminating some of the circumstances in which perjuries were most likely to occur. A few weeks after the Graef trial, for example, the conservative *Dresdner Nachrichten* chimed in from Saxony to suggest that the best solution for reducing the number of perjury cases was for judges to avoid administering "unnecessary" oaths that might (accidentally or willfully) be violated and thus *require* eventual prosecution.[17] The key here is that the law did not threaten punishment for false testimony as such but only for the violation of the oath, which was still considered a sacred and quasi-religious ritual.[18] The goal of the *Dresdner Nachrichten* editors, therefore, was not specifically to ensure more truthful testimony in court—although that would have been a worthy goal—but to protect the sanctity of the oath by limiting its administration to instances where it was absolutely necessary for the proceedings.[19]

Other critics pointed to additional problems with the use of the oath. Meyer Heckscher, in his legal commentary on the Graef case, suggested that Gustav Graef had been put in an untenable situation by being asked to testify about an alleged extramarital affair. Before Gustav Graef was questioned, he had been repeatedly advised by Judge Bachmann that he had the right to refuse to answer questions about any extramarital affairs based on §54 of the Code of Criminal Procedure—which allowed witnesses to refuse to answer questions that might incriminate them. This law applied to Graef because any admission of a sexual liaison with Bertha Rother could have subjected him to prosecution for adultery. Heckscher argued that the legal protection of §54 here was not sufficient to serve its original purpose. If Graef had refused to testify and invoked the protection of §54, he suggested, it would have naturally led observers to assume that an adulterous relationship had actually taken place. Thus, while perhaps saving him from the threat of prosecution for adultery, a refusal to testify would have subjected him instead to public dishonor. What should such a man choose, Heckscher asked his readers, "perjury or dishonor?"[20] His solution to this conundrum was an extension of legal protection for witnesses. In a society where personal honor is sacred, he argued, witnesses should be allowed to refuse to testify not only if their testimony could lead to potential prosecution, but also if it might lead to their own dishonor or to the dishonor of family members.[21] Heckscher, of course, did not pay as much attention to protecting the honor of alleged victims of sexual abuse in this case—something that is not entirely surprising. Although legislation in Germany today protects the alleged victims of physical and sexual abuse from any questions that might unfairly target their private lives or lead to their dishonor, those laws were not enacted until the 1970s, almost a century after the Graef trial.[22]

These are only a few examples of what was a very robust and complex debate about the oath. Critics also suggested measures ranging from changing the timing of the oath to altering the nature of the ceremony used to administer the oath to increase its solemnity.[23] Although reform recommendations varied, there was general agreement that the oath as it was had ceased to function effectively. Perjury, that most grievous violation of honor, was now running rampant. Ironically, despite all the energy and hand-wringing expended on these debates, both in public newspapers and specialized legal journals, concrete changes to the administration of the oath did not take place during this period.[24]

ART AND OBSCENITY

In October of 1972, almost ninety years after the end of the Graef trial, the local historian Kurt Pomplun published an article in the *Berliner Morgenpost* that briefly summarized the case.[25] This article was part of a regular feature called "Houses and Their History," and it was printed alongside an old photograph of the building at Lützowplatz 10, where Gustav Graef and his family had once lived. The headline of Pomplun's article emphatically referred to the Graef case as Germany's first "porno trial," a description that, although inaccurate, is not entirely surprising. The Graef trial itself, of course, was not directly about pornography, but about alleged perjury and sexual exploitation; there is good reason, however, for Pomplun's confusion. At the time of the Graef trial, there was substantial concern about the public display and sale of reproductions of Gustav Graef's nude paintings, which were often available for purchase alongside ordinary photographs of Graef and his model, Bertha Rother. Displays of these images prompted demands for a government crackdown, especially by the conservative and Catholic press.

Prussian police officials had struggled mightily to combat the spread of obscene texts and images throughout the nineteenth century, and especially since the Revolution of 1848.[26] More than twenty years before the Graef case, the Prussian Minister of Culture (*Kultusminister*) Heinrich von Mühler had complained bitterly about an increase in inappropriate photographs displayed in the windows of Berlin bookstores and art dealers, a trend he attributed to the new availability of stereoscopic imagery for public consumption.[27] Over the next two decades, these concerns only intensified as cardboard-backed "art cards" (*Kunstkarten*) became increasingly popular. Such cards were revolutionary in that they made reproductions of classical artworks available at a reasonable price to the general public. They were also seen as dangerous for the same reason: now potentially salacious images (including both pornography and classical female nudes) would be available to people who lacked the refinement and cultivation to distinguish fine art from smut. The widespread circulation of these art cards was unsettling enough; however, the public display of such cards in the front windows of bookstores and art shops would prompt an ever-increasing number of complaints to police authorities.[28]

The law that prosecutors usually relied on for such cases was §184 of the Penal Code, often referred to as the obscenity statute, which threatened a stiff fine or a jail sentence of up to six months for the public sale, display, or distribution of lewd literature, pictures, or illustrations. In 1878, the Minister of the Interior, Botho Graf zu Eulenburg, responded to multiple complaints about the public sale of obscene literature and images by sending out a decree to all provincial and regional government officials urging them to crack down on such activities. In his decree, Eulenburg bemoaned the fact that the obscenity statute might not be up to the task and suggested that "experience has shown us that the prosecution and suppression of such literature and images is made more difficult by the fact that there is a significant amount of latitude in determining what exactly is considered 'lewd' [*unzüchtig*]. There are a variety of people, therefore, who would like to see this provision amended or strengthened."[29] Despite the potential weakness of the obscenity statute, Eulenburg insisted that government officials, prosecutors, and police should act quickly to bring charges against those who engaged in the display of vulgar imagery—even sending a public message by appealing cases that didn't end in convictions.[30] It is not completely clear how successful this campaign against obscenity was; however, a report submitted eight months later to the Interior Ministry claimed that eight men had been convicted under the obscenity statute in five separate prosecutions—just in the city of Königsberg alone.[31]

The issue of the public display of lewd images once again came to the attention of the Interior Ministry in 1881, when Berlin police-president Guido von Madai sent a query to the new Prussian interior minister, Robert von Puttkamer. Like his predecessors, Puttkamer was intent on curbing obscene images and literature, and he suggested to Madai that there might actually be a broader range of legal tools available to help get the job done. In a decree sent to the Berlin Police-Presidium on May 9, 1881, Puttkamer proposed that if a court was reluctant to find a work or image obscene in violation of §184 of the Penal Code, police might instead be able to rely on other, more flexible statutes such as §10, part II, title 17 of the Prussian General Code or ALR (*Allgemeinen Landrecht für die preußischen Staaten*). This particular statute, from a law code that had been enacted more than a century earlier, granted police broad authority to prevent any threats to public safety or breaches of the public peace. The law thus gave police the power to intervene in cases where the display of particular images might cause a public disturbance, while at the same time sidestepping the question of what might constitute "lewdness" or obscenity. Of course, this law left the question of what might count as a "threat to public order" up to the discretion of local police officials.

Puttkamer also mentioned a third statute, §68 of the Law on the Organization of the General State Government of July 26, 1880 (*Gesetz über die Organisation der allgemeinen Landesverwaltung vom 26. Juli 1880*), which allowed police officials in certain circumstances to use either the threat of fines or outright force in order to carry out their duties. In his decree, Puttkamer did not try to tease out specific guidelines about when police should act, except to refer generally to displays that violated a sense of public decency. He did add, however, that "a public nuisance will be considered a given in cases where pictures are arranged or grouped in a way that seems designed to inflame sexual feelings in viewers."[32] This was an explicit reference to recent decisions by the Supreme Court (*Reichsgericht*) in Leipzig that defined as obscene "anything that offends the public's sense of modesty and shame [*Schamgefühl*] in a sexual sense."[33] While such a definition allowed for wide discretion in whom or what the authorities might choose to prosecute, it did not necessarily solve the problem of defining obscenity—only shifting the uncertainty instead to the question of what exactly constituted an injury to "public modesty." In dealing with the aftermath of the Graef trial, these vague legal

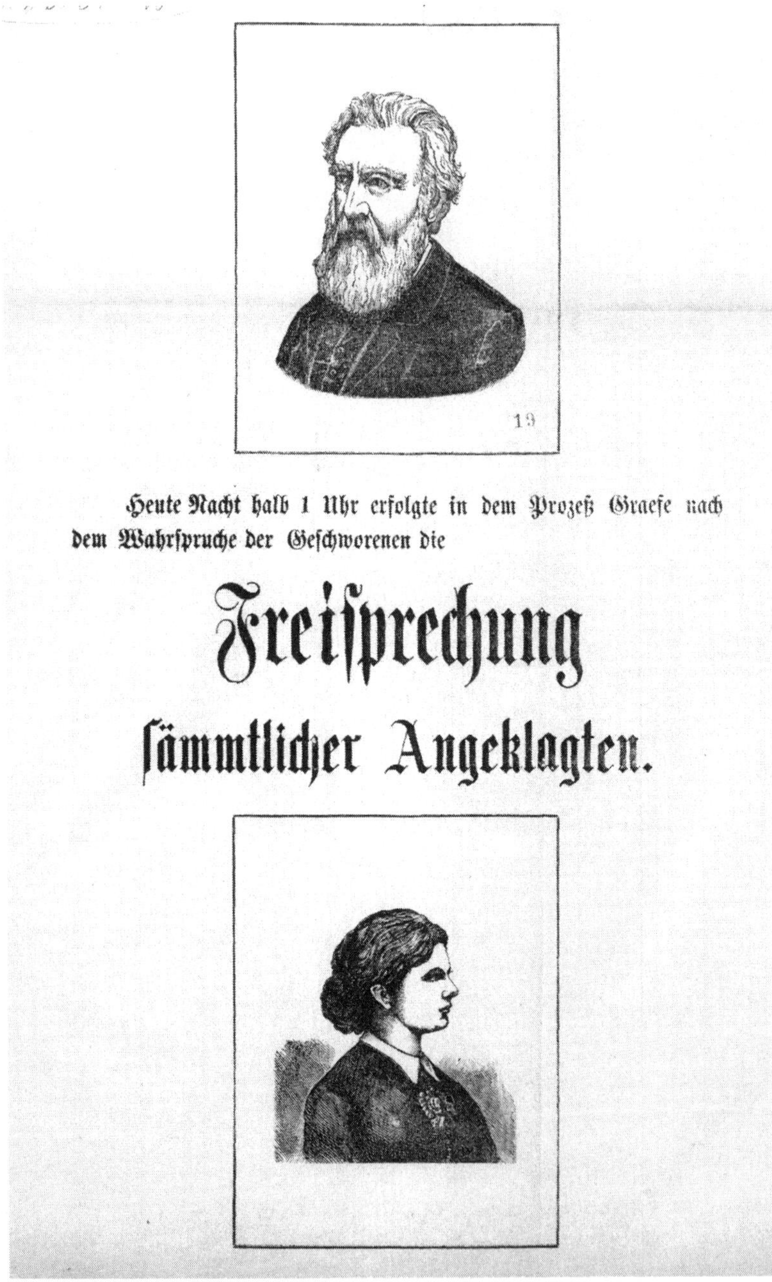

FIGURE 15. A flyer from the Schulze publishing house reporting the trial verdict. It was found in police records. With permission from the Landesarchiv Berlin (LAB A pr. br. rep. 30 Berlin C, nr. 14751, 19).

definitions would be put to the test, as would the legal tactics of Interior Minister von Puttkamer and Police-President von Madai.

As I described in chapter four, sensational coverage of the Graef trial helped to produce an intense public obsession over images of Bertha Rother. Even before the verdict was announced, Berlin book and art dealers stocked their shop windows with photographs and sketches of Bertha, as well as art cards featuring Graef's paintings *The Fairy Tale* and *Félicie*. These public displays attracted crowds of onlookers, and sales were reportedly so brisk that new art cards were often hastily and poorly composed in a rush to keep up with demand.[34] This public obsession drew the ire of those who thought the fascination with nude images of a known prostitute was a clear sign of cultural degeneracy. The Catholic *Germania*, for example, commented sarcastically that it could only find a few local art dealers that had not stooped to placing art cards of *The Fairy Tale* or photographs of Graef and Rother in their store windows. The editors singled out one particular Berlin shop owner who had not lowered his own moral standards for a quick profit, and they suggested that readers should spend their money only in this kind of "Christian" business.[35]

Police were also concerned. On October 8, the day after the verdict, the Berlin Police-Presidium sent out a telegram to all police officials ordering that any pamphlets or flyers sold on the street that featured images of Bertha Rother or Gustav Graef were to be confiscated immediately. The telegram was careful to add that this was *not an act of censorship*, and that no copies were to be confiscated directly from publishers or booksellers. The order was justified simply as an attempt to avoid the "ugliest of public scenes" (*einem Unfug gröbster Art*), which had already been reported in different parts of the city.[36]

Not everyone was satisfied by police actions. The Catholic *Germania* and ultra-conservative newspapers such as the *Reichsbote* were incensed by what they perceived to be a half-hearted and inconsistent response to the situation by the Berlin Police-Presidium. From their perspective, some pamphlets were being banned but not others, just as some art cards featuring Graef paintings seemed to have been confiscated while others had been left untouched. As a contrast, the *Germania* pointed to a much clearer and stronger reaction by Police-President von Brandt in Hannover, where the cult of Bertha Rother had also spread. Brandt had sent an open letter to a local newspaper, the *Hannover'sche Courier*, angrily denying that he had allowed the public display of reproductions of the Graef nudes. In this letter, he insisted that in his opinion, no nude images should ever be considered acceptable for public display:

> From my point of view, no photographs, copies, or even original works of art that contain nudity should be displayed publicly in shop windows—even if those artworks are by the great master artists of the past—and no such displays will be tolerated by the police. . . . The Graef pictures include the naked bodies of two female figures, in part standing and in part lying down, and their public display will be banned not only on the grounds stated above, but also particularly because it has become common knowledge through the Graef investigation that the paintings in question are portraits of the debauched prostitute Bertha Rother.[37]

The *Germania* used Brandt's public statement as a direct challenge to local authorities: "What do the Berlin police have to say about this? Is there a different moral code in the capital of the Reich than there is in Hannover?"[38]

The simple answer to this question was yes. What the *Germania* perceived as a lack of concern by police officials was defended by members of the Berlin Police-Presidium as a more thoughtful and nuanced response that took into account both existing legal precedents and concerns about public order. In a long report to the Prussian interior minister, Robert von Puttkamer, the acting police-president of Berlin, *Oberregierungsrat* Otto Friedheim—writing as a proxy for the retiring police-president Guido von Madai—directly responded to the accusations made by the *Germania*. Friedheim explicitly rejected the suggestion by Police-President Brandt of Hannover that all artwork that featured nudity must be kept from public display regardless of artistic quality. He argued instead that the Berlin police had closely followed Puttkamer's own decree of May 9, 1881, and acted based on their own sense of whether the images being displayed would likely be considered a violation of the obscenity statute (StGB §184). Friedheim then provided his own analysis of the two images being most widely circulated on art cards: Graef's *The Fairy Tale* and *Félicie*. Despite the fact that both paintings depicted nude women and that both figures were modeled at least in part on Bertha Rother, Friedheim suggested that the paintings represented very different levels of artistic value. As he stated in his report:

> Despite the nudity of the main figure, *The Fairy Tale* is a modern artistic work that portrays a perfectly-formed female body in an ideal, pure, and noble manner, and the position of the nude figure does not seem especially designed to provoke sexual arousal in viewers. The figure in the painting *Félicie*, on the other hand, is positioned and drawn in such a lewd and lascivious manner that it seems especially designed to elicit sexual arousal, and therefore to create a public nuisance. Based on this view of

> the artistic character and moral worth of the two above-mentioned paintings, and based on your decree of May 9, 1881, I decided to order that the public display of reproductions of *The Fairy Tale* was to be tolerated, while any photos of *Félicie* were to be immediately confiscated by the vice squad.[39]

Friedheim added that neither the fact that Bertha Rother had become infamous because of her role in the Graef case, nor the fact that she had been a prostitute under police supervision, nor the fact that she had now apparently returned to a sinful lifestyle in Berlin, had led him to change his own opinion about the best approach to these images. In order to reassure his supervisor, Robert von Puttkamer, that he was not being too lax in preventing possible public disturbances, Friedheim added that extra police officers had been put on guard in key places, and he announced that any art cards with Bertha Rother's name printed directly next to her nude painted image were to be confiscated immediately.

Friedheim's delicate distinction between classical nudity and vulgarity in the two Graef paintings was consistent with the newest legal scholarship on defining lewdness. Three years earlier, for example, Professor Karl Binding at the University of Leipzig had advised that "if the [text or image] is aimed at the sexual arousal of the reader or viewer . . . only then is the text or image immoral—otherwise it is not."[40] Of course, this definition did not necessarily make such decisions easier or prevent outside criticism. We should note, for example, the contrasting opinion offered just a few years earlier by the art critic Adolf Rosenberg (see chapter one), who had denied that *Félicie* was a scandalous or provocative image and described it instead as the childlike and innocent countenance of the young woman lost in graceful reverie.[41] One can imagine both Friedheim and Rosenberg agreeing with the American justice Potter Stewart's famous comment eighty years later about the nature of obscenity: "I know it when I see it." Even for the most discerning viewers, it seems, obscenity, like beauty, is in the eye of the beholder.

Otto Friedheim's attempt to distinguish the artistic value of the two paintings was also complicated by a similar case in Cologne that was already attracting significant public attention across the country. Five months before the Graef trial, in May of 1885, the police-president in Cologne, Wilhelm von König, received multiple complaints about the public display of small terracotta statuettes in the Langfeld'schen Book and Art Store in the center of the city. König ordered the store owner, Alexander Ganz, to remove these artworks from his window since they were creating a public nuisance in the busy Schildergasse shopping area. Ganz refused, claiming that the statues were miniaturized copies of master works by respected artists, including copies of the famous Danish sculptor Bertel Thorvaldsen's most popular works: *The Three Graces, Venus, Night*, and *Morning*. Police-President König refused to back down, and he told Ganz that the statuettes were especially inappropriate since their terracotta color mimicked the actual color of flesh. After repeated warnings, König finally ordered officers to forcibly remove the figures from the store, and he asked prosecutors to file charges against Ganz under the obscenity statute. Local prosecutors refused his request. Apparently, they were convinced of the artistic merit of these statuettes, and perhaps the high price of these items also persuaded them that the display was intended for artistic appreciation and not public titillation. At the same time, the store owner, Alexander Ganz, filed his own complaint with the Royal Government of Cologne (*Königliche Regierung zu Köln*) in which he claimed that the police confiscation of the statues had been entirely unwarranted and had hurt his business. Government officials agreed with Ganz—a conclusion that further infuriated Police-President von König.

At the end of July 1885, König submitted his own protest against the decision of the government of Cologne directly to the Prussian minister of the interior, Robert von Puttkamer. This was not simply the product of philosophical disagreement or personal resentment; it was also clearly part of a turf battle in Cologne. In his complaint, König ridiculed the idea that there must be a presumption of criminal behavior by the bookstore owner before police officials could take action, and he cited both the local *Rheinischen Ressort-Reglement* and the Prussian General Code (ALR)—the last of which Puttkamer himself had formerly cited as a potential tool against obscene images—as explicitly guaranteeing police authorities the right to intervene if they perceived a threat to public order. Since, in his opinion, these artworks offended a public sense of modesty, this was more than enough cause to assume a threat to public order also existed. Puttkamer eventually rejected König's complaint; however, the exercise was not a total loss. Although the Cologne government stood behind their rejection of any prosecution of Ganz under the obscenity statute (StGB §184), they did admit that police had a right to preemptively act against potential threats to public order. Thus, they suggested that if König felt he had sufficient cause to file charges against Ganz for a disturbance of the peace (*grober Unfug*) under §360, part 1, no. 11 of the Penal Code, they would not stand in his way.[42]

What followed was a rather surreal prosecution of Alexander Ganz for disturbance of the peace, argued before the Cologne Court of Lay Assessors on November 24, 1885—less than six weeks after the end of the Graef trial. Its surreal nature stemmed from the fact that the prosecution and defense attorneys seemed to be arguing entirely different issues. Prosecutors justified their charges of disturbing the peace against Ganz by arguing that the figures were displayed on one of the busiest streets in town and very close to two different schools. Not only were the schoolchildren spiritually and morally corrupted through their viewing of the figures, it was suggested, but even many upstanding adults who passed by had to turn away from the window in disgust.[43] The defense responded by defending the artworks as perfectly acceptable and not in any way obscene—an argument that might have been more powerful if Ganz was actually charged with obscenity under §184 of the Penal Code. Defense attorneys called three art experts to testify to the artistic value of the pieces, and they also pointed out that the same artworks were sold across Germany without any objections. The attorneys described the case as unreasonable artistic censorship, and they suggested that a guilty verdict against Ganz would necessitate the removal of famous paintings from museums and the covering of numerous outdoor classical sculptures with fig leaves. All of this argument about artistic value went for naught. In a verdict that was noted by newspapers across the country, including back in Berlin, the judges convicted Ganz and sentenced him to a fifty-Mark fine.[44] The verdict itself noted that a disturbance of the peace had been proven by the testimony of witnesses and police officials, and such things as the reputation of the artist, the quality of the artworks, or the fact that such works had been exhibited elsewhere in Germany were irrelevant to the case. Instead, the only factors that judges could consider were the actual effects that the display in question had on the local populace.[45] Two well-publicized appeals of the Ganz case were unsuccessful.[46]

The handling of the Ganz case points to another common approach to obscene materials by German authorities, what the historian Gary Stark has called the idea of "relative obscenity." During the Imperial Period, both jurists and police authorities came to view obscenity as not necessarily inherently tied to the nature of a work, but instead to the way it was presented and to the audience for which it was intended.[47] A sketch of a nude female figure, for example, was perfectly acceptable as an aid to training new artists inside a painter's studio; the same drawing, however, could be considered obscene if it were passed around a neighborhood tavern. The key here was purpose and audience: in the first case, the image was a tool to build artistic skill that transcended any prurient interest in the figure; in the second case, the image was intended to provoke the basest instincts of the untrained and uncultured. This approach to obscenity explains what otherwise seems to be a truly hypocritical and contradictory policy: the idea that a display of Thorvaldsen's sculptures in a museum was a celebration of free cultural expression, while the display of reproductions in a public shop window—especially colored in terra cotta—was a clear danger to public order.[48] One should notice, as Gary Stark rightly points out, the class distinctions inherent in this definition of "relative obscenity." While an image might be deemed as valuable if shared within cultured circles for "higher" purposes, it was much more likely to be characterized as obscene if it was available to a general audience—and more specifically if it was available to uncultured and unsophisticated populations such as women, children, and members of the working classes.[49] Not surprisingly, legal approaches to obscenity during this period gradually came to reflect a deeply embedded sense of class prejudice and a fear of social outsiders.

Meanwhile, back in Berlin, the craze over *The Fairy Tale* and *Félicie* had not yet diminished. The painting *Félicie* had been purchased by the art collector Louis Simon in Hamburg, who wrote almost immediately to the Royal Academy of Arts to ask if they would make gallery space available in Berlin for the painting's display. Not surprisingly, Simon's request was refused.[50] Simon also sent a formal request to the new police-president of Berlin, Bernhard von Richthofen, for permission to exhibit his new acquisition. At about the same time, a collector named Otto Kaufmann in Potsdam also contacted Richthofen for the same kind of permission for his newly purchased painting, *The Fairy Tale*. Richthofen responded by rejecting both of these requests outright. Unlike Friedheim before him, Richthofen did not justify his decision with a lengthy analysis of the artistic value of the two paintings. He simply issued a decree banning either of the two collectors from displaying their paintings in the city.

Like the bookseller Alexander Ganz in Cologne, Otto Kaufmann refused to idly accept this ruling. Kaufmann immediately filed a protest with the governor (*Ober-Präsident*) of the province of Brandenburg, and when this was rejected, he submitted a formal complaint to the Superior Administrative Court (*Oberverwaltungsgericht*) in Potsdam in January of 1886. Kaufmann's argument was simple: it was impossible for the Berlin police to define the exhibition of a recognized artwork like *The Fairy Tale* as a threat to public order, especially when during the Graef trial itself police had decided to *allow photographic reproductions of the same image* to be displayed in storefront windows across the city (based on the order of acting police-president Otto Friedheim). In those bookstores, Kaufmann argued, art cards featuring the Graef paintings had been offered for sale alongside actual photographs of the trial participants in order to make them seem especially titillating. All he wanted to do, he suggested, was to exhibit a collection of serious works of art, displayed behind closed doors in a respected establishment, with absolutely no connection to the Graef trial. The mere fact that Bertha Rother was the model for the painting could not empower the police to ban it from being exhibited. Finally, Kaufmann suggested in his complaint that this ban would mean that "police officials could now decide in an arbitrary way, based on their own whims and without relying on any specific law, to intervene in a business enterprise and interfere in the private use of property whenever they so wished."[51]

The Superior Administrative Court rejected Kaufmann's complaint, and it upheld the decision to forbid him from exhibiting *The Fairy Tale* under §10.17.II of the ALR—the section that gave the police powers to protect public order. In their decision, the judges rejected the idea that Richthofen had made an arbitrary judgment about the quality of the artwork or the guilt or innocence of the artist involved. It was obvious, they claimed, that many viewers would be attracted to Kaufmann's exhibit not for the love of art, but because of the notoriety of this particular model and the potential arousal that might come from the viewing of her naked body. The judges also added that Bertha Rother was still living in Berlin and drawing attention to herself—a fact that suggested there was good reason for police to fear that the exhibit could cause a public disturbance. The court refused to acknowledge any precedent set by earlier police tolerance of photographic reproductions of *The Fairy Tale*. The only thing for them to decide here, the judges claimed, was the facts in this particular complaint.[52]

Otto Kaufmann did not relent in his efforts to display *The Fairy Tale* in Berlin, but even three years later the ban was still firmly in place. Finally, in 1888 both Kaufmann and the new owner of *Félicie* sent separate letters to Police-President von Richthofen, and to the new interior minster Ernst Ludwig Herrfurth, which again begged for the chance to display their paintings in Berlin. Although a significant amount of time had passed since the end of the trial, Police-President Richthofen was still adamant about maintaining the ban. It was true that Bertha Rother had left Berlin by this time; however, Richthofen suggested that she was still a common topic of discussion—especially since news of her impending marriage to the son of a wealthy Viennese industrialist had spread throughout the city. His superior, Minister Herrfurth, however, thought that these concerns were perhaps a bit exaggerated, and he pressed Richthofen to change his mind. After an exchange of letters, Richthofen finally relented, and both paintings were allowed in the city.[53] There is no record of any public disturbances caused by the first displays of Graef's work in Berlin. By the time these exhibits opened, police were more concerned about the appearance of other images in book and art-store windows, including photographs of the beautiful Baroness Marie Veczera, who had recently died as part of a murder-suicide pact with her lover, Crown Prince Rudolf of Austria.

So what can we conclude about this rather complex series of events? In one sense, this story helps to demonstrate what Gary Stark argued in his wonderful 2009 book *Banned in Berlin*: namely, that censorship in Imperial Germany was not always the simple story of a rigidly conservative police state cracking down on liberal artistic freedom. As we can see here, there was often inconsistency and internal disagreement about when and how the government should intervene. In some cases, conservative government officials at state or local levels could act aggressively to prohibit things they found objectionable. In other cases, they refused—much to the chagrin of segments of the conservative and Catholic press. It is also true here, as Stark argues, that when police or prosecutors did choose to intervene, they could use broad powers and even laws *not* explicitly dealing with censorship to do so.[54]

Despite conservative complaints, and despite considerable dissatisfaction among many police and justice officials, there were no real attempts in the aftermath of the Graef case to pass new legislation against the public display of art cards or to stifle the distribution of obscene works. Only a few years later, however, the public uproar surrounding a sensational murder trial (the Heinze case), and the activism of a new young kaiser who was determined that his government should rein in obscene literature and imagery, would lead to more systematic efforts to revise the law. Those efforts would eventually culminate in the so-called *Lex Heinze*, a topic to which we will return a bit later in the chapter.

CLOSING THE COURTROOM

Of all the legal controversies debated in the aftermath of the Graef trial, the one that provoked the most widespread consternation was the decision by Judge Boguslaw Müller to close the courtroom to the public and yet still allow court reporters to attend the trial and publish detailed accounts in the daily press. Almost all of the postmortem reports on the Graef trial expressed astonishment at this ruling. Not everyone agreed, however, on what should be done to prevent this kind of farce in the future. While some observers sought explicit legislation to limit public (and especially press) access to sensitive trials, others were more protective of the principles of a free press and an open courtroom. Once again, the public debates would be fierce in both the Reichstag and the press, and the path to forging new legislation would be long and complex.[55]

Here, as in the case of debates about the oath and about obscenity, class prejudices and conceptions of bourgeois masculine honor would be central to the public discourse. As Alexandra Ortmann has argued, the concept of legal openness (*Öffentlichkeit*) had been a key principle of liberal legal reformers throughout the nineteenth century. By the time of unification, however, "the public" for many bourgeois jurists had gradually come to describe a population whose education and level of civility was incomplete, and who were therefore naïve, vulnerable, and easily corrupted.[56] This broader public, which included women, children, and men from the lower classes, required guardianship by their social betters and also a rigorous protection from a sensationalist and manipulative press. In sum, this impressionable and malleable public now needed to be protected both from the salacious details of sensational trials and from those journalists who used such trials to appeal to the basest of human instincts.

Why, then, did Boguslaw Müller allow the press into the courtroom in the Graef case? As the judge took great pains to explain during the trial itself, he believed he had sufficient legal grounds to close the courtroom and still allow press representation. Müller had ordered the general public to be excluded under §173 of the German Court Organization Law (*Gerichtsverfassungsgesetz* or *GVG*), which gave judges the discretion to close trial proceedings in cases where public order or public morality was threatened.[57] Section 176 of the same code, however, granted the lead judge the power to allow specific individuals access to a closed courtroom—although the law gave no specific guidance on how broad or how limited those exceptions should be. Thus Müller apparently decided to close the courtroom as a matter of decorum, but he allowed entry to journalists in the general interest of openness and transparency. This was a decision that Müller very quickly came to regret. His long speech to the jurors denouncing press coverage of the trial was not simply a knee-jerk attack on a sensationalist press, it was also an attempt at self-defense that he knew would be read (or heard) by his own superiors. In this speech, Müller claimed he had made his ruling because he believed that press coverage of high-profile criminal cases was essential to protect public confidence in the justice system (*öffentliche Rechtsbewußtsein*), and also because he had trusted that these reporters and editors would act professionally. It was the improper, dishonorable, and ungentlemanly behavior of individual journalists that had created the public controversy, therefore, not his own decision to admit those reporters into the courtroom.

Ultraconservative newspapers such as the *Kreuzzeitung*, which were otherwise quite supportive of Judge Müller, suggested that he had been extraordinarily naïve about the possible consequences of such a ruling. As this newspaper put it:

> This exclusion of the public was purely a symbolic measure, at least compared to what we would ordinarily assume such an exclusion to mean. Regular exceptions were made . . . not simply for people against whom one could hardly raise any objection, such as those who had a scientific or psychological interest in the proceedings, or even a few carefully chosen upstanding gentlemen for whom an exposure to the sexual filth of such a trial would not pose a real danger. No! Exceptions were made for exactly the kind of people who make a living by spreading those things that should normally be kept behind closed doors: namely, court reporters employed by the press.[58]

Several prominent jurists weighed in publicly and echoed the sentiments of the *Kreuzzeitung*. Otto Mittelstädt, a judge at the Supreme Court in Leipzig, ridiculed Müller's decision in a long critique of the trial published in the prominent journal *Preußische Jahrbücher*. Common sense, Mittelstädt suggested, would demand that if any class of people were restricted from the courtroom, it should be members of the press:

> They desired absolutely nothing more or less than to carry out the profession by which they live; they wanted to quickly turn what they heard in court into readable newspaper articles, and then through the daily press to scream out their accounts, just as a seller in the marketplace or as a call to prayer from church towers, *urbi et orbi*, in a manner best designed to attract the most attention possible. If this kind of publicity was acceptable and innocuous, then why all the secretiveness and the closing of the courtroom?[59]

It was especially naïve, according to Mittelstädt, for Müller to suggest that he had relied on reporters to self-edit the most salacious testimony. Such editing, he suggested, could be even more dangerous than verbatim transcripts since any gaps, euphemisms, and circumlocutions would only provoke readers to rely on conjecture or their own lecherous imaginations. For both Mittelstädt and the *Kreuzzeitung*, then, journalists—and especially liberal journalists—could simply not be trusted to act properly in fulfilling their important social role.

Even many liberal newspapers that ordinarily defended freedom of the press and the principle of legal transparency agreed that scandalous trials such as the

Graef case could be a clear danger to the public. The *Frankfurter Zeitung*, a very successful paper affiliated with the fringe left-liberal German People's Party, staunchly reaffirmed its support for the principle of an open courtroom and for the specific right of court reporters to have access to trials; the principle of openness was essential, as the newspaper put it, because it "placed an additional judge above the presiding judge in the case—namely, the conscience of the people."[60] The *Frankfurter Zeitung* also suggested, however, that judges must remember that "the public" is not constituted by the few idlers and "students of criminality" who regularly attend court proceedings because of their addiction to scandal, but instead by hundreds of thousands of newspaper readers as well as their families and friends. The *Frankfurter Zeitung* suggested, therefore, that closing the trial to the public must also mean shutting out the press, and the newspaper argued that no one would have faulted Judge Müller for excluding reporters, especially since the principle of openness was already protected by the panel of lay jurors who would decide the question of guilt or innocence.[61] Apparently for the *Frankfurter Zeitung*, the potential benefit provided by public oversight of the legal process in such cases could not outweigh the potential damage caused by public exposure to indecent subject matter.

Of course, not everyone believed that the exclusion of court reporters would be in the public interest—even for cases as salacious as the Graef trial. The left-liberal *Berliner Börsen-Courier*, one of those organs commonly targeted for their sensationalized trial commentary, argued that allowing reporters inside the courtroom was not only constitutionally protected but also in the best interests of the nation.[62] An open courtroom, the newspaper asserted, had often aided in the search for truth, and press coverage had long proven useful in explaining convoluted legal questions to the public, encouraging a better understanding of the legal code and even serving as a deterrent to criminal behavior. "The newspapers could do without transcripts of trial proceedings," the *Börsen-Courier* claimed, "and they would do without them if the government insisted on restricting or controlling them . . . it is rather the interests of the state which cannot be served without such publically available trial transcripts."[63]

Certainly, government officials were attuned to this debate; however, it is not entirely clear if formal legislation would have made any progress if another legal crisis had not come along. In late 1885, Christian von Sarauw, a military historian and former captain in the Danish Army, was arrested and charged with treason for allegedly bribing German military officers for access to sensitive documents that he then passed on to the French. Sarauw was tried and convicted in February of 1886 and sentenced to twelve years of hard labor. The press coverage of the

Sarauw trial had greatly concerned Otto von Bismarck and his son Herbert, who at the time was serving as the state secretary of the Foreign Office. In a letter to Hermann von Schelling in the Imperial Justice Office, Herbert von Bismarck complained that although the Sarauw proceedings had been closed to the public, detailed reports on the evidence had still appeared in the press after the trial. The published information was specific enough that a key witness, who had testified only on condition of anonymity, was easily identifiable even without his name being explicitly mentioned.[64]

The source of the problem was a loophole in §174 of the German Court Organization Law, which explicitly required that all trial verdicts be delivered publicly. When this law had first been proposed, there was a debate about whether it should pertain to the simple trial verdict itself, or also to the legal grounds (*Gründe* or *ratio decidendi*) for the decision—a long written summary of the evidence and all relevant legal paragraphs. Before unification, most German states had only required the publication of the simple verdict form; however, after contentious negotiations during the 1870s, the Reichstag insisted that in the interests of openness the new law should also make the grounds for a verdict a part of the public record. At the time, a Reichstag Committee suggested that individual judges should be able to compose the *ratio decidendi* in a clever enough manner to avoid releasing any sensitive information. It was not the job of lawmakers, they concluded, to sacrifice a basic principle in order to account for the potential lack of skill of individual judges.[65] In other words, even in closed proceedings, judges had a legal obligation to make detailed information about the trial evidence public; if the judges happened to include sensitive information divulged during the trial, that information was now in the public domain and the press could obviously not be prosecuted for printing it.[66]

This situation was clearly unacceptable. Herbert von Bismarck advised Schelling that new legislation should be drafted quickly which removed judicial discretion about attendance of "outsiders" in closed trials, required the appointment of specially approved lawyers for defendants in cases of treason, established an oath of silence for all participants in a trial involving state secrets, and held out the threat of severe punishment for any press reports on such sensitive cases. Bismarck believed these changes were a matter of national security, and he instructed Schelling to push new legislation through the Reichstag as quickly as possible.[67] Schelling, however, worried that some of Bismarck's proposals were either unnecessary or would provoke too much opposition within the Reichstag. Eliminating a defendant's choice of counsel in cases of treason, for example, or excluding his family from the entire proceedings might be perceived by some legislators as too heavy-handed. Schelling also suggested making exceptions to allow scientific or criminological experts access to trials that were otherwise closed. Finally, Schelling also pointed out one way that the proposed restrictions on the press should be *expanded*. As he saw it, this was an opportunity to make headway not just against irresponsible press reporting on trials that involved military secrets, but also cases where sensational trial reporting could violate a sense of public shame and decency as well—especially for proceedings such as the Graef trial.[68]

Herbert von Bismarck agreed to many of Schelling's changes, and after some additional tinkering, a package of legal reforms entitled "The Law Regarding Court Proceedings Closed to the Public" was passed through the Bundesrat and sent to the Reichstag on May 18, 1886.[69] This proposal sought four major changes:

1. It would now be required that judges make the verdict form (*Urteilsformell*) public, but not necessarily the detailed grounds for the verdict. (Change in §174 GVG)
2. Judges could now require participants in trials that involved a danger to national security to swear an oath to keep the proceedings (or portions of the proceedings) secret. Violation of this oath was punishable by fines of up to 1,000 Marks or up to six months in jail. (Addition to §175 GVG and a new free-standing Article II)
3. Judges would no longer have an explicit right to make exceptions for the attendance of nonparticipants in a closed trial, although a specific exemption was added for those government officials who had a supervisory responsibility for court officials. (Change to §176 GVG)
4. Journalists would now be forbidden from publishing any reports on trials that had been closed to the public. Violation of this law was punishable by fines of up to 1,000 Marks or up to six months in jail. (Free-standing Article III of this law)

Despite the acute concerns expressed by government officials about threats to national security, this new law proposal was not discussed on the floor of the Reichstag during the summer of 1886 nor after it was reintroduced by Schelling during the following session in December. One must remember that the Reichstag majority at this time was fairly antagonistic toward the policies of Otto von Bismarck. In the federal elections of 1884, the left-liberal *Freisinnige* Party, one of Bismarck's main antagonists, had lost a substantial amount of seats (from 106 to 67), while the friendlier German Conservative Party had seen the largest electoral gains (from 50 to 78 seats). The Conservatives, however, were still not able to hand Bismarck an easy majority for legislation—even when they cooperated with their most likely allies, the Free Conservatives (28 seats) and National Liberals (51 seats).[70] The biggest obstacle for Bismarck was now the Catholic Center Party, which controlled a very large bloc of 99 seats. Still stinging from the impact of Bismarck's *Kulturkampf* legislation of the 1870s, the Center Party was often wary of the chancellor's motives and could not be counted on as a reliable partner. Over the next several years, therefore, Bismarck was continually frustrated by his inability to get key legislation passed.[71]

Many members of the Reichstag, including both liberals and members of the Catholic Center Party, were actually quite sympathetic to the idea of tightening up the legal code to protect national security; there was, however, deep suspicion about government motives and a firm commitment to the principle of an open courtroom. Most conservatives could be counted on to support the new law, but other legislators were wary that broad labels such as "national security" (*Staatssicherheit*) and "morality" (*Sittlichkeit*) might be used to restrict public and press access to a broad range of trials and thus effectively vitiate the principle of an open courtroom. Socialists and Catholic politicians were especially vigorous in their opposition to this legislation, in part because both groups had a long history of facing government prosecution. In fact, at the same time the Graef trial was commencing in Berlin, several Socialist leaders, including August Bebel, were standing trial in the city of Chemnitz for allegedly participating in a meeting that violated the Anti-Socialist Laws. The Chemnitz trial resulted in an acquittal for all defendants and a sensational public relations victory for the Socialist Party. Protecting public and press access to such trials was thus understandably a vital priority for the Socialists, especially since an acquittal (or even a conviction) in a court of law could provide a valuable propaganda opportunity.[72]

It is also important to note that earlier in 1885, Chancellor Otto von Bismarck had proposed a separate slate of legal reforms that would have limited both the size of juries and the range of trials that could be held before them. These reforms, Bismarck had claimed, were intended to aid the efficiency of the criminal justice system. They were instead seen by many critics in the Reichstag as a rather brazen attempt to remove laypeople as a potential complicating factor in obtaining verdicts that were reliably favorable to government prosecutors. That legislative proposal ran into substantial opposition and stalled in the Reichstag in mid-1885. It is no surprise, then, that this new "Law Regarding Court Proceedings Closed to the Public" was met with equal suspicion a year later. Although Schelling, as head of the Imperial Justice Office, repeatedly insisted that this new law would not endanger legal openness but merely make existing statutes more enforceable, his critics viewed this proposal as something potentially far more sinister.[73]

While the new legislation was stalled in the Reichstag, debates about it continued both in the press and within the legal community itself. In June of 1886, a judge at the Berlin District Court named Hermann Jastrow gave a lecture on the new proposal in the Berlin *Juristische Gesellschaft*, which he later published as an essay in a specialized legal journal.[74] Jastrow argued that in trials that involved sensitive military information, it made perfect sense to have all participants swear to keep the proceedings secret and also to ban the press from reporting significant details of the case. The problem with the new law proposal, he suggested, was that it sought in a heavy-handed manner to restrict access to *all* trials that had been closed to the public. First of all, Jastrow suggested, not all trials that are closed to a public audience must inherently be off-limits to press reporting. There were many reasons for closing a courtroom—including disruptions in the audience or attempts to influence witnesses—that didn't necessitate either shutting out the press or keeping the grounds for the verdict secret. Secondly, passing a blanket restriction on who can attend a closed proceeding would necessarily exclude social scientists, doctors, and others for whom the trial might be instructive and beneficial. And finally, a ban on all reporting about closed trials would also prevent acquitted defendants from regaining their public honor. In a society where honor was paramount, Jastrow argued, it was not sufficient for a defendant accused of grave crimes to have proven his innocence if that proof was kept secret. Without a right to proclaim his vindication in a pamphlet or through the press, the acquitted defendant would be powerless to completely remove the injury to his honor inflicted by the charges against him.[75]

Jastrow acknowledged that the breadth of the new legislation was sparked by the unseemly behavior of some newspapers during the Graef trial. However, he suggested that this could all have been prevented if Judge Müller had chosen to exclude the press—a decision that had been entirely within his power. After Müller's experience, Jastrow claimed, judges would now undoubtedly be more mindful about limiting press access to such scandalous cases. New legislation to restrict press access was thus unnecessary and might actually do more harm than good.

Jastrow did, however, suggest one other means for limiting press reporting that transgressed the moral norms of society. He pointed to existing laws that pertained to public nuisances, including blasphemy in public (§166 StGB), animal cruelty (§360 StGB), and lewd behavior (§183 StGB). Jastrow saw no reason why a clause could not also be added to the Penal Code restricting press reporting that created a public nuisance. He even suggested a wording for such a law:

> Those who publish reports in the press about court proceedings that were closed to the public, and who do so in a manner designed to create a public nuisance will be . . . punished. However, publications by trial participants that are released after the end of the proceedings and seek openly to defend rights or exercise legitimate interests will not be subject to this regulation.[76]

Although Jastrow's speech and subsequent article were aimed particularly at jurists, his conclusions were discussed in the general press as well, including a review in the *Hamburger Nachrichten* that urged lawmakers to follow his advice in rewriting the government's law proposal.[77]

Meanwhile, both the chancellor and his son were seething over the delay in passing this important legislation. In a stern letter to Schelling, Herbert von Bismarck pointed out that while the proposal was floundering in the Reichstag, several other treason cases had been heard at the Supreme Court in Leipzig, and detailed press reports on these cases had once again divulged state secrets for everyone to read. As an example, Bismarck attached a page-long article from the *Berliner Börsen-Zeitung*. This article described the treason trial of one of Christian von Sarauw's confederates and summarized all of the evidence against him, including information about a secret factory that manufactured the ignition devices for torpedoes, the existence of a special new sealing cap for an underwater torpedo bay, the methods used by the German Navy to lay sea mines, and the fact that the navy had conducted tests of particular ships to gauge their seaworthiness when partially flooded.[78] Since all of this information had been included in the legal grounds that substantiated the verdict, there was no explicit legal restriction on its publication.

Schelling introduced his legislation into the Reichstag once again (for a third time) on March 18, 1887. Interestingly, he chose to begin his reintroduction of the bill not with a call for urgent action to protect military secrets, but with a not-so-subtle reference to another kind of case still apparently fresh in the public mind:

> First of all, the public has developed such a fondness for reading about interesting court cases that even the most respectable newspapers can't free themselves from the compulsion to write about them. However, this desire for sensation is no longer

> hidden behind closed doors; it instead seeks new kinds of stimuli to help achieve its satisfaction. I need only refer here to the lessons of that widely-discussed case from one and one-half years ago which came before the local *Landgericht*, which I only mention here as evidence of the irresistible nature of public curiosity once it has been aroused.[79]

Schelling said he sincerely wished that §184 of the Penal Code, the "obscenity paragraph" that banned the sale or distribution of obscene books and images, could be applied to newspaper reports as well. He lamented, however, that the obscenity statute was designed only for the most extreme examples of moral decadence. Only after this long discussion about press reports on morally repugnant trials did Schelling move on to talk about the recent treason cases and the grave danger to national security posed by press reports on closed treason trials.[80]

It is important to note that the makeup of this new Reichstag was considerably different than it had been during previous sessions. First of all, the National Liberals, under the leadership of Johannes Miquel, had been drifting steadily to the right since 1884 and now firmly supported Bismarck's major priorities—including protectionism, anti-Socialist legislation, and state intervention in the economy.[81] Secondly, Otto von Bismarck had dissolved the previous Reichstag and used the saber-rattling rhetoric of the French war minister, Georges Boulanger, to attack German opposition parties for refusing to finance a military buildup. His strategy worked. In elections that February, the National Liberals increased their share of the eligible popular vote from 11 to 18 percent and the two conservative parties from 13 to 19 percent. This resulted in an overall increase of about seventy seats in the Reichstag for these three parties—enough to secure a majority if members of the three parties worked together.[82] Thus, in this new Reichstag, Bismarck could more confidently hope to build a majority among a "*Kartell*" of Conservatives, the Free Conservatives, and the National Liberals without having to rely on support from the Catholic Center Party.

Despite a potentially more receptive audience, the "Law Regarding Court Proceedings Closed to the Public" still encountered substantial resistance. Even after serious revisions in committee, the proposal still garnered over a dozen significant amendments when it came to the full Reichstag. Some of these amendments even came from members of the so-called Kartell parties, including the National Liberals and Free Conservatives—groups that were normally expected to support government initiatives. Clearly, significant numbers of delegates even from these "loyal" parties still worried that the legislation went too far. Not surprisingly, therefore, the law proposal languished once again and remained unpassed at the end of a third consecutive Reichstag session.

In the meantime, Herbert von Bismarck complained bitterly to Schelling about yet another treason trial that had once again yielded embarrassing and potentially damaging information through the press.[83] Bismarck now instructed Schelling to do whatever was necessary to get the essential parts of legislation through the Reichstag immediately, including fully accepting almost all of the changes offered by the previous Reichstag committee and even adopting further amendments proposed by the National Liberals. Bismarck's hope was to attract enough support from the National Liberal and Catholic Center parties to push the legislation through over opposition from leftist parties. Schelling agreed, although he also argued that Conservative members of the Reichstag would be displeased since they strongly favored press restrictions in cases involving morality and would be unhappy with any further watering down of the proposal.

In December of 1887, Schelling brought a revised bill to the Reichstag floor that was very close to the previous Reichstag committee version. The new proposal won over many critics in the National Liberal Party but not enough to prevent it from being once again sent to committee for a thorough reworking. The new committee suggested a number of changes, some major and some minor. For example, the committee accepted the government's insistence on a blanket ban of press reports on closed trials that dealt with matters of national security. However, instead of accepting the government's proposal of judicial discretion on banning the press in cases involving moral issues, the committee turned instead to amendments previously offered by the National Liberal deputy Wilhelm Kulemann and the Catholic Center Party deputy Viktor Rintelen. These amendments adopted an idea first put forward by Hermann Jastrow: to forgo a new press law for trials dealing with moral issues and instead add a new clause to the obscenity statute (§184 StGB) dealing specifically with egregious press coverage of sensational trials. The paragraph suggested by the committee read: "The same penalty [as for the distribution of obscene literature or imagery] applies to those who publicly report on trials that were closed to the public on the grounds of a danger to morality, or who report about official documents that pertain to such a case, in a manner that is likely to cause a public nuisance."[84] The Reichstag committee defended this change as a more effective method of cracking down against the excesses of the press while avoiding unnecessary restrictions on the right of "responsible" journalists to report on trials in a reasonable manner. Judges could still choose to close the courtroom if they felt the matters at hand were too salacious; however, journalists would not be precluded from reporting on such trials, and they would only be vulnerable to prosecution if their reportage on such cases was later judged to be beyond the pale.[85]

Once the overall proposal returned to the Reichstag floor, the legislation was picked apart once again in several contentious days of debate. One more significant change was approved from the floor. August Munckel, a well-known defense lawyer and left-liberal *Freisinnige* deputy, once again insisted that publication of the full legal grounds for a verdict (*ratio decidendi*) should be the norm, unless a judge explicitly decided that such information posed a threat to either national security or public decency. This amendment, which was similar to one proposed by the Free Conservative Paul von Rheinbaben in a previous session, was now accepted by the Reichstag.

After these changes, the National Liberals finally expressed their support for the new law. Wilhelm Kulemann, the chief National Liberal spokesman on legal issues, defended the law as a necessary balance between legal openness, freedom of the press, and the good of the nation. He insisted that the new laws would only restrict press access to a small number of very sensitive cases, and he chided opponents of the legislation for seeking to adhere obsessively to legal abstractions such as the principle of an open courtroom (*Öffentlichkeit*) without regard to practical considerations. Kulemann also stressed that the revised legislation had largely restored judicial discretion on questions of public and press access to closed trials except when national security was at stake. This, he suggested, should allow for much greater confidence in the independence of the courts—unless, of course, one was already convinced that judges themselves were criminals just waiting for their chance to abuse their judicial power behind closed doors.[86]

Members of most opposition parties still rejected the legislation, and they accused the National Liberals of abandoning their core principles. Speaking for the Socialists, Paul Singer claimed it would be a simple matter under existing law to close courts to public access in cases of a real danger to national security or public morality; he argued, however, that the sweeping legislation under consideration—even in its watered-down form—was designed primarily to restrict press access to a broad range of political trials, especially those targeting the Socialists. As proof, Singer pointed to an offhand comment made by a representative from the Bundesrat, Paul Kayser, which suggested that threats to national security (*Staatssicherheit*) that might serve as excuses to close the courtroom and ban the press could be either "external" or "internal" in nature. Singer used this statement to rebuke the National Liberals, whom he accused of continuing to voice their commitment to an open courtroom and freedom of the press even as they sacrificed those very ideals.[87]

Attitudes were more mixed within the Catholic Center Party. While some delegates, such as Viktor Rintelen, seemed to be supportive (at least initially), other Center Party leaders, such as Ludwig Windthorst, were adamantly opposed to the legislation. Windthorst dismissed government assurances that the new laws would not be a violation of the principle of legal openness. Instead, he suggested that they were a direct attack on the foundations of the modern legal system and a first step toward instituting a form of Star Chamber in Germany.[88] The left-liberal *Freisinnige* Party expressed similar grounds for their continued opposition. As the deputy Alexander Meyer argued: "In certain circumstances, legal openness (*Öffentlichkeit*) may lead to difficulties; however, under any circumstances, attempts to restrict openness always prove to be the greater evil."[89]

Despite this vigorous opposition, the approval of the National Liberals (in cooperation with the Conservatives and Free-Conservatives) made passage of the revised law a fait accompli. The "Law Regarding Court Proceedings Closed to the Public," which included what might be referred to as a "Lex Graef"—an obscenity law dealing with salacious press coverage of closed trials—passed the Reichstag and went into effect on April 5, 1888.

FROM LEX GRAEF TO LEX HEINZE

Not surprisingly, the 1888 law did not herald the end of debates about restricting press coverage of controversial trials, but only the beginning. On September 28, 1891, exactly six years after the opening of the Graef trial, another sensational trial which would eventually have even greater legal repercussions would take place in the same Berlin courthouse. The new case involved murder charges against the twenty-seven-year-old Gotthilf Heinze and his forty-two-year-old wife Anna for killing a night watchman named Friedrich Braun in September of 1887. The defendants were already well known to police at the time, and they had very long criminal records that included theft, fencing, embezzlement, forgery, counterfeiting of coinage, assault, and rape. The couple were also involved in procuring (pimping) and prostitution, with Anna Heinze having forty-four previous arrests for moral offenses alone.

Like the Graef trial six years earlier, the Heinze case had attracted considerable public attention even before the start of the proceedings. Faced with the prospect of a packed courtroom that included members of the press, and a case that was sure to delve deeply into the salacious details of the criminal underworld of Berlin, Judge Otto Rieck consulted carefully with the prosecution about whether or not to close the trial to both press and public. Rieck announced his decision in court: in the interests of protecting public confidence in the justice system (*öffentliche Rechtsbewußtsein*), he would allow the courtroom to remain open to the public. He did, however, politely ask members of the press to maintain a sense of decency in reporting on the trial so as not to endanger public morality.[90] The consequences, at least in hindsight, were predictable.

The initial hearing of the Heinze trial lasted only four days before it was postponed indefinitely while the court summoned a witness from Chicago. These four days of sensational testimony, however, were enough to raise the hackles of many newspaper readers, including the young German emperor, Wilhelm II, who had assumed the throne three years earlier. The day after the trial was temporarily adjourned, Wilhelm had his adjutant send an urgent telegram to Berlin from his hunting lodge in East Prussia expressing his outrage at press reports on the disturbing details of the case. His telegram demanded immediate responses from the head of the Secret Civil Cabinet, Hermann von Lucanus, and the Prussian justice minister, Hermann von Schelling. Wilhelm wanted action, and he demanded not only the strict enforcement of existing laws but also the immediate drafting of new legislation that would target pimps, limit the distribution and display of obscene images and literature, and curb the excesses of the German press. The emperor would now take a direct personal interest in rectifying the problems in society and within the justice system that the Heinze trial had exposed.[91]

The Heinze case sparked what many historians have called a "moral panic" in Germany and began a decade-long public battle over the so-called Lex Heinze: a series of laws pushed by a coalition of "morality associations" designed to root out the moral corruption that was poisoning the social body.[92] Although the Heinze case was certainly a trigger for a more intense period of public (and parliamentary) debate about issues such as prostitution and obscenity, these concerns were not—as we have seen—altogether new. In fact, a number of these new morality associations had already begun to form in the years between the Graef trial and the Heinze case. Religious opposition to prostitution, for example, had begun to coalesce as a political force several years earlier. In 1885, Pastor Ludwig Weber had formed the West German Morality Association (*Westdeutscher Sittlichkeitsverein*) in Mönchen-Gladbach and two years later Wilhelm Philipps formed the Berlin Men's Alliance for Combating Public Immorality (*Berliner Männerbund zur Bekämpfung der Unsittlichkeit*), both of which were conservatively oriented morality associations with ties to Adolf Stöcker and his Berlin City Mission.[93] In 1888, these two groups and many others joined forces to form the General Conference of German Morality Associations (*Allgemeine Konferenz der deutschen Sittlichkeitsvereine*) under the leadership of Weber. This national organization was led primarily by Evangelical clergy, allowed only male members, and had strong support from the lower-middle classes.[94] Within a year of its founding, the General Conference included branch organizations in almost a dozen cities as well as links to City Missions, houses for "fallen women," and even associations for the rehabilitation of prisoners.[95] After the start of the Heinze trial, the General Conference issued a pamphlet entitled *The Struggle Against Immorality*, which demanded that prostitution be rooted out of German society and suggested that the nation would follow down the same decadent path that had destroyed Ancient Babylon, Greece, and Rome if the situation were not improved immediately. This pamphlet went through a first printing of 65,000 issues.[96]

At the same time, women were also becoming more vocal in debates about morality. In 1889, Hanna Bieber-Böhm founded the Association for the Protection of Youth (*Verein Jugendschutz*) in Berlin, which called both for an end to regulated prostitution and an improvement in the treatment of prostitutes within the existing system. Although their rhetoric and proposals differed from those of the morality associations, members of this group also tended to support efforts to improve morality among the German youth, especially poor young women who often turned to prostitution out of necessity.[97] These improvements would include education and housing programs for "endangered" women and the employment of female police officials and doctors to supervise them.[98]

These kinds of organizations, along with a loose coalition of conservatives, Catholics, and anti-Semites, pressured government officials to be more aggressive in prosecuting not only "filth" in the form of simple smut and pornography, but also a broader range of artistic and literary "trash" that violated moral standards. This meant combating literary and artistic naturalism, which continued to feature frank and open discussions of social conflict, human depravity, and worst of all, immoral sexual behavior.[99] Thus, the debates about the corruptive influence of naturalism, prominent in the aftermath of the Graef trial, would continue throughout the 1880s and early 1890s in regard to newer authors such as Karl Bleibtreu, Gerhart Hauptmann, and Hermann Sudermann.[100]

At times, this grassroots pressure could be quite successful, especially in encouraging crackdowns against salacious live theater performances, which German officials had always regarded as potentially more dangerous than the printed word.[101] In an infamous incident in October of 1890, for example, the Lessing Theater in Berlin had been banned from staging Hermann Sudermann's play *Sodom's End*. When the theater director appealed in person to Police-President von Richthofen about how he might alter the play to please censors, Richthofen, the same official who had gruffly banned the display of Graef's *Fairy Tale* and *Félicie* in Berlin for three years, dismissed the notion that any changes to the play would alter his decision. He simply replied to the director: "The whole direction [of the play] doesn't suit us!"[102] Sudermann's play featured a rather sharp attack on the morals of the upper class in Berlin, including rather frank portrayals of extramarital relationships. Perhaps coincidentally, one of its main characters, a young artist named Willy Janikow, is seduced by an older married woman named Adah Barczinowski, and the artist's obsession with her leads him to lose all creative power and eventually commit suicide. Despite the age reversal, some critics who saw the play would later compare Adah's character to Bertha Rother.[103] As in the case of Graef's paintings, von Richthofen's decision to ban the play was appealed to the Prussian justice minister, Ernst Herrfurth. After screening the play himself and insisting on some minor edits, Herrfurth approved it over Richthofen's objections. This time, however, an even higher authority became involved. Wilhelm II, the thirty-one-year-old emperor who considered himself a defender of traditional German art and culture, demanded an explanation from Herrfurth about how such a scandalous play could be approved. Despite the emperor's outrage and the protests and complaints from conservative Christian groups, the die was already cast. The play was performed in Berlin and in many other places around Germany.[104] This incident occurred more than a year before the start of the Heinze trial. Thus, the Heinze case did not occur in a vacuum but in an atmosphere where debates about a perceived crisis in German morality had been steadily intensifying since the end of the Graef trial.

While the legal reforms passed by the Reichstag after the Graef trial had been fairly limited—an addition to the obscenity statute dealing with press reports on closed trials—the legal reforms pursued by the government in the wake of the Heinze case would now be much more comprehensive. As a whole, the Lex Heinze proposal was intended as an offensive against three major sources of moral corruption in German society: pimps, pornographers, and the press. First of all, several revisions to the Penal Code (§180, §181, §181a StGB) were intended to strengthen punishments for pandering (increasing the minimum sentence from one day to one month) and to add especially harsh penalties for husbands who prostituted their wives (no less than one year of hard labor). Landlords who knowingly rented rooms for the purpose of prostitution were also subject to prosecution, although the *Bundesrat* insisted on an exception for those prostitutes who were under the supervision of police. Those defendants who were convicted of moral crimes were also now to be treated with much harsher sentences: the first Lex Heinze proposal even included a new paragraph (§16a StGB) that would subject the most bestial and immoral of criminals to hard beddings and a diet of bread and water for up to the first six weeks of their incarceration. This punishment was justified with the argument that pimps and other members of the criminal underclass often found the care and nourishment offered in prison to be superior to their ordinary life and thus no real hardship at all.[105]

A second target of the Lex Heinze was a strengthening of the obscenity statute (§184 StGB). Previously, most works considered obscene could only be confiscated (and their creators prosecuted) after they had first been printed and distributed. The proposed new law would be more proactive and more comprehensive. It entitled prosecutors to charge those who manufactured, stored, or distributed obscene literature, images, and drawings, and also those who advertised in publications seeking lewd relations. In addition, the text or image in question need not have been judged to be lewd (*unzüchtig*) to provoke prosecution. Texts and images that caused a public nuisance and violated a public sense of shame and morality could also be confiscated even if they were not considered lewd in and of themselves. Images displayed in public places—including art cards placed in the front windows of bookstores—could thus be prosecuted as a violation of obscenity laws even if the images themselves had never been judged to be obscene. As we have seen, police and prosecutors had previously relied on other laws dealing with "disturbances of the peace" to sidestep the requirement of proving that a text or artwork was obscene; now this legal "end run" would no longer be necessary since it would be an explicit part of the obscenity statute.

Finally, the Lex Heinze proposal also attempted to return to the issue of press reporting on sensational trials. The Lex Graef, the recently added part of the obscenity statute dealing with press reports on closed trials (§184 Abs. 2 StGB), remained untouched in the new proposal except for the fact that the penalties were raised slightly. In addition to the Lex Graef, however, the government now proposed a new addition to §173 of the German Court Organization Law. This law would give judges the option to restrict press reports about trials that involved moral issues—*even if those trials had not been closed to the public.* Although discretion for such restrictions would be left in the hands of judges and not government officials, this change nevertheless signaled a potentially dramatic limitation on freedom of the press to report on trial proceedings.

Predictably, a fierce battle ensued when the Lex Heinze came to the Reichstag for debate. Conservative and Catholic deputies, who now held just short of a majority of Reichstag seats, pushed for even more radical measures in committee discussions of the legislation, including another addition to the obscenity statute (§184b of the Criminal Code) that would have made it easier to prosecute those who staged theater performances that were offensive to the public. Under this committee proposal, any play that violated the public's sense of shame and morality could be prosecuted for obscenity *even if censors had allowed the play to be performed*. This proposal was very controversial and was rejected by the Reichstag committee in a very close vote.[106] The committee did, however, accept additional Center Party recommendations to raise the "age of consent" from sixteen to eighteen and to create a new law (§182a of the Criminal Code) that would protect working women from being sexually exploited by their employers.[107] When this revised legislation returned to the Reichstag floor, it again faced substantial resistance, and even the Imperial government itself was lukewarm about the changes that had been made. Debates on the Lex Heinze were eventually halted when the parliament was dissolved in May of 1893, and government officials, uncomfortable with the course of events, did not reintroduce the legislation in the following session. Despite the urgency of the emperor's original admonitions, therefore, this first attempt at a Lex Heinze did not create new law.[108]

The failure of the original Lex Heinze was only the first salvo in a legislative battle that would last through the turn of the century. Morality associations continued to push the government to reintroduce the Lex Heinze, and in the mid-1890s, the Reichstag was deluged with petitions about everything from ending government regulation of prostitution to suppressing newspaper ads for prophylactics. When the government and the Bundesrat ignored these petitions and refused to revive the Lex Heinze, leaders of the Center Party decided to take matters into their own hands. In December of 1897, several Catholic leaders, including Franz von Arenberg, Adolf Gröber, and Viktor Rintelen, proposed their own revised version of the Lex Heinze legislation. As the largest political party in the German parliament during the 1890s, the Catholic Center Party had substantial clout, and their new Lex Heinze proposal sought to include many of the controversial amendments to the original legislation that had helped cause it to stall in 1893. These additional measures included raising the "age of consent" from sixteen to eighteen, criminalizing the conscious spread of venereal disease, and most controversially a stronger paragraph on the censorship of theatrical plays and other public performances.[109] The new bill also carried forward controversial paragraphs from the original legislation that criminalized the renting of rooms to known prostitutes for immoral purposes and allowed prosecution of artists and authors for works that caused public offense—even if those works had not been formally censored. Emboldened by their own substantial political power, by a temporary alliance with conservatives and anti-Semites, and by the growing influence of morality associations and other conservative interest groups, the Center Party had now proposed legislation that was even more comprehensive than the first Lex Heinze and far more wide-ranging than most government officials were comfortable with.[110]

By the time this new and stricter version of the Lex Heinze proposal was introduced in 1898, however, a substantial parliamentary and public resistance to the bill had begun to form. Liberals and Social Democrats (whose party had been freed from the shackles of the Anti-Socialist Laws in 1890) vigorously opposed the legislation in the Reichstag and sought to use obstructive tactics to prevent it from passing. Meanwhile, a coalition of artists, writers, and publishers had joined with other members of the public to form the so-called "Goethe Leagues for the Protection of Free Art and Learning" (*Goethebund zum Schutze freier Kunst und Wissenschaft*) in at least a dozen German cities. The Goethe Leagues drafted petitions signed by leading artists and scholars, organized public rallies, and actively lobbied the federal government in opposition to the new laws.[111] This movement was fed by the growth of a more robust and self-confident cadre of literary and artistic naturalists, who bristled at attempts by cultural conservatives to limit works that were adjudged as unnecessarily salacious or subversive. These battles, of course, were in many ways extensions of the battles begun by Karl Frenzel and Max Heinemann in the wake of the Graef trial.

This time, however, the overall reaction of Berlin's artistic community was quite different. Not surprisingly, the impressionist painter Max Liebermann, who had only recently helped found the Berlin Secession, served as a leading member of the Berlin *Goethebund* and expressed his deep opposition to passages that seemed to threaten artistic freedom (especially §184 and §184a StGB). But Liebermann was far from alone. Among the vocal critics of the new legislation were also paragons of the old artistic regime, including Anton von Werner and Adolph Menzel. Despite their antipathy toward Liebermann and toward modernism in general, these artists worried that the proposed Lex Heinze would cut too deeply into artistic freedom. The Royal Academy of Arts, now led by the architect Hermann Ende, even submitted a petition to the Reichstag strongly opposing the new theater paragraph in the Lex Heinze.[112] Quite a bit had changed, apparently, in the decade since the Graef trial.

The Lex Heinze finally did pass into law in 1900, although in a modified form that many contemporaries (and modern historians) have described as a victory for opponents of the law rather than its supporters. The main achievement for those opponents of the Lex Heinze was the complete defeat of proposed new restrictions on theater performances. This particular paragraph (intended to be §184b StGB) had drawn the most ire from liberal and socialist delegates as well as from artists and intellectuals outside the parliament. Several other measures present in various versions of the Lex Heinze had also been dropped or softened. The draconian punishments for the most heinous offenders, for example, originally proposed under §16a of the Penal Code, had been abandoned long before; in fact, almost every law against the creation or distribution of obscene texts and images now included a specific clause allowing lesser punishments for mitigating circumstances. As for the Lex Graef—the part of the obscenity clause (§184 StGB) that threatened punishment for inappropriate reporting on trials involving sensitive moral content—it was now relabeled as a new §184b StGB, but otherwise left intact. Efforts by Catholics and conservatives to further restrict press reporting through an amendment to §173 of the German Court Organization Law had been scrapped.

Editorials, public complaints, and petitions to the Reichstag about the need to further restrict press coverage of sensational trials would continue throughout the course of the *Kaiserreich*. There was predictable consternation in 1907, during the so-called Eulenburg Affair, when a trial judge once again decided to close his courtroom to the public, while still allowing press representatives to attend and report explosive testimony about alleged homosexual trysts involving members of Emperor Wilhelm II's entourage. Both experts and lay critics decried the seeming incongruity of barring a few dozen local spectators for reasons of decorum and yet allowing an international audience to salivate over printed accounts of every sordid trial detail.[113] However, despite multiple mass petitions to the Reichstag demanding new legal restrictions on the press, no further legislation was forthcoming.[114] The Lex Graef would remain on the books not only through the remainder of Imperial Germany, but also through the World War, the Weimar Republic, the Nazi regime, and the first twenty-five years of the Federal Republic of Germany, before finally being stricken in 1973 and replaced by a law against child pornography.

What conclusions can we draw from this battle over the principle and practice of an open courtroom? There is no question that, as Alexandra Ortmann suggests, the Imperial German government attempted to use cases such as the Graef and Sarauw trials to restrict public and press access to certain criminal proceedings. There is also no question that both politicians and professional jurists from across the political spectrum were becoming increasingly concerned with the damaging influence of legal openness on the criminal justice system, especially in regard to the constant drumbeat of press coverage of various sensational *causes* célèbres. What is not entirely clear, however, is to what degree such concerns resulted in significant *actual limitations* on the openness of criminal courts. Although Ortmann does admit that the general principle of openness remained sacrosanct throughout the *Kaiserreich*, she also tends to emphasize the willingness of liberal politicians and jurists to compromise this principle when faced with concerns about the behavior of the press. Ortmann particularly identifies the 1888 "Law Regarding Court Proceedings Closed to the Public" as a key success in government efforts to close the courtroom for sensitive moral or political trials. The oath of secrecy and the banning of reportage for closed trials involving national security, she claims, were part of a planned government offensive to keep controversial political trials behind closed doors. "If one considers the fact that the original ideal of open courtrooms was implemented primarily to prevent arbitrary verdicts from being pronounced in political trials," Ortmann argues, "it is clear just how serious an attack this was against the foundations of this [legal] principle."[115] Ortmann also identifies the passage of §184b of the Penal Code—which I have described as the "Lex Graef"—as a serious curtailment of the freedom of newspapers to report on trials that involved a potential threat to public decency. Altogether, she insists, these laws demonstrate the degree to which the principle of legal transparency was already on shaky legal ground during this era.[116]

The evidence I have presented above, however, suggests a more nuanced interpretation. Firstly, while Bismarck and his ministers were certainly interested in using all possible means to limit public and press access to political trials, this was far from the only issue at hand during the consideration of this legislation, and the federal government was far from the sole driver in this political process. Although Bismarck's government did eventually get laws that tightened up legal loopholes, especially in limiting press reporting on cases involving national security, these measures passed only after substantial delays and significant concessions and revisions. Where Hermann von Schelling had tried to push a blanket ban on reporting about any closed trials, members of the Reichstag insisted on differentiated responses between trials involving national security and those that involved a danger to public morality. Even a friendlier "*Kartell*" Reichstag ended up passing a law that was substantially less restrictive—on either type of case—than Herbert von Bismarck and Hermann von Schelling had originally wished.

There were, admittedly, a few politicians in the debates on the 1888 law who openly questioned just how essential open courtrooms were to achieving just and fair verdicts; however, both government officials and even the most conservative of deputies repeatedly insisted that the principle of legal openness was sacrosanct and would not be substantially harmed by the proposed measures. These repeated government assurances were undoubtedly directed at the National Liberal Party in the hope of convincing them that the limited press restrictions at issue would not violate their core principles. Even if such statements were as much about pandering as principle, however, they are still a demonstration of just how embedded the ideal of legal openness was in Imperial German society.

In response to accusations that the National Liberals had abandoned their principles by backing the revised legislation, the deputy Georg Meyer countered that it was not they but the government that had been forced to make compromises: "Thus, gentlemen, the objections that I originally held [against the legislation] were not overcome by the fact that *I myself* was *won over to a new opinion* of the proposal, but because in the meantime *the Federated Governments* [a reference to the Bundesrat] undertook *a thorough reworking of the proposal.*"[117] It was clear, he argued, that the Bundesrat "had on many points come to adopt the points of view that were first expressed here in this house."[118] Georg Meyer's self-evaluation here does not seem entirely unreasonable. The changes forced on the government suggest a National Liberal Party that was far from powerless, feckless, or gullible. If National Liberals were keen to look for areas of compromise with the government, and if their nationalism made them relatively unsympathetic to Socialist claims that the new laws could be easily abused, it is also true that National Liberal resistance to the original government proposals seems to have been driven by a belief in the independence of judicial proceedings, the value of a free press, and the necessity for checks to government power. Deeply concerned about preserving the openness of legal proceedings and assuring the freedom of the press to report on trials, the National Liberals had joined with other opposition parties to repeatedly stymie restrictive legislation that the government deemed vital to national security. The compromises they forced were significant limitations on governmental power even if they did not preclude the government from manipulating the legal process against its political enemies in other ways. In the end, even if one still interprets National Liberal acceptance of the final law as a compromise of liberal principles (especially in the concessions made for trials regarding national security), it is clear that Bismarck's government was forced to compromise in important ways as well.

It is also worth noting that much of the new restrictions on public and press access to the courtroom contained in the 1888 law were left up to judicial discretion and not governmental fiat. One might interject here that this was an important victory for the National Liberals in that it left most decisions about press access to the courtroom in the hands of a largely bourgeois cadre of professional jurists, who may have assumed that as "experts" they were best qualified to properly regulate the principle of *Öffentlichkeit*. Certainly, for Socialists, who often viewed German judges as sharing the same elite social status and political priorities as the government, this was cold comfort. However, as the historian Benjamin Hett asserted in his book on criminal justice in the Wilhelmine era, it is difficult to argue that German courts went on to abuse the discretion stemming from this law.[119] Sensational cases such as the later Heinze trial and Eulenburg Affair clearly demonstrated that judicial discretion would continue to fall consistently on the side of maintaining openness—even for trials that were salacious or embarrassing to the government. Despite the continuing outrage at press coverage of such cases, further efforts to restrict press access or reporting on such trials were almost entirely ineffective.

It is also true that the Reichstag's approval of a "Lex Graef" in 1888 can in part be understood as a compromise offered by Catholics and National Liberals to prevent the possibility of far more powerful legal restrictions on trial coverage in the press, and as a measure that could in theory be difficult for justice officials to enforce—much less abuse. Prosecutors across Germany had long complained that obscenity charges were difficult to sustain in court and that "lewdness" was an almost impossible standard to define. Thus, the successful conviction of journalists for inappropriately lewd or sensational trial coverage *after the fact* promised to be a much more daunting task for public prosecutors than the *proactive* enforcement of a ban on all press accounts.[120]

We must remember, however, that the Lex Graef was not simply a reluctant compromise made under government pressure; it was a novel approach that reflected real and widespread concern in the aftermath of the Graef trial about the corruptive power of a sensationalist and potentially "obscene" press. While seemingly in conflict with general liberal ideals such as legal openness and freedom of the press, it should also be noted that this law was actually fairly consistent with liberal legal reforms from earlier in the century. As Sarah Leonard argues in her history of obscenity in nineteenth-century Germany, "the invention of obscenity as a distinct offense, separate from assaults on the state, the sovereign, and religion . . . happened in the decades before the Revolution of 1848 (the *Vormärz*), a period of liberalization and growing expectations for reform. These laws were not adopted by reactionary governments but by states whose population had recently achieved liberal concessions."[121] In other words, there had always been a tension within German liberalism between advocacy of legal openness and press freedoms on the one hand, and belief in the potentially harmful effects of obscenity and salacious press reports on the other. If the pendulum had perhaps swung toward the side of legal openness at midcentury, it was now perhaps starting to swing back in the other direction.

Ironically, Prussian justice officials had for decades been reluctant to pursue any revision or expansion of the obscenity statute to deal with the public display of lewd images—perhaps in part because of the anticipated difficulty of getting such changes approved in a hostile Reichstag. However, after Hermann von Schelling, the state secretary of the Imperial Justice Office, had bluntly dismissed the possibility of using an expansion of the obscenity statute to restrict the press, it was Catholic and National Liberal politicians—truly convinced that press coverage of salacious trials was a real danger to public morality—who pushed forward legislation to do just that.

CHAPTER SEVEN

POWER CONFLICTS IN THE COURTROOM

On the penultimate day of the Graef trial, a rather curious episode occurred in an anteroom just outside the courtroom. Although it received scant attention compared to the drama inside the court, it nonetheless offers a window into the profound tensions that existed within the legal profession at the time. Because of occasional disturbances during the trial, Judge Müller had ordered the general public to be restricted not only from the courtroom but from the hallways outside the court as well. On this day, a local lawyer named Dr. Matthias Quenstedt arrived on the scene and demanded access to an internal hallway in order to talk to a fellow lawyer. He was sternly rebuffed by a guard at the front entrance. Quenstedt, who had no connection to the Graef case, was livid. Although not as well known as other defense lawyers in Berlin, Quenstedt had previously served as a personal attorney for that great arch-nemesis of Bismarck, Prince Harry von Arnim, and he had also served as Arnim's legal and financial representative in Berlin once he left for voluntary exile in France. Quenstedt refused to take no for an answer. He first insisted he had to speak to his colleague, Wilhelm Kleinholz (who was one of Graef's defense attorneys), and then he simply pushed his way past the guard into the special lawyers' chambers (*Anwaltszimmer*) inside the courthouse. After being told of this incursion, Judge Müller stormed into the lawyers' chambers and demanded to know what made Quenstedt think he could violate a sitting judge's orders. According to the liberal *Berliner Börsen-Courier*, Quenstedt responded by physically confronting Müller in front of several other lawyers and screaming at him: "You are not my superior! We are equal factors in the court. You studied law and I studied law. What do you want in here? This is *our* room. You have nothing to say to me. That's my final word!"[1] According to reports, the stunned judge did not answer and instead quickly left the room. The *Börsen-Courier* claimed that at least one fellow attorney openly congratulated

Quenstedt and told him: "You have spoken up for all of us." In fact, a week later, the *Volkszeitung* reported that some Berlin lawyers had signed a letter to the Prussian justice minister, Heinrich von Friedberg, supporting Quenstedt and emphasizing their own authority (*Hausrecht*) within the lawyers' chambers.[2] In the aftermath of the incident, the *Berliner Börsen-Courier* strongly suggested that the Prussian Justice Ministry publicly comment on its interpretation of §177 of the Court Organization Law (*Gerichtsverfassungsgesetz*), which gave judges the right to keep order in the court, to explain just how far outside the physical courtroom those powers extended.[3]

Despite the public attention drawn by Quenstedt's actions, there is good reason to believe that he did not enjoy the full support of all of his fellow attorneys. In 1882, Quenstedt had been censured and fined 600 Marks by the Honor Court of German Lawyers for employing an untrained "hack lawyer" (*Winkeladvokat*) to pose as an attorney and attract new clients to his civil practice. Such hack lawyers were also known pejoratively as "people's lawyers" (*Volksadvokaten*), "agents" (*Agenten*), or even "counselors of lefts" (*Linksanwälte*)—a play on the common German term for private lawyers, "*Rechtsanwälte*" or "counselors of rights." These terms applied to a variety of lay lawyers, usually lacking any formal legal training, who waited in the halls of courthouses or in nearby taverns hoping to poach a few clients with promises of cheap and effective representation. The implication behind the labels was not only that such lay attorneys were insufficiently trained, but also that they tended to be unethical.

Winkeladvokaten, however, were not all scoundrels and hucksters. According to Alexandra Ortmann, informal legal advisers often played an important role in the justice system of Imperial Germany—especially in rural areas, where trained jurists were lacking. These lay jurists took a fee for legal advice, for composing legal papers, and for appearing as a representative in civil proceedings. They were organized as a profession, and by the end of the nineteenth century their guild had almost 8,000 members.[4] In crowded cities such as Berlin, on the other hand, where professional attorneys already faced substantial competition for business, such lay attorneys were viewed with utter contempt. Krischen—the infamous representative of Antonie Hammermann, who sought to squeeze Gustav Graef for money—was one such "agent," whom Paul Lindau, son of a former high justice official, had described at trial with appropriate disdain.

In associating with such ungentlemanly rabble, therefore, Quenstedt had been guilty of betraying his guild and aiding an illegitimate class of pretenders in stealing business from qualified lawyers. Reputable attorneys would likely have shunned Quenstedt, just as they tended to shun the *Winkeladvokaten* themselves. In addition to his previous censure, Quenstedt was also awaiting additional disciplinary hearings at the time of the Graef trial for the alleged overcharging and intimidation of clients as well as a case of improper behavior towards a young woman. Only a few months after his run-in with Judge Müller, Quenstedt was disbarred.[5] Quenstedt's confrontation with Judge Müller was, of course, a rather silly turf battle with no lasting impact on the Graef trial or on German legal culture. It does shed light, however, on just how intense conflicts over questions of class, status, and honor could be within the justice system.

In previous chapters I have made passing reference to a famous indictment of the Imperial German legal system delivered by the Socialist activist Karl Liebknecht in a 1907 speech. In this speech, made more than twenty years after the Graef trial, Liebknecht argued that despite all the public rhetoric about the "rule of law," the government of Imperial Germany had carefully maintained a system of "class justice" rather than one that protected either individual rights or the interests of Germans as a whole. For Liebknecht, the entire legal system was stacked against ordinary Germans. The most obvious example was the enormous power held by prosecutors, who were seen as representatives of government authority and thus enjoyed a superior status in the courtroom. Judges, in his opinion, were also biased and unreliable. Although they were often celebrated publicly for a tradition of independence within the German legal system, Liebknecht suggested that the independence of the judiciary was undermined by several factors, including the purging of "politically unacceptable" candidates and close oversight (and occasional intervention) by the Justice Ministry. Finally, Liebknecht condemned the elite composition of lay judges and juries, and the relative unwillingness of any of these judicial participants to challenge either the testimony or the power of the police.[6] The criminal justice system, therefore, was an institution designed by German elites primarily to benefit themselves.

Anyone who studies the German legal system during this era will recognize elements of truth within Karl Liebknecht's critique. Surely, not all defendants could expect to get the same treatment in court, and the government (through the extensive power afforded to police, prosecutors, and judges) could use prosecutions to make life very difficult for political enemies of the regime. Still, as a number of historians such as Uwe Wilhelm, Kenneth Ledford, Alexandra Ortmann, and Benjamin Hett have recently argued, the power balance within the German justice system was far more nuanced and contentious than Liebknecht acknowledged.[7] Most litigants or defendants in Imperial Germany imagined the Imperial

German courtroom as a place where they could seek a redress of their grievances or a restoration of their reputations. Even if many trial participants were unsure of their prospects for victory, they would often relish a public trial as a platform to make their own case, tell their own stories, and seek sympathy from the public. This was especially true of "political" trials, which could often be as valuable for defendants hoping to gain publicity as they were for the government in intimidating or silencing dissent. We must remember that many Socialist defendants, including Karl Liebknecht's father Wilhelm Liebknecht, were quite successful at using their own trials (and even their eventual convictions) as political propaganda against the German state.

Karl Liebknecht's analysis of the legal system also failed to acknowledge the dramatic changes in German legal culture that had taken place before the turn of the century. Just as it is misleading to view particular legal codes as existing in stasis, so it is equally mistaken to view the roles of prosecutors, judges, and defense attorneys as essentially stable within a given society. This was especially true in the first decades after German unification—a time when rapidly transforming social conditions, new theories of criminality, and public dissatisfaction with the German legal code all led to fierce debates about the proper roles and powers of officers of the court.

In general, criminal justice in Imperial Germany was a hybrid of an older "inquisitorial" system and an "adversarial" system more familiar to American readers. In the old inquisitorial system, judges had been responsible for bringing charges, hearing the evidence, and coming to a verdict; that is, judges combined many of the functions of modern prosecutors, judges, and juries.[8] It was only beginning in the early nineteenth century that Prussia began to move decisively away from the inquisitorial model toward an adversarial model where prosecutors, judges, and defense attorneys played separate and distinct roles. Although the Imperial German legal system preserved parts of the older inquisitorial model in the extensive powers it granted to judges and especially prosecutors, defendants and defense attorneys were hardly powerless. As these various court officers accommodated themselves to new legal realities and to the growing power and frequent presence of the press, they often fought desperately—both inside and outside the courtroom—to protect or enhance their power and prestige. If the superior class and status of German jurists often put members of the lower classes (and their Socialist advocates) at a disadvantage in the courtroom, class pressures also worked very powerfully to create tensions and divisions within these juristic elites as well.

THE ALMIGHTY PROSECUTOR

In Karl Liebknecht's estimation, the institution of the state prosecutor (*Staatsanwalt*) was the key to the intrusion of state power into the nominally "independent" courts. Prosecutors, after all, were representatives of government authority, who in Berlin answered directly to officials in the Prussian Justice Ministry. Aside from his direct link to the state, the core of the prosecutor's power came through the so-called *Anklagemonopol*—the exclusive power to file charges or indict a defendant. During his initial inquiry into the facts of a case, the prosecutor had all local police authorities at his disposal. It was the prosecutor who ran the initial investigation, and it was his decision whether or not to move the case forward. Although §152 of the Code of Criminal Procedure obligated prosecutors to file charges whenever they believed a crime had been committed, and although a prosecutor's decision to file charges (or not to file charges) could often be appealed to a court, in reality prosecutors by and large enjoyed wide discretion about which cases to prosecute and which to ignore.[9]

This is not to say that the role of the prosecutor as agent of the state was universally accepted—even among prosecutors themselves. Prevailing theory stemming from midcentury legal reforms regarded prosecutors as *Gesetzwächter* or "guardians of the law," whose purpose was to enforce all laws dispassionately regardless of the defendants involved. This conception conflicted with the idea that a prosecutor was an agent of state interests—or it at least took a more idealistic view of state interests, in that it placed prosecutors next to judges as officers of the court who were tasked with pursuing justice free from political influence.[10] In reality, however, prosecutors did answer to their superiors within the government, and they were often tasked directly with the prosecution of enemies of the state and the suppression of dissent. It is no surprise, then, that the great arch-nemesis of Socialist leaders such as August Bebel and Wilhelm Liebknecht was not one of the judges they faced at trial, but the infamous representative of state power, First Prosecutor of the Berlin Municipal Court (and later Chief Prosecutor at the Supreme Court in Leipzig) Hermann Tessendorf.

Prosecutors such as Tessendorf were often accused of an "addiction to prosecution" (*Verfolgungssucht*), in which even flimsy evidence or false denunciations were enough to imprison someone in investigative custody for months without a trial.[11] This long-standing criticism of state prosecutors seemed to be increasing in frequency and intensity during the 1880s, not only for political prosecutions, but also for the most ordinary of crimes. Legal journals and political newspapers frequently described cases where innocents had been convicted based solely on flimsy evidence and the gravitas of the prosecutor. In fact, just a few months before the Graef trial, the new chief prosecutor (*Generalstaatsanwalt*) in Saxony, Hermann Gustav Held, attracted attention from across the country when he personally participated in the appeal for a defendant previously convicted of theft. Held not only asked for an acquittal based on insufficient evidence, but he also made a long speech to the court that discussed past prosecutorial abuses. He suggested that prosecutors in general needed to be much more careful to file charges not based on mere strong suspicions, but instead based only on the actual strength of the evidence. He also reminded all prosecutors that it was their duty to make sure that no innocent defendant could be convicted since "every conviction of an innocent, and even every conviction of a defendant whose guilt is not demonstrably proven, is an attack on our legal protections and thus an attack on both the function and the very existence of the state."[12] This speech, widely discussed both in legal journals and the political press, foreshadowed much of the criticism of the prosecutor in the Graef case, Max Heinemann, a short time later.

It is also important to note that despite their substantial power and ties to state authority, prosecutors in the German Empire never operated in a political vacuum, and they were often very sensitive to public opinion. There are, for example, a number of cases in the Prussian Justice Ministry files where prosecutors expressed serious doubts about evidence and yet still filed charges in the hopes that a public airing of the case might dampen popular anger against particular defendants.[13] Prosecutors were also clearly understaffed and overworked, especially in major German cities. Just a few years before the Graef trial, Justice Minister Heinrich von Friedberg had complained that it was all too common for first prosecutors in Prussia to be so overwhelmed with administrative business that they left actual litigation to younger or lower-ranking attorneys. Friedberg also sent out a directive that "such criminal cases, which take on an added importance either because of the personality of the defendants or the nature of the case, should be overseen closely at every stage by the First Prosecutor if they are not directly under his control."[14] It is not entirely clear why, despite this admonition, the Graef case was assigned to Max Heinemann, whom the *Kreuzzeitung* referred to as a "second-level" prosecutor in Berlin. It may either have been a sign of his exceptional talent as a young litigator, or a suggestion of just how impacted the prosecutors' office was during this time.

Heinemann's handling of the Graef case brought criticism from both legal experts and lay observers. He was taken to task for his decision to file charges based mostly on circumstantial evidence and his unwillingness to accept the testimony of expert witnesses about Anna Rother's mental state. Critics also loudly mocked his alleged statement to jurors during closing arguments that "it would be a terrible thing to convict an innocent man, but it would be even more terrible to let a guilty man go free"—a comment that would naturally cause consternation in light of all the recent criticism about "trigger-happy" prosecutors.[15] Many observers of the trial were especially critical of Heinemann's decision to enter Gustav Graef's poetry and private papers into evidence. Expert legal analysts such as Otto Mittelstädt, as well as prominent outsiders such as Paul Lindau and Theodor Fontane, all agreed that such evidence did not prove that an adulterous relationship had occurred and therefore only served to needlessly besmirch the reputation of the defendant.[16] At best this was seen as an error in judgment, and at worst as an example of prosecutorial abuse.

As the trial went on, the attacks on Heinemann became more personal. Some critics suggested that he was a "cultural Philistine," a careerist looking to build a reputation, and worst of all, an incompetent boob who did not understand basic moral or legal norms. Newspapers such as the *Volkszeitung* were relentless in their attacks, suggesting that Heinemann sought a conviction of Gustav Graef at any cost rather than engaging in a simple pursuit of truth. Max Heinemann's very public reaction to the criticism aimed at him must be understood in this context. He had been sensitive about public criticism from the start of the trial, even writing to ask newspapers for retractions and corrections to their reports. After the trial, Heinemann's published response to Karl Frenzel's essay demonstrated that he was perfectly capable of using his skill as a rhetorician to fight his critics in the public sphere; however, he also made clear to these critics that he could bring traditional prosecutorial powers to bear as well. In the first paragraph of his pamphlet, he included a not-so-veiled threat to his critics in the press: "their outcries against the partisan prosecutor who enjoys persecuting innocents . . . may receive their proper response at another time and place."[17] Here, Heinemann's rhetoric can have a double meaning. On the one hand, it can be read as holding out the prospect of a duel if attacks against his honor continued. His critics, however, may have interpreted this comment as a more straightforward flexing of "prosecutorial muscle." In an era when prosecutions of newspaper editors were still relatively common and libel charges were regularly filed against journalists, such a threat would have to be taken very seriously.

This is not to suggest that Heinemann was without supporters. Aside from the faint praise offered by conservative and Catholic newspapers, and the letter of support from the Association of Berlin Artists, the prosecutor also drew sympathy from the novelist Theodor Fontane. Although Fontane believed that Graef was likely guilty of all charges, he also suggested that if he had been in the place of the jurors he might also have been forced to acquit due to insufficient credible evidence.[18] He did not conclude, however, that Heinemann had been irresponsible in taking the case to trial or in his behavior afterwards. In a letter to his friend Georg Friedländer, Fontane expressed his own dismay about the trial's unfortunate legacy:

> The outcome of this trial demonstrates that the sexual domain is a realm in which circumstantial evidence is no longer enough for a conviction because the modern world does not wish it to be so. This is a severe blow for the entire legal world, and especially for the prosecutor—a man who I believe to be both sharp and sensible—who now has to stand there looking like a twit.[19]

Less than a week after Heinemann's pamphlet criticizing Lindau and Frenzel was published, Fontane sent Heinemann a personal letter expressing both his congratulations and his sympathy:

> Allow me to express to you my complete agreement with *everything* (with the possible exception of the dissection of the poetry) and my admiration of your courage. You disturbed a wasp's nest, and the hours in the courtroom must have been, at least in the end, more painful for you than for the accused. There are many, perhaps more than you know, who are grateful for this sacrifice.[20]

Over the next several weeks, Fontane, perhaps eager for more gossip about the case, developed an acquaintanceship with Heinemann through their mutual friend, Friedrich Stephany—editor of the liberal *Vossische Zeitung*. For Fontane, as for many other observers in German society, the Graef case and its aftermath was far from a story of an almighty prosecutor who had abused his power. In Fontane's estimation, it was not the defendants but both Heinemann and the institution of the prosecutor that had been victimized by this ordeal.[21]

Heinemann's harshest critics believed that his involvement in the Graef case might have a lasting impact on his career. The prosecutor was rumored to have pursued the case over the objections of the justice minister, Heinrich von Friedberg, who would likely also have been less than pleased with the outcome. Not surprisingly, many liberal newspapers speculated that Heinemann would soon be sacked or demoted.[22] This turned out not to be the case. Less than a year after the Graef trial, Heinemann applied for a promotion to first prosecutor in the city of Göttingen; the glowing recommendation sent by his superior, the *Oberstaatsanwalt* Ludolf von Luck, pointed to his "astute and shrewd decision-making skills, careful attention to detail, exceptional energy, and his thorough understanding of his role as prosecutor."[23] This was just the beginning of what would be a rather dramatic career ascent. After eight years in Göttingen, Heinemann became a prosecutor at the Higher Regional Court (*Oberlandesgericht*) in Stettin. Then, in 1895, he was promoted to prosecutor at the Supreme Court (*Reichsanwalt*) in Leipzig; finally, only five years later, at the age of fifty-nine, he reached the pinnacle of his career when he was appointed as a judge in the Second Criminal Division of the German Supreme Court, a position he would retain for over a decade until his retirement in 1911.

It is also clear that Heinemann's involvement in the Graef case did not teach him to keep his head down and shy away from controversy. In fact, shortly after his promotion and transfer to Stettin as a prosecutor, Heinemann became involved in a rather nasty feud with one of the leading criminologists in Germany: Franz von Liszt. Liszt had achieved prominence as a legal theorist during the previous decade primarily for his view that punishments should be tailored to the individual criminal defendant rather than to the crime. In place of the traditional positivist approach, which viewed crimes as choices to violate legal norms by people endowed with free will, Liszt stressed the social and psychological forces that help to shape human actions. Any punishment, therefore, should not simply be punitive but should also take into account the possibility of rehabilitation and the subjective factors that may have driven a person to act.[24]

The dispute between Liszt and Heinemann began when Heinemann published a review of the fifth edition of Liszt's *Textbook for German Penal Law* (*Lehrbuch des deutschen Strafrechts*). While praising individual portions of the book, Heinemann claimed that the "fundamental philosophical assumptions present in the work will continue to have the effect of corrupting any healthy idealism that young students of the law have carried with them into their studies."[25] Although this review was published in a specialized legal journal, Liszt interpreted it as a personal attack, and he took to the pages of Maximilian Harden's popular journal *Die Zukunft* for a very angry and very public response. Liszt suggested that Heinemann's attacks amounted to a personal denunciation, and he felt that Heinemann's assertion that he—a man who had dedicated his life to teaching—was responsible for corrupting the idealism of German law students was especially outrageous. Rather than attempt any substantial intellectual refutation in his short response, Liszt provided names of other legal theorists who had adopted his views—including the Supreme Court justice Otto Mittelstädt, who had once been one of the leading proponents of retributive justice. Liszt then simply dismissed Heinemann as a "harmless" and "insignificant" unknown.[26]

Heinemann could not leave this unanswered. He did, however, choose again to respond to Liszt in a specialized law journal rather than a newspaper, since he claimed wider public opinion did not interest him and he "already knew the feelings of his colleagues."[27] Although Heinemann insisted that he wanted to rise above personal insults to focus instead on the crucial legal questions, his response to Liszt was both an impassioned attack on Liszt's ideas and an indignant response to the man who had insulted him publicly. Heinemann, for example, took great pains within the article to defend his status and reputation. He insisted that he was far from "insignificant" and "unknown" to Liszt since he had previously published a well-regarded journal article effectively refuting Liszt's statistical arguments about the effectiveness of prison sentences. He also emphasized that he was both a professional peer and an equal in status (*Fach- und Standesgenossen*) to Liszt, and was "certainly no less affected by concerns about the practical effectiveness of jurists than an academic law professor."[28] Finally, Heinemann ended his response to Liszt with a bit of bluster: "I am not as generous and noble as [Liszt], who claims to 'take a degree of pleasure in a well-landed blow, even one that is delivered against him.' He might like to test this claim out—whenever and wherever he prefers. He will find me if he looks."[29] Clearly, when it came to defending his own ideals, his personal honor, or his status as a public prosecutor, Max Heinemann was always ready for a fight.[30]

THE ABSOLUTE DISCRETION OF JUDGES

There is a famous German legend about a simple miller named Arnold who stood up to the illustrious Frederick the Great. In the common version of this story, passed down through generations, Frederick had traveled to visit Arnold, who owned a small piece of property that he refused to sell to the Prussian king. When Frederick hinted that he could simply take the land if he wished, the miller allegedly responded that he was not afraid because "there are still courts in Berlin."[31] This statement, transformed over the years by various poets and storytellers into the French "Il y a des juges à Berlin" or "There are still judges in Berlin," was still a very public symbol of the power and independence of Prussian judges even a century after Frederick's death.[32] In reality, however, the independence of judges in Imperial Germany was far from secure. The role of judges in the legal process was much more complex, and perhaps even more contested and controversial, than the position of the state prosecutor.

Although judges were not direct representatives of the state, their power was still substantial. As Benjamin Hett argues in his book *Death in the Tiergarten*, judges in Imperial Germany tended to be the "star of the show" in their individual courtrooms. It was judges, not prosecutors or defense attorneys, who questioned witnesses first. The other attorneys could then ask questions only with the judge's permission (which he was required to grant). Section 177 of the Court Organization Law (*Gerichtsverfassungsgesetz*) also gave judges the right to maintain order in their court—a power that they could interpret quite broadly.[33] In addition to all this, one of the most important pillars of judicial power in criminal trials was the so-called "*Freie Ermessen des Richters*"—the absolute discretion that judges held over what evidence to admit. In the old Prussian inquisitorial system, judges would often hear all the evidence available and then decide for themselves what testimony was credible. In Imperial Germany, judges still had wide latitude to decide what evidence and testimony was presented in court.

Public complaints about judicial overreach were relatively common throughout this era. The most frequent target for criticism was Judge Boguslaw Müller's controversial colleague at the Berlin Regional Court: Georg Robert Brausewetter. In a long series of sensational trials spanning the 1880s and early 1890s, Brausewetter became infamous for repeatedly cutting off defendants, attacking defense attorneys, and suggesting guilt to jurors before deliberations had started. As Benjamin Hett points out, Brausewetter frequently battled with defense lawyers over perceived slights of honor, and his courtroom antics brought complaints from lawyers' associations, defendants, and journalists across the political spectrum. Far from being a tool of state authority, however, Brausewetter was also a thorn in the side of his superiors, and he repeatedly ignored missives from officials in the Justice Ministry that all judges should avoid the appearance of bias.[34] Brausewetter was not necessarily motivated by ideology; he had a reputation for being equally rude, abrasive, and prejudiced toward a range of defendants regardless of their political leanings or social origin.[35] By the mid-1890s, Brausewetter's behavior had become even more erratic, and his behavior toward attorneys and defendants in an 1894 trial provoked a special meeting of the Association of Berlin Lawyers. As Benjamin Hett reports, just a year later Brausewetter was taken directly from the courtroom and committed to a mental institution. He was there diagnosed with signs of a "progressive paralysis" stemming from a disease that especially targets "businessmen, scholars, and officers." Just a few days later, Brausewetter was dead.[36]

Another of Müller's colleagues at the Berlin Regional Court, Hermann Lüty, was also a frequent target for public criticism. The noted defense attorney Fritz Friedmann described Lüty as a generally genial and half-blind old man; however, Friedmann also criticized Lüty's habit of delivering a long *Resumé*—a judge's speech to jurors before they entered into deliberations. Although judges were required only to give jurors instructions about the law and discouraged from making any comments about the credibility of particular witnesses or pieces of evidence, Lüty was infamous for crossing the line.[37] Lüty had also been thrust into the limelight for his actions in the so-called Stöcker-Bäcker Affair, a case that had aroused controversy just a few months before the Graef trial. In this trial, the liberal editor Heinrich Bäcker was found guilty of libeling the prominent pastor, anti-Semite, and leader of the Christian-Social Party, Adolf Stöcker. In Lüty's reading of the grounds for his verdict, however, he included his own opinion that Stöcker, a coplaintiff (*Nebenkläger*) in the case, had himself been rather careless with the truth. This comment brought cheers from the liberal press, who had hoped that the trial would result in Stöcker's public shaming. Other observers, however, were incensed at Lüty's extraneous comments.

In a long article after the Stöcker-Bäcker trial, entitled "The Absolute Discretion of Judges," the ultraconservative *Kreuzzeitung* blasted not only Judge Lüty, but the entire modern judicial system: "The prosecutor now functions as a party to the case and stands under the authority of the judge. He is detached from the idea of law (*Recht*), just as the court itself is detached from the idea of state . . . this disgusting 'Laskerish' Jewish-liberal legal conception satisfies neither the notion of the state nor of justice."[38] The National Liberal jurist Otto Bähr also expressed his dismay in the journal *Grenzboten*, where he lamented the effects of the twin principles of orality and openness on the German court system. Perhaps, he argued, it was too late to prevent prosecutors and defense attorneys from performing for a public audience or engaging in the kind of flowery rhetoric normally reserved for a parliamentary debate. It was absolutely unacceptable, however, for *judges* to engage in such speechifying.[39] In reflecting on Judge Lüty and the Stöcker-Bäcker case, Bähr concluded:

> In earlier times, judges earned a reputation for being as clear and concise as possible, and for not saying a word more than absolutely necessary. . . . Today many judges

> see the delivery of the verdict as a chance to give voice to their private opinions and feelings. . . . It would be in the interest of justice if those responsible within the government use their powers to discourage judges from going down this path. Certainly the engagement in such pointless speech-making has no place in the independence and autonomy of judges.[40]

A later *Grenzboten* article on the Graef trial suggested that not all of this was the fault of the judges themselves. It was perhaps impossible for judges to resist the opportunity to get their name in the headlines and to hear themselves praised as great men. The real fault here, therefore, was the growth of a dishonorable press and a legal system that did not prevent its incursion into the sanctity of the courtroom. As a result, serious trials were turned into theater pieces, and judges into fellow actors. As the *Grenzboten* complained: "It seems as if the robe has become just another theatrical prop in the courtroom, as if instead of judges we had actors in front of us who could not rest comfortably until they had surpassed the fame of all other virtuosos."[41]

More than a decade after his involvement in the Stöcker-Bäcker trial, critics were still bitter at Judge Lüty. In an 1896 speech to the Christian Social Youth League, a group associated with Stöcker's Christian-Social Party, the editor Helmut von Gerlach claimed that Lüty had recently died as a result of a softening of the brain (*Gehirnerweichung*)—a common symptom of advanced syphilis. Gerlach implied that this diagnosis might help explain his behavior in the Stöcker-Bäcker trial (perhaps in the same way it could explain the erratic behavior of Judge Brausewetter). *Die Post*, a moderate conservative newspaper, immediately responded by suggesting that not only was Lüty alive and well, but he was enjoying an active retirement in Heidelberg. At the time, Prussian justice officials noted the two conflicting reports about the retired judge but declined to investigate which version was correct.[42]

It is important to note again that many on the political left were also unsatisfied with the behavior of judges during this period. Socialists, who were still being actively targeted for prosecution by the government, tended to be just as critical of judicial power as they were of prosecutorial power. Just a year before the Stöcker trial, in a Reichstag speech about compensation for unjustly convicted defendants, the Socialist politician Max Kayser blasted politically biased judges for using their position on the bench to influence jury verdicts. He particularly stressed the misuse of the *Resumé* by judges to push impressionable jurors toward their own desired verdict. Kayser, perhaps motivated by his recent history of multiple convictions and jail terms for political crimes, went as far as to suggest that it was not the state that should be forced to compensate unjustly convicted defendants, but the presiding judges in cases that ended in wrongful conviction.[43]

In comparison to the behavior of Brausewetter and Lüty, then, the behavior of Judge Müller in the Graef case seems relatively mild. For many supporters of the defense, however, there was still serious cause for concern. Bertha Rother's defense attorney, for example, complained about the broad powers used by Müller and other judges to admit evidence in a jury trial, and he suggested that German courts should follow the English example and eliminate the admission of hearsay evidence.[44] Several liberal newspapers also suggested that Judge Müller had unfairly pressured witnesses—even making some of them cry—and they also pointed to his repeated open criticism of press coverage of the case. The *Berliner Börsen-Courier* even attacked the judge from the original Hammermann case, *Landgerichtsdirektor* Bachmann, for claiming that he did not regularly allow attorneys to ask questions of witnesses. The *Börsen-Courier* expressed alarm at behavior that seemed clearly at odds with §§239–241 of the Code of Criminal Procedure, and the newspaper insisted that the Justice Ministry should intervene to protect the rights of attorneys against judicial abuse.[45]

Boguslaw Müller's long diatribes against the press in open court, however, are a clear demonstration that he, like the prosecutor Max Heinemann, felt the need to publicly defend both his own reputation and his position as a judge. He clearly knew that the attacks on his decision to admit the press could have devastating repercussions not only for his own reputation and career, but for future judicial discretion in such matters as well. When rumors surfaced shortly after the trial that Judge Müller would be transferring to a civil court, the conservative *Kreuzzeitung* was quick to suggest that this move was not a punishment for his actions in the Graef case but had been planned long before the trial began. Such a transfer was not a demotion, the *Kreuzzeitung* added, and was known to be favored by those in the criminal courts.[46] These rumors were unfounded, however. There is no evidence of any censure in Boguslaw Müller's personnel file, and he would remain a judge at the Berlin Regional Court until his death in 1889.[47]

A LAWYERS' WORLD

The last decades of the nineteenth century were in many ways a golden era for German lawyers. The same legal reforms that moved Germany on the path toward a *Rechtsstaat*—a society governed by laws rather than by arbitrary state authority—also carved out a new and increasingly independent role for defense attorneys. In addition to reforming civil and criminal procedure and setting up a new hierarchy of German courts, the Imperial Justice Laws of the late 1870s initiated the free private practice of law (*freie Advokatur*). Previously in Prussia, the number of lawyers permitted to appear before any particular court had been strictly limited by a *numerus clausus,* and those positions were approved by government authority.[48] The Lawyers' Statute (*Rechtsanwaltsordnung*) of 1879, however, opened admission to the bar and freed private lawyers from state interference. While there were still some restrictions on lawyers, such as localizations and fixed fee schedules, the new system allowed attorneys "to champion anything and anyone, regardless of reason of state, as long as he does not show himself unworthy of the respect and trust which his profession demands."[49] The Lawyers' Statute also created institutions such as Lawyers' Chambers and Lawyers' Honor Courts, which empowered private attorneys in Germany for the most part to govern and police themselves.[50]

For many lawyers, these reforms were the culmination of a long struggle to establish independence within the justice system. However, as the historian Kenneth Ledford notes, attorneys also tended to believe these reforms were not simply in their own professional interests, but also in the general interests of the German people. From midcentury onward, liberal legal theorists such as Rudolf von Gneist had viewed the private legal profession as a key bulwark against judicial overreach and arbitrary state authority. In addition to merely serving their private clients, therefore, many lawyers viewed themselves as guarantors of individual rights and representatives who worked for the good of the German public.[51] It is not surprising, then, that some of the most prominent private lawyers in the 1870s and 1880s, such as August Munckel, also tended to be active in liberal politics and as members of the German parliament.

In this newly reformed legal system, the most able defense attorneys could achieve both prosperity and a degree of public prestige. Munckel, for example, became known for representing high-profile clients, especially in politically tinged cases. He was the attorney who had skewered the anti-Semitic pastor Adolf Stöcker on the stand during the Stöcker-Bäcker slander trial, just as he had previously defended the Jewish businessman Hermann Kontorowicz in 1881 for having assaulted the anti-Semitic activist Bernhard Förster. Munckel, however, was not linked only to defending liberal activists and causes. In 1874, he had represented Bismarck's political nemesis Count Harry von Arnim, and a few years later he defended the editors of the *Reichsglocke*—a radical anti-Semitic newspaper that had launched slanderous attacks on Bismarck in the mid-1870s. As the Graef trial was under way, Munckel was engaged as the lead defense attorney in the Chemnitz Socialist trial, which included prominent Socialist leaders such as August Bebel as defendants. Munckel's defense of Bebel was spirited enough to inspire the Berlin police to open a surveillance file to keep tabs on his political activities.[52] Despite his involvement in such controversial cases, Munckel was far from a grandstander or demagogue. He enjoyed nearly universal respect amongst his fellow lawyers and judges, who suggested that he brought the defense of clients to "high artistic fulfillment" through a combination of juristic brilliance and eloquence.[53]

Gustav Graef's defense attorney, John Simson, was less famous as a litigator than August Munckel, and his own career was eclipsed by that of his famous older brother Eduard von Simson—with whom he had founded a very successful law practice. Eduard had served as president of the Frankfurt parliament during the Revolution of 1848, president of the German Reichstag from 1871 to 1874, and then president of the German Supreme Court (*Reichsgericht*) until his retirement in 1891. A second brother, Georg Bernhard Simson, had also been active in the Frankfurt parliament and forged a successful law career. Although there is very little information on the career of John Simson, it is clear that he was prominent enough to have earned the honorific title of *Justizrat* along with a Grand Cross from the French Legion of Honor. The Simson family law firm, housed at the eminently respectable address Pariser Platz 1 (directly in front of the Brandenburg Gate), was one of the most prestigious and successful in the city.[54] Just a short time after the Graef trial, the firm would take on a bright young attorney named Max Weber as a legal intern.[55] John Simson also happened to be an old friend of Gustav Graef. Both were born and raised in Königsberg, and the two became close while attending the Albertina University.

Although John Simson could be aggressive in representing his clients and attacking the credibility of hostile witnesses, his behavior at the Graef trial does not mark him as any more of a grandstander than August Munckel. His long defense of Graef was generally praised by observers, and although he defended the reporting of the liberal press and took the prosecutor to task for having filed criminal charges, his attitude toward the court was generally respectful and deferential. Both Simson and the prosecutor, Max Heinemann, praised each other's skill as rhetoricians—even as they told jurors that they would have to rely on the truth to overcome the brilliance of their courtroom opponents.

If the success of men such as August Munckel and John Simson seemed to herald a golden age for defense lawyers, it is also clear that defense attorneys as a whole felt their power and status were under serious threat. The legal reforms of the 1870s, which had created a world in which private attorneys could thrive, had also resulted in an exponential growth in the number of attorneys and thus to dramatically increased economic competition. A career that had once been limited to a relatively small band of liberal "notables" now began to transform itself into a modern profession. The regular reports of the chairs of the Berlin Lawyers' Chamber (*Anwaltskammer*) are filled with lamentations about the new commercial nature of the profession, which turned members into profit-seeking individuals rather than members of an honorable guild. The first chairs of this organization, Rudolf Ulfert and Carl Laué, bemoaned the flood of young lawyers in Berlin—especially the high numbers assigned to the Regional Court—which made it challenging to sustain a practice, made the forging of any common cause among lawyers difficult, and made ethical violations much more likely. Both chairs thought that the opening of the legal profession had been a mistake, and they urged immediate reforms. As spokesmen for their guild, they expressed the fear that younger attorneys, who might not understand how to treat judges or interact with the public, would soon assume control of the guild and bring about a precipitous drop in the decorum, honor, and public prestige of the profession.[56]

Not surprisingly, many of these "younger attorneys" were irritated by the attitudes of men like Ulfert and Laué and the deference and honor often expected by their older and more established peers. A generation of younger attorneys such as Erich Sello, Fritz Friedmann, and Max Wronker were becoming both famed and feared, not because of their connections or social background but for their rhetorical skills and their willingness to openly confront prosecutors and judges in court.[57] Their behavior was not simply a difference in style but also a change in the fundamental self-perception of many attorneys. Traditionally, defense lawyers were expected to act both as advocates for their clients *and* as officers of the court. The latter responsibility was expected to take precedence; that is, the primary task of a defense attorney was to assist the court in its search for truth—not to assist his clients in hiding or evading the truth. At least in theory, this meant that a defense attorney who had knowledge of his client's guilt must not try to help him evade punishment. For a younger generation of attorneys, these priorities seemed to have been reversed, as both renown and financial success now depended more on achieving acquittals than on maintaining honor. Perhaps the most egregious case of lawyerly misbehavior arose in the infamous Heinze murder trial in 1891, where the two defense attorneys, Alfred Ballien and Richard Cossmann, frequently challenged the judges and prosecutors, used repeated motions to delay the trial, and even sipped champagne at the defense table. Ballien and Cossmann were disciplined for their actions, and Ballien was later disbarred for other ethical violations—but this did not prevent other attorneys from pandering to a public audience or being very aggressive advocates of their clients.[58] For critics, these kinds of publicity-hungry defense attorneys were a perfect example of all that was wrong with the justice system in Germany; instead of aspiring to join an honorable cohort of lawyers, they had become sophists and demagogues, who sought to muddy and mislead rather than seek truth and justice.[59] With a sensationalist media as their potential allies, it was feared, these new defense lawyers had both prosecutors and judges at a serious disadvantage.

One last anecdote, this time involving the nephew of Gustav Graef's defense attorney, will show how close to the surface these tensions between attorneys could often lie. In his memoirs, the famed defense attorney Fritz Friedmann related a confrontation with the lawyer August von Simson, which took place at an 1887 meeting of the Berlin Lawyers' Chamber—an association that all lawyers in the city were required to join. Although only fifty years old at the time, August von Simson, the nephew of Graef defense attorney John Simson, had already become one of the clear leaders of the Berlin Lawyers' Chamber. Friedmann, fifteen years Simson's junior, clearly had little respect for the man he described as "the little son of the big father"—a reference to Simson's famous father and president of the Supreme Court, Eduard von Simson. During a formal dinner preceding the 1887 meeting of the Lawyers' Chamber, Friedmann apparently took it upon himself to make a toast that singled out the new younger generation of lawyers for special praise. After his address, he walked by the area where leaders of the organization—including August von Simson—were seated. Simson immediately took Friedmann aside and started to criticize his toast, but he quickly saw something else that bothered him even more: Friedmann was wearing a medal presented to him earlier that afternoon by the Russian tsar. This, Simson believed, was a clear violation of decorum by Friedmann, since German citizens were not allowed to wear medals granted by foreign powers without the express permission of the German kaiser. In response to Simson's pointed questions, Friedmann mocked him for being envious and brusquely claimed that he needed no one's permission to wear the medal. As Simson began to get angry, Friedmann haughtily recounted a story that decades earlier the Prussian king Friedrich Wilhelm III had made an exception to this rule for all Russian medals in order to avoid offending his son-in-law Tsar Nikolaus I; because of this exception, Friedmann smirked, he did not need the kaiser's permission, and certainly did not need August von Simson's permission, to wear such a decoration. According to Friedmann's own account, he quickly turned his back on the red-faced Simson and returned in triumph to his young colleagues on the other side of the room.[60] This may seem a rather trivial personal clash. However, the glee with which Friedmann recounted this story decades later in his memoirs is not simply a sign of his lack of modesty; it also gives some representation of the real tensions and divisions within the community of lawyers in Berlin before the turn of the century. Such tensions would only continue to grow well into the twentieth century.

THERE ARE STILL JURIES IN BERLIN!

Unfortunately, we know very little about the jurors in the Graef case, their social composition, their deliberations, or their feelings about the defendants. Unlike some sensational trials in contemporary America, no jurors gave public interviews or published tell-all books about their role in the proceedings. There was also absolutely no indication in the press that the jury had acted improperly or failed to carry out their responsibilities in a fair and balanced manner. Even those critics who believed Graef was clearly guilty tended to agree that contradictions in witness testimony, the prosecutor's reliance on circumstantial evidence, and the lack of actual court transcripts from the Hammermann case would have made it difficult for any jury to reach a guilty verdict. The absence of controversy surrounding this particular jury, however, did not mean that the institution of the jury trial escaped criticism. In fact, the Graef case helped to unleash a fierce public debate about the potential benefits and risks of including untrained members of the public in the judging of major criminal cases.

The jury trial was a relatively recent development within the German legal system. It had been one of the key demands of political liberalism coming out of the Enlightenment, and these demands were aided by both the popularity of French writers such as Montesquieu and the experience of German states under Napoleonic rule. Although the adoption of the jury system spread slowly, in the aftermath of the Revolutions of 1848 almost every German state was moving toward implementing some form of a trial by jury.[61] This is not to say that juries were universally acclaimed. While the popularity of juries seemed to increase both among the populace and among many jurists over the course of the century, conservative hostility toward the jury system festered. In fact, the debate over the adoption and expansion of jury trials was especially fierce in Prussia, where conservatives liked neither the revolutionary origins of the institution nor the idea that lay people would be entrusted with power that counterbalanced the authority of trained legal experts. The Prussian government also feared the unpredictability of juries—especially in political cases. After a number of 1848 revolutionaries were acquitted in jury trials, the Prussian government embarked on a long and concerted effort to limit the purview of such courts.[62]

As Alexandra Ortmann has argued in her book *Machtvolle Verhandlungen* (Powerful Proceedings), liberal enthusiasm toward direct public participation in the criminal justice system had already begun to wane as early as midcentury. In the early 1800s, members of the liberal bourgeoisie had considered public participation in the finding of criminal verdicts to be an important assertion of power against reactionary landed elites who dominated the legal system. By the 1870s, however, members of the bourgeoisie had thoroughly infiltrated both the parliament and judiciary. If the principle of public participation was still viewed by jurists as an essential protection against government power and caprice, it was now also seen as potentially opening the door to members of society outside either the landed elites or the bourgeoisie, including the lower classes, women, and Jews. These "outsiders," it was suggested, lacked the education, experience, and moral character to properly execute their duties as lay jurors and reach fair verdicts in a courtroom setting. Increasing numbers of liberal jurists were becoming convinced, therefore, that it was now more appropriate to place important matters of the law in the hands of experts rather than leaving them to laypeople who lacked sufficient training and cultivation to apply the law in an appropriate manner.[63]

Perhaps the most influential voice to express doubts about the jury courts as an institution was Friedrich Oskar von Schwarze, the chief prosecutor (*Generalstaatsanwalt*) in Saxony and later a Free Conservative member of the German Reichstag.[64] While Schwarze supported the idea of popular inclusion in decision-making at criminal courts, he viewed the jury system as a French invention that was inimical to German traditions. Schwarze also believed that jury courts had an "unnatural" split between the functions of judges and jurors, and he argued that untrained jurors were prone to erroneous judgments. Schwarze's solution was the *Schöffengericht*, or court of lay assessors, in which professional judges would be joined by a small panel of lay judges (*Schöffen*). This compromise was intended to preserve what was popular about the jury system while also limiting the negative impacts of inexperienced jurors and restoring traditional powers to German judges. The new lay judges would be able to work with professional judges as an organic whole, rather than as two separate bodies with oddly conflicting and overlapping responsibilities.[65] In the first proposals for a German Court Organization Law in the early 1870s, the Prussian justice minister Adolph Leonhardt pushed for the inclusion of courts of lay assessors as a replacement for jury courts. His proposals, however, faced strong opposition from liberals and from the governments of some southern German states that did not want to give up the jury as an institution.

In the end, the German Court Organization Law, finally completed in 1877, was a compromise. Criminal courts in Germany would now have a tripartite division of responsibilities. Courts of lay assessors (*Schöffengerichte*), comprised of a professional judge and two lay judges, heard misdemeanors and cases that could result in either fines or sentences of less than three months in jail. The most egregious cases would be left to the jury courts (*Schwurgerichte*), which had a panel of three judges that decided questions of law, and a panel of twelve jurors that heard evidence and decided guilt or innocence based on questions formulated by the court. In between these two institutions were the criminal chambers (*Strafkammern*), which were made up solely of a panel of professional judges and heard middle-range cases.[66] Importantly, as part of the division of labor between these three court systems, Bismarck insisted that political trials and press trials (often for libel against government officials) would be heard in front of the criminal chambers (*Strafkammern*) and thus not in front of jurors or lay assessors. This measure, a result of government worries about the reliability of juries in political trials, was understandably unpopular with many opponents of the regime.[67] From the beginning, therefore, the jury court in the German Reich was a controversial institution and one that was under fire.

A set of new criminal justice reforms proposed by Otto von Bismarck in early 1885 once again set off heated debates inside legal journals, in the political press, and also inside the Reichstag. These reforms would have reduced the size of juries from twelve to six members and reassigned many kinds of cases away from jury courts to the courts of lay assessors—including perjury, forgery, abuse of office (*Amtsverbrechen*), and any criminal charges to which a defendant had already confessed. For Socialists and liberals—even the right-wing National Liberals who ordinarily supported Bismarck's proposals—these reforms were a direct threat to the jury as an institution. The liberal *Berliner Tageblatt*, for example, addressed the 1885 legislation proposals with the headline: "The Jury Court is in Danger!" The newspaper argued that the proposed reduction of jury size and the accompanying plan to reduce the jurisdiction for jury courts would only be the first steps in the gradual phasing out of juries as a whole. This, it was argued, would be a shocking reversal in the long campaign to include ordinary people in the justice system as a counterbalance to state power. These debates over Bismarck's proposals to restrict the jury courts were ongoing when Gustav Graef was arrested and held over for trial.[68]

After the verdict in the Graef trial, many liberal observers wasted no time in painting the case as a shining example of the role that juries could play in checking the power of overeager prosecutors such as Max Heinemann. The *Berliner Tageblatt*, for example, claimed that "the doctrine of the jurisdiction of jury courts, against which the enemies of free and popular institutions have already started to agitate, has proven itself magnificently in this episode—and that alone is a result that can provide some compensation for all the horrible dirt dredged up by this trial and for all the sad and sickening impressions that were brought along with it."[69] Despite efforts by the prosecutor and judge to suggest that the liberal press was prejudiced on behalf of the defendant, the *Tageblatt* argued, it was clear that the verdict of the jury put to rest any notion that the press had falsified or misrepresented popular sentiment: "**The verdict of the jurors, with which the press overwhelmingly agrees**, demonstrates that the press can justifiably claim to speak in the name of public opinion. Press and jury courts belong together; he who casts aspersions on one undermines the foundation of the other. Both institutions speak with the same voice, one that in our age may be scorned only at one's own risk. '**The voice of the people—the voice of God!**'"[70] The editor of a published trial summary agreed with this interpretation and suggested that there was only one lesson from the Graef trial that could give people some sense of comfort: "There are still jurors in Berlin!"[71] More conservative newspapers, of course, were quite critical of this interpretation. The *Reichsbote* condemned such newspapers for opportunism, suggesting that in the aftermath of the trial involving Adolf Stöcker the previous summer, the same newspapers had sung the praises of the independent judiciary; however, now that a judge was critical of their own reporting, they instead resorted to praising the jury.[72]

Debates in the press soon included the opinions of prominent jurists as well. One of the earliest and most significant commentaries came from Otto Mittelstädt, a judge at the Supreme Court (*Reichsgericht*) in Leipzig. Mittelstädt was no stranger to controversy, and his blunt and provocative critiques of legal issues had already won him admirers as well as entrenched enemies. In 1879, when still a judge at the Higher Regional Court (*Oberlandesgericht*) in Hamburg, Mittelstädt had created a firestorm with his pamphlet *Against Prison Sentences* (*Gegen die Freiheitsstrafe*), in which he proposed replacing short prison terms with hefty fines that would threaten the livelihood of defendants, and jettisoning rehabilitation as the main goal of imprisonment in favor of a return to traditional deterrence. Although his critique of the idea of prison rehabilitation was complex and multifaceted, he was widely maligned over his most controversial suggestions, including the implementation of food deprivation, corporal punishment, and perhaps even the pillory.[73] It was this essay that eventually motivated the criminologist Franz von Liszt to write his famous response "The Concept of Purpose in Criminal Law," which launched a movement to support rehabilitation and the tailoring of sentences to individual defendants.[74]

In response to the Graef trial, Mittelstädt was no less provocative in his opinions. In a long essay in the November 1885 issue of the prestigious journal *Preußische Jahrbücher*, he blasted Judge Boguslaw Müller for deciding to close the courtroom and yet allow the press, and he also criticized the prosecutor, Max Heinemann, for reading Graef's poetry out loud in court—an act he suggested provoked more sympathy than disdain for the defendant among jurors and the general public.[75] Mittelstädt's blunt critique of these officials was enough to inspire editors of the liberal *Volkszeitung* to claim that his essay had substantiated their own critiques of the trial and vindicated the role of the press in the Graef affair.[76] This interpretation, however, could have only been extracted from his essay through a highly selective reading and cherry-picked quotations. The core of Mittelstädt's article was a stern warning about the growing power of public opinion and the threat that it posed to the integrity of the justice system. In his view, public opinion was a loud and irrational interloper in the courtroom, a "multi-headed demon," which "works with the incalculable power of the great forces of nature, and whose meteorology will require careful study."[77] In modern times, he argued, such a powerful force cannot be ignored and should not be underestimated by statesmen and politicians; he added, however, that all efforts to control this terrible force would inevitably be futile. One cannot simply reason with these strange powers (*fremdartige Gewalten*), he suggested, nor simply rebuff them as bothersome interlopers (*unbequemen Eindringlings*) without provoking even more popular anger. On the other hand, any jurist who attempted to kowtow to public opinion would assuredly meet an even worse fate in the end. A jurist might initially be showered with coquettish praise; however, once the *aura popularis* (wind of popular favor) shifted, it would "whip the hat right off his head."[78] The only solution, Mittelstädt concluded, was for German judges to prepare for battle:

> That the judiciary must protect its independence against interference from both above and below seems self-evident. Courage and fearlessness seem especially

> necessary these days, perhaps even more so against democratic rather than against monarchical demands. Thus, our judges must gird themselves in triple armor [*dreifachem Erz*] against all those things which call themselves public opinion, and they must scrupulously avoid any suspicion of submissiveness to the *aura popularis* as well as any other possible grounds that might cast doubt on their impartiality and neutrality.[79]

Mittelstädt's language here is telling. His call is for judges to observe a chivalric code of courage and self-control when entering into battle with the "many-headed demon" of public opinion. A judge, he explicitly suggests, can only preserve his dignity in the courtroom and protect his class identity (*Standesbewusstsein*) outside the courtroom by making himself impervious to the temptations of public praise and the fire of public criticism. Only through such fearless stoicism, Mittelstädt argues, is there any hope of taming the beast.[80]

Not surprisingly, Mittelstädt's essay included substantial doubt about the efficacy and benefit of the jury system. Although he was not particularly critical of the Graef jury, he denounced newspapers that hailed the jurors in this case as if they had stepped in to prevent a "judicial murder." A panel of professional judges, he argued, would likely have come to the same verdict if faced with the same contradictory testimony and circumstantial evidence. This particular case, therefore, provided absolutely no support to the argument that jury courts were necessary to protect civic freedom and individual rights.[81] In fact, Mittelstädt lamented that since jurors were drawn from the general public, they were especially vulnerable to being influenced by public opinion—particularly since they were not sequestered during the course of a trial. Repeated warnings to jurors about avoiding outside influences and disregarding press coverage, such as those delivered by Judge Müller in the Graef case, would only serve to antagonize the jury and perhaps drive them consciously or unconsciously to disregard the judge's comments. Jurors, in other words, were ill-equipped to resist the corruptive power of public opinion, and they might actually try to turn themselves into representatives of it rather than simple arbiters of fact within a particular proceeding.[82] Although Mittelstädt argued that the general principle of an open courtroom was essential to prevent governmental interference, popular mistrust, gossip, and overall ignorance about the court system, he clearly did not believe that a full jury system was an ideal solution. Nevertheless, he seemed resigned to accept this flawed institution since "whoever dares to touch this cornerstone is labeled a reactionary and an obscurantist."[83]

Mittelstädt's argument was seconded by another prominent jurist, Carl Fuchs, who was a former prosecutor and judge at the Higher Regional Court in Jena. In his own review of the legal lessons of the Graef trial, Fuchs provided a full-throated defense of professional jurists and a withering attack on the jury system. After a vigorous defense of the conduct of Max Heinemann during the Graef trial, Fuchs took issue with those journalists who claimed that the trial had somehow proven the necessity of protecting jury courts from any potential reform. While the institution of the jury may have been adopted for historical and political reasons (associated with the Revolution of 1848), he argued it must now be eliminated for practical reasons. Not only did the jury courts put unreasonable burdens on the laymen who served, they also delegated responsibilities to people who were often unprepared and unable to exercise them properly. Whereas professional jurists had been trained to weigh evidence and apply complicated legal provisions, jurors were motivated by such things as "unjustified compassion, political prejudices, petty concerns about the families of defendants, or even hostility toward allegedly unjust laws."[84] In his opinion, the eventual demise of the jury courts was inevitable: "The time will come when one will perceive the importance and verity in the question of whether all decisions on questions of law—as all questions put before juries inevitably are—are best left to men who understand the law or men who do not."[85] In the interest of society, in the interest of justice, and in the interest of individual defendants, Fuchs argued, crucial functions within the legal system must be left to those with an appropriate education and expert training.

The essays by Mittelstädt and Fuchs were just the opening salvos. Just a short time later, the Association of German Jurists (*Deutscher Juristentag*) announced that the question of the efficacy of jury courts—especially as compared to that of the courts of lay assessors—would be a main topic of debate for their general meeting planned for September of 1886. In advance of the meeting, the organization commissioned two expert opinions on the matter from Justus von Olshausen, a regional court director in Schneidemühl (today Piła) who was already widely respected for his published commentaries on the German Penal Code, and Gustav von Elben, a prosecutor at the Regional Court in Ravensburg. Neither opinion turned out to be very supportive of the jury system in general nor of the capacity of ordinary jurors to weigh complex evidence free of bias. Olshausen, for example, advised that the jury system be abandoned entirely in favor of "great courts of lay assessors" (*Grosse Schöffengerichte*). In his opinion, the division between judges and juries was unnatural and led to conflicts between the two forces in court. Even worse, jurors were often influenced by inappropriate considerations, including private knowledge and sympathy or aversion to a particular defendant.[86] In his opinion, therefore, the jury courts had never demonstrated their usefulness and were undeserving of the praise that had been lavished on them in some quarters.

One other prominent voice to condemn the jury system at this time was Gustav Otto, a prosecutorial colleague of Max Heinemann at the Regional Court in Berlin. In early 1886, Otto had published an anonymous essay entitled "The Criminal World of Berlin," in which he explored the social and economic distress that helped criminality to fester within the modern city.[87] Otto's experiences as prosecutor in the infamous Dickhoff trial had also convinced him that popular sympathy for defendants was often misplaced, and that to make any progress against crime one must free himself from "sentimental theories of humaneness and the dignity of men, sympathetic cantatas about the poor who are led astray and fall victim to temptation, and specious theorems about the close connections between criminality and insanity which would eventually lead to the extreme conclusion that every offender should be freed from criminal accountability."[88] The only way to fight the criminal underworld of Berlin, Otto concluded, was to "mercilessly cut out the roots of this evil, and to cut without scruple as deeply as necessary to carve out all of the damaged tissue, as painful as this operation might be."[89] In his conclusion to this pamphlet and in a separate sequel entitled *Against the Jury Courts*, Otto insisted that the juries—and in fact all lay participation in criminal trials—must be eliminated as a part of this new ruthless campaign. Citing his long experience with criminal proceedings, Otto suggested that juries were not only ineffective and unpredictable, but downright dangerous. He claimed the problem was especially obvious in Berlin, where over 60 percent of criminal defendants were acquitted, as opposed to the lower but still unreasonably high 10–30 percent acquittal rate in the countryside. Otto blamed the high acquittal rate not only on juror biases but also on the inferior education (and occasionally moral qualities) of jurors, who were given the power to place their own personal judgments over and above the wisdom of judges and the spirit and letter of the law. The leniency of jury courts in Berlin had actually allowed criminals to enter the courtroom without real fear of conviction or punishment, and, according to Otto, it also emboldened them to mock judges and ridicule the legal proceedings themselves. It was highly desirable, therefore, to place the key parts of the German criminal justice system in the hands of highly trained and educated jurists rather than in the hands of ordinary people.[90]

Otto also suggested that the incompetence of jurors was actually encouraged by a new type of defense attorney who sought to purposely weed out any jurors with a modicum of intelligence or moral judgment so that he could manipulate the rest. These new professional attorneys, he suggested, were now in the majority and overshadowed those few good old-school lawyers who only reluctantly practiced in front of a jury.[91] Despite his claim to have had some initial optimism for the institution of the jury, Otto now claimed that "the end result of all my considerations and observations has been, and still remains, that I cannot see a single advantage to having a jury court system; indeed, I believe the entire institution to be so thoroughly flawed, and so gravely dangerous to the public good, that I must challenge it with all means available to me."[92]

The provocative arguments of Olshausen, Elben, and Otto prompted further public reactions both in the press and from other prominent jurists, including direct formal responses from prominent liberal attorneys such as Fritz Friedmann, Ludwig Fuld, and August Munckel—all of whom strongly favored retention of the jury system.[93] In the meantime, the conflict came to a head at the 1886 meeting of the Association of German Jurists in Wiesbaden, for which the original opinions by Elben and Olshausen had been solicited. Although the gathering was a restricted professional meeting for approximately three hundred legal specialists from across Germany, it received widespread attention because of the political stakes and public interest in debates about the usefulness of juries. Within the conference, discussions about the jury system occurred first in one of three major subcommittees. After vigorous debates, this subcommittee came to a rather startling conclusion. They voted, albeit by a very slim majority, for a resolution that the jury system did not deserve the trust placed in it, and they approved a recommendation that jury courts be replaced with courts of lay assessors. This resolution was then sent to the general plenum of the Association, where it was *rejected* by a majority. Instead, a substitute resolution was approved that characterized the jury system as an institution in immediate need of reform.[94] Although this final vote was a relief to many defenders of the jury system, it nonetheless left many with the sense that support for this institution had seriously eroded among members of the legal profession.[95]

In a summary of the conference, the liberal lawyer August Munckel suggested that although a majority of jurists still supported the inclusion of lay voices in determining criminal verdicts, a significant number now seemed willing to abandon the jury system. Even Rudolf von Gneist, a prominent old campaigner for the jury system, had started to put forward compromise proposals. Munckel, an enthusiastic supporter of the jury courts, clearly feared for the future of this institution in Germany. He ended his commentary on the conference with the hope that public opinion might step in to save the day: "Jurists have had their say; now it is perhaps time for laymen to make their voices heard."[96]

At least temporarily, August Munckel's hopes were answered. Over the next several decades, support for juries among the general public, resistance from particular state governments, and opposition from liberal and Socialist politicians helped to stymie repeated efforts to scrap the jury system. The intense debates in the wake of the Graef trial do suggest, however, that a high-water mark of support for juries had been reached—especially among professional jurists. During a later attempt by the German government to end the jury system in 1906, the liberal law professor Wolfgang Mittermaier lamented the degree to which his colleagues had already turned against the institution. He estimated that opposition had dramatically increased since the 1886 meeting of the Association of German Jurists in Wiesbaden and that a substantial number—perhaps a majority—now enthusiastically favored the replacement of jury courts with courts of lay assessors.[97]

The jury system would survive these continued attacks and eventually outlast the German Empire itself—but not by much. In 1924, Erich Emminger, justice minister of the Weimar Republic, approved an ordinance that scrapped the jury courts and formally replaced them with courts of lay assessors. Emminger was empowered to make such changes because of an Enabling Act (*Ermächtigungsgesetz*) passed by the Reichstag in December of 1923, which allowed the Weimar government extraordinary powers in the wake of the hyperinflation that was devastating the German economy. This dramatic reform, which was enacted despite angry protests among leftist parties in the Reichstag, was justified as a cost-saving measure. It was also the final blow for juries in Germany. Although the old title of the jury courts (*Schwurgerichte*) was retained after 1924 for criminal chambers of Regional Courts and still exists to this day, the epithet is now only a relic of a long and complicated history. Although there are still lay judges, today there are no more juries in Berlin.

EPILOGUE

The End of the Fairy Tale

Let us, at long last, return fully to the stories of the major characters in this drama—stories that are both rich in pathos and also in lessons about the world in which these men and women lived. On the night of his acquittal, Gustav Graef returned home with great relief to the embraces of his wife and children. His apartment quickly filled with flowers and congratulatory telegrams, and a small crowd gathered as friends arrived to pay their respects. But all was not well. Amidst the well-wishers, a muckraking journalist named Gustav Preusse had also found his way into the home, and he announced that he would publish an especially salacious account of the entire affair if he was not paid off. Preusse was quickly expelled from the household, but as we know, the scandal surrounding the family would not go away anytime soon.[1] For the next several weeks Graef's photograph was almost unavoidable as it sat in bookstore windows alongside photos of Bertha Rother and art card reproductions of his paintings. Thereafter, of course, came the public dispute between Karl Frenzel and the prosecutor Max Heinemann, which led Graef's colleagues in the Berlin Artists' Association to side with Heinemann, and—at least in public perception—against Graef. After his resignation from the Berlin Artists' Association, Graef struggled to get public recognition for his work. Although he did keep some contacts within the group, many artists shunned him, and he was too timid to approach still others for fear of rejection.[2]

In the months after the trial, it appears that Graef spent considerable time working on a memoir about his ordeal that would recount his experiences and publicly defend his reputation. In a recent article, Klaus-Peter Möller, an archivist at the Theodor Fontane Archive in Potsdam, reported that he discovered a handwritten copy of this document in the hands of a private collector, in which Graef carefully recounted his innocent relationship with Bertha Rother, his martyrdom during the trial, and his stunned sadness at the infamous Artists' Declaration—all over the course of more than two hundred pages.[3] For Graef, the writing of such a manuscript may have helped to vent his frustration at being a social outcast, but his memoir remained unpublished and it thus had absolutely no effect on his public reputation.

Not that infamy was without its benefits. Several newspapers reported that the art collector Otto Kaufmann had paid Graef approximately 30,000 Marks for the purchase of *The Fairy Tale*. This was a substantial sum, approximately equal to an entire year's income for Graef during the height of his career. This one payment, by the way, recouped almost all of the money Graef had spent on Bertha Rother and her family during their long association.[4] The windfall from this painting, however, could not provide full recompense for Graef's disastrous loss of status and prestige. In 1889, he wrote a letter to the Prussian minister of culture, Gustav von Goßler, all but begging him to visit Kaufmann's Berlin exhibit of his paintings in order to see for himself the "artistic worthiness" of his work. In his letter, Graef listed several artworks in addition to *The Fairy Tale* that were included in the show, and he specifically emphasized two sketches (*Vorwürfe*) that he hoped Goßler might find especially pleasing: *The Apotheosis of Kaiser Wilhelm I* and *The Apotheosis of Kaiser Friedrich III*. These sketches were obviously nationalistic works that hearkened back to Graef's famous historical paintings from midcentury while at the same time paying tribute to the two recently deceased German emperors. Graef's appeal seems to have been unsuccessful; there is no record of any answer from Goßler, no evidence that he ever visited the exhibit, and no surviving copy of either of the two sketches.[5]

Gustav Graef's attempts to win the approval of Goßler did not mean that he had given up his own experimentations with nude figures. In fact, Otto Kaufmann's 1889 Berlin exhibit, staged in a hall on Friedrichstrasse in central Berlin, featured several new works, including *Persecuted Fantasy* (*Der verfolgte Phantasie*), an idealized nude figure floating upwards and away from the chained rabble beneath. Contemporaries interpreted this work as Graef's acerbic response to those moral Philistines who had prosecuted, persecuted, and shunned him—and many were not pleased by it. A review of the exhibit in the popular journal *Die Gegenwart*, a weekly that was once led by Paul Lindau, savaged this painting and reminded Graef that he had been on trial for perjury, not for his art. The newspaper criticized both the idea and the execution of the work, characterizing it as a "complete flop" (*Schlag ins Wasser*). A collection of clothed female half-figures in the exhibit, entitled *The Four Elements*, was described by the reviewer as banal, insignificant, and unworthy even for placement on packages of chocolates.[6] Despite Graef's continued experimentation, then, it is clear that his most productive period—and certainly his most successful work—was behind him.[7]

This is not to suggest that Graef was without friends, supporters, and admirers. Almost immediately after hearing of Graef's acquittal, the respected scientist Emil du Bois Reymond sent him a sympathetic note of support and made arrangements to have his portrait painted.[8] Du Bois Reymond, a professor at the University of Berlin, was already internationally known for his discoveries in electrophysiology—including nerve action potential. Graef also painted a portrait of the politician Ferdinand von Hansemann in 1891, as well as a portrait of Robert Koch—an internationally famous scientist, who was one of the founders of modern microbiology and would eventually win the Nobel Prize for his work on tuberculosis.[9] In some cases, those who commissioned portraits did so as gestures of support, but in other cases it seems that the immense skill of Graef as a portraitist trumped any sense of shame that might have come from engaging him as an artist. For example, Robert Koch apparently first contacted Graef to commission a portrait after marveling at a painting of Graef's brother in-law, Oskar Liebreich, who was a prominent pharmacologist and professor at the University of Berlin.[10] In 1892, Malwine von Arnim, the sister of Otto von Bismarck, wrote to Graef to ask about the price he might charge for a portrait. She said she had written on behalf of several of her close acquaintances who had been moved by Graef's portrait of Malwine's daughter, Sybille von Bismarck, painted more than a decade earlier.[11]

These occasional commissions do not seem to have been enough to stave off some financial difficulties. In fact, Gustav Graef's letters to his daughter Sabine reveal the degree to which the family was facing financial instability by the early 1890s. Because Graef's income still came primarily from portraits of the aristocratic and bourgeois elite, the maintenance of social networks had always been absolutely essential to his work. Portraits tended to be displayed prominently in the homes of wealthy benefactors, making them visible for all the guests. As I suggested earlier, this would often lead to a "snowball effect," where one prominently displayed portrait could lead to multiple new commissions. With those fertile social connections now limited by the scandal, the most lucrative source of family income was undoubtedly affected.[12] In an 1893 letter to his daughter Sabine, Gustav Graef suggested that it was essential for both of them to take any commission that was offered, and he encouraged her to pursue friends and acquaintances to have their portraits painted. At the same time, he told his daughter that he pined for a life where he would be free from his dependence on painting for income.[13] In her memoirs, Sabine Lepsius suggested that her father's estate had been diminished enough by the time of his death that it was relatively easy to manage and divide among his children.

Gustav Graef died on January 6, 1895, at the age of seventy-four. His eulogy was delivered by the pastor Johannes Lepsius, who was the brother-in-law of Graef's daughter Sabine. The funeral was attended by a large crowd, and representatives from the Royal Academy of Arts—to which Graef still belonged—participated in both the funeral ceremony and the burial.[14] Even this sad occasion, however, did not come without its minor scandals. Sabine Lepsius later bitterly complained about the ridiculous "satyr play" that immediately followed her father's funeral, as young models bombarded the family with pleas for support after the death of their patron.[15] Although Sabine had been a fierce defender of her father at trial, some of their letters during the last years of his life suggest a fairly troubled relationship—in part because of her father's behavior. For example, in a letter sent less than a year after the death of his wife Franziska in 1893, Graef included a point-by-point refutation of several accusations that Sabine had made against him, including escorting young models around the city and hosting wild late-night Skat parties with strange women. Graef proclaimed his innocence, and he suggested that all the alleged incidents were the product of misunderstandings, misperceptions, and mistaken identity. He acknowledged she would be difficult to convince, but wondered mournfully: "What hope remains for me to be judged more favorably by the powerful people who manufacture sentiments and reputations, when you—who wish me well—view the facts in such an exaggerated way as the three sins mentioned at the start of this letter."[16] It is not clear how successful Gustav Graef was in persuading his daughter of his good character or to what degree they had reconciled before his death.

Of course, Sabine's letters and memoirs remind us how severely the psychological and emotional toll of this ordeal must have affected Gustav Graef's family. Although there are no surviving letters from Franziska Graef, a letter written to her by her friend Robert von Keudell gives some insight into the torment she must have suffered at the time of her husband's arrest. "After a few weeks," he had tried to reassure her, "we will all look back on this as a bad dream . . . and then everything will go back to normal, and the power of the mind to forget such things will not fail you."[17] Of course, the arrest was just the beginning of what must have seemed an interminable nightmare. As Graef's daughter Sabine described it in her own memoirs: "Our intimate life was thrown into the public spotlight; despite the eventual triumph we lost our sense of security in society, something that was only restored very gradually."[18] This was not just idle talk. At the time of the trial, Sabine had been secretly engaged to Ludwig Traube, who would later become a classical philologist at the Ludwig-Maximilian-Universität in Munich. After the verdict, Traube offered to make their engagement public as a gesture of support for the

Graef family. Sabine refused, and—at least in part due to the stresses surrounding the trial and its aftermath—the engagement was soon called off. Also, although Sabine's memoirs do not mention the anti-Semitic attacks on Graef after the trial, there is good reason to believe that her mother's Jewish heritage made the injury to the family's reputation all the more painful and frightening, particularly given how common social discrimination and prejudice were in Germany during that time.[19]

It is interesting to note that controversy—and even public sex scandals—affected several people within Graef's circle of friends and supporters over the next few years. The scientist Robert Koch, for example, had been embroiled in controversy starting in 1890 when he suddenly announced that he had discovered a vaccine for tuberculosis. Koch's cure, however, did not seem to achieve the results that his experiments had first promised. He resigned his professorship to work on the vaccine more closely, but his reputation—at least temporarily—was seriously damaged. At about the same time, Koch also divorced his wife and scandalously married the seventeen-year-old Hedwig Freiburg—a woman whom he had allegedly met at the studio of her art teacher: Gustav Graef.[20] According to one biography of Koch, the real story was even more salacious. Johannes Grüntzig and Heinz Mehlhorn suggest that Robert Koch actually met Hedwig Freiburg much earlier—when she was a very young actress in Ludwig Barnay's Berliner Theater. If true, this would mean that Hedwig was younger than seventeen when the relationship started, and that their affair occurred at a time when Koch was still married to his first wife. The suggestion made by Grüntzig and Mehlhorn is that Koch had originally requested Graef to paint his portrait not solely because of his skill as an artist, but also because it would make a convenient cover story about the start of his relationship with Hedwig. After all, a relationship with a seventeen-year-old budding artist was controversial enough, but far more palatable than an *adulterous* relationship with an even younger actress—a profession that still had some negative connotations at the time. Whatever the truth, just a few years later Gustav Graef would serve as the best man at their wedding.

The author and critic Paul Lindau, whose coverage of the Graef trial we have reviewed in depth, also ran into trouble. In 1888, three years after the trial, Lindau's wife of fifteen years—the same woman for whom he had demanded a painting from Graef as a "gift"—left him for the French journalist Jacques Saint-Cère. Although the novelist Theodore Fontane described Lindau as "happy as a clam" (*kreuzfidel*) as he waited for the divorce to be completed, the scandalous story had to have been humiliating for him. Jacques Saint-Cère was one of several aliases for Jacob Rosenthal, a journalist who had himself just broken off an adulterous affair with Wanda von Dunajew, the former wife (and dominatrix) of Leopold von Sacher-Masoch.[21]

Soon after his divorce, Lindau began a new relationship with the Russian author and actress Elsa von Schabelsky, who was twenty years his junior and worked in the same Berliner Theater that had employed Robert Koch's second wife, Hedwig Freiberg. A year later, however, Schabelsky left Lindau for the younger journalist and actor Maximilian Harden.[22] This time, Lindau did not take the news well. He wrote a series of letters to Schabelsky insisting that she leave town immediately or face the consequences. Over the next several months, Lindau apparently used his influence to make Schabelsky's life miserable; he had her fired from the Berliner Theater and used his connections to make sure her work as an aspiring playwright was rejected by theaters and publishers.[23]

In response, Schabelsky turned to the editor of the leftist *Berliner Volkszeitung*, Franz Mehring, for help. Mehring energetically took Schabelsky's side against Lindau, and he penned several harsh attacks against him. Mehring printed verbatim the threatening letters that Lindau had sent Schabelsky, and in numerous articles, he skewered Lindau and his friends. Lindau's allies, such as the director of the *Freie Volksbühne*, Otto Brahm, responded with their own public defense of Lindau, and as a result of the vitriolic exchanges, Mehring was eventually forced out as editor of the *Berliner Volksblatt*. But this did not end the conflict. Mehring sought revenge against Lindau by publishing two angry books, and Schabelsky even published a play called *Der berühmte Mann* (The Famous Man) that openly mocked him.[24] After a while, Lindau was shamed enough by this extended public spectacle that he left the country for a long trip to the United States. He eventually returned to Germany, but he did not pick up his work in Berlin until almost a decade later.

Perhaps fittingly, many of the artworks produced by Gustav Graef also had their own complex and even bizarre histories in the years after the death of the artist. Several of his early nationalist paintings are currently owned by museums such as the *Alte Nationalgalerie* in Berlin and the *Kunstforum Ostdeutsche Galerie* in Regensburg. The *Landesmuseum für Kultur und Geschichte Berlins* owns several of his portraits, and his painting of Sir Francis Galton is owned by the National Portrait Gallery in London. *The Fairy Tale*, the most infamous of Gustav Graef's paintings, is still in private hands. This painting toured Europe in the years after the trial, including stops in Vienna and Amsterdam, where it attracted significant attention and mixed reviews. A photogravure of the painting was included in an 1891 book published in Philadelphia, which purported to be a list of the one

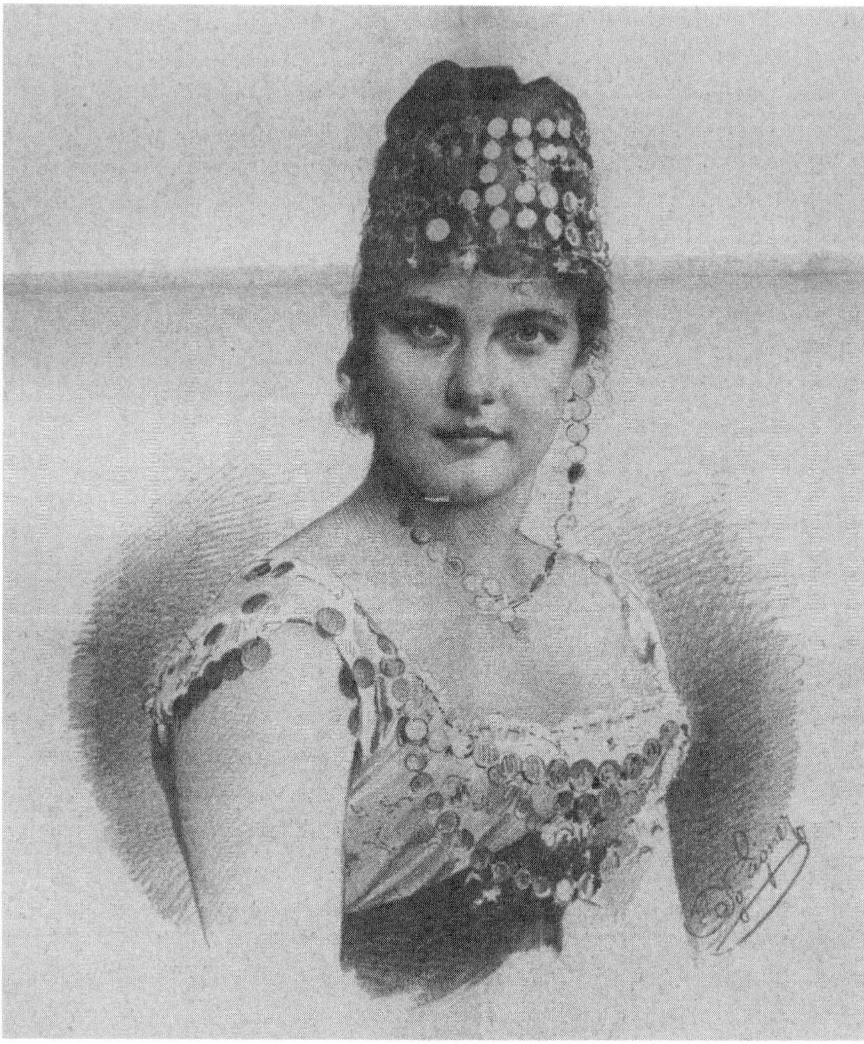

FIGURE 16. Sketch of Bertha Rother in costume. *Der Humorist* (Vienna), no. 5 (March 1, 1887): 1. Courtesy of ANNO / Österreichische Nationalbibliothek.

hundred most important works of modern art.[25] The painting itself, however, soon completely faded from view. In 1972, a reader of the *Berliner Morgenpost* claimed to have encountered it hanging in a private home in El Paso, Texas.[26] Finally, a private art dealer claimed to have rediscovered the painting, which had been retitled *Meeresjungfrau* (The Naiad), and it was placed on auction in 1988. It is not entirely clear if this work is an earlier or later version of the painting; as of this writing, however, it is still listed as available for sale.[27]

An even stranger story involves Gustav Graef's famous early painting *Ferdinande von Schmettau Sacrificing her Hair at the Altar of the Fatherland.* This patriotic painting was originally part of a traveling exhibit in the 1860s sponsored by the Prussian government for the fiftieth anniversary of the Wars of Liberation. During the Imperial era, the image was commonly featured in German school textbooks as a lesson for young children on the importance of patriotism and self-sacrifice for the Fatherland. The painting would continue to be used for such purposes long after Graef's death and well into the twentieth century. In fact, it was even adopted for propaganda purposes by the National Socialists. During the hard winter of 1933/1934, the Nazi government placed reproductions of Graef's image on postcards, which it sold publicly to help fund the Winter Relief Charities (*Winterhilfswerk*).[28] In Graef's image of Ferdinande von Schmettau sacrificing during a time of need, the Nazis found a historical precedent to support their ideal of personal sacrifice for a German "people's community" (*Volksgemeinschaft*). Perhaps not surprisingly, the name of Graef did not appear on these Nazi postcards. It is one of those unique and sad ironies of history that Gustav Graef—a non-Jewish painter whose art had been publicly attacked for its "Jewishness"—would eventually have his most famous painting used as propaganda by a Nazi regime that was already beginning to persecute and would soon be attempting to annihilate all of European Jewry. This painting, by the way, is still owned by the *Nationalgalerie* in Berlin, although it is rarely exhibited.

It is perhaps appropriate to finish this epilogue with a few brief notes about the fate of the Rother family. As for Anna Rother and her mother Auguste, there is relatively little information. Immediately after the verdict, the *Berliner Börsen-Courier* reported that, unlike the celebrations held for Gustav Graef, there had been no happy homecoming for Auguste and Anna. Since the family had been unable to pay rent during their incarceration, their apartment had been leased to someone else. Most of their furniture and belongings had apparently either been pilfered by neighbors or confiscated by the creditors to whom Auguste Rother owed substantial sums of money.[29] With no home and no income, without Bertha or Professor Graef to support them, and with little Lieschen (Auguste's youngest daughter) already on her deathbed—one can only imagine how difficult it was for the two to make ends meet over the next several years. Perhaps, then, it should not surprise us entirely to read that in February 1899 Auguste Rother had once again been arrested for aggravated pandering (*schweren Küppelei*), apparently involving the pimping out of her own daughter Anna Rother.[30]

Bertha Rother's fate was significantly more complicated. What information we do have about her life after the trial comes in brief snippets, often from unlikely places, and almost always written in a sarcastic or critical tone. Truth is not always easy to discern in these accounts, but interesting stories abound. As Paul Lindau might say, a description of Bertha's life after the trial would be an undertaking worthy of a Zola—and in fact, her life story unfolds in newspaper accounts with an eerie similarity to the tragic main character of Émile Zola's *Nana*.[31]

In the immediate aftermath of the trial, police officials reported that Bertha quickly returned to an "immoral lifestyle" and sought to capitalize on public attention generated by the case.[32] She was seen shortly after the trial in the company of the young Swiss artist Karl Stauffer-Bern, who painted her portrait and was widely rumored to be her new lover.[33] Within a few months, however, Bertha had decided to abandon Berlin completely and move on to Vienna, where she would attempt a career as a singer and performer on stage.[34] The monthly theater magazine *Der Humorist* published very positive reviews of her shows at the Orpheum Theater, which were said to be popular with Viennese audiences. The editor of this journal, Isidor Kohn, praised both Bertha's surprising vocal range and her stunning beauty—the latter of which he demonstrated for his readers by the inclusion of large sketches of her in various alluring costumes (see figure 16). In what may have revealed a slight conflict of interest, Kohn also praised Bertha for generously performing two of his own musical compositions in her show.[35]

Bertha's stay in Vienna was not without controversy. According to a newspaper in New Zealand, which followed her exploits rather closely, Bertha soon became involved with a married diplomat, whom she tried to blackmail once he decided to end the affair. Allegedly, police searched her apartment and found incriminating evidence, and—at least according to the newspaper—only her "substantial charms" helped her escape an order of expulsion from the country.[36] Bertha then became engaged to Josef Edler von Schroll, the young son of a wealthy industrialist of the same name, who had made his money in textiles. According to a small newspaper in the German region of Mecklenburg, Bertha and her fiancé blew through enormous amounts of money before his father could intervene.[37]

Apparently, before this last relationship was forcibly ended, the younger Schroll purchased his fiancée a substantial estate called Flessenow on the Schweriner See in Mecklenburg. This estate of 240,000 Ruthen (approximately 1,300 acres) provided Bertha Rother with luxurious accommodations in a manor house within the village of Flessenow, along with fertile fields, forests, and hunting grounds; it also potentially came with special status and rights as a "lady of the manor" (*Rittergutsbesitzerin*). In the still quasi-feudalistic society of the eastern provinces, the owner of such an estate (if male) had automatic membership in the local parliament (*Landtag*). Thus, any man Bertha married could now automatically become a parliamentary official. In addition, if she submitted a simple application for citizenship of Mecklenburg, she could also wield substantial local rights as a magistrate, including the authority to imprison for twenty-four hours anyone who endangered public order. One newspaper took great delight in mocking the idea of a former prostitute and nude model now holding court in an old manor: "It is reported that the lady of the castle has taken to her new duties quite seriously and is delighted with her station. There is a fine smack of the opera-bouffe in the offhand theatrical style with which she boldly delivers her judgments to the intense wonderment of the country folk who are subject to her jurisdiction."[38]

Perhaps predictably, this rags-to-riches story—like that of Zola's Nana Coupeau—would not have a happy ending. Less than a year after taking possession of her Mecklenburg estate, Bertha was reported to have sold it to a Herr Paasch from Lübeck, and to have fled in a desperate attempt to escape the boredom of the countryside.[39] The *Chicago Tribune* reported that in the spring of 1894, she launched a tour of European cities as a "skirt-dancer" under the management of a man named Joseph Deutsch. This tour came to a sudden end, however, when Deutsch was arrested in Frankfurt for forging bank drafts.[40] Bertha Rother apparently surfaced some months later back in Berlin, living in a shabby apartment in the Prenzlauer Berg district. The *Dresdner Nachrichten* reported that word had spread around the capital that she was once again appearing at the courthouse in Moabit, this time as a witness. The newspaper almost gleefully reported that the crowds which had gathered spontaneously to get a look at the legendary "Fairy Tale Model" eventually left in disappointment once it became clear that Bertha no longer possessed the perfect beauty of her youth.[41] One newspaper later described a wan Bertha Rother as one of the women who had caused a scene at Gustav Graef's funeral in January of 1895, apparently after being turned away by police at the request of the Graef family.[42]

After this incident, the trail of evidence becomes more sparse. In 1896, at the age of thirty-two, Bertha apparently entered into a brief and brutal marriage with a salesman, who managed to spend most of her remaining money before their eventual divorce.[43] More than a decade later, the author Fedor von Zobeltitz, who maintained a detailed chronicle of life in Berlin in the years before World War I, mentioned in his entry for August 8, 1910 that Bertha Rother had been arrested for shoplifting. According to Zobeltitz, Bertha had apparently opened a small paper shop in the Rixdorf neighborhood of Berlin under the name Bertha Stein; she was arrested for allegedly shoplifting several postcards from another store and put on trial at a District Court (*Amtsgericht*) in Berlin. According to Zobeltitz, after she cried in front of the judge and complained that the entire thing was a misunderstanding, he let her off with a mild sentence. What is especially notable about Zobeltitz's account is how freshly he seemed to remember the Graef trial almost twenty-five years earlier and how joyfully he recounted it in extensive detail. As he concluded his diary entry: "And so Graef's *Fairy Tale* once again becomes a topic of discussion—and the old men, who back in that time were in the prime of their youth, begin to smile somewhat wistfully . . ."[44] Apparently, even decades after the trial, wherever Bertha Rother went, the memory of "The Fairy Tale Model" was sure to follow.

The final pieces of evidence about Bertha Rother's fate come from an article memorializing the fiftieth anniversary of the Graef case. According to this story, Bertha had quickly sunk into alcoholism after her return to Berlin, and by 1912 she was homeless and wandering the streets. There is, of course, some reason to believe that syphilis, first diagnosed during compulsory health checks required by the Berlin vice squad when Bertha was a young teen, may have also been finally taking its toll on her health and mental state. Although syphilitic patients were often treated with various mercury compounds, such cures were not always effective and might have their own severe long-term impacts. Regardless of the causes of her long slow decline, Bertha Rother would not survive long on the streets of Berlin. On New Year's Eve 1913, Bertha was found lying in a pool of blood along a public street. She had apparently been brutally raped, beaten, and then left for dead. Bertha Rother was taken to the hospital, where she died one week later—just a few days before her forty-ninth birthday.[45]

CONCLUSION

There is no doubt that the Graef trial makes for a compelling story. A good story alone, however, does not make for good history. What matters for a historian is not simply patterns of character development, dramatic plot twists, or a final climax and dénouement; what is essential instead are the insights that such a story can provide about the complex and nuanced world in which the story took place. If the Graef case may seem ripe for novelization or screenplay development, it is also a nearly ideal episode for leveraging historical insights.

The fact that a story like this is appealing to us speaks to some similarities between our own culture and that of Imperial Germany. One could certainly argue that we are at least as fixated (or perhaps more fixated!) on sensational trials and public scandals than the Germans were 130 years ago. Our news flashes may come more quickly and via electronic means rather than by broadsheet, but then as now, such public events merged easily into contemporary political debates and could quickly become touchstones of public memory. And yet, one cannot imagine a Graef trial occurring today in the same way it did in 1885 Berlin. Too much of this episode appears strange to us, the product of a world that is remote in both distance and time.

Perhaps the most obvious bit of "strangeness" that the Graef trial exposes is the pervasiveness of a complex honor culture within Imperial Germany. Although no physical duels occurred between the main figures of this drama, we can very much see an alternate type of duel taking place constantly both inside and outside the courtroom—this one fought with speeches, pens, and print rather than swords or pistols. For Gustav Graef especially, but also for jurists such as Boguslaw Müller and Max Heinemann, the courtroom and the press became public battlegrounds where they fought desperately to defend and repair their injured personal honor.

Standards of honor were also frequently deployed in this historical episode as a method of asserting the status and influence of one professional group over another. This was part of a longer process of professionalization that began in the late nineteenth century, as a variety of occupations sought to distinguish expert practitioners from lay people so as to make claims to special value and status, and to defend themselves against increased competition and the demands of social "outsiders."[1] In the field of journalism, for example, many editors and writers pushed back against the ungentlemanly forms of sensational "new journalism" that seemed to aim at the lowest common denominator of public tastes rather than reporting objectively and in a manner that educated and ennobled readers. Of course, this anger was in part borne out of jealousy, as liberal newspapers tended to outsell their conservative and Catholic counterparts. We have also seen it in the Association of Berlin Artists, which had no problem abandoning a member who was perceived as having acted dishonorably—especially once he had enlisted the public support of an art critic and sworn enemy of the guild. Finally, we have seen this defensiveness most powerfully evident in the actions of professional jurists, who battled fiercely against the influence of "lay people," against those that occupied rival positions within the courtroom, and even against rebellious or dishonorable members of their own profession. To serve as a prosecutor, judge, or defense attorney during this era was to be a member of an occupation seemingly at risk of losing status and influence in a rapidly changing world.

If claims of honor, education, and experience were frequently deployed as justifications for special power and prestige in Imperial German society, stereotypes of immorality, ignorance, and criminality were also commonly used by the same elites to justify the exclusion of social outsiders—especially the urban lower classes. Summaries of the Graef trial by journalists such as Paul Lindau juxtaposed the behavior of witnesses such as the Rothers, the Hammermanns, and especially Intrau and Kühnle with the conduct of more distinguished witnesses, including the defendant Gustav Graef himself. In both Lindau's essay and the shocking "revelations" about the Berlin criminal underworld penned shortly after the trial by the prosecutor Gustav Otto, we can see representations of the lower classes not simply as immoral and uncultured but as inherently dangerous to the stability of German society. If the modern metropolis of Berlin held promise as a locus of culture, as a source of economic power, and as a symbol of the unified empire, it was also viewed as containing an especially virulent strain of moral depravity and criminality that would be passed down hereditarily across generations. These stereotypes, reinforced by a growing fear of working-class militancy, led to the sense that the urban slums of Berlin (and other cities) were a potential powder keg that might eventually destroy German civilization.

The tenor of trial coverage in the Graef case also tended to reflect stereotypes about women within this culture of honor. On the one hand, the opinions of bourgeois women about the Graef case were not recorded for public consumption; these conspicuous public silences were both enforced and voluntary, as legal restrictions made public comments on such sensitive matters dangerous, and bourgeois norms about female behavior made any such comments seem ignoble. Women such as Sabine and Franziska Graef were not expected to speak out publicly in such circumstances—even if their own honor and social status were also at stake. Lower-class women, on the other hand, were heavily criticized for their failure to silence themselves at appropriate times. Paul Lindau consistently portrayed working-class women as inappropriately vocal, assertive, and irrational, and he held up their demeanor and actions in court as proof of their moral depravity and cultural backwardness. Women's voices in debates about the Graef case were not just silenced or criticized, they were also appropriated by male authors who provided satirical proof that a woman's contribution to public debates could only be worthy of public scorn. Bertha Rother, of course, is perhaps the most powerful example here. Held up both as an ideal of feminine beauty and an exemplar of sexual depravity, mercilessly mocked by depictions that emphasized her physical appearance and dismissed any intellectual or moral substance, Bertha could never quite escape the fairy tale that both defined and confined her.

The Graef trial, improbably, also served as a potent piece of evidence for anti-Semites that Jewish influence had corrupted German high culture, infiltrated the press, inhibited the functioning of the criminal justice system, and lowered general standards of morality. For Jewish participants in the trial (or those who were converts from Judaism), including Gustav Graef's wife, his lawyer John Simson, and the prosecutor Max Heinemann, the trial served as a reminder that almost every public event or scandal could serve as anti-Semitic propaganda—even those examples where Jews operated on opposing sides and had conflicting interests. Although the public attacks launched by men such as Otto Glagau, Adolf Stöcker, and Carl Paasch seem extreme and even paranoid from our perspective, we should remember that these sorts of accusations were a common part of political discourse at the time. If most Germans would probably not have identified themselves explicitly as anti-Semites in the 1880s, there would undoubtedly still have been some sympathy with Glagau's assertion that the Graef case was a powerful example of the Jewish Question.

In general, the political and intellectual culture of early Imperial Germany was marked far more by the rhetoric of exclusion than the rhetoric of inclusion. In the aftermath of unification, German political discourse included the conspicuous labeling of opposition parties (including members of the Socialist Party, Catholic Center Party, and even some ultraconservatives) as *Reichsfeinde*, or "enemies of the Reich." While political opponents were not deported to concentration camps in the Second Reich as they would be in the Third, they were still targeted for sustained police harassment and aggressive prosecution. In this atmosphere, political debates (both in the Reichstag and in newspapers) were often imbued with rhetoric that emphasized the disloyalty, untrustworthiness, and un-Germanness of those with alternate points of view. In the process of forging a common identity as Germans, this kind of "othering" became common far beyond the political sphere as well. National and religious minorities within Germany and Imperial subjects outside of Germany often faced crude stereotypes and treatment that could range from subtle discrimination to overt brutality. As we saw in chapter three, even modern trends in art, literature, and music could also be labeled as "foreign" and portrayed as inimical to indigenous German traditions.

In tracing the story of the Graef case, then, this book paints a rather frightful picture of a culture riven with deep social and political divisions, plagued by fear in the midst of a tremendous social and economic transformation, and troubled by both a "crisis of masculinity" and a perceived cultural decline. This is an accurate representation, but it is also only half of the true picture. To dismiss or underestimate the presence of substantial "progressive" and democratizing tendencies within Imperial Germany is necessarily to misread the history of this era. The story of the Graef trial is *not* simply the story of a society moving backward, with bourgeois elites abandoning liberal principles in a desperate rearguard action to prevent the rise of modern mass society. Indeed, the political, cultural, and legal clashes described here represent the growing pains of an often wrenching and disorienting transformation, but one that was inexorably and unavoidably moving forward.

Until relatively recently, many historians had described the development of German liberalism during the *Kaiserreich* as a story of weakness, "ideological and strategic emptiness," and hypocrisy.[2] Hans-Ulrich Wehler's classic 1975 work, *The German Empire,* for example, described the failed efforts of the liberal bourgeoisie to achieve meaningful democratic reforms during this period. Despite new law codes and the granting of universal manhood suffrage for elections to the German Reichstag, Wehler argued, the German bourgeoisie had failed to push for further democratization, and instead compromised key liberal principles in order to protect their elite status and ensure government support. This failure of principle, he suggested, not only helped to preserve archaic and authoritarian institutions in

Imperial Germany (including oppressive elements of the criminal justice system), it also put Germany on a *Sonderweg* or "special path" that led away from modern democratic principles and toward an eventual fascist dictatorship.[3]

Wehler's powerful critique of German liberalism was countered just a few years later in a landmark study by David Blackbourn and Geoff Eley. Blackbourn and Eley challenged Wehler's portrayal of the German bourgeoisie as being weak and ineffective; more specifically, they accused Wehler of being too focused on legislative and electoral setbacks in estimating the success of German liberalism, and they pointed instead to significant transformations in German culture as evidence of the *embourgeoisment* of German society. Even if the German bourgeoisie never achieved an actual political revolution, the hegemony of liberal values itself constituted a kind of "silent revolution."[4]

Recent scholarship has tended to side with Blackbourn and Eley, but it has also provided an even more nuanced analysis. Both Margaret Anderson and Alexandra Ortmann, for example, have emphasized that despite the distinct advantages held by aristocratic and economic elites in Germany's political and legal systems, the German Empire was, in fact, undergoing a gradual process of political and legal democratization. In the political sphere, Margaret Anderson argues, the institution of universal manhood suffrage and a (relatively) free press led to the development of a powerful grassroots political culture and greater opportunities for dissent and resistance to government initiatives.[5] Ortmann suggests a similar story for German legal culture. Despite increasing hostility voiced by many professional jurists against recent liberal reforms such as the open courtroom, the open bar, and the jury court, such institutions remained a vital part of the legal culture of the *Kaiserreich*. Ortmann adds that over the course of Imperial Germany ordinary people were able to have a substantial effect on the criminal justice system as they closely followed newspaper coverage of legal affairs, understood the function of the justice system, demanded their legal rights, and pursued their personal interests. If complaints about "class justice" still echoed throughout this period, ordinary Germans nonetheless grew to believe in the courtroom as a legitimate site for conflict resolution and the pursuit of justice. This, Ortmann suggests, was not the outlook of humble subjects (*Untertanen*) but of self-conscious citizens.[6]

What we see in the story of the Graef trial, therefore, is not just personal and professional resistance by the bourgeoisie against modernization, democratization, and social change, but also an underlying commitment to preserving liberal legal reforms that ran fairly deep within German society. It is true, for example, that the Graef trial (along with the Sarauw trial soon afterward) sparked a government effort to restrict press coverage of trials closed to the public for reasons of moral sensibilities and national security. However, what is remarkable here is *not* that the government, aided by an alliance of conservative and National Liberal lawmakers, successfully passed laws that restricted press freedoms and the openness of court proceedings. What is noteworthy instead is that this legislation was passed only after three long years of resistance by the Reichstag, which in the end produced a bill fundamentally different from—and fundamentally weaker than—government officials had wished. This resistance, of course, came despite the fact that the legislation was viewed by Otto von Bismarck and his son Herbert as an immediate priority that was absolutely vital for national security.

It is also important to note that the Lex Graef, the 1888 law which threatened punishment for newspaper trial coverage that violated standards of public decency, does not seem to have had any meaningful impact on the future press coverage of such trials. For better or worse, despite repeated complaints and additional failed legislative initiatives, German judges would still tend to favor an open courtroom and German journalists would still continue to bring the most scandalous details of criminal trials to public attention. The same would be true even after the gruesome Heinze murder trial of 1891, the salacious Kotze Affair of the mid-1890s, and the notorious Eulenburg Affair of 1907—the last two of which were publicly humiliating for the kaiser and his entourage. Press coverage of scandalous trials may not seem the best measure of the strength of liberal ideals in Imperial Germany—and yet, as Martin Kohlrausch points out, the requisite preconditions for public scandals usually include a government that respects the rule of law, a substantial freedom of the press, and a variegated political landscape.[7]

The same kind of argument can be made about the institution of the jury courts. Although the jury in the Graef trial did nothing unseemly, and while their vote for acquittal was not entirely unexpected, the case nonetheless became a launching pad for attacks against the qualifications of lay jurors and fierce defenses of their role in dispensing criminal justice. The rhetoric of this public debate, as well as the contentious 1886 conference of the Association of German Jurists, clearly demonstrate the growing resistance among professional jurists to having untrained laypeople decide questions of guilt or innocence. However, even if, as Alexandra Ortmann rightly suggests, German jurists were turning decisively away from the jury courts in an attempt to distinguish their own expertise and experience from those untrained in the law, we must remember that all attempts to root out the jury courts and replace them with courts of lay assessors were completely unsuccessful during the Imperial period. Dogged resistance from Social Democrats and left-liberals in the Reichstag (as well as significant resistance within the bar itself) meant that juries remained in operation despite the growing ambivalence. It was not Hermann von Schelling, the secretary of state of the Imperial Justice Office (and later Prussian justice minister) who eventually presided over the dismantling of the jury system, but Erich Emminger, the centrist minister of justice in the Weimar Republic. In other words, the jury courts were not scrapped after public debates within a quasi-authoritarian state, but by an emergency decree within a democratic republic.

A revolution in the German art world was also slowly and inexorably taking place in Germany just as it was elsewhere in Europe—despite the efforts of idealists such as Anton von Werner. The decision of the Berlin Artists' Association to side with the prosecutor in the Graef case, Max Heinemann, in his public dispute with Karl Frenzel had been both an attempt to defend the honor of the profession and an effort to rebuke lay critics such as Frenzel as untrained and unqualified outsiders. This collective public response, however, concealed a growing split within the Berlin (and German) art world that would fracture it permanently over the next decade. Attempts by the Berlin Artists' Association to restrict German art to "proper" topics and themes, as well as all efforts to shield German art from French influence, would eventually fail as new generations of artists and a newly invigorated private art market fed a growing secession from artistic norms and a rebellion against control from "above." The Graef case did not cause this artistic revolution, but we can sense the growing rifts in the rhetoric surrounding the trial.

Despite the ugly anti-Semitic propaganda associated with the trial, we should also be careful not to assume that such rhetoric represented part of an inexorable decline into the vicious anti-Semitism that would later aid the rise of Adolf Hitler and the Nazi Party. In our own historical imagination, the "Second German Reich" often exists within the ominous shadow of the Third. Hindsight, which can be both a valued ally and dangerous adversary to the historian, naturally predisposes us to search within Imperial Germany for the signs of social forces and the roots of prejudices that would help to pave the long and twisted road to Auschwitz. Certainly those signs and roots are evident if we look. Imperial Germany, however, was not only a time of danger, but also a time of opportunity for German Jews. The Imperial German government had extended full political rights to all Jewish citizens, and both Jews and converts now numbered among the most prominent and most visible political and economic leaders of the new nation. Furthermore, even with the frequent employment of anti-Jewish rhetoric in the press and the persistence of formal and informal slights and exclusions within German society, we should also note that anti-Semitic leaders in Imperial Germany did not succeed in reaching any of their major goals: they failed to pass any significant anti-Jewish legislation, failed to build a grassroots movement, and failed to elect more than a few isolated candidates to the Reichstag.[8] During this era it was still much easier for most German Jews to envision a future of tolerance and inclusion in their homeland rather than the social exclusion and genocidal violence that would come fifty years later. Such hopes only seem naïve in retrospect.

Finally, although this book has not made any systematic effort to compare the Graef case to similar episodes in other European countries, what limited comparisons have been offered with the work of Judith Walkowitz on the Maiden Tribute Affair have tended to suggest as many similarities as areas of significant difference. If the kind of public activism of Josephine Butler in England was made difficult in Germany by oppressive legislation that restricted women's participation in the public sphere, and if organized campaigns to outlaw prostitution developed decades later in Germany than they did in England, many other differences in the way these cases unfolded can be explained by the circumstances of each case and the strikingly dissimilar depictions of the two female "victims." Otherwise, many important aspects of the cases investigated by Walkowitz seem largely consistent with the Graef Affair, including the widespread condemnation of sensationalist journalism, the stereotypes used to describe lower-class urban residents, and the employment of anti-Semitic rhetoric.

Perhaps the most reasonable conclusion, based on this very limited data, is that the German experience here was peculiar but not special. If the Graef case reveals social and cultural tensions undoubtedly unique to the German experience, this episode was also broadly consistent with the wide range of experiences in other European societies. This conclusion is in line with the far more exhaustive comparative study by Frank Bösch, entitled *Öffentliche Geheimnisse* (Open Secrets), which analyzes a series of public scandals in both Imperial Germany and late Victorian and Edwardian England. Bösch describes the very different political and media landscapes in Germany and Britain and then clearly explains how these differences affected individual scandals emerging in each milieu. His overall analysis, however, points to far more similarities than differences. In both countries, a newly powerful press could instrumentalize public scandals for political goals, and in both societies dominant social and political elites grew to fear the power of a scandal-hungry press as much as they feared a revolutionary conspiracy.[9] Bösch argues that while such public scandals in England demonstrated the often surprising limits of political and cultural liberality, in Germany they were more frequently "an important indicator of the varied boundaries placed on the authoritarian state by the Reichstag, the media, and the wider public."[10] The Graef trial, then, was neither evidence of a particularly German moral and cultural decline (as it was often then perceived), nor an indication of a special German path toward fascism. It was instead simply evidence of a particularly contentious and difficult transition into the modern world.

NOTES

Prologue

1. Graef's long pretrial detention (*Untersuchungshaft*) was probably based more on the fear that he might collude with witnesses and his fellow defendants before trial rather than a fear that he might flee Germany. He was, after all, charged with perjury and influencing others to commit perjury. Long periods of detention before trial were not entirely uncommon in Imperial Germany, but the practice was becoming increasingly controversial. See a record of public debates about compensating those held in *Untersuchungshaft* without an eventual conviction in BArch R 3001/5557.

2. "The Best Known Woman in Germany," *The Daily Colonist* (Victoria, British Columbia), October 9, 1892, no. 101, p. 1, accessed April 9, 2014, http://archive.org/stream/dailycolonist18921009uvic/18921009#page/n0/mode/1up.

3. This description comes from Paul Lindau, "Idealismus und Naturalismus in Berlin. Prozess Graef," *Nord und Süd* 35, no. 104 (November 1885): 243, and it is consistent with the description of the painting in the catalog for the 1881 Exhibit of the Royal Academy of Arts. Later sources erroneously describe the girl in the painting being transformed from a "water dragon" or a mermaid. See also Theresia Bach, "'Sie haben in ein Wespennest gestochen.' Unbek. Dokumente zum Prozeß gegen Gustav Graef," *Fontane Blätter* 78 (2004): 11.

Introduction

1. The new German Empire did, of course, exclude the German-speaking lands of the Austro-Hungarian Empire—an omission that displeased many southern Germans at the time, and that later nationalists, including Adolf Hitler, would seek to redress.

2. Eric Johnson, *Urbanization and Crime: Germany 1871–1914* (Cambridge: Cambridge University 2002), 157. Johnson makes the case that rapid industrial and population growth in cities did *not* necessarily lead to increased crime. Nonetheless, the jarring changes to urban life spurred government officials and bourgeois elites to become obsessed with crime, perversion, and the immoral nature of the city.

3. See Andrew Lees, *Cities, Sin, and Social Reform in Imperial Germany* (Ann Arbor: University of Michigan Press, 2002), 81.

4. Margaret Lavinia Anderson, *Practicing Democracy: Elections and Political Culture in Imperial Germany* (Princeton, NJ: Princeton University Press, 2000), 20.

5. Ibid., 17.

6. For an excellent summary of historical debates on the nature of the German bourgeoisie initiated in the 1980s and 1990s by historians such as Jürgen Kocka, Werner Conze, and Reinhart Koselleck, see Jonathan Sperber, "Bürger, Bürgertum, Bürgerlichkeit, Bürgerliche Gesellschaft: Studies of the German (Upper) Middle Class and Its Sociocultural World," *The Journal of Modern History* 69, no. 2 (June 1997): 271–297.

7. Ann Goldberg, *Honor, Politics, and the Law in Imperial Germany, 1871–1914* (Cambridge: Cambridge University Press, 2010), 45.

8. Ibid., 2.

9. Kevin McAleer, *Dueling: The Cult of Honor in Fin-de-Siècle Germany* (Princeton, NJ: Princeton University Press, 1994), 23. This book differs from two previous works on the subject of dueling: V. G. Kiernan's *The Duel in European History: Honor and the Reign of the Aristocracy* (Oxford:

Oxford University Press, 1988), and Ute Frevert's *Men of Honour: A Social and Cultural History of the Duel*, trans. Anthony Williams (Cambridge: Polity Press, 1995). On the one hand, Kiernan and McAleer suggest that the duel was the last bastion of aristocratic honor in modern society, and they suggest that members of the bourgeoisie began to adopt this archaic ritual in the hopes of mimicking the Junker aristocracy and demonstrating their own *Standesehre* (class honor). For Frevert, however, although the duel had originated in aristocratic practices, it was gradually adapted to bourgeois ideas of masculine honor, and thus became a thoroughly bourgeois institution.

10. Barnet Hartston, *Sensationalizing the Jewish Question: Anti-Semitic Trials and the Press in the Early German Empire* (Leiden: Brill, 2005), 35; McAleer, *Dueling*, 89.

11. Goldberg, *Honor, Politics, and the Law*, 2–5, 35.

12. Ibid., 61–62; Alexandra Ortmann, *Machtvolle Verhandlungen: Zur Kulturgeschichte der deutschen Strafjustiz, 1879–1924* (Göttingen: Vandenhoeck and Ruprecht, 2014), 70.

13. See chapter three for more about the very interesting reaction to the Graef scandal within the Association of Berlin Artists.

14. Goldberg, *Honor, Politics, and the Law*, 9.

15. See Sarah Leonard, *Fragile Minds and Vulnerable Souls: The Matter of Obscenity in Nineteenth-Century Germany* (Philadelphia: University of Pennsylvania Press, 2015), 172.

16. Goldberg, *Honor, Politics, and the Law*, 10. See also Goldberg's discussion of attempts by young women who had been committed to mental asylums to restore their own honor through the publication of pamphlets recounting their unfair treatment on her pp. 168–191.

17. Frevert, *Men of Honour*, 183.

18. Ibid., 180–187.

19. For a French exception that proves the rule, see Edward Berenson's account of the 1914 trial of Henriette Caillaux, who violated social mores by killing the journalist who had published embarrassing letters from her husband (the politician Joseph Caillaux) to a mistress. Madame Caillaux was eventually acquitted since it was determined that she, like other women, were invariably ruled by their passions. Edward Berenson, *The Trial of Madame Caillaux* (Berkeley: University of California Press, 1993).

20. §166 of the Penal Code threatened up to three years in prison for the public slander of any established religious organization. Prosecutors, however, were often hesitant to file charges using this statute against anti-Semitic agitators. See for example, the failed efforts by the Deutsch-Israelitischer Gemeindebund to encourage a prosecution of the notorious August Rohling in Hartston, *Sensationalizing the Jewish Question*, 195–204.

21. Hirsch Hildesheimer was the son of the prominent Orthodox rabbi Ezriel Hildesheimer, founder of the *Berliner Rabbinerseminar*, who is often called the father of Modern Orthodox Judaism. For more on Hirsch Hildesheimer and his public campaigns against anti-Semitism, see Hartston, *Sensationalizing the Jewish Question*, 87–101.

22. See again the work of Goldberg, *Honor, Politics, and the Law*, 59.

23. Ibid.

24. Edward Ross Dickinson, *Sex, Freedom, and Power in Imperial Germany, 1880–1914* (New York: Cambridge University Press, 2013), 30.

25. Gary Stark, "Pornography, Society, and the Law in Imperial Germany," *Peer Reviewed Articles*, Paper 21 (2014), p. 212, http://scholarworks.gvsu.edu/hst_articles/21.

26. On the Heinze case as the start of a moral panic, see Benjamin Hett, *Death in the Tiergarten: Murder and Criminal Justice in the Kaiser's Berlin* (Cambridge, MA: Harvard University Press, 2004), 78, and Edward Ross Dickinson, "The Men's Christian Morality Movement in Germany, 1880–1914: Some Reflections on Sex, Politics, and Sexual Politics," *Journal of Modern History* 75, no. 1 (2003): 59–110. On the struggle against "filth and trash," see also Gideon Reuveni, "Der Aufstieg der Bürgerlichkeit und die bürgerliche Selbstauflösung," *Zeitschrift für Geschichtswissenschaft* 51 (2003): 131–143; Stark, "Pornography, Society, and the Law in Imperial Germany"; and Gary Stark, *Banned in Berlin: Literary Censorship in Imperial Germany, 1871–1918* (New York: Berghahn, 2012).

27. Dickinson, *Sex, Freedom, and Power*, 30.

28. Ibid., 30–33; Stark, "Pornography, Society, and the Law," 212–213.

29. Stark, "Pornography, Society, and the Law," 203–204. On Gobineau, see Peter Pulzer, *The Rise of Political Anti-Semitism in Germany and Austria* (Cambridge, MA: Harvard University Press, 1988), 47.

30. Stark, "Pornography, Society, and the Law," 201, 202–203.

31. See Carlo Ginsburg, *The Cheese and the Worms: The Cosmos of a Sixteenth-Century Miller* (Baltimore: Johns Hopkins University Press, 1980); Natalie Zemon Davis, *The Return of Martin Guerre* (Cambridge, MA: Harvard University Press, 1983); Edward Berenson, *The Trial of Madame Caillaux* (Berkeley: University of California Press, 1993); Helmut Walser Smith, *The Butcher's Tale: Murder and Anti-Semitism in a German Town* (New York: W. W. Norton, 2002); and also Judith Walkowitz, *City of Dreadful Delight: Narratives of Sexual Danger in Late Victorian London* (Chicago: University of Chicago Press, 1992). The last three of these have been especially influential for my approach to this book.

32. There are a number of excellent books that focus on political scandals and the press in Imperial Germany, including Alex Hall, *Scandal, Sensation and Social Democracy: The SPD Press and Wilhelmine Germany 1890–1914* (New York: Cambridge University Press, 1977); Philipp Müller, *Auf der Suche nach dem Täter: Die öffentliche Dramatisierung von Verbrechen im Berlin des Kaiserreichs* (New York: Campus, 1985); Martin Kohlrausch, *Der Monarch im Skandal: Die Logik der Massenmedien und die Transformation der wilhelminischen Monarchie* (Berlin: Akademie, 2005); and Frank Bösch, *Öffentliche Geheimnisse. Skandale, Politik und Medien in Deutschland und Großbritannien 1880–1914* (Munich: Oldenburg, 2009). See also my own *Sensationalizing the Jewish Question: Anti-Semitic Trials and the Press in the Early German Empire* (Leiden: Brill, 2005). There are a number of works specifically on the Kotze and Eulenburg Affairs, including Wolfgang Wipperman's *Skandal im Jagdschloss Grunewald. Männlichkeit und Ehre im deutschen Kaiserreich* (Darmstadt: Primus, 2010), and Norman Domeier's *The Eulenburg Affair. A Cultural History of Politics in Imperial Germany*, trans. Deborah Lucas Schneider (New York: Camden House, 2015).

33. Martin Kohlrausch, *Der Monarch im Skandal: Die Logik der Massenmedien und die Transformation der wilhelminischen Monarchie* (Berlin: Akademie, 2005).

34. For an argument against the notion that the 1890s were a watershed moment signaling the development of "politics in a new key," see James Retallack, "The Authoritarian State and the Political Mass Market," in *Imperial Germany Revisited: Continuing Debates and New Perspectives*, ed. Sven Oliver Müller and Cornelius Torp (New York: Berghahn, 2011), 88–92. Retallack identifies Carl Schorske as one of the most strident advocates of the idea of the 1890s as a transformative decade—although Schorske's famous article is focused primarily on Austria. See Carl Schorske, "Politics in a New Key: An Austrian Triptych," *Journal of Modern History* 39 (1967): 343–386.

35. Alexandra Ortmann, *Machtvolle Verhandlungen: Zur Kulturgeschichte der deutschen Strafjustiz 1879–1924* (Göttingen: Vandenhoeck and Ruprecht, 2014), 13.

36. Bösch, *Öffentliche Geheimnisse*, 3–4.

37. Dagmar Reese, *Akt und Anstand: Die Skandal um den Gustav Graef Prozess, Berlin 1885* (Vienna: Böhlau, 2014). I should also acknowledge here the valuable contributions of Klaus-Peter Möller on the Graef trial. See, for example, his "'Entartete Kunst' als 'Gefahr für die Sittlichkeit des ganzen Volkes': Die 'Ächtung' des Malers Gustav Graef—Hintergrunde und Folgen," in *Erledigungen-Pamphlete, Polemiken und Proteste*, ed. Marcel Atze and Volker Kaukoreit (Vienna: Praesens, 2014), 118–137, accessed July 18, 2014, http://www.wilnitsky.com/pictures/Erledigungen_Artikel_Gustav%20Graef.pdf.

Chapter One

1. Christian Krollmann, ed., *Altpreußische Biographie*, vol. 1 (Marburg/Lahn: Elwert, 1974), 227.

2. Hans Prutz, *Die Königliche Albertus-Universität zu Königsberg i. Pr. Im neunzehnten Jahrhundert. Zur Feier ihres 350jährigen Bestehens* (Königsberg: Hartung, 1894), 32.

3. This epithet is present in a poem penned to honor the king by the Königliche Deutsche Gesellschaft in 1798. GStA PK, XX. HA Historisches Staatsarchiv Königsberg, Rep. 100 A Kleine Erwerbungen, Nr. 388, Bl. 3.

4. Sabine Graef Lepsius, *Ein Berliner Künstlerleben um die Jahrhundertwende: Erinnerungen* (Munich: G. Müller, 1972), 13.

5. Johann August Ferdinand Graef, *Zur Feier des Geburtstagfestes Sr. Majestät des Königes* (Königsberg: Degen, 1808).

6. Lepsius, *Ein Berliner Künstlerleben*, 13–14. See also Hugo von Tschudi, *Ausstellung von Werken des Malers Gustav Graef* (Berlin: Mittler und Sohn, 1896), 3.

7. Gustav Graef, *Die Corpslandsmannschaft Normannia I zu Königsberg* (1843).

8. Peter Paret, *Art as History: Episodes in the Culture and Politics of Nineteenth-Century Germany* (Princeton, NJ: Princeton University Press, 1988), 81.

9. Annette Dorgerloh, *Das Künstlerehepaar Lepsius: zur Berliner Porträtmalerei um 1900* (Oldenburg: Akademie, 2003), 61n2.

10. This claim is made by Annette Dorgerloh in her biography of Gustav Graef's daughter Sabine and her husband, Reinhold Lepsius. It is important to note that in Prussian society status was not absolutely dependent on wealth, and so Graef's poverty would not *necessarily* have erased the prestige of his own ancestral ties. Nonetheless, this assertion should be taken as a sign of just how well established and respected the Liebreich family had been in Königsberg. See ibid., 62.

11. Ibid., 61.

12. All of these artworks were eventually lost due to the destruction caused by World War Two.

13. Paret, *Art as History*, 20.

14. Ibid., 24–26.

15. Ibid., 21.

16. Gustav Graef, *Der Auszug der ostpreußischen Landwehr ins Feld 1813 nach deren Einsegnung in der Kirche zu Königsberg* (1860–61) Canvas. 101x131.5 cm. [Regensburg Kunstforum Ostdeutsche Galerie: Inv. 6130].

17. As Amos Elon suggests, the real story of Jewish life in Prussia at the time of the Napoleonic Wars was much more complicated than the painting might suggest. Although Frederick Wilhelm III approved an edict of emancipation in 1812, Jews were still restricted from government positions and teaching posts. In addition, the widows of Jewish veterans such as the one portrayed in Graef's painting would not have been eligible for pensions. Amos Elon, *The Pity of It All: A History of Jews in Germany, 1743–1933* (New York: Metropolitan Books, 2002), 95–96. Interestingly, Elon uses a sketch similar to Graef's image as an illustration in his book; however, he leaves it uncredited and lists it as a "contemporary woodcut" from the Napoleonic Era. It is not clear if Graef's painting was modeled on this older woodcut or (as seems more likely) the woodcut itself was actually of much later origin and based on Graef's painting.

18. Gustav Graef, *Vaterlandsliebe. Ferdinande von Schmettau opfert ihr Haar auf dem Alter des Vaterlandes* (c. 1863). Canvas. 98x125cm. [Alte Nationalgalerie: Inv. A I 2].

19. See three letters from Fontane to Graef about the painting in Theodor Fontane, *Briefe*, vol. 3, 1879–1889, 3rd ed., ed. Otto Drude et al., part 4 of *Werke, Schriften und Briefe* (Munich: Carl Hanser, 1980), 91–92, 94–95.

20. Lepsius, *Ein Berliner Künstlerleben*, 18.

21. Dorgerloh, *Das Künstlerehepaar Lepsius*, 62.

22. Gustav Graef, *Abschied eines lithauischen Landwehrmannes von seiner Geliebten, 1813* (1862–1863).

23. Tschudi, *Ausstellung von Werken*, 4.

24. See Gustav Graef, *Bildnis Henry Bethel Strousberg* (1868) Canvas. 131.5x101.5cm. [Stiftung Stadtmuseum Berlin. Landesmuseum für Kultur und Geschichte Berlins: Inv. VII 60/585x]; and *Bildnis Mary Ann Strousberg* (1868) Canvas. 131x99.5cm. [Stiftung Stadtmuseum Berlin. Landesmuseum für Kultur und Geschichte Berlins: Inv. VII 60/568x].

25. No record of such a painting exists in the biographical literature about Graef or in the guide to his posthumous exhibit in the Berlin National Gallery. However, in several letters sent to Graef in 1892 by Sybille von Bismarck and her mother Malvine von Arnim, they discuss Graef's request to

publicly display the painting and their desire to have it back. See letters in DLA Marbach A: Lepsius (1892) [71.762/1–3] and [71.765/1–3].

26. DLA Marbach A: Lepsius, letter from Marie (Gräfin von) Bismarck-Schönhausen to Gustav Graef (August 8, 1877).

27. *Berliner Morgenpost*, October 8, 1885, no. 235, 8.

28. Petra Wilhelmy-Dollinger, *Der Berliner Salon im 19. Jahrhundert (1780–1914)* (New York: De Gruyter, 1989), 649. See also pp. 253–254 on Babette Meyer, the daughter of a Jewish banker, who married the director of the Weimar school of art, Stanislaus Graf Kalckreuth, only to separate from him soon after. Meyer (now Gräfin Kalckreuth) cultivated close ties to the family of Otto von Bismarck before the two had a rather mysterious falling out. Meyer went on to be one of the more popular salonnières and salon guests in Berlin.

29. George Ritzer, *The Blackwell Companion to Major Classical Social Theorists* (Malden, MA: John Wiley and Sons, 2008), 240–241.

30. Dorgerloh, *Das Künstlerehepaar Lepsius*, 61.

31. Annette Dorgerloh, "Beseelung der Bilderscheinung: Porträt und Selbstbildnis im 19. Jahrhundert" in *Vom Biedermeier zum Impressionismus*, vol. 7 of *Geschichte der bildenden Kunst*, ed. Hubertus Kohle (Munich: Prestel, 2008), 438.

32. See Dagmar Reese, *Akt und Anstand: Der Skandal um den Gustav Graef Prozess, Berlin 1885* (Vienna: Böhlau, 2014), 44, 56n57. Reese describes *Pensierosa* as one of a series of allegorical nude paintings by Graef which began in 1877 and continued in 1878 with *Rubinella*, *Maria Gila*, and finally *Félicie*. The painting *Pensierosa*, however, was mentioned as early as 1875 in Paul Lindau's *Die Gegenwart* (see issue from December 18, 1875, no. 51, 407).

33. Paul Lindau, "Idealismus und Naturalismus in Berlin. Prozess Graef," *Nord und Süd* 35, no. 104 (November 1885): 242.

34. See Hollis Clayson, *Painted Love: Prostitution in French Art of the Impressionist Era* (Los Angeles: Getty Research Institute, 2003), 79–93. Dagmar Reese also suggests that Graef's *Félicie* is likely an homage to other famous odalisques, including Titian's *Venus of Urbino*, Giorgione's *Venus*, Ingres's *La Grande Odalisque*, or Manet's *Olympia*. See Dagmar Reese, *Akt und Anstand*, 146n6.

35. Lindau, "Idealismus und Naturalismus," 242.

36. Adolf Rosenberg, "Die akademische Kunstausstellung in Berlin I.," *Die Grenzboten* 38, no. 3 (1879), 460.

37. Ibid.

38. Adolf Rosenberg, "Die vierte allgemeine deutsche Kunstausstellung in Düsseldorf," *Die Grenzboten* 39, no. 3 (1880), 383.

39. Lepsius, *Ein Berliner Künstlerleben*, 88.

40. See "Von der Kunstausstellung," *Im neuen Reich* 11, no. 2 (1881), 451. This was the last issue of this particular journal, which the editor, Wilhelm Lang, ceased publication due to tastes in Germany having become more conservative. See Johannes Heinssen, *Historismus und Kulturkritik: Studien zur deutschen Geschichtskultur im späten 19. Jahrhundert* (Göttingen: Vandenhoeck and Ruprecht, 2003), 309–310.

41. Adolf Rosenberg, "Die akademische Kunstausstellung in Berlin I.," *Die Grenzboten* 40, no. 3 (1881), 512. It should be noted that it is reasonably likely that the version of *The Fairy Tale* reviewed by Rosenberg is not the one depicted in this book. This image is perhaps more likely a revised version of the image finished shortly before the trial in 1885.

42. Adolf Rosenberg, "Die große Kunstausstellung in Berlin," *Die Grenzboten* 43, nno. 3 (1884), 562.

43. Theresia Bach, "'Sie haben in ein Wespennest gestochen'. Unbek. Dokumente zum Prozeß gegen Gustav Graef," *Fontane Blätter* 78 (2004): 10.

44. This account is from H. Holz, "Prozess Graef: Dargestellt von Herrn Rechtsanwalt Holz in Berlin," *Das Tribunal: Zeitschrift für praktische Strafrechtspflege* 1, nno. 12 (December 1885): 663–664. Since Holz served as a defense lawyer for Bertha Rother in the Graef trial, he would have had direct

access to testimony from the Hammermann trial. One must remember that his position in the Graef trial would also mean he was not at all favorably disposed to Helene Hammermann.

45. Although he claimed only to be a kindly salesman who just wanted to help his neighbors, Krischen was consistently described by others as a *Volksanwalt* (people's lawyer) or *Winkeladvokat* (shyster), a paid representative with little or no legal training who performed simple legal tasks. These terms were *always* meant in a derogatory sense. See chapter seven for more on the running conflict between professional lawyers and such lay advocates.

46. Holz, "Prozess Graef," 663.

47. Ibid., 664.

48. This is according to the closing argument of the prosecutor, Max Heinemann, who claimed he would otherwise have filed these charges against Graef as well. See *Berliner Gerichtszeitung*, October 8, 1885, no. 118, 2.

49. For more detail on the importance of perjury charges in an honor-bound society, and a discussion of contemporary concerns about an alleged "perjury fever" that was gripping the county, see chapter six.

Chapter Two

1. *Prozeß (Gustav) Graef, verhandelt vom 29. September bis 7. October 1885 vor dem Geschworenengericht zu Berlin* (Berlin: Bartels, 1885), i.

2. Uwe Wilhelm, *Das Deutsche Kaiserreich und seine Justiz. Justizkritik—politische Strafrechtsprechung—Justizpolitik* (Berlin: Duncker and Humblot, 2010), 300–301.

3. Kurt Koszyk, *Deutsche Presse im 19. Jahrhundert* (Berlin: Colloquium, 1966), 281.

4. Benjamin Hett, *Death in the Tiergarten: Murder and Criminal Justice in the Kaiser's Berlin* (Cambridge, MA: Harvard University Press, 2004), 65.

5. Ibid., 16, 66.

6. Ibid., 65.

7. *Prozeß (Gustav) Graef*, 1.

8. As a prosecutor during the 1870s, Tessendorf was both hated and feared for his role in carrying out a campaign of prosecutions against perceived enemies of the state, including Socialist leaders such as August Bebel and Wilhelm Liebknecht. At the time of the Graef trial, Tessendorf had recently assumed the position of president of the Criminal Division of the Berlin *Kammergericht*, and this makes it likely he was attending the Graef trial to observe the performance of the prosecutor, Max Heinemann. Tessendorf would be promoted to chief prosecutor at the Supreme Court (*Oberreichsanwalt*) in Leipzig the following year.

9. GStA PK, I. HA Rep. 89 Geheimes Zivilkabinett, Nr. 17112, Bd. 1 (1879–1887), Bl. 125.

10. Several sources name Schäfer as the foreman, including the *Nationalzeitung*, as referenced in Theresia Bach, "'Sie haben in ein Wespennest gestochen.' Unbek. Dokumente zum Prozeß gegen Gustav Graef," *Fontane Blätter* 78 (2004): 16.

11. The evidence is not completely clear on this point. Several sources mention Hermann Kleinholz as a prominent member of the *Berliner Anwaltsverein* during the 1880s, while most sources suggest the attorney for Harden was named Wilhelm Kleinholz. Since the *Handbuch über den Königlich Preussischen Hof und Staat* lists only one Kleinholz as actively assigned to the Landgericht Berlin during this period, it seems reasonable to assume that this may have been the same person.

12. The last is likely Oskar Cassel, who had started his career as a lawyer only a few years earlier. Cassel would later be elected as a delegate to the Prussian *Abgeordnetenhaus*, and he would serve for many years as a Berlin city councilman—becoming powerful enough for the Free-Conservative politician Wilhelm von Kardorff to refer to him as the "uncrowned king of Berlin." Cassel was also a practicing Jew and would eventually become chair of the Organization of German Jews (*Verband Deutscher Juden*). See Ernest Hamburger, *Juden im öffentlichen Leben Deutschlands:*

Regierungsmitglieder, Beamte und Parlamentarier in der monarchischen Zeit 1848–1918 (Tübingen: Mohr Siebeck, 1968), 368–369.

13. Heinemann was the son of a doctor from the East Prussian town of Bischofsburg. See BArch R3002/347, Bl. 39. See chapter seven for more on his career after the Graef trial.

14. Hugo Friedländer, *Interessante Kriminal-Prozesse von kulturhistorischer Bedeutung: Darstellung merkwürdiger Strafrechtsfälle aus Gegenwart und Jüngstvergangenheit nach eigenen Erlebnissen* (Berlin: Barsdorf, 1910–1914).

15. For more on controversies about court reporting, including judicial hostility to unqualified laymen "telling stories" about judicial proceedings, see Alexandra Ortmann, *Machtvolle Verhandlungen: Zur Kulturgeschichte der deutschen Strafjustiz, 1879–1924* (Göttingen: Vandenhoeck and Ruprecht, 2014), 163–164.

16. *Prozeß (Gustav) Graef*, 10.

17. Johann Herrmann Kretzschmer (1811–1890) was a decade older than Graef but followed a fairly similar career path. As a young man he studied with Wilhelm von Schadow in Düsseldorf before later dedicating himself to large-scale historical paintings. Kretzschmer was also well known for his sketches of peasant life, and after a trip to Greece, Egypt, and the Ottoman Empire in 1840 he apparently became the first painter in Berlin to follow the French fashion of painting scenes from the "Orient," including Ottoman sultans. See Gustav Ebe, *Der deutsche Cicerone: Malerei deutsche Schulen* (Leipzig: Spamer, 1898), 371.

18. *Prozeß (Gustav) Graef*, 14.

19. Ibid., 20.

20. H. Holz, "Prozess Graef: Dargestellt von Herrn Rechtsanwalt Holz in Berlin," *Das Tribunal: Zeitschrift für praktische Strafrechtspflege* 1, no. 12 (December 1885): 670.

21. *Prozeß (Gustav) Graef*, 56.

22. Ibid., 31.

23. A *Halspinsel*, or laryngeal throat brush, was sometimes used by doctors in the late nineteenth century to apply medicine for throat ailments.

24. *Prozeß (Gustav) Graef*, 40.

25. Holz, "Prozess Graef," 680.

26. *Prozeß (Gustav) Graef*, 27.

27. Ibid., 54.

28. Ibid., 38.

29. Ibid., 42–43. Entries from Graef's diary were later used to confirm his yearly income from 1881 at 31,656 deutsche marks, from 1882 at 61,280 marks, and from 1883 at 30,612 marks. One should note that in comparison, the prosecutor, Max Heinemann, earned 4,200 marks per year at the time of the trial with a small apartment allowance. Eight months after the trial, Judge Boguslaw Müller was given a raise to 5,400 marks per year with an apartment allowance of an extra 600 marks. Even fifteen years later when Max Heinemann was appointed as a Supreme Court Judge in Leipzig, his annual salary had reached only 12,000 marks. See *Prozeß (Gustav) Graef*, 50; BArch R3002/347, Bd. 3, Bl. 27; BArch R3002/346, Bl. 1; GStA PK, I. HA Rep. 84a Justizministerium, Nr. 40323, Bl. 18.

30. *Prozeß (Gustav) Graef*, 35. The rhyme scheme is altered slightly here. To be fair, the phrase "give me bliss" is not present in the original poem. A verbatim translation of the original line is simply "open your fresh blossom!" and was changed to fit the new rhyme scheme. The original poem is:

Blühend blondes Kind herein!
Einzig blaues Augenpaar.
Reizend winkt dein froher Schein,
Tief hineinschaun bringt Gefahr,
Heißen Wunsch, von vollen Lippen
Ach nur einen Kuß zu nippen.

Rose schlanke wilde Rose,
Oeffene deine frische Blüthe!
Thau aus Deinem jungen Schooße,
Haucht mir Jugend in's Gemüthe.
Es durchströmt mich Lieb und Lust,
Rose, blüh' an meiner Brust!

31. Ibid., 45. The original poem:

Du hast mir ja, o Kunst gegeben
Des Lebens Bilder schön zu schauen,
Mich dem Gemeinen zu entheben,
Die Himmelsleiter mir zu bauen.
Mich hebend auf die Täuschung schwingen
Treibt mich die Macht der Phantasie,
Auch die dem Staube zu entringen
Die meinem Bild das Antlitz lieh.
Sie möge sich so hoch erheben,
Wie meine Phantasie sie trägt,
Dem Bilde wird sie wiedergeben
Was ich in sie hineingelegt.
O, möchte noch der Zauber walten
Blieb noch so lang der schöne Schein,
Bis ich zum Bilde mag gestalten
Das Märchen, das ich sah so rein.
Fand unter Unkraut wilde Ranken
Manch' schönen Trieb doch tief versteckt,
Nun strebend sorgen die Gedanken
Bis ich zur Reife sie geweckt.
Ist ja zum Guten, wie zum Bösen
In jede Brust gelegt der Keim.
Vom uebel möcht ich sie erlösen
Die durch's Geschick mir fiel anheim.
Zwei Wege liegen da zu wandern:
Könnt' ich doch wählen ihre Wahl
Zu gehen den, zu flehen den andern
Zu flieh'n der Reue ew'ge Qual.
Ist einmal so das Loos gefallen,
Dann kennet sie nicht mehr mein Herz,
Denn ich muß strebend weiter wallen
Mit hehrem Blicke himmelwärts.

32. Ibid., 44.

33. Holz, "Prozess Graef," 683.

34. *Prozeß (Gustav) Graef*, 45.

35. Ibid., 53.

36. Ibid., 53–54.

37. Lindau, as we will see in later chapters, had both the predilection and perhaps also an ulterior motive to exaggerate such episodes. See Paul Lindau, "Laienhafte Glossen zum Graef'schen Prozess," *Nationalzeitung*, October 8, 1885, no. 558, Morgen Ausgabe, 1, and Theresia Bach, "'Sie haben in ein Wespennest gestochen,'" 13–14.

38. See *Germania*, October 9, 1885, no. 231, Erstes Blatt, 1. The Catholic *Westfälische Zeitung* even suggested that coverage of the Graef case by the Berlin liberal press made it seem as if all of their newspapers were edited by "Louis." This reference to "Louis" was not only a slang word for a pimp, but perhaps also in this case a snide pun on the name of Arthur *Levysohn*, editor of the liberal *Berliner Tageblatt*. Levysohn was apparently insulted enough by this comment to file a private suit for slander. See *Kreuzzeitung*, October 31, 1885, no. 255, 2.

39. Two infamous assassination attempts on Kaiser Wilhelm in 1878 led to the banning of the Socialist Party. Otto von Bismarck had also been targeted by assassins in both 1866 and 1874.

40. Judith Walkowitz, *City of Dreadful Delight: Narratives of Sexual Danger in Late Victorian London* (Chicago: University of Chicago Press, 1992). For an example of such comparisons, see *Grenzboten* 44, no. 4 (1885): 143, in which the author refers to the Graef trial and suggests that anyone who thought that something as horrible as the Maiden Tribute Affair could not happen in Germany now knew differently.

41. Walkowitz, *City of Dreadful Delight*, 81.

42. Ibid., 84.

43. There were no sexual charges against Stead and the other defendants because all witnesses, including Eliza Armstrong, agreed that no actual sexual contact took place. Ibid., 106, 113.

44. Lucia Zedner and Andrew Ashworth, eds., *The Criminological Foundations of Penal Policy: Essays in Honour of Roger Hood* (New York: Oxford University Press, 2003), 241.

45. *Kreuzzeitung*, October 4, 1885, no. 232, 3.

46. *Reichsbote*, September 30, 1885, no. 228, 1.

47. *Kreuzzeitung*, October 18, 1885, no. 244, 1.

48. *Prozeß (Gustav) Graef*, 59; *Berliner Gerichtszeitung*, October 8, 1885, no. 118, 2.

49. *Prozeß (Gustav) Graef*, 60; *Berliner Gerichtszeitung*, October 8, 1885, no. 118, 2.

50. *Prozeß (Gustav) Graef*, 60.

51. *Berliner Gerichtszeitung*, October 8, 1885, no. 118, 2.

52. *Prozeß (Gustav) Graef*, 60.

53. Ibid., 63. Heinemann described it as a "jammervolles Gefühl." Before ending his closing argument, Heinemann did advise the jury to *acquit* the defendants on some of the charges. This may seem a bit strange from our own perspective; however, it was actually fairly common in the German court system for prosecutors to bring charges against a defendant and then end up admitting in closing arguments that some (or even all) charges should be dismissed for lack of substantial proof. In fact, according to §154 of the Code of Criminal Procedure, German prosecutors were *not allowed* to withdraw charges once they had been filed, and they were expected to instruct the jury to find defendants not guilty if in their estimation the evidence did not reach the proper threshold of proof.

54. Ibid., 63–64.

55. Ibid., 70. Estimate of the crowd from Bach, "'Sie haben in ein Wespennest gestochen,'" 15.

Chapter Three

1. Irmgard Wirth, *Berliner Malerei im 19. Jahrhundert: von der Zeit Friedrichs des Grossen bis zum ersten Weltkrieg* (Berlin: W. J. Siedler, 1990), 260.

2. See Fritz Stern, *The Politics of Cultural Despair* (Berkeley: University of California Press, 1974). Paul de Lagarde had penned his "Deutsche Schriften" between 1878 and 1881, and Julius Langbehn's *Rembrandt als Erzieher* would be published five years after the Graef trial in 1890. Both Lagarde and Langbehn would also add the allegedly pernicious Jewish influence on German culture to their list of targets. Nietzsche, however, tended to reject anti-Semitism as intolerant and ignorant.

3. The conservative and Lutheran *Kreuzzeitung* (officially known as the *Neue Preußische Zeitung*) was a leading advocate for the cause of ultraconservative Junkers in Germany, many of whom were patriotic but also critical of Otto von Bismarck's compromises with political liberals in the 1870s and early 1880s. The *Germania* was a Berlin Catholic paper that also tended to be critical of Bismarck and political liberals, and to push rather conservative opinions within the Catholic Center Party. Because of their common enemies and shared commitments, these two papers often echoed one another even while representing two quite different constituencies. As we will see below, the two newspapers were often most strident in their condemnation of the liberal press, and especially newspapers such as the *Berliner Tageblatt* and *Berliner Börsen-Courier*.

4. Mary Stewart, "German Naturalism and the Novel," *The Modern Language Review* 71, no. 4 (October 1976): 846.

5. Quoted from Zola's introduction to the novel in Rolf Sätzer, *Entwicklungslinien der deutschen Zola—Rezeption von den Anfängen bis zum Tode des Autors* (Bern: Peter Lang, 1989), 34.

6. This quote is from an anonymous reviewer in the *Magazin für die Literatur des in- und Auslandes*, which appears in Sätzer, *Entwicklungslinien*, 16, 34.

7. As quoted in Martin Gubser, *Literarischer Antisemitismus: Untersuchungen zu Gustav Freytag und anderen bürgerlichen Schriftstellern des 19. Jahrhunderts* (Göttingen: Wallstein, 1998), 187.

8. Sätzer, *Entwicklungslinien*, 45.

9. Ibid., 44.

10. Ibid., 44–46.

11. Julian Schmidt, "Adolf Menzel," *Preußische Jahrbücher* 56, no. 6 (1885): 629.

12. The key role played by the Brothers Hart in the spread of Zola's ideas came despite their criticism of some aspects of his philosophy and method. See Sätzer, *Entwicklungslinien*, 78–84 for a more thorough account of their critiques.

13. As Sätzer goes on to argue, these German naturalists were inspired by Zola and defended his work against German critics, but they also developed their own versions of naturalism, which emphasized their particular interpretations of what it should encompass. Ibid., 107.

14. Gary Stark, *Banned in Berlin: Literary Censorship in Imperial Germany* (New York: Berghahn, 2012), xviii.

15. Volker Berghahn, *Imperial Germany, 1871–1914: Economy, Society, Culture, and Politics* (Providence, RI: Berghahn, 1994), 133.

16. As quoted in Robin Lenman, *Artists and Society in Germany, 1850–1914* (New York: Manchester University Press, 1997), 51.

17. As described by the modern historian Robin Lenman. See ibid., 51.

18. Ibid., 81.

19. Ibid., 4.

20. *Germania*, October 9, 1885, no. 231, Erstes Blatt, 1.

21. Ibid.

22. Original in *Die Post*, October 11, 1885, no. 278, 1; reprinted in *Berliner Börsen-Courier*, October 12, 1885, no. 517, Morgen Ausgabe, 2–3.

23. The *Börsen-Courier* attributed the summary judgment by the Aereopagus more to fear than to lust, since they would have been afraid to sentence a woman who seemed beautiful enough to be a priestess of Aphrodite. *Berliner Börsen-Courier*, October 18, 1885, no. 529, 1. Beilage, 2.

24. *Berliner Börsen-Courier*, October 18, 1885, no. 529, 1. Beilage, 2.

25. *Berliner Börsen-Courier*, October 10, 1885, no. 514, 1. Beilage, 1. The French term "Bohème" may be a reference to the popular play *La Vie de Bohème* by Henri Murger and Théodore Barrière. The Puccini opera based on this play was not written until a decade after the Graef trial.

26. *Berliner Börsen-Courier*, October 10, 1885, no. 514, 1. Beilage, 1. Many other interesting personalities are described among the models, including a brief mention of the only black model, John Walker, who sat for Carl Becker's painting *Othello* in 1880.

27. For more on the relationship between artists and models as a common site for the transgression of social and moral norms, see Dagmar Reese, *Akt und Anstand: Der Skandal um den Gustav Graef Prozess, Berlin 1885* (Vienna: Böhlau, 2014), 26–29, 43–64. As Reese suggests, criticism of the use of young girls as nude models took place outside of Germany as well. In England, William Knighton cited the Graef trial as evidence that nude models were not only unnecessary for great art, but also only one half step above prostitution. Knighton agreed with John Calcott Horsley, an English painter and longtime campaigner against the use of nude models. See William Knighton, *Struggles for Life* (London: Williams and Norgate, 1886), 226–235.

28. Karl Frenzel, *Die Kunst und das Strafgesetz* (Berlin: Walther und Apolant, 1885), 5.

29. Ibid., 12.

30. Ibid., 3.

31. Ibid., 4.

32. Ibid., 4–5. These are references to the main characters of Shakespeare's *Othello* and Schiller's *Maria Stuart*, respectively.

33. Frenzel, *Die Kunst und das Strafgesetz*, 7.

34. Ibid., 8.

35. This fact is mentioned without any elucidation in Ruth Stummann-Bowert's *Malwida von Meysenburg—Paul Rée: Briefe an einen Freund* (Würzburg: Königshausen and Neumann, 1998), 86. The social circle reportedly included a variety of intellectuals, including the philosopher Ferdinand Tönnies, the psychologist Hermann Ebbinghaus, and the historian Hans Delbrück.

36. Max Heinemann, *Der Prozeß Graef und die deutsche Kunst: Eine Antwort auf Dr. Karl Frenzel's Abhandlung in der Nationalzeitung: "Die Kunst und das Strafgesetz"* (Berlin: Friedrich Luckhardt, 1885), 6–7.

37. Ibid., 9. Bold in original.

38. Ibid., 10. The reference to Jupiter comes from Ovid's "Ars Amatoria."

39. Heinemann, *Der Prozeß Graef*, 11.

40. Ibid., 12.

41. Ibid., 14. The reference is to Schiller's 1795 poem "Das Ideal und das Leben."

42. Heinemann, *Der Prozeß Graef*, 15.

43. Ibid., 16.

44. Paul Lindau, "Laienhafte Glossen zum Graef'schen Prozess," *Nationalzeitung*, October 8, 1885, no. 558, Morgen Ausgabe, 1. According to Dagmar Reese, this article appeared in the space normally reserved for the commentary of Karl Frenzel. See Dagmar Reese, *Akt und Anstand*, 38n41.

45. Heinemann, *Der Prozeß Graef*, 3. Lindau allegedly used the phrase "Den Staatsanwalt werden wir hochfliegen lassen."

46. *Berliner Börsen-Courier*, October 14, 1885, no. 521, Morgen Ausgabe, 4. Although written for the November issue of his own journal, Lindau allowed excerpts of his article to be published in the *Berliner Börsen-Courier* as early as October 23, 1885—just over two weeks after the end of the trial.

47. Paul Lindau, "Idealismus und Naturalismus in Berlin. Prozess Graef," *Nord und Süd* 35, no. 104 (November 1885): 205.

48. Ibid., 241.

49. Ibid., 243–244.

50. Ibid., 244.

51. Lindau's assertions here, which echoed those of Frenzel and the *Börsen-Courier*, were also supported by other commenters on the trial. In an essay published in a specialized law journal, Bertha Rother's attorney suggested that writers as diverse as Petrarch, Goethe, and Heinrich Heine had all been inspired by intense sensual feelings that had gone unrequited and unfulfilled. If one wanted to take their poetry as truth and as proof of immoral behavior, he suggested, then perhaps a special kind of court would have to be set up to pursue these sorts of literary crimes. See H. Holz, "Prozess Graef: Dargestellt von Herrn Rechtsanwalt Holz in Berlin," *Das Tribunal: Zeitschrift für praktische Strafrechtspflege* 1, no. 12 (December 1885): 684.

52. Lindau, "Idealismus und Naturalismus," 250. Klaus-Peter Möller has recently located a memoir written by Gustav Graef after his trial that was intended to help clear his name, but which was never published. It is entirely possible that the "diaries" referred to in Lindau's essay were an early version of this document. See Klaus-Peter Möller, "'Entartete Kunst' als 'Gefahr für die Sittlichkeit des ganzen Volkes': Die 'Ächtung' des Malers Gustav Graef—Hintergrunde und Folgen," in *Erledigungen—Pamphlete, Polemiken und Proteste*, vol. 14/15, ed. Marcel Atze and Volker Kaukoreit (Vienna: Praesens, 2014), 129, accessed July 18, 2014, http://www.wilnitsky.com/pictures/Erledigungen_Artikel_Gustav%20Graef.pdf.

53. Lindau, "Idealismus und Naturalismus," 248. Lindau cleverly cites Goethe's famous epigraph here: "Märchen, noch so wunderbar/ Dichterkünste machen's wahr." (Fairy-tale so wonderous / a poet's art does make it thus).

54. DLA Marbach A: Lepsius, letter from Paul Lindau to Gustav Graef (December 21, 1885).

55. DLA Marbach A: Lepsius, letter from Paul Lindau to Gustav Graef (December 22, 1885).

56. See Fritz Stern, *Gold and Iron: Bismarck, Bleichröder, and the Building of the German Empire* (New York: Knopf, 1977), 275. Also, in an unpublished memoir originally written for public consumption, Gustav Graef apparently felt compelled to deny rumors that Karl Frenzel had penned his own essay at Graef's personal request. See Möller, "'Entartete Kunst,'" 131.

57. *Kölnische Volkszeitung*, October 10, 1885, no. 279, Zweites Blatt.

58. *Reichsbote*, October 8, 1885, no. 235, 1.

59. As quoted in the *Kreuzzeitung*, October 10, 1885, no. 237, 1.

60. As quoted in the *Leipziger Zeitung*, October 13, 1885, no. 239.

61. As quoted in ibid. This language, of course, is fairly ominous in retrospect. The notion that "degenerate art" (*entartete Kunst*) was a danger to the morality of the people would be used explicitly less than fifty years later to justify the persecution of artists and the confiscation and destruction of modern art by the National Socialist regime.

62. Theresia Bach, "'Sie haben in ein Wespennest gestochen.' Unbek. Dokumente zum Prozeß gegen Gustav Graef," *Fontane Blätter* 78 (2004): 22.

63. According to Dagmar Reese, 172 of the 334 members of the Association signed the declaration. She also suggests, however, that the original list of signers was identical with the list of meeting attendees, which may suggest that names were included without explicit consent. See Reese, *Akt und Anstand*, 71–72.

64. *Kreuzzeitung*, October 28, 1885, no. 252, 2.

65. *Kreuzzeitung*, November 6, 1885, no. 260, 3. The other member of the Association known to have refused to sign the declaration was Karl Gussow, who had also been a witness at the Graef trial.

66. To add insult to injury, student leaders at the *Hochschule der bildende Kunst* (Berlin State School of Fine Arts) rushed to publicly refute rumors in the press that they were considering a celebration to mark Graef's acquittal. *Kreuzzeitung*, November 6, 1885, no. 260, 3.

67. *Berliner Zeitung*, November 3, 1885 in GStA PK, I. HA Rep. 76 Kultusministerium, VIII Sekt L., Pers. Lit. G., Nr. 45, Bl. 11.

68. Bach, "'Sie haben in ein Wespennest gestochen,'" 28.

69. Ibid., 29.

70. I should note that there is some evidence that officials within the government wanted art organizations to distance themselves from Graef. According to the *Berliner Tageblatt*, the Prussian *Kultusminister*, Gustav von Goßler (who sat on the *Landeskunstkommission* as a nonvoting member), reacted angrily to rumors that students at the Royal Academy of Arts planned a torchlight procession to honor Graef after his acquittal. The newspaper claimed that Goßler sent a letter to the Academy threatening any student who participated in such a demonstration with expulsion. I was unable, however, to find such a letter in the records of the *Kultusministerium* at the *Geheimes Staatsarchiv Preußischer Kulturbesitz*.

71. Lenman, *Artists and Society*, 36. Lenman quotes Anton von Werner as denouncing French-influenced painters as supporters of "modern anarchism and terrorism in art."

72. Christopher With, *The Prussian Landeskunstkommission, 1862–1911* (Berlin: Gebr. Mann, 1986), 46, 49. See also ibid., 56–57.

73. Quidam [Julius Stinde], *Berliner Kunstkritik mit Randglossen* (Berlin: Freund and Jeckel, 1884).

74. *Nationalzeitung*, November 23, 1883, no. 551, Morgen-Ausgabe, 2.

75. See *Nationalzeitung*, November 27, 1883, no. 561, Morgen-Ausgabe, 2–3 and December 2, 1883, no. 568, Erstes Beiblatt, 3. Anton von Werner's account of the conflict is in his memoirs: *Erlebnisse und Erinnerungen 1870–1890* (Berlin: Mittler, 1913), 390.

76. With, *The Prussian Landeskunstkommission*, 37–38.

77. As quoted in Reese, *Akt und Anstand*, 72.

78. *Reichsbote*, October 10, 1885, no. 237, 2.

79. *Reichsbote* as quoted in *Leipziger Zeitung*, November 5, 1885, no. 258, 1

80. Ibid.

81. *Reichsbote* as quoted in *Leipziger Zeitung*, November 5, 1885, no. 258, Beiblatt, 3.

82. According to Irmgard Wirth, Menzel's *An Afternoon in the Tuileries Garden* (*Ein Nachmittag im Tuileriengarten*) (1867) and *A Weekday in Paris* (*Pariser Wochentag*) (1869) were painted after repeated visits to Paris—where Menzel was well known—and the former has a remarkable similarity to Manet's *Music at the Tuileries* (*La Musique aux Tuileries*) (1862), which had been exhibited just a few years earlier. See Wirth, *Berliner Malerei im 19. Jahrhundert*, 289–290.

83. Lenman, *Artists and Society*, 32–33.

84. Ibid., 36, 113. It should be added that according to Diane Guido, Werner was also one of the leading intellectuals of the so-called Anti-League, or the German League for the Prevention of Women's Emancipation. See Diane Guido, *The German League for the Prevention of Women's Emancipation: Antifeminism in Germany, 1912–1920* (New York: Peter Lang, 2010), 99.

85. Wirth, *Berliner Malerei im 19. Jahrhundert*, 326.

86. See Lenman, *Artists and Society*, 57; John C. G. Röhl, *Wilhelm II: der Aufbau der persönlichen Monarchie, 1888–1900* (Munich: Beck, 2001), 1025.

87. Petra Wilhelmy-Dollinger, *Der Berliner Salon im 19. Jahrhundert, 1780–1914* (New York: De Gruyter, 1989), 312.

88. As quoted in ibid., 310–311.

89. As quoted in Lenman, *Artists and Society*, 51.

90. Wirth, *Berliner Malerei im 19. Jahrhundert*, 448–449; ibid., 114–115. Lenman also rightly points out the growing tension over the pending Lex Heinze, an attempt by Wilhelm II and

conservatives to crack down on obscenity in art and literature. A brief discussion of the controversy over the Lex Heinze will follow in chapter six.

91. Lenman, *Artists and Society*, 55, 57–58.

92. Ibid., 115–116.

93. Ibid., 58–59.

94. Hugo von Tschudi, *Ausstellung von Werken des Malers Gustav Graef* (Berlin: Mittler und Sohn, 1896).

95. See Adolf Rosenberg, "Sammlungen und Ausstellungen," *Zeitschrift für bildende Kunst* 31 (1896): 305–306. Ironically, the famous artist whose show Graef's posthumous exhibit displaced, Peter von Cornelius, was an early member of the "Nazarene School" of German romantic art and later a director of the Düsseldorf School. Cornelius, however, had left Düsseldorf long before Gustav Graef came there to study.

96. See ibid., 305–306. This, of course, flies in the face of Rosenberg's earlier praise of paintings such as *Félicie* (as discussed in chapter one).

97. The essay, from the March 1896 issue of *Die Zeit*, is reprinted in David Frisby, ed., *Georg Simmel in Wien: Texte und Kontexte aus dem Wien der Jahrhundertwende* (Vienna: Facultas WUV, 2000), 50–53.

98. See ibid., 50–51.

99. As quoted in David Frisby, *Simmel and Since: Essays on Georg Simmel's Social Theory* (New York: Routledge 1992), 106.

100. See Frisby, *Georg Simmel in Wien*, 51.

Chapter Four

1. Letter from Bertha Rother to the Polizei Präsidium von Berlin, April 27, 1887 LAB A Pr. Br. Rep. 30 Berlin C—Polizeipräsidium Berlin, Nr. 14751. Veröffentlichungen über den Prozeß Prof. Gräfs. (1885–1887), pp. 35–36.

2. Letter from Bertha Rother to the Polizei Präsidium von Berlin, April 27, 1887 LAB A Pr. Br. Rep. 30 Berlin C—Polizeipräsidium Berlin Nr. 14751. Veröffentlichungen über den Prozeß Prof. Gräfs. (1885–1887), pp. 35–36. For more detailed information on the tragic fate of Bertha Rother, see the epilogue.

3. Dagmar Reese cites an additional letter from Bertha Rother, which was apparently printed in the *Berliner Volksblatt* just a few weeks after the trial verdict. In this letter, she complained about being the constant focus of public stares, as if she were some kind of a "sea monster" (*Meerwunder*). See Dagmar Reese, *Akt und Anstand: Der Skandal um den Gustav Graef Prozess, Berlin 1885* (Vienna: Böhlau, 2014), 80.

4. Some of this record was discussed in the *Berliner Gerichtszeitung* and then summarized in more detail by Bertha Rother's lawyer, H. Holz, in his posttrial article. Holz suggested that the prosecutor, Max Heinemann, had unfairly used evidence of Bertha's past behavior to establish a pattern of current conduct. For Holz, this was not only unfair to Bertha, but also entirely improper since her history as a prostitute had no bearing on the charge of perjury. *Berliner Gerichtszeitung*, October 6, 1885, no. 117, 1; H. Holz, "Prozess Graef: Dargestellt von Herrn Rechtsanwalt Holz in Berlin," *Das Tribunal: Zeitschrift für praktische Strafrechtspflege* 1, no. 12 (December 1885): 680.

5. Holz, "Prozess Graef," 680.

6. Hartwig Gebhardt and Ulla Wischermann, eds., *Die Staatsbürgerin: Originaltreuer Nachdruck der ersten Arbeiterinnenzeitschrift Deutschlands* (Munich: K. G. Saur, 1988), 9.

7. Michael Häusler and Bettina Hitzer, ed., *Zwischen Tanzboden und Bordell: Lebensbilder Berliner Prostituierter aus dem Jahr 1869* (Berlin: be.bra wissenschaft, 2010), 33.

8. Reese, *Akt und Anstand*, 24.

9. For examples of this attitude among government officials, see an 1890 letter from Police Constable Lorey in Kiel to Senior Prosecutor (*Oberstaatsanwalt*) Starke in which he deeply laments the banning of bordellos in a city that had a significant university population, served as home for half the

German fleet, and included large shipyards and factories. Lorey specifically worried that prosecutions would inevitably multiply the number of unregulated "secret whores" and push young men to target upstanding women of higher classes. He was also convinced that the outright banning of prostitution would never be effective since "the consummation of coitus will not stop as long as there are two human genders, and extramarital intercourse will exist as long as people are still unmarried after puberty." Letter from the Polizeibehörde in Kiel (signed Lorey) to Oberstaatsanwalt Starke on August 14, 1890 in GStA PK, I. HA Rep. 84a Justizministerium, Nr. 8094, Bd. 3, Bl. 203.

10. Marek Czapliński, "Prostitution as a problem of the city of Wrocław in the 19th century," *Silesian Historical Quarterly "Sobótka,"* accessed January 12, 2014, http://sobotka.uni.wroc.pl/1.pdf. Original Polish text in *Śląski Kwartalnik Historyczny Sobótka* 54, no. 3 (1999): 315–331.

11. For debates on the eve of German unification, see Häusler and Hitzer, *Zwischen Tanzboden und Bordell*, 10–12.

12. My summary of this episode is distilled from Tanja Hommen, *Sittlichkeitsverbrechen. Sexuelle Gewalt im Kaiserreich* (Frankfurt: Campus, 1999), 69–72.

13. Czapliński, "Prostitution as a problem of the city of Wrocław."

14. Häusler and Hitzer, *Zwischen Tanzboden und Bordell*, 62n143.

15. See the comparison of nineteenth-century Frankfurt and Breslau in Czapliński, "Prostitution as a problem of the city of Wrocław."

16. Philipps later moved to Berlin, becoming an assistant to Adolf Stöcker at the Berlin City Mission and an important figure in the Christian-Social Party. In 1887 he formed the Men's Alliance for Combatting Public Immorality (*Berliner Männerbund zur Bekämpfung der Unsittlichkeit*), in which he continued his campaigns against prostitution.

17. [Gustav Otto], *Die Verbrecherwelt von Berlin* (Berlin: Guttentag, 1886), 180.

18. Letter from the Magistrat zu Greifswald to Innenminister Puttkamer on May 4, 1886 in GStA PK, I. HA Rep. 84a Justizministerium, Nr. 8094, Bd. 3, Bl. 131.

19. See letter from the Oberstaatsanwalt in Stettin to Prussian Justice Minister Friedberg from May 18, 1886 and a report from Ernst Herrfurth to Justice Minister Friedberg and Kultusminister Goßler on July 28, 1886, both in GStA PK, I. HA Rep. 84a Justizministerium, Nr. 8094, Bd. 3, Bl. 137–139, 141.

20. It should be noted that this "concealment" was often only symbolic. In a conflict between prosecutors in Kiel about whether or not to target apartment owners for renting to prostitutes, Senior Prosecutor Starke mentioned that almost every building in the narrow alley "Hinter der Mauer" was occupied by prostitutes, and that these buildings happened to abut the High Regional Court (*Oberlandesgericht*). See letter from the Königliche Oberstaatsanwalt Starke in Kiel to Prussian Justice Minister Schelling on October 21, 1889 GStA PK, I. HA Rep. 84a Justizministerium, Nr. 8094, Bd. 3, Bl. 156.

21. For a look at the Berlin Regulations on Prostitutes from 1869 and 1911, see respectively Häusler and Hitzer, *Zwischen Tanzboden und Bordell*, 12–13, and Abraham Flexner, *Prostitution in Europe* (New York: Century Co., 1914), 415–419. Flexner also provides a comparison to other European cities.

22. Häusler and Hitzer, *Zwischen Tanzboden und Bordell*, 13, 15.

23. Richard Evans, "Prostitution, State, and Society in Imperial Germany," *Past and Present* 70, no. 1 (1976): 109.

24. Gebhardt and Wischermann, *Die Staatsbürgerin*, 9.

25. Flexner, *Prostitution in Europe*, 120–121. For an interesting history of prostitution in Berlin that veers from the anecdotal to the statistical and back, see also Hans Ostwald, *Berliner Kultur- und Sittengeschichte* (1911; repr., Paderborn: Voltmedia, 2006).

26. Otto, *Die Verbrecherwelt von Berlin*, 181; Evans, "Prostitution, State, and Society," 108.

27. In 1886, the Supreme Court in Leipzig ruled that doctors could examine alleged victims of sexual assault even against their will. Such exams usually included a determination of whether or not the victim had an intact hymen. According to the historian Tanja Hommen, there was considerable disagreement among medical experts at the time about the value and accuracy of such

"virginity examinations"; despite this fact, many courts not only commonly allowed such evidence to be presented, but also attributed significant weight to the conclusions drawn by doctors. In the Graef trial, a Dr. Wolff testified to having performed physical examinations on both Helene Hammermann and Lieschen Rother and reported that he found their virginity "to be fully intact." There is no evidence about whether Helene Hammermann and Lieschen Rother gave their permission for these examinations, the latter of whom was already on her deathbed suffering from tuberculosis. See *Berliner Gerichtszeitung*, October 6, 1885, no. 117, 3; *Berliner Gerichtszeitung* October 8, 1885, no. 118, 1; Hommen, *Sittlichkeitsverbrechen*, 69–73; and H. Holz, "Prozess Graef," 677 on Lieschen's condition.

28. Hommen, *Sittlichkeitsverbrechen*, 70; Angelika Schaser, *Frauenbewegung in Deutschland 1848–1933* (Darmstadt: Wiss. Buchges., 2006), 70.

29. Häusler and Hitzer, *Zwischen Tanzboden und Bordell*, 15–17.

30. Ibid., 38–39, 49–50.

31. *Prozeß (Gustav) Graef, verhandelt vom 29. September bis 7. October 1885 vor dem Geschworenengericht zu Berlin* (Berlin: Bartels, 1885), 31.

32. The term *unblemished* (*unbescholten*) remained a part of the German and later West German Criminal Code until 1973.

33. Hommen, *Sittlichkeitsverbrechen*, 66–67.

34. *Prozeß (Gustav) Graef*, 60.

35. *Berliner Gerichtszeitung*, September 29, 1885, no. 114, 2.

36. As quoted in *Kreuzzeitung*, October 11, 1885, no. 238, 1. Beilage, 2.

37. *Die Post*, October 10, 1885, no. 277, 3.

38. Comments like this were attributed to an unnamed left-liberal (*Freisinnige*) newspaper by the ultraconservative *Reichsbote*, which condemned the sentiments as a typical liberal attempt to diminish individual responsibility while at the same time embracing immoral behavior. See *Reichsbote*, October 10, 1885, no. 237, 2.

39. *Reichsbote*, September 30, 1885, no. 228, 1.

40. As reprinted in ibid.

41. Émile Zola, *Nana* (London: Penguin, 1972), 44–45.

42. As we will see, Bertha's life after the trial would be portrayed in ways similar to the dramatic downfall of Nana Coupeau. For additional comparisons, see the epilogue.

43. Gustav Braun [Martin Böhm], *Im Atelier oder der Maler und sein Modell. Genrebild mit Gesang in 1 Akt* (Berlin: H. Schmidt, 1885).

44. See Ulysses, *Das Märchenmodell: Ein Modellmärchen für Kinder der Zeit* (Berlin: M. Schulze, 1886).

45. Judith Walkowitz, *City of Dreadful Delight: Narratives of Sexual Danger in Late Victorian London* (Chicago: University of Chicago Press, 1992), 107.

46. For accounts of the fascinating and troubling life of Bertha Rother after the trial, see the epilogue. There are a number of studies on prostitutes and "fallen women" in Europe and America during this era. See, for example, Walkowitz, *City of Dreadful Delight*; Jill Suzanne Smith, *Berlin Coquette: Prostitution and the New German Woman, 1890–1933* (Ithaca, NY: Cornell University Press, 2013); Regina Kunzel, *Fallen Women, Problem Girls: Unmarried Mothers and the Professionalization of Social Work, 1890–1945* (New Haven, CT: Yale University Press, 1993); and Amanda Anderson, *Tainted Souls and Painted Faces: The Rhetoric of Fallenness in Victorian Culture* (Ithaca, NY: Cornell University Press, 1993).

47. Ingrid Sharp and Jane Jordan, eds., *Josephine Butler and the Prostitution Campaigns: Diseases of the Body Politic* (New York: Routledge Curzon, 2003), ix.

48. Walkowitz, *City of Dreadful Delight*, 132–133.

49. Ibid., 24, 105.

50. Ibid., 133.

51. Chris Weedon, "Gender, Feminism, and Fiction in Germany, 1880–1914," in *Gender, Sexuality, Culture*, Volume 5, ed. William J. Spurlin (New York: Peter Lang, 2006), 23.

52. Ibid., 23–24.

53. Ute Gerhard, *Frauenbewegung und Feminismus: Eine Geschichte seit 1789* (Munich: C. H. Beck, 2009), 33.

54. Ibid., 42.

55. Ibid., 56.

56. See ibid.

57. Ruth-Ellen Joeres, *Respectability and Deviance: Nineteenth-Century German Women Writers and the Ambiguity of Representation* (Chicago: University of Chicago Press, 1998), 120–121.

58. Gebhardt and Wischermann, *Die Staatsbürgerin*, 9.

59. Helene Lange, *Lebenserinnerungen* (Berlin: F. A. Herbig, 1928), 231.

60. Gebhardt and Wischermann, *Die Staatsbürgerin*, 12.

61. Although Guillaume-Schack would at first be a regular guest at the home of Friedrich Engels in London, her work in organizing women of the working class was later dismissed by Engels as "pure bourgeois shenanigans" (*reine Bourgeoisspielerei*). Guillaume-Schack increasingly withdrew from her public activism and was nearly forgotten by the time she passed away in 1905. See Gerhard, *Frauenbewegung und Feminismus*, 134.

62. Edward Dickinson, *Sex, Freedom, and Power in Imperial Germany, 1880–1914* (New York: Cambridge University Press, 2013), 17.

63. The author also counters Guillaume-Schack's description of the exploitation of poor young women by soldiers, suggesting that honorable men are just as often seduced by the presence of provocative young women: "What the morality associations call an attack (*Attentat*) on the chastity of young girls is in such cases really an attack by the young girl on the wallet of the man." See *Die Gefallene Mädchen und die Sittenpolizei* (Berlin: Wilhelm Ißleib [Gustav Schuhr], 1887), 1–7.

64. Ibid., 29.

65. Portia, "Das Fundament des Urtheils," *Nation* 3 (1885/1886): 43.

66. To confuse the analogy even further, Portia begins her article with an epigraph from Act Four, Scene One of *The Merchant of Venice*: "What judgment shall I dread, doing no wrong?" Although this may seem an appropriate opening for an article that paints Graef as an innocent martyr, it is a phrase spoken by Shylock, the putative villain of the play, and not Bassanio.

67. See Siegfried Mews and James Hardin, eds., *Nineteenth-Century German Writers: 1841–1900* (Detroit: Gale Research, 1993), 179.

68. Poem and brief commentary printed in the *Berliner Volksblatt*, October 16, no. 242, Beilage, 4. The untranslated last stanza:

> Doch des Volks Gerichte
> Sprachen ja dich frei.
> Fleck der Weltgeschichte!
> Gut, daß es vorbei.

69. Thanks here for a suggestion from Ann Goldberg, e-mail message to the author, July 6, 2016.

70. Based on a report from the *Nationalzeitung*, printed in *Kreuzzeitung*, October 10, 1885, no. 237, 3.

Chapter Five

1. Paul Lindau, "Idealismus und Naturalismus in Berlin. Prozess Graef," *Nord und Süd* 35, no. 104 (November 1885): 221.

2. Norbert Bachleitner, *Der englische und französische Sozialroman des 19. Jahrhunderts und seine Rezeption in Deutschland* (Atlanta: Rodopi, 1993), 272–273. Lindau, by the way, was not the only observer to use literary comparisons to describe the Graef trial. Editors of the left-liberal *Berliner Börsen-Zeitung*, for example, seconded Lindau's allusion to Zola, but also suggested stories by Guy de

Maupassant, or perhaps a combination of the first half of *Manon Lescaut* by Abbé Prévost and *The Lady of the Camellias* by Alexander Dumas—a novel that later inspired Verdi's opera *La Traviata*. Rother's defense attorney, on the other hand, half-seriously suggested that Boccaccio's *Decameron* was a better comparison. See *Berliner Börsen-Courier*, October 8, 1885, no. 469, Beilage; H. Holz, "Prozess Graef: Dargestellt von Herrn Rechtsanwalt Holz in Berlin," *Das Tribunal: Zeitschrift für praktische Strafrechtspflege* 1, no. 12 (December 1885): 687.

3. Mary Stewart, "German Naturalism and the Novel," *The Modern Language Review* 71, no. 4 (October 1976): 846.

4. Paul Lindau, it should be noted, was not entirely uncritical of Zola and naturalism. In fact, he frequently complained about the gruesome and immoral subjects chosen by Zola, and the necessarily corruptive effects that these kinds of books might have on ordinary readers. As Lena Marie Olbrisch points out, however, Lindau's point of view towards Zola and naturalism was often quite flexible. Not only did he rave about many of Zola's books, including *La Bête Humaine*, he also helped to spread Zola's popularity by regularly publishing his stories in his literary journal, *Nord und Süd*. Lindau's opinions about Zola were not only "flexible" but also blatantly hypocritical. His repeated criticism of Zola for corrupting his audience by sensationalizing the "sickening, tasteless, and gruesome" elements of society seems especially ironic considering the content of Lindau's essay on the Graef trial and his later series of books that would focus on other sensational criminal cases. Lena Marie Olbrisch, "Paul Lindaus 'Der Andere': Vom Fall zum Film" (Masterarbeit, Institut für Germanistik, Universität Potsdam, 2011), 32n109, accessed June 21, 2014, http://opus.kobv.de/ubp/volltexte/2013/6513/pdf/master_olbrisch.pdf. See also John Osborne, *Gerhard Hauptmann and the Naturalist Drama* (Amsterdam: Harwood Academic, 1998), 6–8.

5. Statistics come from Charles W. Haxthausen and Heidrun Suhr, "Introduction," in *Berlin: Culture and Metropolis*, ed. Charles W. Haxthausen and Heidrun Suhr (Minneapolis: University of Minnesota Press, 1990), xv n13.

6. See Andrew Lees, *Cities, Sin, and Social Reform in Imperial Germany* (Ann Arbor: University of Michigan Press, 2002), 4.

7. Ibid., 4.

8. Ibid., 81.

9. Amos Elon, *The Pity of It All: A History of the Jews in Germany 1743–1933* (New York: Metropolitan Books, 2002), 205.

10. Barnet Hartston, *Sensationalizing the Jewish Question: Anti-Semitic Trials and the Press in the Early German Empire* (Leiden: Brill, 2005), 1–2.

11. Ibid., 1–2.

12. As quoted in Derek J. Penslar, "Philanthropy, the 'Social Question,' and Jewish Identity in Imperial Germany," *Leo Baeck Institute Yearbook* 38 (1993): 51.

13. Lindau's work here was part of a tradition of sensationalistic reporting on the criminal world of Berlin that extended back to the mid-nineteenth century. In the 1860s, for example, Gustav Rasch was tipped off by police before raids against prostitutes or bands of criminals and then published his observations. Lindau was also not alone in treating the Graef case as if it were a rare opportunity to examine the real lives of the dregs of Berlin society. Pamphlets, newspaper editorials, and even accounts written by court reporters described the case as if the lives of the lowest classes and the secrets of the artists' studio were suddenly now exposed to public view for the first time. On Gustav Rasch, see Michael Häusler and Bettina Hitzer, eds., *Zwischen Tanzboden und Bordell: Lebensbilder Berliner Prostituierter aus dem Jahr 1869* (Berlin: be.bra wissenschaft, 2010), 11.

14. Olbrisch, "Paul Lindaus Der Andere," 37 n128.

15. Paul Lindau, "Laienhafte Glossen zum Graef'schen Prozess," *Nationalzeitung*, October 8, 1885, no. 558, Morgen Ausgabe, 1–3.

16. Ibid.

17. Meyer Heckscher, *Der Prozess Graef: Ein Mahnruf an die Gesetzgebung* (Berlin: Stahn, 1885), 4.

18. Lindau, "Idealismus und Naturalismus," 231.

19. Olbrisch, "Paul Lindaus 'Der Andere,'" 38.

20. Ibid., 39.

21. Lindau, "Idealismus und Naturalismus," 208.

22. *Prozeß (Gustav) Graef, verhandelt vom 29. September bis 7. October 1885 vor dem Geschworenengericht zu Berlin* (Berlin: Bartels, 1885), 11.

23. Sabine Graef had been called as a witness to offer testimony that refuted Helene Hammermann's accusations against her father. She claimed to have been present at home during Helene's visits and to have neither seen nor heard any evidence of a sexual assault. It is often assumed that the details of Sabine's testimony had been excluded from the court transcripts because of her youth. However, at the time of trial Sabine was 21 years old—exactly the same age as Helene Hammermann and Bertha Rother. Sabine's testimony was expunged because she was assumed to possess honor that could be damaged by her involvement in such a salacious affair; Helene Hammermann, on the other hand, whom Graef's defense attorney labeled as "Canaille" (filthy dog or piece of scum) during his closing arguments, was obviously not treated with the same sensitivity.

24. Ellen Ross, "'Fierce Questions and Taunts': Married Life in Working-Class London," *Feminist Studies* 8, no. 3 (Fall 1982): 575–576, as quoted in Walkowitz, *City of Dreadful Delight*, 35.

25. Lindau, "Idealismus und Naturalismus," 222.

26. *Prozeß (Gustav) Graef*, 4–5.

27. *Germania*, October 9, 1885, no. 231, Erstes Blatt, 1.

28. As quoted in *Leipziger Zeitung*, October 13, 1885, no. 239.

29. Max Heinemann, *Der Prozeß Graef und die deutsche Kunst: Eine Antwort auf Dr. Karl Frenzel's Abhandlung in der Nationalzeitung: "Die Kunst und das Strafgesetz"* (Berlin: Friedrich Luckhardt, 1885), 3–4.

30. Maximilian Harden, "Lex Heinze," *Die Zukunft* 30 (1900): 457–458.

31. [Gustav Otto], *Die Verbrecherwelt von Berlin* (Berlin: Guttentag, 1886), 4, 6.

32. Ibid., 4, 35.

33. See ibid., 8–35 for a summary of the Dickhoff case. The judge in the Dickhoff trial, by the way, was Boguslaw Müller.

34. Otto, *Die Verbrecherwelt von Berlin*, 47–48.

35. Ibid., 190–191.

36. *Berliner Gerichtszeitung*, October 1, 1885, no. 115, 2. After the trial, Bertha Rother's attorney described her courtroom demeanor much differently—as a woman who acted with quiet grace and dignity, except for the few occasions when she cried openly out of embarrassment at the public airing of the details of her past life. See Holz, "Prozess Graef," 690.

37. There are many works on the rise of expert testimony in the German courtroom, especially medical and psychological testimony, and its impact on German legal culture. See, for example, Benjamin Hett, *Death in the Tiergarten: Murder and Criminal Justice in the Kaiser's Berlin* (Cambridge, MA: Harvard University Press, 2004), 206–219.

38. Dr. Carl (also Karl) Liman was appointed as an official court physician (*Gerichtliche Stadt-Physiker*) and was attached in that capacity to the Berlin Police-Presidium. Along with his colleague Dr. Wolff (see below), Liman was often called into court to testify in such cases. By this time, Liman had already practiced medicine in Berlin for nearly forty years. He also served as director of the Applied School for State Pharmacology (*praktischen Unterrichtsanstalt für die Staatsarzneikunde*) and had issued new editions of the well-regarded *Handbook of Forensic Medicine* (Handbuch der gerichtlichen Medicin), which had first been compiled by his uncle, J. L. Casper. See Julius Leopold Pagel, "Liman, Karl," *Allgemeine Deutsche Biographie* (1906), S. [Onlinefassung], accessed April 9, 2014, http://www.deutsche-biographie.de/pnd11906555X.html?anchor=adb.

39. *Prozeß (Gustav) Graef*, 21–22.

40. Ibid., 33.

41. Ibid., 30.

42. A few years later, this same Lewin was publicly accused by the anti-Semitic agitators Hermann Ahlwardt and Carl Paasch of being part of a wide-ranging Jewish conspiracy that had involved the two assassination attempts on Kaiser Wilhelm I in 1878. Both Ahlwardt and Paasch used

this conspiracy story as an excuse to refuse Lewin's attempts to examine them while they were in pretrial custody on charges of libel. See Hartston, *Sensationalizing the Jewish Question*, 227, 256–257. Note: I have compressed the timeline of the Graef trial a bit here for the sake of simplification. The topic of Anna Rother's competence and the expert testimony itself was scattered over several days of the trial.

43. *Prozeß (Gustav) Graef*, 47–48.

44. *Berliner Gerichtszeitung*, October 6, 1885, no. 117, 2.

45. Ibid.; *Prozeß (Gustav) Graef*, 48.

46. *Prozeß (Gustav) Graef*, 50.

47. Ibid., 62.

48. Simone de Beauvoir, *The Second Sex* (New York: Vintage Books, 1989), 610–611.

49. For more on the interplay between judicial proceedings and "community justice," see Barbara Yngvesson, "Inventing Law in Local Settings: Rethinking Popular Legal Culture," *Yale Law Review* 98, No. 8 (1989): 1689–1709 (here especially 1699–1701).

50. *Dresdner Tageblatt*, October 12, 1885.

51. *Der Sozialdemokrat* (Zürich), October 22, 1885, no. 43, 2.

52. Dagmar Reese reports that workers in Berlin took it upon themselves to organize a meeting where they would decide how to respond to the Graef trial and the issues that it raised. Those present allegedly decided that Graef's behavior was to be condemned. Reese cites the description of the meeting as coming from the liberal *Berliner Zeitung*, but she provides few details about who organized or attended the gathering. See Reese, *Akt und Anstand*, 92.

53. See Walkowitz, *City of Dreadful Delight*, 19, 34–35.

54. See Otto Glagau, *Der Börsen und Gründungsschwindel in Berlin* (Leipzig: P. Frohberg, 1876) and *Der Börsen und Gründungsschwindel in Deutschland* (Leipzig: P. Frohberg, 1877).

55. Peter Pulzer, *The Rise of Political Anti-Semitism in Germany and Austria* (Cambridge, MA: Harvard University Press, 1988), 89.

56. Peter Pulzer, *The Rise of Political Anti-Semitism*, 50–51.

57. Ibid.

58. See Hartston, *Sensationalizing the Jewish Question*; Jacob Katz, *From Prejudice to Destruction* (Cambridge, MA: Harvard University Press, 1980), 261. See also Massimo Ferrari Zumbini, *Die Wurzeln des Bösen: Gründerjahre des Antisemitismus von der Bismarckzeit zu Hitler* (Frankfurt: Klostermann, 2003), 168–174.

59. Importantly, the Graef case occurred not long after two additional trials that had been widely covered by the press and served as useful anti-Jewish propaganda: the Tisza-Eszlar Ritual Murder trial (June–July 1883) and the Neustettin Synagogue Arson trial (October 1883/March 1884). For more on the impact of these cases, see chapters three and four of Hartston, *Sensationalizing the Jewish Question*.

60. Bernhard Förster, *Das Verhältniss des modernen Judenthums zur deutschen Kunst* (Berlin: M. Schulze, 1881), 7, accessed February 9, 2012, http://books.google.com/books.

61. Ibid., 36,

62. Ibid., 38.

63. *Freie Zeitung*, October 1884, Extra-Blatt, in LAB A Pr. Br. Rep. 30 Berlin C—Polizeipräsidium Berlin Nr. 14754, Die Verhandlungen gegen Karl Paasch wegen der Herausgabe und Veröffentlichung von antisemitischen Schriften (1892–1901), p. 7 (bold in original).

64. *Zeuge Stöcker: Ein Zeitbild aus dem Jahre 1885. Die Prozeßverhandlungen wegen Beleidigung des Hofpredigers Stöcker vor der II. Strafkammer des Landgerichts Berlin I am 9., 10., 13. Und 16. Juni nebst erläuternden und ergänzenden Anmerkungen* (Berlin: Verlag "Fortschritt, Aktiengesellschaft," 1885), 59–60.

65. This summary is taken from a more thorough discussion of the Stöcker-Bäcker trial in the context of similar cases within chapter two of Hartston, *Sensationalizing the Jewish Question*.

66. Otto Glagau, ed., *Der Kulturkämpfer: Zeitschrift für öffentliche Angelegenheiten* 6, no. 123 (October 1885): 35.

67. Glagau, *Der Kulturkämpfer* 6, no. 123 (October 1885): 14.

68. Ibid., 35.

69. *Kreuzzeitung*, October 13, 1885, no. 239, 1.

70. *Nationalzeitung*, October 15, 1885, no. 570, Erstes Beiblatt, 2. For more on the history of the phrase "There are still judges in Berlin!" (*il y a des juges à Berlin!*), which comes from the era of Frederick the Great, see chapter six. In her book on the Graef trial, Dagmar Reese points out that many anti-Semites linked the Graef trial with the perjury allegations made against the prominent Jewish banker Gerson von Bleichröder a few years earlier. See Reese, *Akt und Anstand*, 103–104.

71. As quoted in *Kreuzzeitung*, October 16, 1885, no. 242, Beilage, 3.

72. *Nationalzeitung*, October 15, 1885, no. 571, Abend-Ausgabe, 2.

73. As reported in *Kreuzzeitung*, October 25, 1885, no. 250, Beilage, 2.

74. Ibid.

75. In what was a rather unusual path, Max Heinemann had apparently first converted as a young man to Catholicism, and then later converted again to Evangelical Protestantism after his first marriage. See Reese, *Akt und Anstand*, 105.

76. Glagau, *Der Kulturkämpfer* 6, no. 123 (October 1885), 35.

77. Carl Paasch, *Die kaiserlich deutsche Gesandtschaft in China. Eine Denkschrift über den Fall Carl Paasch, für die deutschen Landesvertretungen, insbesondere den Reichstag* (Leipzig: Selbstverlag, 1892), in Landesarchiv Berlin Pr. Br. Rep. 30 Berlin C—Polizeipräsidium Berlin, Nr. 14754, 28. John Simson, Paul Lindau, and Karl Frenzel are already well known to the reader from their roles in the Graef trial. Both Simson's and Lindau's ancestors had converted from Judaism. Wolff, Lewin, and Siegmund were almost certainly references to the doctors that participated in the Graef trial and perhaps also in Paasch's own examination while in custody. Other prominent names on the list were liberal journalists or editors, including Carl Robert Lessing (*Vossische Zeitung*), Robert Davidsohn (*Berliner Börsen-Courier*), Friedrich Dernburg (*Nationalzeitung*), and Aaron Bernstein, Hermann Holdheim, and Adolph Phillips (*Volkszeitung*). Salomonsohn is probably a reference to the Jewish banker Adolf Salomonsohn, who was active in the controversial *Disconto-Gesellschaft*.

78. Paasch, *Die kaiserlich deutsche Gesandtschaft*, 28. These kinds of accusations against Schelling eventually resulted in Paasch's prosecution for slander and a sentence of fifteen months in prison, which he apparently escaped by fleeing to Zurich. See Report to the Polizei-Präsident Abtheilung VII from Oberstaatsanwalt, December 21, 1901 in Landesarchiv Berlin Pr. Br. Rep. 30 Berlin C Polizeipräsidium Berlin, Nr. 14754, 147.

79. Walkowitz, *City of Dreadful Delight*, 203.

80. Ibid., 203–204.

81. On the complex issues surrounding the 1881 pogroms, see Hartston, *Sensationalizing the Jewish Question*, 105–127, and Christhard Hoffmann, "Political Culture and Violence against Minorities: The Antisemitic Violence in Pomerania and West Prussia," in *Exclusionary Violence: Antisemitic Riots in Modern German History*, ed. Christhard Hoffmann, Werner Bergmann, and Helmut Walser Smith (Ann Arbor: University of Michigan Press, 2002).

Chapter Six

1. *Prozeß (Gustav) Graef, verhandelt vom 29. September bis 7. October 1885 vor dem Geschworenengericht zu Berlin* (Berlin: Bartels, 1885), 9–10.

2. Ibid., 10.

3. The writers Karl Frenzel and Paul Lindau later repeated the defense attorney Kleinholz's arguments on this point. See chapter three as well as Paul Lindau, "Idealismus und Naturalismus in Berlin. Prozess Graef," *Nord und Süd* 35, no. 104 (November 1885): 255.

4. *Berliner Gerichtszeitung*, October 1, 1885, no. 115, 1; *Prozeß (Gustav) Graef*, 10, 13.

5. Benjamin Hett, *Death in the Tiergarten: Murder and Criminal Justice in the Kaiser's Berlin* (Cambridge, MA: Harvard University Press, 2004), 19; Richard Wetzell, "From Retributive Justice to

Social Defense: Penal Reform in Fin-de-Siècle Germany," in *Germany at the Fin de Siècle: Culture, Politics, and Ideas*, ed. Suzanne Marchand and David Lindenfeld (Baton Rouge: Louisiana State University Press, 2004), 59.

6. Kenneth Ledford, *From General Estate to Special Interest: German Lawyers, 1878–1933* (New York: Cambridge University Press, 1996), xxvii.

7. See Alexandra Ortmann, *Machtvolle Verhandlungen: Zur Kulturgeschichte der deutschen Strafjustiz, 1879–1924* (Göttingen: Vandenhoeck and Ruprecht, 2014), 109.

8. Hett, *Death in the Tiergarten*, 19. See Karl Liebknecht, *Rechtsstaat und Klassenjustiz: Vortrag, gehalten zu Stuttgart am 23. August 1907* (Stuttgart: Singer, 1907). Karl Liebknecht claimed that in Germany, there was a thin facade of a system of laws (*Rechtsstaat*) that only partially covered the police state (*Polizeistaat*) underneath. In reality, he suggested, Germany was perhaps three-quarters or even nine-tenths police state.

9. Uwe Wilhelm, *Das deutsche Kaiserreich und seine Justiz. Justizkritik, politische Strafrechtsprechung, Justizpolitik* (Berlin: Duncker and Humblot, 2010), 236–237. Kauffmann was a lawyer at the Berlin Landgericht and also a Reichstag deputy for the liberal Free-Thinking Party. He later became a city councilman (*Stadtrat*), and eventually had his election for mayor by the council in 1901 rescinded by Wilhelm II—perhaps for his leftist political leanings or because he had chosen not to have his son baptized.

10. As quoted in ibid., 242.

11. Ortmann, *Machtvolle Verhandlungen*, 80–85.

12. All of this controversy over potential reforms to the Criminal Code was exacerbated by the long and contentious process of developing a new Civil Code (*Bürgerliche Gesetzbuch*), which was intended to replace the various civil law codes of individual states. This project began in 1881, and it was so controversial that it would only be completed decades later after several false starts.

13. *Prozeß (Gustav) Graef*, 60.

14. *Vossische Zeitung*, March 10, 1883 in GStA PK, I. HA Rep. 84a Justizministerium, Nr. 8255, Bd. 2, Bl. 38.

15. The text and rationale for the 1885 legal reforms are in BArch R3001/5277, starting on page 61.

16. See "Allgemeine Verfügung von November 2, 1885,—betreffend die Protokolle über die Verhandlungen in Strafsachen," in *Justiz-Ministerial-Blatt für die Preußische Gesetzgebung und Rechtspflege* (Berlin: R. Von Decker, 1885), 359–360.

17. *Dresdner Nachrichten*, November 1, 1885.

18. Ortmann, *Machtvolle Verhandlungen*, 29.

19. This view was shared by other commentators, many of whom had quite different opinions of the Graef case. See Meyer Heckscher, *Der Prozeß Graef: Ein Mahnruf an die Gesetzgebung* (Berlin: Stahn, 1885) and H. Holz, "Prozess Graef: Dargestellt von Herrn Rechtsanwalt Holz in Berlin," *Das Tribunal: Zeitschrift für praktische Strafrechtspflege* 1, no. 12 (December 1885): 697–698 for additional commentaries. See also the long letter from "R. B." in Dresden to the *Leipziger Zeitung* calling for reform. *Leipziger Zeitung*, October 17, 1885.

20. Heckscher, *Der Prozeß Graef*, 19.

21. Ibid., 16.

22. Beginning in the 1970s, the West German government passed several Victim Protection Laws (*Opferschutzgesetze*). These reforms included a revision to §68a of the Code of Criminal Procedure which put off-limits any questions that might unnecessarily lead to the dishonor of a witness (or his or her relatives) or that unfairly target his or her private life. See Kirsten Stang and Ulrich Sasse, *Trauma und Justiz: juristische Grundlagen für Psychotherapeuten; psychotherapeutische Grundlagen für Juristen* (Stuttgart: Schattauer, 2007), 150.

23. This includes debates between supporters of the "attestory oath" (*Nacheid*), the practice of swearing in witnesses *after* their testimony, and supporters of the "promissory oath" (*Voreid*), the swearing in of witnesses *before* their testimony. The attestory oath had been common practice in Prussia and much of northern Germany for much of the nineteenth century. New law codes in the German

Empire, however, favored the promissory oath, which had been more common in southern Germany. Critics of the promissory oath suggested that once a witness began lying, a promissory oath was quickly forgotten. An oath (and threat of punishment) at the end of their testimony, however, might test the conscience of a witness more thoroughly and force them to recant any untruths. See Holz, "Prozess Graef," 697–698 for one such argument relating to the Graef case. See also an unsuccessful 1885 proposal for reform of the timing of the oath that was scuttled by the Reichstag shortly before the Graef trial began in BArch R3001/5277, Bl. 61.

24. The timing of the oath was, in fact, finally changed in November 1933, when the new Nazi government passed a Law to Reduce Oaths in Criminal Proceedings. The attestory oath implemented by the Nazis has remained the norm for German criminal trials ever since.

25. Kurt Pomplun, "Die erste Porno-Prozess Berlins brachte Maler und Modell vor Gericht," *Berliner Morgenpost*, October 8, 1972, no. 235, 8.

26. See Sarah Leonard, *Fragile Minds and Vulnerable Souls: The Matter of Obscenity in Nineteenth-Century Germany* (Philadelphia: University of Pennsylvania Press, 2015), 168–170.

27. Letter from Innenminister to the Polizei-Präsident of Berlin on August 15, 1862 in GStA PK, I. HA Rep. 77 Preußisches Innenministerium, Tit. 2772, Nr. 15, Bl. 3–4.

28. See the voluminous reports and police complaints in GStA PK, I. HA Rep. 77 Preußisches Innenministerium, Tit. 657, Nr. 3.

29. GStA PK, I. HA Rep. 77 Preußisches Innenministerium, Tit. 657, Nr. 3, Bd. 1, Bl. 83.

30. Eulenburg was particularly concerned with newspaper ads for rubber condoms and other prophylactics that he considered inappropriate. In December of 1879, the German Supreme Court (*Reichsgericht*) upheld the decision that such ads were inappropriate and illegal. GStA PK, I. HA Rep. 77 Preußisches Innenministerium, Tit. 657, Nr. 3, Bd. 1, Bl. 91.

31. GStA PK, I. HA Rep. 77 Preußisches Innenministerium, Tit. 657, Nr. 3, Bd. 1, Bl. 90.

32. GStA PK, I. HA Rep. 77 Preußisches Innenministerium, Tit. 657, Nr. 3, Bd. 1, Bl. 100–101.

33. Gary Stark, "Pornography, Society, and the Law in Imperial Germany," *Peer Reviewed Articles*. Paper 21 (2014): 213. http://scholarworks.gvsu.edu/hst_articles/21. Stark lists the important *Reichsgericht* decisions as taking place on December 15, 1879, February 16, 1881, and February 19, 1883.

34. *Berliner Volksblatt*, October 6, 1885, no. 233, Beilage, 1.

35. *Germania*, October 20, 1885, no. 240, Erstes Blatt, 2.

36. LAB A Pr. Br. Rep. 30 Berlin C—Polizeipräsidium Berlin Nr. 14751. Veröffentlichungen über den Prozeß Prof. Gräf. (1885–1887), pp. 17–18.

37. *Germania*, excerpted in GStA PK, I. HA Rep. 77 Preußisches Innenministerium, Tit. 657, Nr. 3, Bd. 1, Bl. 127.

38. Ibid..

39. Report by Friedheim in GStA PK, I. HA Rep. 77 Preußisches Innenministerium, Tit. 657, Nr. 3, Bd. 1, Bl. 128–134. Friedheim, by the way, was put forward by the liberal *Nationalzeitung* as a perfect replacement for Madai because of "his tireless work ethic, his prudence, as well as the amiable and humane nature that won him sympathy from wide sections of the population." He didn't get the job. See *Nationalzeitung*, October 6, 1885, no. 555, Abend-Ausgabe, 1.

40. Karl Binding, "Unzüchtige Handlungen und unzüchtige Schriften: Gutachten des Leipziger Spruchkolleges, Entworfen von Professor Karl Binding in Leipzig," *Zeitschrift für die gesamte Strafrechtswissenschaft* 2 (1882) as quoted in Sarah Leonard, *Fragile Minds*, 174.

41. Adolf Rosenberg, "Die akademische Kunstausstellung in Berlin I.," *Die Grenzboten* 38, no. 3 (1879), 460.

42. Report from the Königliche Regierung zu Köln, Abtheilung des Innern to Puttkamer on August 15, 1885 in GStA PK, I. HA Rep. 77 Preußisches Innenministerium, Tit. 657, Nr. 3, Bl. 115–119. Prosecutions for disturbance of the peace would be a common instrument in tackling offensive literature, especially in South Germany. According to Gary Stark, police tended to become frustrated with government reluctance to pursue obscenity cases it might not win in front of juries, and they therefore would frequently turn to the *Grober Unfug* statute instead—which did not require a jury trial

or any proof that the text or image in question was obscene. See Gary Stark, *Banned in Berlin: Literary Censorship in Imperial Germany* (New York: Berghahn, 2009), 5–6.

43. *Berliner Börsen-Zeitung*, October 28, 1885, Morgen Ausgabe, 3. Beilage in GStA PK, I. HA Rep. 77 Preußisches Innenministerium, Tit. 657, Nr. 3, Bd. 1, Bl. 139.

44. See, for example, *Die Post*, October 26, 1885, no. 293 and *Berliner Börsen-Courier*, November 26, 1885, no. 325, I. Beilage in LAB A Pr. Br. Rep. 30 Berlin C—Polizeipräsidium Berlin, Nr. 14542, p. 73.

45. A copy of the verdict is in GStA PK, I. HA Rep. 77 Preußisches Innenministerium, Tit. 657, Nr. 3, Bd. 1, Bl. 155–161.

46. Citing the legal importance of the appeals, the *Kölner Gerichts-Zeitung* printed the closing arguments of the defense in full. See *Kölner Gerichts-Zeitung*, April 4, 1886, no. 104 in GStA PK, I. HA Rep. 77 Preußisches Innenministerium, Tit. 657, Nr. 3, Bd. 1, Bl. 147–148.

47. Stark, "Pornography, Society, and the Law," 223.

48. Stark also notes that Zola's *Nana* was allowed to be circulated in its original French edition, but was banned in German translation, where its salacious nature might be more accessible to a general audience. Stark, "Pornography, Society, and the Law," 225.

49. Ibid., 224.

50. PrAdK, 2.3/111 (film Nr. 310), Bl. 355.

51. GStA PK, I. HA Rep. 77 Preußisches Innenministerium, Tit. 657 Nr. 3 Bd. 1, Bl. 150–153.

52. Ibid.

53. See exchange of letters between the Poliziei-Präsidium and the Interior Ministry in GStA PK, I. HA Rep. 77 Preußisches Innenministerium, Tit. 657 Nr. 3 Bd. 1, Bl. 178–190. In the meantime, Kaufmann's painting circulated around Europe, including stops in Amsterdam and Vienna. It was greeted by mixed reviews at best.

54. See Stark, *Banned in Berlin*, xxv.

55. Substantial parts of this section of the book appear in the article "Closing the Courtroom: Press Restrictions and Criminal Trials in Late Nineteenth-Century Germany," *Law and History Review* (forthcoming). My gratitude to Elizabeth Dale, editor of *Law and History Review*, for permission to use that material here.

56. See Stark, *Banned in Berlin*, xxiii–xxiv.

57. The term *Gerichtsverfassungsgesetz* does not have an obvious English translation. Scholars have used a variety of terms, including "Constitution of the Courts," "Judiciary Act," or "Court Organization Law," and I have chosen the latter for the sake of clarity. This law, passed in 1877, set out the hierarchy of courts, and such things as the qualifications and presiding powers of judges, and the rules for jury trials. For an explanation in English, see Kenneth Ledford, "Lawyers, Liberalism, and Procedure: The German Imperial Justice Laws of 1877–79," *Central European History* 26 (1993): 165–193.

58. *Kreuzzeitung*, October 2, 1885, no. 230, 1.

59. Otto Mittelstädt, "Strafjustiz und öffentliche Meinung," *Preußischer Jahrbücher* 56, no. 5 (1885): 501. Similar opinions were voiced by Carl Fuchs, a judge at the Higher Regional Court (Oberlandesgericht) in Jena, who suggested the trial demonstrated the need to amend press laws to restrict reporting on closed trials. See [Carl] Fuchs, "Zum Prozess Graef," *Goltdammer's Archiv für Strafrecht* 33, no. 6 (1885): 403–430. Mittelstädt was a fascinating character. Although he identified as a liberal, he is occasionally characterized by historians as an arch-conservative because of his controversial call for a renewed emphasis on corporal punishment in prisons rather than a focus on rehabilitation. For more detail on his career, see Warren Rosenblum, *Beyond the Prison Gates: Punishment and Welfare in Germany* (Chapel Hill: University of North Carolina Press, 2008), especially 34–40.

60. See *Frankfurter Zeitung*, October 11, 1885 Morgen in BArch R3001/4776, Bd. 1, Bl. 2.

61. Ibid.

62. The diversity of liberal reactions should not be surprising. As Michael Gross points out, Leopold Sonnemann, editor of the *Frankfurter Zeitung*, and his People's Party had been staunchly against the anti-Catholic *Kulturkampf* legislation of the 1870s, which many other liberals had supported. Despite this position, the *Frankfurter Zeitung* was commonly lumped in with other liberal

newspapers as part of the "*Judenpresse*." See Michael Gross, *The War Against Catholicism: Liberalism and the Anti-Catholic Imagination* (Ann Arbor: University of Michigan Press, 2005), 272–273.

63. *Berliner Börsen-Courier*, October 17, 1885, no. 527, Morgenausgabe, 2.

64. Bismarck singled out an article from the *Frankfurter Zeitung* as an example. Letter from Herbert Bismarck to Schelling on February 14, 1886 in BArch R3001/4776, Bd. 1, Bl. 4–5.

65. Hermann Jastrow, "Der Deutsche Gesetzentwurf, betreffend die unter Ausschluss der Öffentlichkeit stattfindenden Gerichtshandlungen," *Jahrbuch der Gesetzgebung, Verwaltung und Volkswirthschaft im Deutschen Reiche* 10, no. 4 (1886), included in BArch R3001/4776, Bd. 1, 45. The proposal for this wording of the 1877 law had been made in committee by the Center Party delegate, August Reichensperger. It was adopted against the original opposition of Bundesrat representatives.

66. Legal scholars also pointed to §266 of the Code of Criminal Procedure, which spelled out what must be included in the legal rationale for a verdict.

67. Letter from Bismarck to Schelling on February 14, 1886 in BArch R3001/4776, Bd. 1, Bl. 4–5.

68. See the letters from Schelling to the Auswärtiges Amt on March 2, 1886 and from Herbert von Bismarck to Schelling on March 8, 1886 in BArch R3001/4776, Bd. 1, Bl. 6–10, 11–13.

69. Alexandra Ortmann reports that the original proposal sent to the Bundesrat also included provisions to hold all slander trials and cases against minors behind closed doors. This legislation apparently was rejected by representatives from Württemberg and Bavaria. See Alexandra Ortmann, *Machtvolle Verhandlungen*, 171–172.

70. A majority in the Reichstag at this time required 199 votes.

71. Despite Bismarck's attempts to crush it over the previous six years, the Socialist Party also gained a substantial number of seats in the 1884 election.

72. This would be proven shortly thereafter. Prosecutors quickly appealed the Chemnitz verdict, which was then overturned by the Supreme Court. The case was sent back to the criminal chamber (*Strafkammer*) in Freiberg, which convicted Bebel and his associates in August 1886 and sentenced each to between six and nine months in jail. As in many other such cases, the conviction served as valuable propaganda for Socialist leaders and attracted sympathy even across party lines. This conviction almost certainly did more harm to the government than to the Socialist Party itself. See Franz Mehring, *Geschichte der Deutschen Demokratie*, vol. 4 (1909; repr., Books on Demand, 2011), 285–286, accessed June 7, 2015, https://books.google.com/books?id=QK6BmEVzCaoC&pg=PA285&lpg=PA285&dq=bebel+freiberg+verurteilung&source=bl&ots=etROKcZcVP&sig=ZrLGGv4yOyluCsjGrlQOr4EBUjY&hl=en&sa=X&ei=U2OcVbjyPIq5ggSrnICwBw&ved=0CD8Q6AEwBg#v=onepage&q=bebel%20freiberg%20verurteilung&f=false.

73. It should also be noted that the Bundesrat had angered some liberals by failing to move forward on legal reforms that had substantial liberal support in the Reichstag, including compensation for wrongly convicted defendants and the introduction of a full appeals process for criminal chambers (*Strafkammern*). See Fritz Friedmann, *Die Öffentlichkeit der Gerichtsverhandlungen, ihre Vorzüge und Schäden* (Berlin: Heine, 1887), 1.

74. Jastrow, "Der deutsche Gesetzentwurf."

75. Ibid.

76. Ibid.

77. *Hamburger Nachrichten*, November 18, 1886 in BArch R3001/4776, Bd. 1, Bl. 47–48.

78. The entire issue of the *Berliner Börsen-Zeitung* (November 28, 1886, no. 557, 1. Beilage), which reports on the trial of the newspaper editor Prohl, as well as exchanges between Herbert von Bismarck, Hermann von Schelling, and Leo von Caprivi on their continued national security concerns, is present in BArch R3001/4776, Bd. 1, Bl. 49–57.

79. Stenographic report of the Reichstag session on March 18, 1887 in BArch R3001/4776, Bd. 1, Bl. 75.

80. Ibid.

81. Jonathan Sperber, *The Kaiser's Voters: Electors and Elections in Imperial Germany* (New York: Cambridge University Press, 1997), 190.

82. Ibid., 194, 197. Again, the dramatic changes in the number of seats earned by a party did not always match actual vote totals in the complex electoral system of Imperial Germany. The primary loser of this election, especially in terms of seats lost, was the left-liberal *Freisinnige* Party.

83. This time, the case was against the anarchist Johann Neve. Apparently, Neve had been arrested in Belgium and then secretly transported to Germany for prosecution. Press reports on his apprehension had caused embarrassment for both governments and a strain on relations between the two countries. Letter from Herbert von Bismarck at the Foreign Office to Schelling on October 23, 1887 in BArch, R3001/4776, Bd. 1, 98.

84. The original amendment petitions are in the Reichstag record, available online at www.reichstagprotokolle.de, and are also included in BA R3001/4776, Bd. 1, 92.

85. Verhandlungen des Deutschen Reichstags, (1888, 2), Aktenstück, no. 138, 593, accessed April 10, 2014, http://www.reichstagsprotokolle.de/Blatt3_k7_bsb00018650_00151.html.

86. See Verhandlungen des Deutschen Reichstags, 50. Sitzung 1887/88, 2., 1 März 1888, 1199, accessed June 22, 2015, http://www.reichstagsprotokolle.de/Blatt3_k7_bsb00018648_00509.html.

87. See Verhandlungen des Deutschen Reichstags, 55. Sitzung 1887/88, 2., 7 März 1888, 1340, accessed June 19, 2015, http://www.reichstagsprotokolle.de/Blatt3_k7_bsb00018648_00650.html.

88. See Verhandlungen des Deutschen Reichstags, 47. Sitzung 1887/88, 2., 27 Februär 1888, 1146, accessed June 19, 2015, http://www.reichstagsprotokolle.de/Blatt3_k7_bsb00018648_00456.html.

89. See Verhandlungen des Deutschen Reichstags, 50. Sitzung 1887/88, 2., 1 März 1888, 1197, accessed June 19, 2015, http://www.reichstagsprotokolle.de/Blatt3_k7_bsb00018648_00507.html.

90. This summary comes from *Kreuzzeitung*, September 28, 1891, no. 452, Abend.

91. See GStA PK, I. HA Rep. 89 Geheimes Zivilkabinett, Nr. 17725, Bd. 5, Bl. 44 for the original telegram from *Flügeladjutant* von Scholl on behalf of Kaiser Wilhelm II on October 3, 1891; see also GStA PK, I. HA Rep. 84a Justizministerium, Nr. 8095, Bl. 2 for responses within the Prussian Justice Ministry.

92. On the Heinze case as the start of a moral panic, see Hett, *Death in the Tiergarten*, 78, and Edward Dickinson, "The Men's Christian Morality Movement in Germany, 1880–1914: Some Reflections on Sex, Politics, and Sexual Politics," *Journal of Modern History* 75, no. 1 (2003): 59–110.

93. Edward Dickinson, *Sex, Freedom, and Power in Imperial Germany, 1880–1914* (New York: Cambridge University Press, 2013), 14.

94. Richard Evans, "Prostitution, State, and Society in Imperial Germany," *Past and Present* 70, no. 1 (1976): 120–121.

95. Andrew Lees, "Deviant Sexuality and Other 'Sins': The Views of Protestant Conservatives in Imperial Germany," *German Studies Review* 23, no. 3 (October 2000): 453-476.

96. Evans, "Prostitution, State, and Society," 121.

97. Ibid., 121–122.

98. Angelika Schaser, *Frauenbewegung in Deutschland 1848–1933* (Darmstadt: Wiss. Buchges., 2006), 71–72. In 1894, Bieber-Böhm would go on to play a key role in the formation of the League of German Women's Associations (*Bund deutscher Frauenvereine*), a national umbrella organization for middle-class women's organizations in Germany, and she soon became chair of its committee on issues related to morality. See Dickinson, *Sex, Freedom, and Power*, 78.

99. Stark, *Banned in Berlin*, 196.

100. Ibid., 210.

101. While the press and literature in Germany were usually subjected to a punitive *Nachzensur*, which punished authors and confiscated works after they appeared, plays were much more often subjected to an even stricter *Vorzensur*, in which police reviewed plays before they were ever staged. For a discussion of the traditional importance and also perceived danger of the theater in Germany, see Stark, *Banned in Berlin*, 10.

102. Ibid., 210–211.

103. Adah, however, was a corrupted middle-aged woman of substance rather than a young poor prostitute. Willi was also a younger artist, unlike the much older Graef. See review of the play by

Ernst Dannheiser, who insists that Bertha Rother was not the model for Adah, and that she much more closely resembles the character Diane de Lys created by Alexandre Dumas. Ernst Dannheiser, "Studien zur Weltanschauung und Entwicklungsgeschichte des Dramatikers Alexandre Dumas fils.," *Zeitschrift für Französische Sprache und Literatur* 25 (1902): 191.

104. For a more detailed account of the episode, see Stark, *Banned in Berlin*, 211–213.

105. Carl Werner, *Lex Heinze und ihre Geschichte* (Dortmund: O. Rühmkorf, 1935), 6.

106. Stark, *Banned in Berlin*, 21.

107. Werner, *Lex Heinze*, 10–11.

108. Tanja Hommen, *Sittlichkeitsverbrechen. Sexuelle Gewalt im Kaiserreich* (Frankfurt: Campus, 1999), 85; Stark, *Banned in Berlin*, 21.

109. See the legislative proposal offered on January 12, 1897 by Center delegates Franz von Arenberg, Adolf Gröber, et al. "Entwurf eines Gesetzes betreffend Aenderungen und Ergänzungen des Strafgesetzbuchs." Reichstagsdrucksachen, no. 618 (1897), 2916, accessed April 17, 2014, http://www.reichstagprotokolle.de/Blatt_k9_bsb00002767_00620.html. See also Stark, *Banned in Berlin*, 22.

110. Werner, *Lex Heinze*, 14–15; Stark, *Banned in Berlin*, 263.

111. Stark, *Banned in Berlin*, 23.

112. In his 1935 dissertation on the Lex Heinze debates, Carl Werner suggested that Anton von Werner had endorsed the Lex Heinze legislation after being assured it would only be used by authorities to prosecute the most extreme examples of lewd art and literature; most other sources, however, place Anton von Werner in the opposition. Werner also asserted that a significant number of intellectuals were vocal *supporters* of the more restrictive Lex Heinze, including the *völkisch* anti-Semite Adolf Bartels and the Wagnerite Hans von Wolzogen. See Werner, *Lex Heinze*, 33–34.

113. This was during the Moltke-Harden trial, where the journalist Maximilian Harden was accused of libel for publishing rumors about a homosexual affair between Kuno Graf von Moltke and Philipp Fürst zu Eulenburg-Hertefeld, two close associates of the Kaiser. See Norman Domeier, *The Eulenburg Affair. A Cultural History of Politics in Imperial Germany*, trans. Deborah Lucas Schneider (New York: Camden House, 2015), 75.

114. For an example of such public petitions during the Eulenburg Affair, see the Reichstag petition by a variety of women's organizations in January 1908 asking for a strengthening of the 1888 Law Regarding Court Proceedings Closed to the Public, and especially a sharpening of §184 StGB, the "Lex Graef" in Verhandlungen des Deutschen Reichstags, Aktenstück, no. 813, 4819, accessed June 16, 2015, http://www.reichstagsprotokolle.de/Blatt_k12_bsb00002887_00789.html. On subsequent attempts to limit public and press access to trials, especially those involving private personal or family matters, see Alexandra Ortmann, *Machtvolle Verhandlungen*, 171–172. The Lex Graef was finally dropped as part of the Fourth Criminal Law Reform Act of 1973 due to its "lack of practical usefulness." See Burkhard Jähnke, Heinrich Wilhelm Laufhütte, and Walter Odersky, eds., *Strafgesetzbuch Leipziger Kommentar* 9, 11th ed. (Berlin: De Gruyter, 2006), 59n5, accessed July 1, 2015, https://books.google.com/books?id=8WZbrufr-CLMC&pg=PR4&lpg=PR4&dq=%C2%A7%C2%A7+339-358;+Nachtrag+zum+StGB;+Gesamtreg-ister+2006&source=bl&ots=oX1iMgJ_gh&sig=f_kEPufqqqYkZWkLgvDDf__oxNY&hl=en&sa=X-&ei=rIeUVZ3xL8WTsAWy0Y34Dw&ved=0CB4Q6AEwAA#v=onepage&q=unter%20 hinweis&f=false.

115. Ortmann, *Machtvolle Verhandlungen*, 169.

116. See ibid., 168–170. Part of the problem here is that Ortmann makes minor, but still essential errors in the timeline of these debates. She correctly points to the 1885 Graef trial as an origin point for debates about restricting public access to controversial trials, but she then misattributes concerns about national security to that case rather than to the Sarauw trial. She also wrongly suggests that the oath of secrecy was originally intended to apply to all closed trials (instead of solely those cases posing a threat to national security). Finally, she erroneously claims that §184b StGB, which I refer to here as the "Lex Graef," was passed as part of the 1900 Lex Heinze reforms instead of as part of the 1888 law. This last error allows Ortmann to suggest that the passage of the 1900 measure represented an *additional* successful attack on the open courtroom and the rights of the press. In truth, almost all

attempts to pass additional restrictions on press reporting after the Heinze case—as well as after later scandalous trials—failed completely.

117. See Verhandlungen des Deutschen Reichstags, 50. Sitzung 1887/88, 2., 1 März 1888, 1195, accessed June 21, 2015, http://www.reichstagsprotokolle.de/Blatt3_k7_bsb00018648_00505.html. Emphasis in the original transcript.

118. See ibid. This is actually Meyer quoting his own statement from an earlier Reichstag session.

119. Hett, *Death in the Tiergarten*, 25. Hett mentions that the judge in the retrial of Gotthilf and Anna Heinze ordered that the proceedings be held in a closed court *without* press attendance; Hett also reports, however, that this decision provoked a significant public backlash.

120. For complaints by Prussian leaders about the difficulty of prosecutions under obscenity statutes, see GStA PK, I. HA Rep. 77 Preußisches Innenministerium, Tit. 657, Nr. 3, Bd. 1.

121. Leonard, *Fragile Minds*, 128.

Chapter Seven

1. *Berlin Börsen-Courier*, October 9, 1885, no. 512, 1. Beilage, 2.

2. *Volkszeitung*, October 14, 1885, no. 240, Zweites Blatt, 2.

3. *Berliner Börsen-Courier*, October 9, 1885, no. 512, 1. Beilage, 2.

4. Alexandra Ortmann, *Machtvolle Verhandlungen: Zur Kulturgeschichte der deutschen Strafjustiz 1879–1924* (Göttingen: Vandenhoeck and Ruprecht, 2014), 75–76.

5. In 1886, Quenstedt faced an array of charges, and he successfully petitioned for his case to be moved to the Bar Association (*Anwaltskammer*) in Leipzig since he claimed the leaders of the Berlin Bar Association were biased against him. His final disbarment came despite repeated efforts to delay his hearings and an attempt to forestall punishment by resigning from the bar. See BArch R3005/36 and R3005/126; see also *Volkszeitung*, November 4, 1885, no. 258, Zweites Blatt, 2.

6. Karl Liebknecht, *Rechtsstaat und Klassenjustiz, Vortrag gehalten zu Stuttgart am 23. August 1907* (Stuttgart: Singer, 1907), 14–20.

7. Benjamin Hett, *Death in the Tiergarten: Murder and Criminal Justice in the Kaiser's Berlin* (Cambridge, MA: Harvard University Press, 2004); Kenneth Ledford, *From General Estate to Special Interest: German Lawyers 1878–1933* (New York: Cambridge University Press, 1996); Alexandra Ortmann, *Machtvolle Verhandlungen*; Uwe Wilhelm, *Das Deutsche Kaiserreich und seine Justiz. Justizkritik—politische Strafrechtsprechung—Justizpolitik* (Berlin: Duncker and Humblot, 2010).

8. Hett, *Death in the Tiergarten*, 24.

9. See ibid., 24–25.

10. See, for example, the approaches of Prussian Justice Minister Heinrich von Friedberg and the chief prosecutor of Saxony, Friedrich Oskar von Schwarze, as discussed in Wilhelm, *Das Deutsche Kaiserreich*, 225–227.

11. See, for example, the speech by the Socialist Max Kayser in the Reichstag session on April 30, 1884 in BArch R3001/5590, Bd. 5, Bl. 17.

12. See "Die Aufgabe der Staatsanwaltschaft im Strafverfahren," *Grenzboten* 44, no. 3 (1885): 445, and also Wilhelm, *Das Deutsche Kaiserreich und seine Justiz*, 227.

13. One prominent example of this was the 1892 Xanten ritual murder trial, in which a Jewish butcher was tried for murder despite substantial doubts about his guilt and prosecutors' rejection of "Jewish ritual murder" as a possible motive. The butcher, Wolf Buschhoff, was eventually acquitted after both prosecutors and defense attorneys urged jurors to find him not guilty in their closing arguments. Public anger in and around the Westphalian town of Xanten was still strong enough that Buschhoff and his family fled after the verdict. See Barnet Hartston, *Sensationalizing the Jewish Question: Antisemitic Trials and the Press in the Early German Empire* (Leiden: Brill, 2005), 170–186.

14. See Wilhelm, *Das Deutsche Kaiserreich und seine Justiz*, 228.

15. *Prozeß (Gustav) Graef, verhandelt vom 29. September bis 7. October 1885 vor dem Geschworenengericht zu Berlin* (Berlin: Bartels, 1885), 58. Heinemann, by the way, angrily denied having made this comment and accused the court reporter of having misquoted him. He also demanded a retraction from the *Berliner Börsen-Courier*. Other court observers, including the stenographer himself, stood by their recorded versions. The *Berliner Gerichtszeitung*, however, carried a much milder version of the speech in which Heinemann is reported to have said: "Just as it would be horrible to convict an innocent man, it would be equally horrible to acquit someone who is guilty. You have a sacred double duty to acquit if you have any doubt about the defendants' guilt, but also not to shy away from a conviction if you are convinced of guilt." See *Berliner Gerichtszeitung*, October 8, 1885, no. 118, 2.

16. H. Holz, "Prozess Graef: Dargestellt von Herrn Rechtsanwalt Holz in Berlin," *Das Tribunal: Zeitschrift für praktische Strafrechtspflege* 1, no. 12 (December 1885): 696–697.

17. Max Heinemann, *Der Prozeß Graef und die deutsche Kunst* (Berlin: Friedrich Luckhardt, 1885), 3.

18. Letter from Theodor Fontane to Georg Friedländer, October 7, 1885, as printed in Theodor Fontane, *Briefe*, vol. 3, 1879–1889, 3rd ed., edited by Otto Drude et al., part 4 of *Werke, Schriften und Briefe* (Munich: Carl Hanser, 1980), 433.

19. Letter from Theodor Fontane to Georg Friedländer, October 7, 1885, as printed in Theodor Fontane, *Briefe*, vol. 3, 1879–1889, 433.

20. As quoted in Theresia Bach, "'Sie haben in ein Wespennest gestochen'. Unbek. Dokumente zum Prozeß gegen Gustav Graef," *Fontane Blätter* 78 (2004): 22. Emphasis in original.

21. Heinemann also received vocal support from other jurists, including a vigorous point-by-point defense of his conduct by Carl Fuchs, a judge from Jena. Fuchs concluded that not only was Heinemann justified in bringing charges, but that under the circumstances he was actually *required* to prosecute—the eventual acquittal notwithstanding. See Carl Fuchs, "Zum Prozess Graef," *Goltdammer's Archiv für Strafrecht* 33, no. 6 (1885): 409.

22. See *Berlin Börsen-Courier*, October 11, 1885, no. 516, 1. Beilage, 2.

23. BArch R3002/347, Bd. 3, Bl. 39. Dagmar Reese suggests that leading Justice officials such as Friedberg wanted to demote Heinemann, but they worried that such an action might weaken public perceptions of the legal system or undermine prosecutors. She suggests that Heinemann's glowing recommendation and quick transfer to Göttingen were sensitive ways for these officials to get him out of Berlin. This seems unlikely, since the normal career path for a "second prosecutor" like Heinemann would be to wait for a position as "first prosecutor" (*Erste Staatsanwalt*) to open up, even in a smaller district. Thus, a move to Göttingen as first prosecutor would not have been seen as a demotion. Indeed, even if Reese's allegation were true, Heinemann's behavior in the Graef trial did not prevent his meteoric rise through the highest levels of the German justice system. Dagmar Reese, *Akt und Anstand: Der Skandal um den Gustav Graef Prozess, Berlin 1885* (Vienna: Böhlau, 2014), 113. On the career path of prosecutors, See Fuchs, "Zum Prozess Graef," 415–416.

24. See Hett, *Death in the Tiergarten*, 20.

25. Review in *Beiträge zur Erläuterung des deutschen Rechts* 37 (1893): 779–782.

26. Franz von Liszt, "Herr Staatsanwalt Heinemann und die Willensfreiheit," *Die Zukunft* 5 (December 16, 1893): 497.

27. Max Heinemann, "Eine Auseinandersetzung mit Herrn Professor von Liszt," *Der Gerichtssaal: Zeitschrift für zivil- und militär-Strafrecht und Strafprozess-Recht sowie die ergänzenden Disziplinen* 49 (1894): 241.

28. Ibid., 256.

29. Ibid., 263.

30. It is tempting to see Heinemann as one of the few people who truly benefited from his role in the Graef trial. However, his personnel files in the records of the Justice Ministry do not address his role in the trial at all—either positively or negatively. I should also add that Heinemann's fate was not entirely free from difficulty. When he died of a stroke in 1924, he left his widow penniless—perhaps as

a result of the inflation crisis of 1923. He also left a son, Helmut, who suffered from nervous disorders after his experiences in World War One and was desperate for government support after the death of his mother. See BArch R3002/346, Bl. 36.

31. See David Fraser, *Frederick the Great* (New York: Fromm International, 2000), 224.

32. The statement is still a source of pride today, and was included in 2006 on a plaque commemorating the old Berlin *Kammergericht*, that "nursery of the rule of law" (*Hort der Rechtsstaatlichkeit*).

33. Hett, *Death in the Tiergarten*, 24.

34. For a detailed review of Brausewetter and his controversial career, see ibid., 112–123.

35. A typical example of his ability to offend everyone came in the sensational 1892 trial of the anti-Semitic agitator Hermann Ahlwardt. In the midst of a trial in which Brausewetter repeatedly lost his temper with defense attempts to delay the trial with extraneous motions, Ahlwardt's defense attorney suddenly stood up, claimed Brausewetter was biased against his client, and stormed out of the courtroom. Anti-Semitic followers of Ahlwardt used this incident to attack Brausewetter and declare Ahlwardt and his lawyer to be martyrs to judicial abuse. Once the case resumed, however, Brausewetter also drew the ire of the liberal and Jewish press for giving Ahlwardt a very light sentence and then adding the comment: "I consider anti-Semitism in a certain sense not unjustified." For more on Ahlwardt, see Hett, *Death in the Tiergarten*, 117–118; Hartston, *Sensationalizing the Jewish Question*, 219–259.

36. Hett, *Death in the Tiergarten*, 120–121.

37. See Fritz Friedmann, "Juristische Glossen zum Ahlwardt Prozeß," *Die Zukunft* 1 (December 17, 1892): 550. The relevant law on judicial instructions was §300 of the Code of Criminal Procedure (*Strafprozessordnung*).

38. *Kreuzzeitung*, July 22, 1885, no. 168. Eduard Lasker was a National Liberal parliamentarian and former judge who played an enormous role in the judicial reforms of the 1870s.

39. See Otto Bähr, "Das richterliche Urtheil und die Phrase," *Grenzboten* 44, no. 3 (1885): 7–14.

40. Ibid., 14.

41. "Der jüngste Berliner Skandalprozess," *Grenzboten* 44, no. 4 (1885): 145.

42. Judge Lüty and his doctors, by the way, had claimed his blindness and nervous condition were a result of overwork, especially in the corruption trials of the early 1880s. By 1888, the 64-year-old Lüty had become almost completely blind and was forced to retire from the bench. See article from *Die Zeit*, November 24, 1896 in GStA PK, I. HA Rep. 84a Justizministerium, Nr. 40297, Bl. 28 and also an 1888 letter from Lüty and a report from his doctor on pp. 6–8.

43. Stenographic Reichstag Report in BArch R3001/5590, Bd. 5, Bl. 19.

44. Holz, "Prozess Graef," 698. What critics of Müller did not mention, however, was his reluctant agreement to indulge the defense and bring the painting *The Fairy Tale* into court as an exhibit for the jury.

45. *Berliner Börsen-Courier*, October 21, 1885, no. 534, Morgen Ausgabe, 1. It should be noted here that there seems to be little evidence that Müller and his colleagues at the Berlin *Landgericht* were targeted directly with accusations of *Weltfremdheit*, or unfamiliarity with the lives of ordinary people, during this period. This became a common complaint about judges in general beginning in the 1890s and especially after the turn of the century. Of course, Müller was often unfriendly or openly critical of witnesses from the lower classes in the Graef trial. However, critics did not seem to tie this behavior into a general argument about the social origin or elite status of judges. On *Weltfremdheit*, see, for example, Ortmann, *Machtvolle Verhandlungen*, 159–160.

46. *Kreuzzeitung*, October 21, 1885, no. 246, 1. Beilage, 2–3.

47. GStA PK, I. HA Rep. 84a Justizministerium, Nr. 40323.

48. Ledford, *From General Estate to Special Interest*, 5.

49. The trial lawyer Ernst Fuchs, as quoted in Konrad Jarausch, *The Unfree Professions: German Lawyers, Teachers, and Engineers, 1900–1950* (New York: Oxford University Press, 1990), 9.

50. Ledford, *From General Estate to Special Interest*, 82–83.

51. Ibid., 2–3.

52. See LAB A Pr. Br. Rep. 30 Berlin C—Polizeipräsidium Berlin Nr. 11759. Reichstags—und Landtagsabgeordneter Rechtsanwalt Carl Ludwig Ulrich August Munckel und seine Söhne (1886–1911).

53. The sentiments of fellow lawyers Adolf Weissler and Fritz Friedmann as summarized by Hett, *Death in the Tiergarten*, 123–124. Friedmann also relates an anecdote in his autobiography about a humorous exchange between Munckel and *Landgerichtsdirektor* Bachmann (the judge from the Hammermann case) that also demonstrates both a deep respect and friendship between the two jurists. See Fritz Friedmann, *Was ich erlebte!*, vol. 1 (Berlin: Alfred Pulvermacher, 1908), 188–190.

54. Georg Maier-Reimer, "Ernst Wolff (1877-1959) – Führender Anwalt und oberster Richter," in *Deutscher Juristen jüdischer Herkunft*, ed. Helmut Heinrichs, Harald Franzki, Klaus Schmalz, and Michael Stolleis (Munich: C. H. Beck, 1993), 644. According to Dagmar Reese, the Simson law firm was *not* situated at the Pariser Platz. Berlin address books instead listed it at Mohrenstrasse 43/44, which would have put it south of central Berlin near the Gendarmenarkt. See Dagmar Reese, *Akt und Anstand*, 107.

55. Gerhard Dilcher and Susanne Lepsius, "Editorischer Bericht," for "Zur Geschichte der Handelsgesellschaften im Mittelalter" by Max Weber in *Gesamtausgabe* vol. 1, no. 1, ed. Gerhard Dilcher and Susanne Lepsius (Tübingen: Mohr Siebeck, 2008), 114. According to Georg Maier-Reimer, the law firm run by John Simson and August von Simson was one of the leading firms in Europe, and was almost entirely dedicated to civil law. The German jurist Ernst Wolff, a grandson of Eduard von Simson and later president of the Supreme Court of the British Occupied Zone, was also a successful attorney at the firm after the turn of the century. See Maier-Reimer, "Ernst Wolff," 644.

56. Yearly reports were required from the Berlin *Anwaltskammer* by §61 of the *Rechtsanwaltsordnung*. See especially the report from Ulfert to Justice Minister Friedberg on November 22, 1880 in GStA PK, I. HA Rep. 84a Justizministerium, Nr. 20152, Bl. 5–8, and from Laué on January 13, 1883 (Bl. 40–60). The latter report provided startling statistics to back up his complaints. In 1878 there had been 94 attorneys stationed at Berlin courts (including 73 at the old *Stadtgericht*); by 1890 there were 509 (including a whopping 412 just at the Berlin Regional Court, no. 1).

57. Hett, *Death in the Tiergarten*, 124.

58. See ibid. for more on the Heinze case and the changing culture of lawyers—especially pp. 82–95.

59. The *Norddeutsche Allgemeine Zeitung*, in an article after the postponement of the Heinze trial, attacked this new generation of lawyers and pined away for "the honorable old-Prussian lawyers' estate" (*ehrenwerte alt-Preussische Anwaltsstand*) that had always adhered closely to their responsibilities and to a sense of decorum. *Norddeutsche Allgemeine Zeitung*, October 23, 1891 in GStA PK, I. HA Rep. 89 Geheimes Zivilkabinett, Nr. 17725, Bd. 5, Bl. 52.

60. Friedmann, *Was ich erlebte!*, 306–308.

61. Wilhelm, *Das Deutsche Kaiserreich und seine Justiz*, 39–40.

62. Ibid., 40–41.

63. Ortmann, *Machtvolle Verhandlungen*, 12, 20–21.

64. Wilhelm, *Das Deutsche Kaiserreich und seine Justiz*, 52–53. For a detailed discussion of debates about the jury as a political and legal institution, see also pp. 39–54.

65. Arnd Koch, "Der gescheiterte Reform des reformierten Strafprozesses," *Zeitschrift für internationale Strafrechtsdogmatik* 4, no. 10 (2009): 542–548, accessed December 9, 2013, www.zis-online.com.

66. There does not seem to be a commonly accepted translation for Strafkammer, and the most common ("criminal court" and "criminal division") seem perhaps a bit too easily confused with the criminal courts in general.

67. Adolph Phillips and Julius Lenzmann, two left-liberal Reichstag representatives who also repeatedly sponsored legislation for compensation for unjustly incarcerated defendants, put forward legislation in 1884 to return political and press trials to the jury courts. Their efforts were not successful.

68. *Berliner Tageblatt*, February 7, 1885 in BArch R3001/4341, Bd. 1, n.p.

69. From article "Die Lehren des Prozesses Graef," as reprinted in *Prozeß (Gustav) Graef*, 72.

70. Ibid., 73–74. This phrase is in German, although the same phrase had appeared elsewhere in its Latin form: *vox populi, vox dei*. Bold in original.

71. *Prozeß (Gustav) Graef*, ii. See above for a discussion of the original phrase: "There are still judges in Berlin!"

72. *Reichsbote*, October 10, 1885, no. 237, 2.

73. For a nuanced analysis of Mittelstädt's argument, see Richard F. Wetzell, "From Retributive Justice to Social Defense: Penal Reform in Fin-de-Siècle Germany," in *Germany at the Fin de Siècle: Culture, Politics, and Ideas*, ed. Suzanne Marchand and David Lindenfeld (Baton Rouge: Louisiana State University Press, 2004), 62.

74. Wetzell, "From Retributive Justice to Social Defense," 59, 68.

75. Otto Mittelstädt, "Strafjustiz und öffentliche Meinung," *Preußischer Jahrbücher* 56, no. 5 (1885): 504.

76. "Herr Mittelstädt und die Künstler Adresse," *Volkszeitung*, November 6, 1885, no. 260, Erstes Blatt, 1.

77. Mittelstädt, "Strafjustiz und öffentliche Meinung," 508.

78. Ibid., 499–500.

79. Ibid., 508–509.

80. Ibid., 508.

81. Ibid., 505.

82. Ibid., 502–503.

83. Ibid., 507.

84. Fuchs, "Zum Prozess Graef," 413.

85. Ibid., 411.

86. Summary of Olshausen's opinion from a contemporary report on legal literature in *Zeitschrift für die gesamte Strafwissenschaft* 7 (1887): 251, accessed April 10, 2014, http://babel.hathitrust.org/cgi/pt?id=inu.30000111755652;view=1up;seq=271.

87. See [Gustav Otto], *Die Verbrecherwelt von Berlin* (Berlin: Guttentag, 1886). For more detail on this essay and on the Dickhoff case, see chapter five.

88. See ibid., 192. Otto is clearly jumping into the ongoing debates among criminologists here as well. He is siding with Otto Mittelstädt's more draconian approach to punishing criminals and attacking the growing popularity of the criminal theories of Franz von Liszt, which emphasized rehabilitation, and which critics viewed as far too weak-kneed an approach.

89. See ibid.

90. See [Gustav Otto], "Gegen die Schwurgerichte. Von dem Verfasser von 'Die Verbrecherwelt von Berlin.'" *Zeitschrift für die gesamte Strafwissenschaft* 7 (1887): 2–3. In this later essay, Otto was forced to admit that his original estimates of the number of acquittals in Berlin had been exaggerated and the number was actually closer to 40 per cent rather than 60 percent—although he insisted that if one added the number of convictions on lesser charges that resulted in miniscule punishments, the number would easily surpass 60 per cent.

91. Ibid., 24.

92. Ibid., 9.

93. See Fritz Friedmann, *Über die Schwurgerichte: eine Parallele zu der Abhandlung von O. S. "Gegen die Schwurgerichte"* (Berlin: Dresser, 1886); Ludwig Fuld, "Die Kampf über die Schwurgericht," *Die Gegenwart* 30 (1886): 369; see also a brief discussion of these debates in Wilhelm, *Das Deutsche Kaiserreich und seine Justiz*, 229–230.

94. Wilhelm, *Das Deutsche Kaiserreich und seine Justiz*, 229.

95. Ibid.; August Munckel, "Vom 18. deutschen Juristentage," *Nation*, September 18, 1886, no. 51, 751–754.

96. Munckel, "Vom 18. deutschen Juristentage," 754.

97. Wolfgang Mittermaier, "Zur Frage der Schwurgerichte," *Monatsschrift für Kriminalpsychologie und Strafrechtsreform* 2 (1906): 1–24.

Epilogue

1. Report on the incident from *Berliner Volkszeitung*, October 10, 1885, no. 237, 3.

2. A letter in private possession, dated November 21, 1886—more than a year after the trial—gives a sense of Graef's social desperation. In the letter, Graef asks a friend (perhaps Friedrich Weiß, a fellow member of the Association of German Artists) to get a sense of how the painter Georg Bleibtreu feels about him. Graef claims he hasn't spoken to Bleibtreu in the year since the trial, and although some colleagues have reacted well to him, he has had enough bad experiences not to want to set himself up for a humiliating rebuff. See excerpt from this letter in a collector's catalog at http://www.autographs.de/30_0703_Narzissen.pdf.

3. See Klaus-Peter Möller, "'Entartete Kunst' als 'Gefahr für die Sittlichkeit des ganzen Volkes': Die 'Ächtung' des Malers Gustav Graef—Hintergrunde und Folgen," in *Erledigungen—Pamphlete, Polemiken und Proteste*, ed. Marcel Atze and Volker Kaukoreit (Vienna: Praesens, 2014), 118–137, accessed July 18, 2014, http://www.wilnitsky.com/pictures/Erledigungen_Artikel_Gustav%20Graef.pdf. According to Möller, copies of Graef's memoir may have been circulated to a few friends and associates, including the scientist Emil du Bois-Reymond.

4. See *Reichsbote*, October 16, 1885, no. 242, 3. Klaus-Peter Möller suggests the original purchase price was even higher, at 55,000 Marks. See Möller, "'Entartete Kunst,'" 135n3.

5. GStA PK, I. HA Rep. 76 Kultusministerium, VIII Sekt L., Pers. Lit. G., Nr. 45, Bl. 17.

6. This review also once again slammed the highlight of the exhibit, Graef's *Fairy Tale*. See G. M., "Von den Kunstausstellungen," *Die Gegenwart* 34, no. 50 (December 15, 1888), 379. See also G. Christaller, "Über Modellwesen in der Kunst, besonders im Roman," *Die Gesellschaft* 5, Part 4 (1889): 1473. Christaller does not specifically review the painting, but refers to it briefly in an essay about models, morality, and society.

7. Dagmar Reese suggests that the damage to Graef's career and reputation caused by the trial was far more limited than we might think. She claims that Graef had not been totally abandoned by his colleagues in the Berlin Association of Artists—half of whom did not sign the declaration—and that he continued to enjoy the solidarity and support of the liberal, educated elite in Berlin. This conclusion does not seem to be supported by the evidence in newspaper accounts or by his own exchanges of letters during the last part of his life. See below, and also Dagmar Reese, *Akt und Anstand: Der Skandal um den Gustav Graef Prozess, Berlin 1885* (Vienna: Böhlau, 2014), 74–75, 78.

8. See DLA Marbach A: Lepsius, letter from Emil Heinrich du Bois-Reymond to Gustav Graef (November 12, 1885, Berlin).

9. Sabine Lepsius remembers the portrait as depicting the son of the President David Hansemann; however, the *Neue Deutsche Biographie* claims the 1891 portrait is of David's cousin Ferdinand von Hansemann. See Sabine Lepsius, *Ein Berliner Künstlerleben um die Jahrhundertwende: Erinnerungen* (Munich: G. Müller, 1972), 91, and *Neue Deutsche Biographie*, vol. 7: Grassauer–Hartmann (Berlin: Duncker and Humblot, 1966), 630.

10. Johannes W Grüntzig and Heinz Mehlhorn, *Robert Koch: Seuchenjäger und Nobelpreisträger* (Heidelberg: Spektrum Akademischer, 2010), 209.

11. See DLA Marbach A: Lepsius, letter from Malwine (Gräfin von) Arnim to Gustav Graef (February 1, 1892, Berlin).

12. In her memoirs, Sabine Lepsius discusses her own frustrations at having to spend so much time keeping up social networks with members of the elite. See Lepsius, *Ein Berliner Künstlerleben*, 194. See also the art historian Annette Dorgerloh's depiction of these frustrations in *Das Künstlerehepaar Lepsius: zur Berliner Porträtmalerei um 1900* (Oldenburg: Akademie, 2003), 152–153.

13. See DLA Marbach A: Lepsius, letter from Gustav Graef to Sabine Lepsius (April 06, 1893, Berlin) [#66.1552/1].

14. Letters from Botho von Graef to the Akademie der Künste in PrAdK, 2.2/068 (film Nr. 262), Bl. 11, 32.

15. Lepsius, *Ein Berliner Künstlerleben*, 160–161.

16. DLA Marbach A: Lepsius, letter from Graef, Gustav to Sabine Lepsius (May 11, 1894) [66.1552/2]. In her study on the Graef trial, Dagmar Reese comes to a starkly different conclusion about Graef's behavior in the years after the trial—and about his relationship with Sabine. She cites a letter from Sabine to her husband Reinhold in 1893, in which Sabine sarcastically comments on the polite manner with which her father had introduced her to a young model—in a manner that suggested they were social equals. Reese uses this episode to portray Graef as a brave man who consciously transgressed social norms by treating his young models with respect—as opposed to his daughter Sabine, who had been shocked by the absence of traditional social distinctions. This episode, along with Graef's staunch support for Koch and his young bride Hedwig Freiberg (see below), leads Reese to conclude that Graef, "whose upstanding behavior had commanded great admiration among Berliners in 1885, was never cowed by the scandalizing, despite the burdens placed by this trial on him and his family." Reese, *Akt und Anstand*, 76–78.

17. DLA Marbach A: Lepsius, letter from Robert von Keudell to Franziska Graef (April 17, 1885, Rome) [#71.787].

18. Lepsius, *Ein Berliner Künstlerleben*, 91.

19. No real discussion of anti-Semitism or of fears related to Jewish heritage appears in the memoirs of Sabine Lepsius, something that her biographer Annette Dorgerloh attributes to the fact that the memoirs were compiled in Germany during the late 1930s. Sabine Lepsius does, however, briefly describe some of the long-lasting effects that the trial had upon her own life—including her growing skepticism about "bourgeois moral standards." Sabine's engagement with Ludwig Traube had already been postponed before her father's arrest and trial, so it seems clear that there were other issues involved in the failure of her engagement—including perhaps a fear of having to give up her own artistic pretensions to assume a role as a traditional bourgeois wife. See Dorgerloh, *Das Künstlerehepaar Lepsius*, 84–85.

20. Grüntzig and Mehlhorn, *Robert Koch*, 205.

21. See Theodor Fontane's letter to Emilie Fontane on October 2, 1888 in Theodor Fontane, *Briefe*, vol. 3, 1879–1889, 3rd ed., edited by Otto Drude et al., part 4 of *Werke, Schriften und Briefe* (Munich: Carl Hanser, 1980), 643. On Rosenthal, see Theodor Lessing, *Nachtkritiken: Kleine Schriften 1906–7* (Göttingen: Wallstein, 2006), 507.

22. Maximilian Harden was an actor, editor, theater critic, and outspoken journalist who founded the weekly journal *Die Zukunft*. He became infamous for his attacks against the entourage of the royal family, including his 1906 accusations of homosexuality against Prince Philipp Eulenburg which resulted in a sensational trial and one of the biggest scandals of the German Empire.

23. Helga Neumann and Manfred Neumann, *Maximilian Harden (1861–1927). Ein unerschrockener deutsch-jüdischer Kritiker und Publizist* (Würzburg: Königshausen and Neumann, 2002), 123–125.

24. Mehring's conflict with the *Berliner Volkszeitung* led him to break decisively with progressive liberalism and move towards socialism; his conflicts with Brahm also continued over the next several years—especially over the direction of the *Freie Volksbühne* in Berlin. It is also interesting to note that Mehring's attacks in his second book, *Kapital und Presse*, included pointed rhetoric suggesting a capitalist conspiracy that included the press and even his old boss at the *Volkszeitung*, Emil Cohn. Mehring defended himself against charges of anti-Semitism by claiming that he was neither an anti-Semite nor a "philosemite." See Mehring's *Der Fall Lindau* (Berlin: Brachvogel, 1890) and *Kapital und Presse: ein Nachspiel zum Falle Lindau* (Berlin: Brachvogel, 1891), as well as Otto Brahm"s "Sittliche Entrüstung: Zum Fall Lindau," *Freie Bühne* 1 (1890), 817–820.

25. Henri Sylvestre Jr., *The Triumphs of Modern Art, Containing the Most Notable Paintings of To-day Selected from the Modern Masterpieces of the Whole World of Art* (Philadelphia: The Gebbie Pub. Co., 1891), as mentioned in Theresia Bach, "'Sie haben in ein Wespennest gestochen.' Unbek. Dokumente zum Prozeß gegen Gustav Graef," *Fontane Blätter* 78 (2004), 11.

26. Kurt Pomplun, "Die erste Porno-Prozess Berlins brachte Maler und Modell vor Gericht," *Berliner Morgenpost*, October 8, 1972, no. 235, 8.

27. The painting is currently listed on www.wilnitsky.com.

28. These postcards are still available for sale at online collectors' sites and in German second-hand bookstores, and one was purchased by the author.

29. See *Berlin Börsen-Courier*, October 9, 1885, no. 512, 1. Beilage, 2.

30. *Dresdner Nachrichten*, February 10, 1899.

31. In this novel, Zola follows the rise and fall of Anna Coupeau (Nana), a child subjected to extreme poverty and abuse, whose astonishing beauty turns her from common prostitute into a wealthy courtesan and actress. Nana seduces wealthy men and squanders their fortunes, only in the end to die alone—her visage having been eaten away by the ravages of smallpox.

32. GStA PK, I. HA Rep. 77 Preußisches Innenministerium, Tit. 657, Nr. 3, Bd. 1, Bl. 150–153.

33. Reese, *Akt und Anstand*, 97–101. Reese juxtaposes the apparent superficiality and kitsch of Graef's *Fairy Tale* with a more contemplative and radiant portrait of Bertha by Stauffer-Bern to suggest that the former was the product of an obsolete artist embedded in nineteenth-century traditions, while the latter exemplified the start of a new artistic era.

34. GStA PK, I. HA Rep. 77 Preußisches Innenministerium, Tit. 657, Nr. 3, Bd. 1, Bl. 180.

35. See *Der Humorist*, January 10, 1887, no. 1 and also March 1, 1885, no. 5, accessed April 10, 2014, http://anno.onb.ac.at/cgi-content/anno?aid=hu1.

36. "A Continental Adventuress" in *Tuapeka Times*, vol. 22, no. 176, April 3, 1889, p. 5, accessed April 10, 2014, http://paperspast.natlib.govt.nz.

37. *Wöchentliche Anzeigen für das Fürstenthum Ratzeburg*, June 1, 1888, no. 56, p. 5, accessed April 10, 2014, http://wafr.lbmv.de/show.php?action=1888-07-20. The newspaper reported the two had spent 476,000 Gulden in one year before Schroll's access to his family's money was restricted.

38. "A Continental Adventuress" in *Tuapeka Times*, vol. 22, no. 176, April 3, 1889, p. 5, accessed April 10, 2014, http://paperspast.natlib.govt.nz.

39. *Wöchentliche Anzeigen für das Fürstenthum Ratzeburg* (Schönberger Anzeigen), May 21, 1889, no. 40, p. 5, accessed April 10, 2014, http://wafr.lbmv.de/show.php?action=1889-05-21.

40. *Chicago Sunday Tribune*, January 20, 1895, 9–10, accessed July 6, 2015, http://archives.chicagotribune.com/1895/01/20/page/9/article/the-crispi-linguaglossa-wedding. This article contains some clear inaccuracies in its summary of the Graef Affair from a decade earlier. As is the case for many of these news reports, it is not always easy to separate facts from rumors, faulty memories, or dramatic flair.

41. *Dresdner Nachrichten*, November 25, 1894.

42. *Chicago Sunday Tribune*, January 20, 1895, 9–10, accessed July 6, 2015, http://archives.chicagotribune.com/1895/01/20/page/9/article/the-crispi-linguaglossa-wedding.

43. Reese, *Akt und Anstand*, 90.

44. Fedor von Zobeltitz, *Chronik der Gesellschaft unter dem letzten Kaiserreich*, vol. 2 (Hamburg: Alster, 1922), 227–228. Zobeltitz recounts that during and after the Graef trial, he remembered seeing photography of the paintings featuring Bertha being displayed in bookshop windows as far away as Italy.

45. These last details come from a combination of sources, including an unlabeled and unidentified newspaper clipping, apparently from 1935, listed on the website of a private art collector at www.wilnitsky.com. Johannes Grüntzig and Heinz Mehlhorn report having found a similar unlabeled article in the Theodor-Fontane-Archiv. They attribute it to the journal *Korall* 5 (1935), 104. See Grüntzig and Mehlhorn, *Robert Koch*, 1012n25. Dagmar Reese gleans similar details from Hans Niedermeier's article "Glanz und Elend berühmter Künstler-Modelle," in *Koralle (Neue Folge): Wochenschrift für Unterhaltung, Wissen, Lebensfreude* 9, no. 5 (January 31, 1941). See Reese, *Akt und Anstand*, 90n56.

Conclusion

1. Alexandra Ortmann, *Machtvolle Verhandlungen: Zur Kulturgeschichte der deutschen Strafjustiz, 1879–1924* (Göttingen: Vandenhoeck and Ruprecht, 2014), 23.

2. See a brief summary of the historiography on German liberalism in Dennis Sweeney, "Liberalism, the Worker and the Limits of Öffentlichkeit in Wilhelmine Germany," *German History* 22, no. 1 (2004): 37. Sweeney has taken the quoted phrase itself from James Sheehan's *German Liberalism in the Nineteenth Century* (Chicago: University of Chicago Press, 1978), 272–273.

3. See Hans-Ulrich Wehler, *The German Empire* (New York: Berg, 1997).

4. See David Blackbourn and Geoff Eley, *The Peculiarities of German History* (New York: Oxford University Press, 1984). There has been an enormous array of scholarship since Blackbourn and Eley's landmark study that generally supports and extends their argument in various directions. For examples in English, see Dieter Langewiesche, *Liberalism in Germany* (Basingstoke: Macmillan, 2000); David Blackbourn and Richard Evans, eds., *The German Bourgeoisie: Essays on the Social History of the German Middle Class from the Late Eighteenth Century to the Early Twentieth Century* (New York: Routledge, 1991); and Jonathan Sperber, *The Kaiser's Voters: Electors and Elections in Imperial Germany* (New York: Cambridge University Press, 1997).

5. Margaret Lavinia Anderson, *Practicing Democracy: Elections and Political Culture in Imperial Germany* (Princeton, NJ: Princeton University Press, 2000), 17.

6. Ortmann, *Machtvolle Verhandlungen*, 10–11.

7. Martin Kohlrausch, *Der Monarch im Skandal: Die Logik der Massenmedien und die Transformation der wilhelminischen Monarchie* (Berlin: Akademie, 2005), 456.

8. See Richard Levy, *The Downfall of the Anti-Semitic Political Parties in Imperial Germany* (New Haven, CT: Yale University Press, 1975), 1; Barnet Hartston, *Sensationalizing the Jewish Question: Anti-Semitic Trials and the Press in the Early German Empire* (Leiden: Brill, 2005), 262.

9. Frank Bösch, *Öffentliche Geheimnisse. Skandale, Politik und Medien in Deutschland und Großbritannien 1880–1914* (Munich: Oldenburg, 2009), 469.

10. Ibid., 470.

BIBLIOGRAPHY

I. Newspapers and Journals:

Beiträge zur Erläuterung des deutschen Rechts
Berliner Börsen-Courier
Berliner Börsen-Zeitung
Berliner Gerichtszeitung
Berliner Morgenpost
Berliner Tageblatt
Berliner Volksblatt
The Daily Colonist (Victoria, British Columbia)
Dresdner Nachrichten
Dresdner Tageblatt
Die Gegenwart
Germania
Die Gesellschaft
Die Grenzboten
Der Humorist (Vienna)
Im neuen Reich
Kölnische Volkszeitung
Der Kulturkämpfer: Zeitschrift für öffentliche Angelegenheiten
Justiz-Ministerial-Blatt für die Preußische Gesetzgebung und Rechtspflege
Leipziger Zeitung
Monatsschrift für Kriminalpsychologie und Strafrechtsreform
Die Nation
Nationalzeitung
Neue Preußische "Kreuz"-zeitung
Nord und Süd
Die Post
Preußische Jahrbücher
Reichsbote
Der Sozialdemokrat (Zürich)
Die Staatsbürgerin
Tuapeka Times (New Zealand)
Volkszeitung
Vossische Zeitung
Wöchentliche Anzeigen für das Fürstenthum Ratzeburg
Zeitschrift für bildende Kunst
Zeitschrift für die gesamte Strafwissenschaft
Die Zukunft

II. Archival Sources

Bundesarchiv Berlin-Lichterfelde (BArch)

BArch R 1501 Reichsministerium des Innern

BArch R 3001 Reichsjustizamt/Reichsjustizministerium
BArch R 3002 Reichsgericht
BArch R 3005 Ehrengerichtshof für die deutschen Rechtsanwälte

Deutsches Literaturarchiv Marbach (DLA Marbach)

DLA Marbach A: Lepsius (Nachlass Lepsius)

Geheimes Staatsarchiv Preußischer Kulturbesitz (GStA PK)

GStA PK, I. HA Rep. 76—Kultusministerium
GStA PK, I. HA Rep. 77—Ministerium des Innern
GStA PK, I. HA Rep. 84a—Justizministerium
GStA PK, I. HA Rep. 89—Geheimes Zivilkabinett, jüngere Periode
GStA PK, XX. HA—Historisches Staatsarchiv Königsberg

Historisches Archiv: Archiv der Preußischen Akademie der Künste (PrAdK)

PrAdK, 2.2/068 (film Nr. 262)
PrAdK, 2.3/111 (film Nr. 310)

Landesarchiv Berlin (LAB)

LAB A Pr. Br. Rep. 30 Berlin C—Polizeipräsidium Berlin

III. Published Primary Sources

Bähr, Otto. "Das richterliche Urtheil und die Phrase." *Grenzboten* 44, no. 3 (1885): 7–14.
Boetticher, Friedrich von. *Malerwerke des Neunzehnten Jahrhunderts. Beitrag zur Kunstgeschichte.* Vol. 1, pt. 1. Leipzig: Schmidt and Günther, 1948.
Brahm, Otto. "Sittliche Entrüstung: Zum Fall Lindau." *Freie Bühne* 1 (1890): 817–820.
Braun, Gustav [Martin Böhm]. *Im Atelier oder der Maler und sein Modell. Genrebild mit Gesang in 1 Akt.* Berlin: H. Schmidt, 1885.
Dannheiser, Ernst. "Studien zur Weltanschauung und Entwicklungsgeschichte des Dramatikers Alexandre Dumas fils." *Zeitschrift für Französische Sprache und Literatur* 25 (1902): 144–195.
Flexner, Abraham. *Prostitution in Europe.* New York: The Century Co., 1914.
Fontane, Theodor. *Briefe.* Vol. 3, *1879–1889*, 3rd ed., edited by Otto Drude et al. Part 4 of *Werke, Schriften und Briefe.* Munich: Carl Hanser, 1980.
Förster, Bernhard. *Das Verhältniss des modernen Judenthums zur deutschen Kunst.* Berlin: M. Schulze, 1881.
Frenzel, Karl. *Die Kunst und das Strafgesetz.* Berlin: Walther and Apolant, 1885.
Friedländer, Hugo. *Interessante Kriminal-Prozesse von kulturhistorischer Bedeutung: Darstellung merkwürdiger Strafrechtsfälle aus Gegenwart und Jüngstvergangenheit nach eigenen Erlebnissen.* Berlin: Barsdorf, 1910–1914.
Friedmann, Fritz. *Die Öffentlichkeit der Gerichtsverhandlungen, ihre Vorzüge und Schäden.* Berlin: Heine, 1887.
———. *Über die Schwurgerichte: eine Parallele zu der Abhandlung von Ö. S. "Gegen die Schwurgerichte."* Berlin: Dresser, 1886.
———. *Was ich erlebte!* Vol. 1. Berlin: Alfred Pulvermacher, 1908.
Fuchs, [Carl]. "Zum Prozess Graef." *Goltdammer's Archiv für Strafrecht* 33, no. 6 (1885): 403–430.
Fuld, Ludwig. "Die Kampf über die Schwurgericht." *Die Gegenwart* 30, no. 50 (1886): 369–370.

Die Gefallene Mädchen und die Sittenpolizei. Berlin: Wilhelm Ißleib [Gustav Schuhr], 1887.

Glagau, Otto. *Der Börsen und Gründungsschwindel in Berlin*. Leipzig: P. Frohberg, 1876.

———. *Der Börsen und Gründungsschwindel in Deutschland*. Leipzig: P. Frohberg, 1877.

Graef, Johann August Ferdinand. *Zur Feier des Geburtstagfestes Sr. Majestät des Königes*. Königsberg: Degen, 1808.

Guillaume-Schack, Gertrud. *Ein Wort zur Sittlichkeitsfrage*. Berlin: Dollfuß, 1881.

Harden, Maximilian. "Lex Heinze." *Die Zukunft* 30 (1900): 457–464.

Heckscher, Meyer. *Der Prozeß Graef: Ein Mahnruf an die Gesetzgebung*. Berlin: Stahn, 1885.

Heinemann, Max. "Eine Auseinandersetzung mit Herrn Professor von Liszt." *Der Gerichtssaal: Zeitschrift für zivil- und militär-Strafrecht und Strafprozessrecht sowie die ergänzenden Disziplinen* 49 (1894): 241–263.

———. *Der Prozeß Graef und die deutsche Kunst: Eine Antwort auf Dr. Karl Frenzel's Abhandlung in der Nationalzeitung: "Die Kunst und das Strafgesetz."* Berlin: Friedrich Luckhardt, 1885.

Holz, H. "Prozess Graef: Dargestellt von Herrn Rechtsanwalt Holz in Berlin." *Das Tribunal: Zeitschrift für praktische Strafrechtspflege* 1, no. 12 (December 1885): 661–699.

Jastrow, Hermann. "Der deutsche Gesetzentwurf, betreffend die unter Ausschluss der Öffentlichkeit stattfindenden Gerichtshandlungen." *Jahrbuch der Gesetzgebung, Verwaltung und Volkswirthschaft im deutschen Reiche* 10, no. 4 (1886): 1109–1134.

Knighton, William. *Struggles for Life*. London: Williams and Norgate, 1886.

Lange, Helene. *Lebenserinnerungen*. Berlin: F. A. Herbig, 1928.

Lessing, Theodor. *Nachtkritiken: Kleine Schriften 1906–7*. Göttingen: Wallstein, 2006.

Liebknecht, Karl. *Rechtsstaat und Klassenjustiz: Vortrag, gehalten zu Stuttgart am 23. August 1907*. Stuttgart: Singer, 1907.

Lindau, Paul. "Idealismus und Naturalismus in Berlin. Prozess Graef." *Nord und Süd* 35, no. 104 (November 1885): 204–269.

Liszt, Franz von. "Herr Staatsanwalt Heinemann und die Willensfreiheit." *Die Zukunft* 5 (December 16, 1893): 497–499.

Mehring, Franz. *Der Fall Lindau*. Berlin: Brachvogel, 1890.

———. *Geschichte der Deutschen Demokratie*. Vol. 4. 1909. Reprint, Books on Demand, 2011. Accessed June 7, 2015, https://books.google.com/books?id=QK6BmEVzCaoC&pg=PA285&lpg=PA285&dq=bebel+freiberg+verurteilung&source=bl&ots=etROKcZcVP&sig=ZrLGGv4yOyluCsjGrlQOr4EBUjY&hl=en&sa=X&ei=U2OcVbjyPIq5ggSrnICwBw&ved=0CD8Q6AEwBg#v=onepage&q=bebel%20freiberg%20verurteilung&f=false.

———. *Kapital und Presse: ein Nachspiel zum Falle Lindau*. Berlin: Brachvogel, 1891.

Mittelstädt, Otto. "Strafjustiz und öffentliche Meinung." *Preußischer Jahrbücher* 56, no. 5 (1885): 499–509.

Mittermaier, Wolfgang. "Zur Frage der Schwurgerichte." *Monatsschrift für Kriminalpsychologie und Strafrechtsreform* 2 (1906): 1–24.

Oehlert, Wilhelm. *Der Kleine Tiergarten. Ein Beitrag zur Geschichte der Entwicklung des Stadtteils Moabit*. Berlin: Loewenthal, 1906.

Ostwald, Hans. *Berliner Kultur- und Sittengeschichte*. 1911. Reprint, Paderborn: Voltmedia, 2006.

[Otto, Gustav]. "Gegen die Schwurgerichte. Von dem Verfasser von 'Die Verbrecherwelt von Berlin.'" *Zeitschrift für die gesamte Strafwissenschaft* 7 (1887): 1–46.

———. *Die Verbrecherwelt von Berlin*. Berlin: Guttentag, 1886.

Paasch, Carl. *Die kaiserlich deutsche Gesandtschaft in China. Eine Denkschrift über den Fall Carl Paasch, für die deutschen Landesvertretungen, insbesondere den Reichstag*. Leipzig: Selbstverlag, 1892.

Portia [pseud.]. "Das Fundament des Urtheils." *Nation* 3 (1885/1886): 43.

Prozess Graef und die Mängel unseres Gerichtsverfahrens. Leipzig: F. Duncker, 1885.

Prozeß (Gustav) Graef, verhandelt vom 29. September bis 7. Oktober 1885 vor dem Geschworenengericht zu Berlin. Berlin: Bartels, 1885.

Prutz, Hans. *Die Königliche Albertus-Universität zu Königsberg i. Pr. im neunzehnten Jahrhundert. Zur Feier ihres 350jährigen Bestehens.* Königsberg: Hartung, 1894.

Quidam [Julius Stinde]. *Berliner Kunstkritik mit Randglossen.* Berlin: Freund and Jeckel, 1884.

Rosenberg, Adolf. "Die akademische Kunstausstellung in Berlin I." *Die Grenzboten* 38, no. 3 (1879): 460.

———. "Die akademische Kunstausstellung in Berlin I." *Die Grenzboten* 40, no. 3 (1881): 512.

———. "Die vierte allgemeine deutsche Kunstausstellung in Düsseldorf." *Die Grenzboten* 39, no. 3 (1880): 383.

———. "Die große Kunstausstellung in Berlin." *Die Grenzboten* 43, no. 3 (1884): 562.

———. "Sammlungen und Ausstellungen." *Zeitschrift für bildende Kunst* 31 (1896): 305–306.

Schmidt, Julian. "Adolf Menzel." *Preußische Jahrbücher* 56, no. 6 (1885): 628–630.

Schwarze, Friedrich Oskar von. "Voreid oder Nacheid?" *Archiv für Gemeines Deutsches und für Preußisches Strafrecht* 23 (Berlin, 1875): 81–87.

Tschudi, Hugo von. *Ausstellung von Werken des Malers Gustav Graef.* Berlin: Mittler und Sohn, 1896.

Ulysses [pseud.]. *Das Märchenmodell: ein Modellmärchen für Kinder der Zeit.* Illustrated by Julius Schlattmann. Berlin: M. Schulze, 1886.

"Von der Kunstausstellung," *Im neuen Reich* 11, no. 2 (1881), 450–454.

Werner, Anton von. *Erlebnisse und Erinnerungen 1870–1890.* Berlin: Mittler, 1913.

Zeuge Stöcker: Ein Zeitbild aus dem Jahre 1885. Die Prozeßverhandlungen wegen Beleidigung des Hofpredigers Stöcker vor der II. Strafkammer des Landgerichts Berlin I am 9., 10., 13. und 16. Juni nebst erläuternden und ergänzenden Anmerkungen. Berlin: Verlag "Fortschritt, Aktiengesellschaft," 1885.

Zobeltitz, Fedor von. *Chronik der Gesellschaft unter dem letzten Kaiserreich.* Vol. 2. Hamburg: Alster, 1922.

Zola, Émile. *Nana.* London: Penguin, 1972.

IV. Secondary Sources

Anderson, Amanda. *Tainted Souls and Painted Faces: The Rhetoric of Fallenness in Victorian Culture.* Ithaca, NY: Cornell University Press, 1993.

Anderson, Margaret Lavinia. *Practicing Democracy: Elections and Political Culture in Imperial Germany.* Princeton, NJ: Princeton University Press, 2000.

Bach, Theresia. "'Sie haben in ein Wespennest gestochen.' Unbek. Dokumente zum Prozeß gegen Gustav Graef." *Fontane Blätter* 78 (2004): 8–35.

Bachleitner, Norbert. *Der englische und französische Sozialroman des 19. Jahrhunderts und seine Rezeption in Deutschland.* Atlanta: Rodopi, 1993.

Beauvoir, Simone de. *The Second Sex.* New York: Vintage Books, 1989.

Berenson, Edward. *The Trial of Madame Caillaux.* Berkeley: University of California Press, 1993.

Berghahn, Volker. *Imperial Germany, 1871–1914: Economy, Society, Culture, and Politics.* Providence, RI: Berghahn Books, 1994.

Bilsky, Emily. *Berlin Metropolis: Jews and the New Culture, 1890–1918.* Berkeley: University of California Press, 1999.

Blackbourn, David, and Geoff Eley. *The Peculiarities of German History.* New York: Oxford University Press, 1984.

Blackbourn, David, and Richard Evans, eds. *The German Bourgeoisie: Essays on the Social History of the German Middle Class from the Late Eighteenth Century to the Early Twentieth Century.* New York: Routledge, 1991.

Börsch-Supan, Helmut. "Der Verein Berliner Künstler im neunzehnten Jahrhundert." In *Verein Berliner Künstler: Versuch einer Bestandsaufnahme von 1841 bis zur Gegenwart,* edited by Verein Berliner Künstler, 9–44. Berlin: Nicolai, 1991.

Bösch, Frank. *Öffentliche Geheimnisse. Skandale, Politik und Medien in Deutschland und Großbritannien 1880–1914.* Munich: Oldenburg, 2009.

Botsch, Gideon, and Christoph Kopke. "Hugo Friedlaenders Gerichtsreportagen—eine Einführung." In *Mörder—Verräter—Attentäter. Gerichtsreportagen aus dem Kaiserreich*, by Hugo Friedländer. Berlin: Verlag für Berlin-Brandenburg, 2008.

Clayson, Hollis. *Painted Love: Prostitution in French Art of the Impressionist Era.* Los Angeles: Getty Research Institute, 2003.

Czapliński, Marek. "Prostitution as a problem of the city of Wrocław in the 19th century." *Silesian Historical Quarterly "Sobótka."* Accessed January 12, 2014, http://sobotka.uni.wroc.pl/1.pdf. Original Polish text in *Śląski Kwartalnik Historyczny Sobótka* 54, no. 3 (1999): 315–331.

Davis, Natalie Zemon. *The Return of Martin Guerre.* Cambridge, MA: Harvard University Press, 1983.

Dickinson, Edward. "The Men's Christian Morality Movement in Germany, 1880–1914: Some Reflections on Sex, Politics, and Sexual Politics." *Journal of Modern History* 75, no. 1 (2003): 59–110.

———. *Sex, Freedom, and Power in Imperial Germany, 1880–1914.* New York: Cambridge University Press, 2013.

Dilcher, Gerhard, and Susanne Lepsius. "Editorischer Bericht" for "Zur Geschichte der Handelsgesellschaften im Mittelalter," by Max Weber in *Gesamtausgabe*, vol. 1, no. 1, edited by Gerhard Dilcher and Susanne Lepsius, 114. Tübingen: Mohr Siebeck, 2008.

Domeier, Norman. *The Eulenburg Affair. A Cultural History of Politics in Imperial Germany.* Translated by Deborah Lucas Schneider. New York: Camden House, 2015.

Dorgerloh, Annette. "Beseelung der Bilderscheinung: Porträt und Selbstbildnis im 19. Jahrhundert." In *Vom Biedermeier zum Impressionismus.* Vol. 7 of *Geschichte der bildenden Kunst*, edited by Hubertus Kohle, 432–453. Munich: Prestel, 2008.

———. *Das Künstlerehepaar Lepsius: zur Berliner Porträtmalerei um 1900.* Oldenburg: Akademie, 2003.

———. "Plastik und Malerei." In *Preußen: Kunst und Architektur*, edited by Gert Streidt and Peter Feierabend, 456–490. Cologne: Könnemann, 1999.

Ebe, Gustav. *Der deutsche Cicerone: Malerei deutsche Schulen.* Leipzig: Spamer, 1898.

Elon, Amos. *The Pity of It All: A History of Jews in Germany, 1743–1933.* New York: Metropolitan Books, 2002.

Evans, Richard. "Prostitution, State, and Society in Imperial Germany." *Past and Present* 70, no. 1 (1976): 106–129.

Ferrari Zumbini, Massimo. *Die Wurzeln des Bösen: Gründerjahre des Antisemitismus von der Bismarckzeit zu Hitler.* Frankfurt: Klostermann, 2003.

Fraser, David. *Frederick the Great.* New York: Fromm International, 2000.

Frevert, Ute. *Men of Honour: A Social and Cultural History of the Duel.* Translated by Anthony Williams. Cambridge, UK: Polity, 1995.

Fried, Michael. *Menzel's Realism: Art and Embodiment in Nineteenth-Century Berlin.* New Haven, CT: Yale University Press, 2006.

Frisby, David, ed. *Georg Simmel in Wien: Texte und Kontexte aus dem Wien der Jahrhundertwende.* Vienna: Facultas WUV, 2000.

———. *Simmel and Since: Essays on Georg Simmel's Social Theory.* New York: Routledge, 1992.

Gebhardt, Hartwig, and Ulla Wischermann, eds. *Die Staatsbürgerin: Originaltreuer Nachdruck der ersten Arbeiterinnenzeitschrift Deutschlands.* Munich: K. G. Saur, 1988.

Gerhard, Ute. *Frauenbewegung und Feminismus: Eine Geschichte seit 1789.* Munich: C. H. Beck, 2009.

Ginsburg, Carlo. *The Cheese and the Worms: The Cosmos of a Sixteenth-Century Miller.* Baltimore: Johns Hopkins University Press, 1980.

Goldberg, Ann. *Honor, Politics, and the Law in Imperial Germany, 1871–1914.* Cambridge: Cambridge University Press, 2010.

Gross, Michael. *The War Against Catholicism: Liberalism and the Anti-Catholic Imagination.* Ann Arbor: University of Michigan Press, 2005.

Grüntzig, Johannes W., and Heinz Mehlhorn. *Robert Koch: Seuchenjäger und Nobelpreisträger.* Heidelberg: Spektrum, 2010.

Gubser, Martin. *Literarischer Antisemitismus: Untersuchungen zu Gustav Freytag und anderen bürgerlichen Schriftstellern des 19. Jahrhunderts.* Göttingen: Wallstein, 1998.

Guido, Diane. *The German League for the Prevention of Women's Emancipation: Antifeminism in Germany, 1912–1920.* New York: Peter Lang, 2010.

Gutbrod, Evelyn. *Die Rezeption des Impressionismus in Deutschland.* Munich: W. Kohlhammer, 1980.

Hall, Alex. *Scandal, Sensation and Social Democracy: The SPD Press and Wilhelmine Germany 1890–1914.* New York: Cambridge University Press, 1977.

Hamburger, Ernest. *Juden im öffentlichen Leben Deutschlands: Regierungsmitglieder, Beamte und Parlamentarier in der monarchischen Zeit 1848–1918.* Tübingen: Mohr Siebeck, 1968.

Hartston, Barnet. "Closing the Courtroom: Press Restrictions and Criminal Trials in Late Nineteenth-Century Germany." *Law and History Review*, 35, no. 1 (February 2017): 201–233.

———. *Sensationalizing the Jewish Question: Anti-Semitic Trials and the Press in the Early German Empire.* Leiden: Brill, 2005.

Häusler, Michael, and Bettina Hitzer, eds. *Zwischen Tanzboden und Bordell: Lebensbilder Berliner Prostituierter aus dem Jahr 1869.* Berlin: be.bra wissenschaft, 2010.

Haxthausen, Charles W., and Heidrun Suhr, eds. *Berlin: Culture and Metropolis.* Minneapolis: University of Minnesota Press, 1990.

Heinssen, Johannes. *Historismus und Kulturkritik: Studien zur deutschen Geschichtskultur im späten 19. Jahrhundert.* Göttingen: Vandenhoeck and Ruprecht, 2003.

Hett, Benjamin. *Death in the Tiergarten: Murder and Criminal Justice in the Kaiser's Berlin.* Cambridge, MA: Harvard University Press, 2004.

Höfele, Karl Heinrich. *Geist und Gesellschaft der Bismarckzeit, 1870–1890.* Göttingen: Musterschmidt, 1967.

Hoffmann, Christhard. "Political Culture and Violence against Minorities: The Antisemitic Violence in Pomerania and West Prussia." In *Exclusionary Violence: Antisemitic Riots in Modern German History*, edited by Christhard Hoffmann, Werner Bergmann, and Helmut Walser Smith. Ann Arbor: University of Michigan Press, 2002.

Hommen, Tanja. *Sittlichkeitsverbrechen. Sexuelle Gewalt im Kaiserreich.* Frankfurt: Campus, 1999.

Jarausch, Konrad. *The Unfree Professions: German Lawyers, Teachers, and Engineers, 1900–1950.* New York: Oxford University Press, 1990.

Jeffries, Matthew. *Contesting the German Empire.* Malden, MA.: Blackwell, 2008.

Joeres, Ruth-Ellen. *Respectability and Deviance: Nineteenth-Century German Women Writers and the Ambiguity of Representation.* Chicago: University of Chicago Press, 1998.

Johnson, Eric. *Urbanization and Crime: Germany 1871–1914.* Cambridge: Cambridge University Press, 2002.

Katz, Jacob. *From Prejudice to Destruction.* Cambridge, MA: Harvard University Press, 1980.

Kiernan, V. G. *The Duel in European History: Honor and the Reign of the Aristocracy.* Oxford: Oxford University Press, 1988.

Koch, Arnd. "Der gescheiterte Reform des reformierten Strafprozesses." *Zeitschrift für internationale Strafrechtsdogmatik* 4, no. 10 (2009): 542–548. Accessed December 9, 2013, http://www.zis-online.com/dat/artikel/2009_10_365.pdf.

Kohlrausch, Martin. *Der Monarch im Skandal: Die Logik der Massenmedien und die Transformation der wilhelminischen Monarchie.* Berlin: Akademie, 2005.

Koszyk, Kurt. *Deutsche Presse im 19. Jahrhundert.* Berlin: Colloquium, 1966.

Krollmann, Christian, ed. *Altpreußische Biographie.* Vol. 1: Abegg-Malten. Marburg/Lahn: Elwert, 1974. Reprint of the first edition by Königsberg, Gräfe und Unzer, 1941.

Kunzel, Regina. *Fallen Women, Problem Girls: Unmarried Mothers and the Professionalization of Social Work, 1890–1945.* New Haven, CT: Yale University Press, 1993.

Langewiesche, Dieter. *Liberalism in Germany.* Basingstoke: Macmillan, 2000.

Ledford, Kenneth. *From General Estate to Special Interest: German Lawyers, 1878–1933*. New York: Cambridge University Press, 1996.

———. "Lawyers, Liberalism, and Procedure: The German Imperial Justice Laws of 1877–79." *Central European History* 26 (1993): 165–193.

Lees, Andrew. *Cities, Sin, and Social Reform in Imperial Germany*. Ann Arbor: University of Michigan Press, 2002.

———. "Deviant Sexuality and other 'Sins': The Views of Protestant Conservatives in Imperial Germany." *German Studies Review* 23, no. 3 (2000): 453–476.

Lenman, Robin. *Artists and Society in Germany, 1850–1914*. New York: Manchester University Press, 1997.

Leonard, Sarah. *Fragile Minds and Vulnerable Souls: The Matter of Obscenity in Nineteenth-Century Germany*. Philadelphia: University of Pennsylvania Press, 2015.

Lepsius, Sabine Graef. *Ein Berliner Künstlerleben um die Jahrhundertwende: Erinnerungen*. Munich: G. Müller, 1972.

Levy, Richard. *The Downfall of the Anti-Semitic Political Parties in Imperial Germany*. New Haven, CT: Yale University Press, 1975.

Lewis, Beth Irwin. *Art for All? The Collision of Modern Art and the Public in Late Nineteenth-Century Germany*. Princeton, NJ: Princeton University Press, 2003.

Maier-Reimer, Georg. "Ernst Wolff (1877–1959)—Führender Anwalt und oberster Richter." In *Deutscher Juristen jüdischer Herkunft*, edited by Helmut Heinrichs, Harald Franzki, Klaus Schmalz, and Michael Stolleis, 643–654. Munich: C. H. Beck, 1993.

McAleer, Kevin. *Dueling: The Cult of Honor in Fin-de-Siècle Germany*. Princeton, NJ: Princeton University Press, 1994.

Mews, Siegfried, and James Hardin, eds. *Nineteenth-Century German Writers: 1841–1900*. Detroit: Gale Research, 1993.

Möller, Klaus-Peter. "'Entartete Kunst' als 'Gefahr für die Sittlichkeit des ganzen Volkes': Die 'Ächtung' des Malers Gustav Graef—Hintergrunde und Folgen." In Erledigungen—Pamphlete, Polemiken und Proteste, vol. 14/15, edited by Marcel Atze and Volker Kaukoreit, 118–137 (Vienna: Praesens, 2014). Accessed July 18, 2014, http://www.wilnitsky.com/pictures/Erledigungen_Artikel_Gustav%20Graef.pdf.

Müller, Philipp. *Auf der Suche nach dem Täter: Die öffentliche Dramatisierung von Verbrechen im Berlin des Kaiserreichs*. New York: Campus, 1985.

Neumann, Helga, and Manfred Neumann. *Maximilian Harden (1861–1927). Ein unerschrockener deutsch-jüdischer Kritiker und Publizist*. Würzburg: Königshausen and Neumann, 2002.

Olbrisch, Lena Marie. "Paul Lindaus 'Der Andere': vom Fall zum Film." Masterarbeit, Institut für Germanistik, Universität Potsdam, 2011. Accessed June 21, 2014, http://opus.kobv.de/ubp/volltexte/2013/6513/pdf/master_olbrisch.pdf.

Ortmann, Alexandra. *Machtvolle Verhandlungen: Zur Kulturgeschichte der deutschen Strafjustiz, 1879–1924*. Göttingen: Vandenhoeck and Ruprecht, 2014.

Osborne, John. *Gerhard Hauptmann and the Naturalist Drama*. Amsterdam: Harwood Academic, 1998.

Paret, Peter. *Art as History: Episodes in the Culture and Politics of Nineteenth-Century Germany*. Princeton, NJ: Princeton University Press, 1988.

———. *Die Berliner Secession. Moderne Kunst und ihre Feinde in Kaiserlichen Deutschland*. Frankfurt: Ullstein, 1983.

———. "Modernism and the 'Alien Element in German Art.'" In *Berlin Metropolis: Jews and the New Culture, 1890–1918*, edited by Emily Bilski. Berkeley: University of California Press, 1999.

Paret, Peter, and Beth Irwin Lewis. "Art, Society, and Politics in Wilhelmine Germany." *Journal of Modern History* 57, no. 4 (1985): 696–710.

Paul, Barbara. *Hugo von Tschudi und die moderne französische Kunst im Deutschen Kaiserreich*. Mainz: P. von Zabern, 1993.

Penslar, Derek J. "Philanthropy, the 'Social Question,' and Jewish Identity in Imperial Germany." *Leo Baeck Institute Yearbook* 38 (1993): 51–73.

Pfefferkorn, Rudolf. *Die Berliner Secession*. Berlin: Haude and Spener, 1972.

Pulzer, Peter. *The Rise of Political Anti-Semitism in Germany and Austria*. Cambridge, MA: Harvard University Press, 1988.

Reese, Dagmar. *Akt und Anstand: Der Skandal um den Gustav Graef Prozess, Berlin 1885*. Vienna: Böhlau, 2014.

Retallack, James. "The Authoritarian State and the Political Mass Market." In *Imperial Germany Revisited: Continuing Debates and New Perspectives*, edited by Sven Oliver Müller and Cornelius Torp, 83–96. New York: Berghahn, 2011.

Reuveni, Gideon. "Der Aufstieg der Bürgerlichkeit und die bürgerliche Selbstauflösung." *Zeitschrift für Geschichtswissenschaft* 51 (2003): 131–143.

Ritzer, George. *The Blackwell Companion to Major Classical Social Theorists*. Malden, MA: John Wiley and Sons, 2008.

Röhl, John C. G. *Wilhelm II: der Aufbau der persönlichen Monarchie, 1888–1900*. Munich: Beck, 2001.

Rosenblum, Warren. *Beyond the Prison Gates: Punishment and Welfare in Germany*. Chapel Hill: University of North Carolina Press, 2008.

Sätzer, Rolf. *Entwicklungslinien der deutschen Zola—Rezeption von den Anfängen bis zum Tode des Autors*. Bern: Peter Lang, 1989.

Schaser, Angelika. *Frauenbewegung in Deutschland 1848–1933*. Darmstadt: Wiss. Buchges., 2006.

Schorske, Carl. "Politics in a New Key: An Austrian Triptych." *Journal of Modern History* 39 (1967): 343–386.

Sharp, Ingrid, and Jane Jordan, eds. *Josephine Butler and the Prostitution Campaigns: Diseases of the Body Politic*. New York: Routledge Curzon, 2003.

Smith, Helmut Walser. *The Butcher's Tale: Murder and Anti-Semitism in a German Town*. New York: W. W. Norton, 2002.

Smith, Jill Suzanne. *Berlin Coquette: Prostitution and the New German Woman, 1890–1933*. Ithaca, NY: Cornell University Press, 2013.

Sperber, Jonathan. "Bürger, Bürgertum, Bürgerlichkeit, Bürgerliche Gesellschaft: Studies of the German (Upper) Middle Class and Its Sociocultural World." *The Journal of Modern History* 69, no. 2 (June 1997): 271–297.

———. *The Kaiser's Voters: Electors and Elections in Imperial Germany*. New York: Cambridge University Press, 1997.

Stang, Kirsten, and Ulrich Sasse. *Trauma und Justiz: juristische Grundlagen für Psychotherapeuten; psychotherapeutische Grundlagen für Juristen*. Stuttgart: Schattauer, 2007.

Stark, Gary. *Banned in Berlin: Literary Censorship in Imperial Germany, 1871–1918*. New York: Berghahn, 2012.

———. "Pornography, Society, and the Law in Imperial Germany." *Peer Reviewed Articles*. Paper 21 (2014), http://scholarworks.gvsu.edu/hst_articles/21.

Stern, Fritz. *Gold and Iron: Bismarck, Bleichröder, and the Building of the German Empire*. New York: Knopf, 1977.

———. *The Politics of Cultural Despair*. Berkeley: University of California Press, 1974.

Stewart, Mary. "German Naturalism and the Novel." *The Modern Language Review* 71, no. 4 (October 1976): 846–856.

Stummann-Bowert, Ruth. *Malwida von Meysenburg—Paul Rée: Briefe an einen Freund*. Würzburg: Königshausen and Neumann, 1998.

Sweeney, Dennis. "Liberalism, the Worker and the Limits of Öffentlichkeit in Wilhelmine Germany." *German History* 22, no. 1 (2004): 37.

Tauber, Rita E. "Annäherungen: Kunst und Prostitution im Kaiserreich." In *Der Potsdamer Platz: Ernst Ludwig Kirchner und Der Untergang Preußens*, edited by Katharina Henkel and Roland März, 208–217. Berlin: Nationalgalerie Berlin, 2001.

———. *Der häßliche Eros: Darstellungen zur Prostitution in der Malerei und Grafik 1855–1930*. Berlin: Gebr. Mann, 1997.

Teeuwisse, Nicolaas. *Vom Salon zur Secession. Berliner Kunstleben zwischen Tradition und Aufbruch zur Moderne: 1871–1900*. Berlin: Deutscher Verlag für Kunstwissenschaft, 1986.

Walkowitz, Judith. *City of Dreadful Delight: Narratives of Sexual Danger in Late Victorian London*. Chicago: University of Chicago Press, 1992.

Watson, Alan. "Legal Change: Sources of Law and Legal Culture." *University of Pennsylvania Law Review* 131, no. 5 (April 1983): 1121–1157.

Weedon, Chris. *Gender, Feminism, and Fiction in Germany, 1880–1914*. Vol. 5 of *Gender, Sexuality, Culture*, edited by William J. Spurlin. New York: Peter Lang, 2006.

Wehler, Hans-Ulrich. *The German Empire*. New York: Berg, 1997.

Werner, Carl. *Lex Heinze und ihre Geschichte*. Dortmund: O. Rühmkorf, 1935.

Wetzell, Richard. "From Retributive Justice to Social Defense: Penal Reform in Fin-de-Siècle Germany." In *Germany at the Fin de Siècle: Culture, Politics, and Ideas*, edited by Suzanne Marchand and David Lindenfeld, 59–77. Baton Rouge: Louisiana State University Press, 2004.

Wilhelm, Uwe. *Das deutsche Kaiserreich und seine Justiz. Justizkritik, politische Strafrechtsprechung, Justizpolitik*. Berlin: Duncker and Humblot, 2010.

Wilhelmy-Dollinger, Petra. *Der Berliner Salon im 19. Jahrhundert (1780–1914)*. New York: De Gruyter, 1989.

Wipperman, Wolfgang. *Skandal im Jagdschloss Grunewald. Männlichkeit und Ehre im deutschen Kaiserreich*. Darmstadt: Primus, 2010.

Wirth, Irmgard. *Berliner Malerei im 19. Jahrhundert: von der Zeit Friedrichs des Grossen bis zum ersten Weltkrieg*. Berlin: W. J. Siedler, 1990.

With, Christopher. *The Prussian Landeskunstkommission, 1862–1911*. Berlin: Gebr. Mann, 1986.

Yngvesson, Barbara. "Inventing Law in Local Settings: Rethinking Popular Legal Culture." *Yale Law Review* 98, no. 8 (1989): 1689–1709.

Zedner, Lucia, and Andrew Ashworth, eds. *The Criminological Foundations of Penal Policy: Essays in Honour of Roger Hood*. New York: Oxford University Press, 2003.

INDEX

Adami (model), 68–69
Adler, Clara, 47, 48
Adler, Minna, 47, 48
adversarial system, 48, 189
age of consent, 103, 108, 179
Albertina (Königsberg), 23–25, 30, 44, 59, 201
Allgemeine deutsche Frauenverein (AdF), 110–111
Ammann, (anti-Semitic agitator), 139–140
Anderson, Margaret, 11, 229
Anti-Semitic League, 134
anti-Semitism
  comparison with England, 142–143, 231–232
  government reluctance to prosecute, 134, 236n20
  growth of, 119, 133–134
  Jewish self-defense, 15–16
  origin of the term, 133–134
  political failures of, 231–232
  in the press, 134, 139–140, 142–143, 200–201, 267n24
  stereotypes: cultural degeneracy, 21, 135–136; financial corruption, 133; "Jew Press," 54, 136, 138, 140; sexual degeneracy, 138, 141, 142–143
  in trials: Ahlwardt case, 252n42, 263n35; Graef trial, 21, 133, 137–141, 218, 227, 267n19; Stöcker-Bäcker case, 136–140, 197–198, 200, 207
  See also names of individual politicians, journalists, and newspapers
Arbeiterinnenverein (Club for the Interests of Working Women), 112
Arenberg, Franz von, 179
Armstrong, Eliza, 56, 107, 110
Arnim, Harry von, 42, 186, 200–201
Arnim, Malwine von, 216
art
  display in shop windows, 4, 116, 152, 155–162, 178, 214, 268n44
  francophobia and, 34, 62–63, 65–66, 82, 86–88, 91, 231, 246n71
  obscenity laws and, 151–162, 178–181
  private market for, 87–88, 160–161, 231
  "relative obscenity," 159–160
  schools of: idealism, 63–67, 82–83, 86–87, 91; impressionism, 20, 62, 65, 86–89; realism, 26–28, 64–65, 83, 86; romanticism, 25–26, 64
  See also names of individual art academies, artists, and paintings
art cards (*Kunstkarten*), 4, 152, 155–157, 160, 162, 178
artists
  art critics and, 83–85, 226
  governmental influence on, 82–83, 86–88
  nude models, use of, 22, 33, 36–38, 47, 102
  social networks, reliance on, 30–33, 82, 216
  special moral codes and, 66–86
  See also Association of Berlin Artists; Royal Academy of Arts; and the names of individual artists
Ashton, Louise, 110
Association for the Protection of Youth, 176
Association of Berlin Artists (*Verein Berliner Künstler*), 14, 61
  Artists' Declaration, 79–86, 193, 214, 226, 231
  conflict with art critics, 83–85, 226
  conservative nature of, 82–83, 88
Association of Berlin Lawyers (*Anwaltsverein*), 196
Association of Female Artists in Berlin (*Verein Berliner Künstlerinnen*), 33
Association of German Jurists (*Deutsche Juristentag*), 210–213, 230

Bach, Theresia, 82
Bachmann (judge), 144, 150, 199
Bäcker, Heinrich, 136–139, 197–198, 200
Bähr, Otto, 197–198
Ballien, Alfred, 202–203
Bamberger, Ludwig, 119
Barnay, Ludwig, 218
Beauvoir, Simone de, 131
Bebel, August, 10, 42, 168, 190, 201
Becker, Carl, 80, 82

Berenson, Edward, 18
Berliner Börsen-Courier, 56, 67–70, 75–76, 165, 186–187, 199, 221
Berliner Börsen-Zeitung, 140, 170
Berliner Gerichtszeitung, 104
Berliner Morgenpost, 151, 220
Berliner Tageblatt, 41, 206–207
Berliner Theater, 218, 219
Berliner Volksblatt, 115, 219
Berliner Zeitung, 80–82
Berlin Lawyers' Chamber (*Anwaltskammer*), 200, 202–203
Berlin Men's Alliance for Combatting Public Immorality, 175–176
Berlin Secession, 20, 87–89, 180
Bernstein, Felicie and Carl, 87
Bieber-Böhm, Hanna, 176
Bildungsbürgertum, 12
Binding, Karl, 157
Bismarck, Herbert von, 166–167, 170–172, 183, 230
Bismarck, Marie von, 31
Bismarck, Otto von, 82, 98, 119, 147, 171
  1885 legal reforms and, 150, 168, 206–207
  contact with Graef circle, 30–31, 32, 216
  German unification, 9–10
  political attacks against, 54–55, 132, 133–134, 200–201, 243n3
  political trials: Arnim case, 42, 186, 200; attempts to divert from jury courts, 206–207; attempts to limit press access, 165–174, 182–183, 206
  Reichsfeinde, political enemies as, 10–11, 13, 112
  Reichstag opposition to, 167–168, 171, 183–184, 229–230
  social legislation, 118
Bismarck, Sybille von (née Arnim), 30–31, 216
Bismarck, Wilhelm von, 31
Blackbourn, David, 229
Bleibtreu, Karl, 176, 266n2
Bleichröder, Gerson von, 78, 119, 133, 254n70
Böhm, Martin [Gustav Braun], 106
Booth, Bramwell, 56
Bösch, Frank, 19–20, 232–233
Boulanger, Georges, 171
Brahm, Otto, 219, 267n24
Brandt, Hermann von, 155–156
Braun, Friedrich, 174
Brausewetter, Georg Robert, 196–199
Breslauer Zeitung, 115
Bundesrat, 98, 167, 173, 178, 179, 183
Buti, Lucretia, 67
Butler, Josephine, 56, 107–109, 111, 232
Byron, Lord, 70

Cassel, Oskar, 44, 240n12
censorship
  government reluctance to engage in, 155, 156–157, 171
  obscene texts and imagery, 17–18, 152–162, 175–185
  politically dangerous texts, 109–110, 112–113, 132
  public resistance against, 157–162, 180–181
  public support for, 17, 155–156, 175–176, 179–180
  "relative obscenity," 159–160
  self-censorship, 44–45, 82, 110–111
  See also Lex Graef; Lex Heinze
Center Party, 168, 171–172, 174, 179–180, 228, 243n3
Chicago Tribune, 223
Christian-Social Party, 10–11, 118–119, 134, 136, 140, 197–198, 227
class justice, 146–147, 188–190, 229
Club for the Interests of Working Women, 112
Code of Criminal Procedure (*Strafprozessordnung*), 21, 38, 146–147, 149, 150, 190, 199
Conrad, Michael Georg, 64
Conservative Party, 167–168, 171, 172, 174, 179
Contagious Disease Acts, 108
Cornelius, Peter von, 89, 247n95
Cossmann, Richard, 202–203
Coupeau, Nana. *See* Zola, Émile; *see also under* Rother, Bertha
Courbet, Gustave, 86, 88
Court Organization Law (*Gerichtsverfassungsgesetz*), 163, 166, 178–179, 181, 187, 196, 206, 257n57
Courts of Lay Assessors (*Schöffengerichte*), 158, 205–206, 210–213, 230–231
Cremer, Christoph, 133
Cremer, Hermann, 98–99
Criminal Chambers (*Strafkammern*), 206, 213, 264n66
Criminal Code (*Strafgesetzbuch*)
  changes in, 145–149, 189
  criticism of, 21, 132, 146–148
  grober Unfug (disturbance of the peace), 155, 158, 256n42
  obscenity, 152–162, 178–181
  publishing of verdicts, 166
  recording of witness statements, 149–150

right to refuse testimony, 38, 150–151
sexual abuse of children, 103
slander and libel, 16, 139, 236n20
See also Lex Graef; Lex Heinze; perjury; prostitution
criminality
fears of increasing, 10, 17, 117–118, 125–126, 235n2
Jews and, 21, 133, 141–142
lower classes and, 120–132
physiognomy and, 121–122
public obsession with, 7, 18–20, 42–45, 53–57, 125–126165
theories of, 122, 194–195, 207–208, 257n59, 265n88
See also perjury; prostitution
cultural pessimism, 62

Davis, Natalie Zemon, 18
democratization, 11–12, 16, 147–148, 228–231
Deutsch, Joseph, 223
Dickhoff, Ernst Wilhelm. *See* Dickhoff trial
Dickhoff trial, 125–126, 211
Dielitz, Konrad, 79
Diest-Daber, Otto von, 133
Dresdner Nachrichten, 150, 223
du Bois-Reymond, Emil, 216
Dühring, Eugen, 139
Dunajew, Wanda von, 219
Dürer, Albrecht, 136
Düsseldorf Royal Art Academy, 25, 27

Elben, Gustav von, 210, 212
Eley, Geoff, 229
Emminger, Erich, 213, 231
Engels, Friedrich, 112, 250n61
Ephrussi, Charles, 87
epilepsy, 129–130
Eulenburg, Botho Graf zu, 152
Eulenburg scandal, 181, 184, 230, 260n113–114, 267n22

Fairy Tale, The (Graef)
creation of, 35–36,
description of, 4–7
display on art cards, 155–157, 91
evidence at trial, 50–53
exhibition of, 89, 160–162, 177, 215, 219–221
reception of, 36–37, 85–86
Fallen Girls and the Vice Squad, The, 112–113
feminism, 107–113
Feuerbach, Anselm, 29
Fichte, Johann Gottlieb, 23
filth and trash literature (*Schmutz- und Schundliteratur*), 17–18, 176–177
Flexner, Abraham, 100
Fontane, Thodore, 29, 84, 192–193, 218
Förster, Bernhard, 134–136, 200
Francophobia, 34, 64–65, 82, 86–87, 91, 205
Frankfurter Zeitung, 78–79, 124, 165, 257n62
Frederick the Great, 27, 64, 195–196
Free Conservative Party, 67, 78, 168, 171, 173, 174, 205, 231
Freiburg, Hedwig, 218
Freie Volksbühne, 219, 267n24
Freie Zeitung, 136, 138
Freisinnige (Free-Thinking) Party, 167, 173, 174
Frenzel, Karl
on artists and sensuality, 69–72
conflict with Max Heinemann, 72–75, 192, 193, 214, 231
conflict with Anton von Werner, 83–84
criticism of, 76–82, 84–85, 141, 180
Frevert, Ute, 13, 15, 235n9
Freytag, Gustav, 63
Friedberg, Heinrich von, 44, 147, 149–150 187, 191, 193
Friedheim, Otto, 156–157, 160, 256n39
Friedländer, Georg, 193
Friedländer, Hugo, 44
Friedmann, Fritz, 197, 202–204, 212
Friedrich, Caspar David, 61
Friedrich Wilhelm III, 24, 203, 238n17
Friedrich Wilhelm IV, 24, 26, 97
Fuchs, Carl, 210, 257n59, 262n21
Fuld, Ludwig, 212

Galton, Francis, 219
Ganz, Alexander, 157–159, 160
Gartenlaube, 133, 137
General Conference of German Morality Associations, 176
Gensichen, Otto Franz, 67
Gerlach, Helmut von, 198
Germania, 54, 62, 66–68, 124, 133–134, 139, 140, 155–156, 243n3
Gervex, Henri, 32–34
Gesellschaft, Die, 64
Ginsburg, Carlo, 18
Glagau, Otto, 119, 133, 136, 137–140, 142, 227
Gneist, Rudolf von, 200, 212
Gobineau, Comte de, 17
Goethe, Johann Wolfgang von, 58, 135, 245n51, 245n53

Goethe League (*Goethebund*), 180–181
Goldberg, Ann, 12–14, 16
Gordon, George, 114
Goßler, Gustav von, 215, 246n70
Graef, Botho, 26, 32
Graef, Christoph Hartmann, 23–24
Graef, Franziska (née Liebreich), 15, 25–26, 31–33, 123, 217, 227
Graef, Gustav
  arrest, 3–4, 37–40
  career: before trial, 25–37; portraiture, 30–31, 33, 216; experiments with nudes, 33–37; *plein air* painting, 36, 89; resignation from the Association of Berlin Artists, 80; after trial, 89–91, 214–217; posthumous exhibit at the National Gallery, 89–90; as a forgotten artist, 61–62
  childhood, 12, 23–25
  criticism by Georg Simmel, 90–91
  death of, 217–218, 223
  depiction: in fiction and poetry, 109, 114–116; by Dagmar Reese, 22, 266n7, 267n16
  famous works: *East Prussian Militia Takes to the Field in 1813, The*, 28–29; *Farewell of a Lithuanian Militiaman, 30*; *Félicie*, 33–35, 36, 89, 155–157, 160–161; *Love of the Fatherland: Ferdinande von Schmettau Sacrifices her Hair*, 29, 31, 221; See also *Fairy Tale, The*
  testimony: at Graef trial, 45, 48–53, 57–60; at Hammermann trial, 38, 144–145, 149–151; "diaries," 77, 245n52
Graef, Johann August Ferdinand, 24
Graef, Johann Friedrich, 24
Graef, Johann Polycarpus Gottfried, 24
Graef, Sabine. *See* Lepsius, Sabine.
Grenzboten, 34, 197–198
Gröber, Adolf, 179
Gropius, Martin, 31
Grüntzig, Johannes, 218
Guillaume-Schack, Gertrud, 111–113, 250n61, 250n63

Hamburger Nachrichten, 170
Hammermann, Antonie, 38–39, 121, 145, 187
Hammermann, Helene, 37–39, 45, 59, 93, 122, 248n27, 252n23
Hammermann, Wilhelm, 39, 59, 121, 122–123, 131
Hammerstein, Wilhelm von, 139
Hannover'sche Courier, 155–156
Hansemann, Ferdinand von, 216
Harden, Maximilian, 44, 125, 194, 219, 260n113, 267n22
Hardy, Thomas, 114
Hart, Heinrich and Julius, 64
Hauptmann, Gerhart, 176
Heckscher, Meyer, 121, 150–151
Heinemann, Max
  anti-Semitism and, 140–141, 227
  Artists' Declaration and, 79–81, 84, 231
  career: before the Graef trial, 44, 254n75; Graef trial, 45, 49, 52, 57–58, 103–104, 115, 130, 148–149, 191, 201, 208; colleague of Gustav Otto, 125, 211; after the Graef trial, 193–195, 241n29, 262n23, 262n30
  criticism of, 191–194, 207–208
  personal honor, defense of, 72–75, 195, 199, 225
  public conflicts: with Karl Frenzel, 70–75, 180, 192, 214; with Paul Lindau, 75–76; with Franz von Liszt, 194–195
  social circle, 72, 192–193
  support for, 192–193, 210
Heinze trial, 17–18, 19, 113, 125, 162, 174–177, 202–203, 230; *See also* Lex Heinze
Held, Hermann Gustav, 191
Herrfurth, Ernst, 99, 161, 177
Hett, Benjamin, 43, 184, 188–189, 196–197
Heydeck, Johannes, 30
Heyden, August von, 37
Hildesheimer, Hirsch, 16, 141, 236n21
Hitler, Adolf, 231
Hobrecht, Arthur, 32
Hommen, Tanja, 101, 248n27
honor
  and adultery, 150–151
  and bourgeoisie, 9, 12–16, 59, 120–122, 148, 163, 169, 188, 208–209, 238n10
  and dueling, 13, 13n9, 15–16, 54–55, 192, 225
  and Honor Courts, 13–14, 187, 200
  and Jews, 14–16, 26, 235–236n10
  and libel, 13–14, 54–55, 136–137
  and lower classes, 14, 16, 21, 120–127, 226–227, 252n23
  and masculinity, 9, 13–16, 37, 54–55, 112–113, 148, 163, 228
  and professionalization: artists, 14, 20, 79–86, 226, 231; journalists, 20, 54–56, 163–165, 198, 226; jurists, 21, 194–195, 196, 202–204, 208–209, 225–226

and women, 14–15, 101, 103–104, 115–116, 227
See also perjury
Humorist, Der (Vienna), 220, 222

idealism, in art, 63–67, 82–83, 86–87, 91
Im neuen Reich, 36, 239n40
impressionism, 20, 62, 65, 86–89
industrialization, impacts of, 9–10, 62–63, 65–66, 117–119, 125, 235n2
Intrau, Concordia, 46–48, 93, 96, 121, 127–128, 131, 226
inquisitorial system, 48, 189

Jack the Ripper, 55, 142
Jastrow, Hermann 169–170, 172
Jews
in Germany, 119, 231–232
in Prussia, 25–26, 29, 238n17
See also under anti-Semitism; honor
Joeres, Ruth-Ellen, 110
Johl (judge), 128–129
Jordan, Max, 90
judges
changes in the profession, 189, 195–196, 202–203
closed courtrooms and, 162–174, 175, 178–179, 181,184, 230
criticism of, 106, 139, 184, 188, 196–199
lay assessors (*Schöffen*) and, 188, 205–213, 230–231
power and status of, 45, 48, 131, 186–188, 195–199
public opinion and, 197–198, 208–209
ratio decidendi and, 166–167, 173
"There are still judges in Berlin!," 139, 195–196
Jüdische Presse, 141
jury courts (*Schwurgerichte*)
changing attitudes toward, 114, 131, 147, 168, 205–213, 229–231
development in Germany, 146, 204–207
elimination of, 213
Graef case and, 204, 207–210, 230

Kant, Immanuel, 23
"Kartell" parties, 171, 182–183
Kauffmann, Gustav, 147, 255n9
Kaufmann, Otto, 160–161, 215
Kaulbach, Wilhelm von, 26, 61
Kayser, Max, 198–199
Kayser, Paul, 173
Kempner, Friederike, 115–116
Keudell, Robert von, 30, 31–32, 217
Kiernan, V. G., 13, 235n9
Kinel, Gertrud, 32
Kleinholz, Wilhelm, 44, 186, 240n11
Koch, Robert, 216, 218–219, 267n16
Kohlrausch, Martin, 19, 230
Kohn, Isidor, 222
Kollwitz, Käthe, 30
König, Wilhelm von, 157–158
Königsberg Art Academy, 30
Kontorowicz, Hermann, 200
Kotze Affair, 230
Krafft-Ebing, Richard von, 103
Kretzschmer, Hermann, 38, 45, 59, 123, 241n17
Kreuzzeitung (Neue Preußische Zeitung)
anti-Semitism in, 133–134, 139–140, 197
on cultural degeneracy, 62, 116, 139
on Graef trial, 56–57, 80, 164, 191, 199
opposition to Bismarck, 243n3, 133–134
Krischen (*Volksadvokat*) 38, 59, 121–122, 187
Kritische Waffengänge, 64
Kugler, Franz, 27
Kühnle (witness), 46–48, 96, 121, 226
Kulemann, Wilhelm, 172–173
Kulturbund (Cultural Alliance for the Abolition of Officially Regulated Prostitution), 111–113
Kulturkampf, 168, 257n62
Kulturkämpfer, Der, 137–138

Lagarde, Paul de, 62, 243n2
Langbehn, Julius, 62, 243n2
Lange (witness), 49
Lange, Helene, 111
Lasker, Eduard, 119, 197, 263n38
Laué, Carl, 202
Law on the Organization of the General State Government of July 26, 1880, 153
Law Regarding Court Proceedings Closed to the Public (1888), 167–174, 182, 229–230, 260n114
lawyers
changes in the profession, 199–203
generational battles, 202–204, 211–212
Lawyers' Chamber (*Anwaltskammer*), 200, 202, 203–204
lawyers' chambers (*Anwaltszimmer*), 186–187
Lawyers' Statute (*Rechtsanwaltsordnung*), 200, 264n56

power and status of, 186–189, 199–204
Ledford, Kenneth, 188, 200
Leistikow, Walter, 88
Lenman, Robin, 65, 86
Leonard, Sarah, 184–185
Leonhardt, Adolph, 206
Lepsius, Johannes, 217
Lepsius, Karl Richard, 90
Lepsius, Reinhold, 26, 90
Lepsius, Sabine (née Graef)
career, 22, 26, 87, 90, 266n12
childhood, 26, 32
Graef trial and, 37, 123, 217–218, 227, 252n23, 267n19
relationship with father, 24–25, 216–217, 267n16
Lewin, Leopold, 129, 141, 252n42
Lex Graef, 169–175, 178–185, 229–230, 260n114, 260n116
Lex Heinze, 17, 162, 174–175, 177–181, 260n112, 260n116
Lex Otto, 109
liberalism
criticism of: economic liberalism, 62, 118–119, 133–134; "Jewish" nature of, 119, 133–140, 142, 197; liberal press, 20, 54–55, 56–57, 104–105, 164
law codes and, 146–148, 200, 205–206
"model markets" and, 68–69
"weakness" of, 181–185, 228–231
See also the names of liberal parties, politicians, and newspapers; See also under *Öffentlichkeit*
Liebermann, Max, 87–89, 180
Liebknecht, Karl, 147, 188–190, 255n8
Liebknecht, Wilhelm, 10, 42, 147, 189–190
Liebreich, Oskar, 216
Liman, Carl, 128–130, 252n38
Lindau, Paul
after Graef trial, 218–219
Graef trial and, 34, 51, 53–54, 75–78, 106, 120–123, 132, 192
conflict with Max Heinemann, 75–77, 121, 124, 192–193
conflict with Friederike Kempner, 115
lower classes, depiction of, 21, 117, 120–124, 126, 127, 187, 222, 226–227
as "objective observer," 76, 120
and Bertha Rother, 75, 92, 94, 102, 124
Lippi, Filippo, 67
Liszt, Franz von, 194–195, 208, 265n88
Lombroso, Cesare, 122
lower classes
depiction of, 14, 21, 117–132, 187, 222, 226–227, 252n23
power of, 16, 130–132
the "Social Question," 14–15, 118–119, 133
See also socialism
Lucanus, Hermann von, 175
Luck, Ludolf von, 194
Lüty, Hermann, 137, 139, 197–199, 263n42

Madai, Guido von, 153, 155, 156
Maiden Tribute Affair, 55–56, 107–108, 110, 113, 132, 232
Manet, Édouard, 86, 87, 88
Märchen, Das (Graef). See *Fairy Tale, The*
Marr, Wilhelm, 133–134, 136
McAleer, Kevin, 13, 235n9
Mehlhorn, Heinz, 218, 268n45
Mehring, Franz, 219, 267n24
Menzel, Adolph, 27–28, 61, 64, 80–82, 86–87, 180
Meyer, Alexander, 174
Meyer, Babette, 32, 239n28
Meyer, Georg, 183
Meyerheim, Paul, 80–82, 86
microhistory, 18–19, 22
Miller, Ferdinand von, 65
Miquel, Johannes, 171
Mittelstädt, Otto, 164, 192, 195, 207–210, 257n59, 265n88
Mittermeier, Wolfgang, 213
models
depiction in satire, 104–107, 223
as rational economic actors, 68–69
relations with artists, 22, 36–38, 57–58, 66–86, 122–124, 138, 148, 244n27
social status, 37, 47, 51, 95, 102, 217, 267n16
Möller, Klaus-Peter, 214, 237n37, 245n52
morality associations, 11, 17, 112–113, 175–176, 179–180, 232
Morgenstern, Lina, 111
Mühler, Heinrich von, 152
Müller, Boguslaw
actions at trial, 43–54, 122, 124, 127–130, 145, 199
conflict with Matthias Quenstedt, 186–188
decision to allow press access, 43–44, 162–165, 169, 186, 208–209, 225
lower-class witnesses, treatment of, 48–49, 122, 124, 127–128, 132
Munch, Edvard, 88

Munckel, August, 137, 138, 173, 200–202, 212–213, 264n53
Mündlichkeit (orality), principle of, 146, 149, 197
Munich Art Academy, 26, 65, 88
Musset, Alfred de, 33

Napoleon III, 10
Napoleonic Wars, 24, 28–30
Nation, Die, 114
National Liberal Party
- anti-Semitism and, 54–55, 119
- elections and, 168, 171
- Law Regarding Court Proceedings Closed to the Public (1888) and, 171–185
- *Öffentlichkeit*, changing attitudes toward, 197, 206, 229–231
- rightward shift under Miquel, 171
- *See also* liberalism

Nationalzeitung, 53, 56, 69, 75, 79, 83, 105, 120, 132, 140
naturalism
- criticism of, 63–66, 78, 82, 85–89, 91, 176,
- Émile Zola and, 62–64, 243n13, 251n4
- German literature and, 64

Neide, Emil, 30
Neue Bahnen, 110
newspapers
- closed trials and, 162–175, 178–185, 229–230
- "New Journalism" and, 53–57, 226
- transformation of, 19, 41–42
- trial coverage and, 19–21, 42–45, 53–57, 175
- obscenity laws (*Lex Graef*), 169–174, 178–181
- *See also names of individual newspapers*

Nietzsche, Friedrich, 62, 72, 135
Nikolaus I, 203
Nord und Süd, 75–77, 251n4

Offenbach, Jacques, 136
Öffentlichkeit, principle of
- changing opinions about, 147–148, 163–165, 172–174, 182–184
- definition, 146
- persistence of, 181–185

Olshausen, Justus von, 210–212
orality. See *Mündlichkeit*
Ortmann, Alexandra, 19, 147–148, 163, 181–182, 187, 188, 205, 229, 203, 260n116
Otto, Gustav, 125–126, 127, 211–212, 226
Otto-Peters, Louise, 109–111

Paasch (buyer of Flessinow estate), 223
Paasch, Carl, 141–142, 227, 252n42, 254n78
Pall Mall Gazette, 55–56, 142–143
Paret, Peter, 25, 26–27
Penal Code. *See* Criminal Code.
perjury
- Hammermann trial, 144–145
- "perjury fever," 148–151
- seriousness of, 16, 39–40, 48, 57–58, 73, 103–104, 121
- Stöcker-Bäcker case, 137

Perrot, Franz, 133
Philipps, Wilhelm, 98–99, 175–176, 248n16
Piotrowski, Maximilian, 30
police
- conflicts with jurists, 98–99, 157–158, 256n42
- modern crime, overmatched by, 100, 125–126
- obscenity and censorship, 4, 6, 17–18, 113, 152–162, 177–178, 259n101
- prostitution, regulation by, 95–101, 108, 176, 178
- surveillance of political opponents, 109–113, 188, 201, 228

Pomplun, Kurt, 151
Portia, 114–115, 116
Post, Die, 67, 78, 104, 198
Potenberg (witness), 47
press. *See* newspapers
Preusse, Gustav, 214
Preußische Jahrbücher, 64, 164, 208
prosecutors, power and status of, 190–195
prostitution
- activism against, 55–56, 107–113, 118–119, 174–180, 232
- bordellos and, 95–99, 247n9
- depiction of, 33–34, 56, 58, 105–107, 251n13
- economic desperation and, 37, 58, 95–96
- Jews and, 136, 138
- legal status of, 95–104, 108, 248n9, 248n20
- Rother family and, 46, 48, 58, 95–96, 104–107, 123, 155–157, 223
- as symptom of decline, 9, 17, 66–68, 118, 126, 244n27
- *See also* morality associations

Prussian Academy of Arts. *See* Royal Academy of Arts
Prussian General Code (or ALR), 153, 158. 161
Prussian National Art Commission (*Landeskunstkommission*), 82–83, 84

public opinion
and judges, 197–199, 208–209
and jury courts, 207–209, 212–213
and the press, 41–43, 57, 58–59, 74–75, 163–174, 207
and prosecutors, 57, 74–75, 191, 195
and public confidence in the law (*öffentliche Rechtsbewußtsein*), 146, 163–165, 175
See also *Öffentlichkeit*
Puttkamer, Robert von, 99, 153, 155–158

Quenstedt, Matthias, 186–188, 261n5

Reé, Paul 72
Reese, Dagmar, 22
Reichsbote, 56–57, 71, 78, 85–86, 104–105, 134, 139, 140, 155, 207
Reichsglocke, 200–201
Reichstag
debates: on jury courts 206–207, 213, 230–231; Law Regarding Court Proceedings Closed to the Public (1888), 163–174, 177–185, 229–230; Lex Heinze, 167–181; "perjury fever," 148–149
political anti-Semitism, failure in, 232
power of, 11–12, 42, 228–233
Reichsfeinde and, 112, 228
Reim, Marie, 48–49, 132
Reuter, Amanda 48, 95
Rheinbaben, Paul von, 173
Rheinischen Ressort-Reglement, 158
Richter, Gustav, 30, 36
Richthofen, Bernhard von, 160–161, 177
Rieck, Otto, 175
Rintelen, Viktor, 172, 174, 179
Rosenberg, Adolf, 34, 36–37, 66–67, 87, 89, 157
Rosenfelder, Ludwig, 30
Ross, Ellen, 123
Rother, Anna
charges, 39–40
fate of, 221–222
and Graef trial, 46, 58, 60, 93
and Hammermann trial, 38, 127, 144–145
"madness" of, 127–131, 192
as rational actor, 130–132
Rother, Auguste
charges, 40
fate of, 221–222
and Graef trial, 46, 47, 49, 60, 128
as operator of a mini-bordello, 95–96, 123
Rother, Bertha
changes in social status, 95, 100–102
depiction: as the "Fairy Tale Model," 7, 20, 105–107, 223–224; general stereotypes, 102, 104–105, 227; as Phryne, 67; as Zola's Nana Coupeau, 105, 222–223
fate of, 222–224
Graef trial and, 33, 36–39, 46–53, 127, 215
as inappropriate model for activism, 110, 113, 132
as lacking in sexual honor, 103–104
letter to the Berlin Police-Presidium, 92–94, 102
public fascination with, 3–4, 18, 20–21, 116, 155–157, 161, 177, 214
Rother, Lieschen, 39, 46–47, 221, 248n27
Royal Academy of Arts (Berlin)
Graef and, 3, 31, 33, 34, 36, 61, 160, 217, 246n70
leadership of, 25, 82, 86, 180
Lex Heinze and, 180–181
"model market" in, 67–69
resistance against, 88–89
Royal German Society of Königsberg, 24
Rudolf, Crown Prince of Austria, 162

Sacher-Masoch, Leopold von, 219
Saint-Cère, Jacques (Jacob Rosenthal), 218–219
Salomé, Lou von, 72
Sand, Georges, 70, 110
Sarauw, Christian von, 165–166
Sarauw case (and related trials), 165–172, 182, 229–230
Schabelsky, Elsa von, 219
Schadow, Gottfried, 25
Schadow, Wilhelm von, 25–26, 61
Schelling, Hermann von, 141, 166–172, 175, 182–183, 185, 231
Schmettau, Ferdinande von, 28–30, 61, 221
Schmidt, Auguste, 110
Schmidt, Julian, 32, 63–64
Schmieden, Heino, 31
Schöffengericht. See Court of Lay Assessors.
Schopenhauer, Arthur, 62
Schroll, Josef Edler von, 222
Schwarze, Friedrich Oskar von, 205
Sello, Erich, 202
sexual abuse of children
emotional consequences, 103, 248n27
legal definitions, 102–104
relative unimportance, 57, 66, 101, 104, 148, 151, 179
Shakespeare, William, 70, 114–115, 132

Simmel, Georg, 32, 89–90
Simon, Louis, 160
Simson, August von, 44, 203–204
Simson, Eduard von, 44, 201, 203
Simson, Georg Bernhard, 201
Simson, John 44, 57, 58–59, 141, 145, 201, 203, 227, 254n77
Singer, Paul, 173–174
Skarbina, Franz, 87–88
Smith, Helmut Walser, 18
socialism
  Anti-Socialist Laws, 112–113, 132, 168, 171, 180
  criticism of legal system, 146–148, 146–147, 168, 173–174, 184, 188–190
  fear of, 10–11, 63–64, 78, 111–112, 117–119, 125, 183
  Graef trial and, 132
  Gertrud Guillaume-Schack and, 111–112
  prosecution of, 11, 13, 42–43, 54–55, 168, 201, 258n72
  prostitution and, 108, 113
  Socialist Workers' Party of Germany (SAPD), 10–11
  See also the names of individual politicians
Sozialdemokrat (Zurich), 132
Staatsbürgerin, Die, 112–113
Stark, Gary, 17–18, 159–160, 162
Stauffer-Bern, Karl, 222
Stead, [W]illiam [T]homas, 55–56, 107–108, 120, 142
Stephany, Friedrich, 193
Stern, Fritz, 62
Stinde, Julius, (Quidam), 83
Stöcker, Adolf
  Christian-Social Party, 10–11, 118–119, 134, 227
  Graef trial and, 140
  Inner Mission and, 118, 126, 176
  Stöcker-Bäcker trial, 136–140, 197–198, 200, 207
Strousberg, Bethel Henry, 30
Sudermann, Hermann, 176–177
Supreme Court (*Reichsgericht*)
  on compulsory gynecological exams, 101, 248n27
  on landlords and prostitutes, 98–100
  on obscenity, 153–154
  See also Sarauw case (and related trials); *individual jurists*

Tessendorf, Hermann, 43, 190, 240n8
Thiele, Oskar, 44
Thorvaldsen, Bertel, 158, 160
Thumann, Paul, 79
Traube, Ludwig, 217–218
trials, dramatic nature of, 45–48; *See also names of individual trials; See also under* newspapers
Tschudi, Hugo von, 87–90

Ulfert, Rudolf, 202
University of Königsberg. *See* Albertina.
Untersuchungshaft (pre-trial detention), 190, 235n1
Ury, Lesser, 87–88

Veczera, Marie, 162
vice squad (*Sittenpolizei*), 95–101, 108, 112–113, 157, 178, 224. *See also* police
Volksadvokat, 59, 121, 187–188
Volkszeitung, 187, 192, 208, 219, 267n24
Vossische Zeitung, 104, 148, 193

Wagner, Richard, 135–136
Wald, Samuel, 24
Walkowitz, Judith, 55, 107–108, 132, 142, 232
Weber, Ludwig, 112, 175–176
Weber, Max, 201
Wehler, Hans-Ulrich, 228–229
Werner, Anton von, 80–89, 180, 231
West German Morality Association, 175
Whitechapel murders (Jack the Ripper), 55, 142–143
Wichern, Johann Heinrich, 118
Wildenbruch, Ernst von, 67
Wilhelm I, 10–11, 29, 82, 112
Wilhelm II
  on German art and theater, 87, 177
  reaction to the Heinze case, 113, 125, 175
  scandals surrounding, 19, 181, 230
  and Adolf Stöcker, 137
Wilhelm, Uwe, 41, 114, 188
Windthorst, Ludwig, 174
Winkeladvokat, see *Volksadvokat*.
Wirth, Irmgard, 86
Wolff (doctor), 129–130, 141, 248n27, 252n38
Wolstenholme, Elizabeth, 108
women
  inverted gender roles and, 121–123, 132
  restrictions on political activities, 109–112
  sexual double standards, 96, 98–99, 111, 122–124, 247n9
  voices mediated by men, 93, 114–116

See also feminism. *See also under* prostitution; honor
Wronker, Max, 202

Zeit, Die (Vienna), 90
Zobeltitz, Fedor von, 223–224
Zola, Émile, 62–64, 85, 105, 117, 222–223, 251n4, 268n31
Zukunft, Die, 194, 267n22